Quicksilver

DATE DUE

ALSO BY RICHARD M. SWIDERSKI

Anthrax: A History (McFarland, 2004)

Multiple Sclerosis Through History and Human Life (McFarland, 1998)

Quicksilver

*A History of the Use,
Lore and Effects
of Mercury*

Richard M. Swiderski

McFarland & Company, Inc., Publishers
Jefferson, North Carolina, and London

LIBRARY OF CONGRESS CATALOGUING-IN-PUBLICATION DATA

Swiderski, Richard M.
    Quicksilver : a history of the use, lore and effects of mercury /
Richard M. Swiderski.
        p.   cm.
    Includes bibliographical references and index.

    ISBN 978-0-7864-3596-8
    softcover : 50# alkaline paper ∞

    1. Mercury — Therapeutic use.   2. Mercury — Social aspects.
I. Title.
RM666.M5S95   2008
615.9'25663 — dc22   2008023041

British Library cataloguing data are available

Cover photograph ©2008 Shutterstock

Manufactured in the United States of America

*McFarland & Company, Inc., Publishers
    Box 611, Jefferson, North Carolina 28640
    www.mcfarlandpub.com*

Table of Contents

Asi seria, dijo Sancho, porque a buena fe que andaba Rocinante como si fuera asno de gitano con azogue en los oiódos. ¡Y como si llevaba azogue! dijo Don Quixote, y aun una legión del demionos, que es el gente que camina y hace caminar sin cansarse todo aquello que se los antoja.

(Thus it would be, said Sancho, because by faith Rocinante went like a Gypsy's ass with mercury in the ears. And as if she was carrying a load of mercury, said Don Quixote, and even driven by a legion of demons, who are the folk who flee and restlessly make flee everything that is before them.)

— Miguel de Cervantes
Don Quixote, Primera Parte, Capitulo XXXI

Mas vale la plata en la bolsa que no en el mercurio.

(Silver is worth more in the purse than it is in the mercury.)

— Ramon Lull
Arbol de los Ejemplares de la Ciencia
(Proverbios de los Flores)

Preface

Don Quixote rejects Sancho Panza's comparison of his suddenly frisky nag Rocinante to a decrepit horse a Gypsy horsetrader has made seem spirited by putting liquid mercury in its ear. A buyer doesn't know that the horse rears its head and gallops about because it is trying to shake the noise from its skull. Don Quixote prefers to think of Rocinante as driven by spirits in some romance he has in mind. Elsewhere in his adventures, the knight speaks of someone trembling as if they were mercurialized, but here he considers Sancho's analogy undignified and unworthy of his noble mare. This is mercury in popular culture: many specialized and hidden uses, not of the best reputation, yet with representatives of the high culture always in mind.

This book had its origins in a memory that can't be mine. An old experimental physics book I was glancing through radiated a smell of laboratories, though it was a sequence of scanned pictures on a computer screen. When I came to the instructions for demonstrating atmospheric pressure, I paused. The experiment was prefaced with a warning about handling liquid mercury which is poisonous when heated. Place the bowl of mercury on a tray so none of it spills and gets lost in cracks, instructions said. The student was to fill a glass column with mercury and then chase out any air bubbles by holding a finger over the end of the tube while inverting it in the bowl of mercury, then removing the finger. To do this the student would have to plunge a finger into the mercury while inhaling the vapor from the admittedly unheated bowl. At that point I had a flash. I smelled, tasted and felt exactly what it was like to do that, though I never had. It was a set of sensations I have been pursuing since then, out of curiosity rather than nostalgia.

Like most in my generation, I had less direct contact with liquid mercury than did foregoing generations. My father, who worked with chemists but was not a chemist himself, gave me a small glass bottle of the silvery essence. I let it roll in the palm of my hand. I showed it to my friends, who had never seen anything like it. I learned its smell and was not tempted to taste it. I didn't have any gold for it to dissolve. I accidentally dropped a globule onto the cement surface of the sidewalk and tried to herd it back into the bottle with a piece of paper but found it dividing and subdividing into an infinity of small globules in the grain of the cement. Eventually the bottle disappeared, a phase of childhood over.

My mother gave me samples of mercury to taste. She was a hygienist employed by a dentist, and she prepared the amalgam by mixing mercury with silver powder and placing it in a container shaken violently up and down by a machine. The mass was served to the dentist on a small piece of marble. He removed it with a bladed spatula and pressed it into the gap his drilling had made in the decayed area of my tooth.

I found that mercury kept appearing in things. It fell out of the silver line of a broken glass thermometer. It chased among the plastic barriers of a hand-held plastic maze. It was what made a plastic capsule with a face painted on it roll around erratically. I only learned much later that it was in the small black tablets which grew into foaming sleeves supposed to resemble snakes when ignited with a match. But I didn't see the gliding silver globules everywhere mercury was. As I discovered its further presence, this book took shape.

Popular culture research, as opposed to science or art research, requires mining sources that were not composed with the thought of conveying popular beliefs, images and values. Mercury is good at preserving once-living things, and popular culture is no exception. The facsimiles of old books and periodicals now digitally available to anyone with a computer and broadband connection were an important resource for making contact with past popular mercuries, but even more provident were the searchable inventories of hundreds of book dealers and libraries around the world, and rapid shipping of unique publications I consulted for this project.

It is fortunate that mercury-related writings have not become collectors' items in and of themselves (as writings about gold and silver have). Even their antiquity was not a bar to acquiring a few of them. To convey popular culture, the nature of a publication (pamphlet, broadside, unbound or bound book), the advertisements in the back, perhaps, and the markings on the pages can be as useful as the print itself. My copy of Walter Bradley's *Quicksilver Resources of California* (1918) has the number of the page of a "test for quicksilver" penciled on the flyleaf, and water spots on the front cover that suggest the book was present when the test was performed. Living in California gave me a purchase on mining and its consequences that none of the books about mercury mines in California, whatever their condition could convey. At least I had the resources to mark out the immediacy of mercury in popular culture, and its persistence in our lives.

Introduction

Mercury in popular culture renders harmless a beautiful essence we discover in ourselves. We want to make it act as it looks, even when it's invisible. It must be possible to release mercury from its toxic envelope and allow it to work freely and deeply to our advantage. If it is hidden and penetrating the depths, how can we draw it back before it goes too far?

A man accidentally washed his hands in molten lead, and his screams of agony summoned Dr. Pontaeus to step forward from the crowd. The good doctor applied a quantity of his green salve to the man's visibly damaged hands, and bandaged them up. The next day the crowd returned to the same spot to find the man unwrapping his completely restored hands. They were ready to buy the miraculous salve. Dr. Thomas Harris, one of the physicians to the recently restored monarch Charles II, marveled at the gullibility of people who could not see that the burningly hot lead really was liquid mercury. Would this display lead them to try the experiment on their own hands?

A twentieth-century magic trick described as "the miniature inferno" doesn't ask anyone to risk their hands in a pot of molten lead. The magician calls for rings and other jewelry from the audience and places them in a crucible where he has apparently melted pieces of lead. He extracts a solid block of lead where the jewelry has been placed, yet restores it intact to the owners afterward, keeping up a patter that the rings are little travelers who have been on a journey. The author of the magic manual that describes this trick cautions anyone performing the trick not to heat the mercury that has secretly flowed from the magician's wand over the sealed box where the jewelry has been placed. And he further cautions them not to let the mercury to come into contact with gold.

Around the same time that this trick was being copied by amateur magicians, the author of a patent for casting battery plates suggested that mercury could be poured into the mold in place of molten metal to test the mold. The mercury for molten metal surrogate had gone from medicine show to technical magic secret to technological instrument. That is generally how it goes with mercury in popular culture: both show and science at the same time. Mercury can be known simply as a chemical element, but that doesn't last long.

Hydrargyrum, "water silver," once was the only name for what we now call mercury or quicksilver. I only understood the term figuratively until one day with it in mind I saw the silvery breast of a turning stream of water. A formerly hidden component of common nature was exposed to my view like the secret of a magic trick exposed and made technological. Hydragyrum is the permanent state of that light of water, which still has to be given the name of another metal, silver, to describe its color and sheen. Mercury has properties of other substances, but properties seen in motion.

Mercury is known through science, which labeled hydragyrum as Hg, a chemical element, and forgot that turn of the water, though I have no doubt that individual scientists saw that turn and tried to measure it. Naming hydragyrum "mercury" called on Roman mythology to describe another physical property of the liquid metal, its rapid movement for such a substantial, weighty body. The messenger god Mercury took flight on winged fleet, delivered messages from afar, conducted the souls of the dead to the other world and was the patron of thieves who stole in everywhere. It took scientists a long time to catch up with the implications of this name, and prove that mercury sublimates (enters the air as a solid) when not being heated and that it steals into the body through skin, food and inhalation. But what does it do in the body?

Science had its answers, but popular culture presented its own restlessly.

Popular culture is a matter of direct sensory impressions, conclusions drawn rapidly and then enshrined in lore and representation. Mercury acquired a third name, quicksilver—*argentum vivum, vif argent, argento vivo*—which gave it another reputation opposed to and supported by scientific measurements. Science has its own popular culture of quicksilver altering state into mercury and back.

Mercury is a very showy substance, and remains the model if not the fact for some forms of video display. Its presence is easily assayed, and it will condense when something that contains it is heated. But that sets up the observer to be tricked by mercury, because it quickly vanishes, seemingly entering other fluids, solids, or the air.

Long before it was formally established that liquid mercury slowly departs into vapor at room temperature, its elusiveness gave it the reputation of being all-penetrating. It combined with, or at least entered, a great many materials and objects, so that it might seem to be a part of everything. Mercury's hidden, vanishing and emerging presence suggested an entire sensual accounting of the material world in which it had a fundamental role in things as they are.

Mercury welcomed physical operations, warming, grinding, mixing, levigating, calcining, distilling, an entire lost vocabulary of processes and instruments, to find what known or unknown body would result. It was a model for what eventually would become the chemical elements, and then it was ready to serve as an instrument to collect and measure the others. It was through mercury that calcium, sodium and potassium were first isolated as metals, and through mercury that gold and silver are mined.

In China, home of an immense and complex popular culture and science, *dan* was the mineral cinnabar and its colors, paints and elixirs. It was the basic form of mercury and its transformations. There was no distinct word for mercury: the written character for *dan,* a graphic showing a dab on a palette, was sufficient until the adoption of western chemistry called for an equivalent to the European word.

The word becomes visual only with the development of moving media. There was some anticipation of that in architecture: the tomb of the first Chinese emperor showed the world in mercury, and a caliph in Muslim Spain built a reflecting pool of mercury. Mercury is not represented in painting, print and still photography, though it is a component of each. It occasionally appears in film and video as a glowing, invasive liquid.

A recent television commercial for a high-speed Internet service uses the image of mercury as popularly understood. A man and woman disconsolately face a kitchen full of dishes and utensils after a gathering. Then they remember that they have high speed. They open the cable that carries data high speed to their computer, and a body of mercury pours out. In a blur, the man puts their household back in order and the woman stands in awe, the end of her utterance blanked out. No one in their right mind watching this commercial would believe that one can tap a computer cable for superhuman energy, but anyone who has waited for sites to come up, for pictures and videos to appear on their computer gets the point. High-speed Internet access works blindingly fast compared to the old tedium.

Another commercial for the same service has a man

Illustration of liquid-mercury-center-of-gravity-toys, from John Ayrton Paris, *Philosophy in Sport Made Science in Earnest* (1861).

opening the high-speed line to release mercury onto the sole of his shoe. He streaks away and then reappears to tell a colleague he's been to Peru. When the colleague doubts him, he vanishes again, this time showing up with an elderly man clad in a serape and asking in Spanish if they are in Lima yet. A neocolonialist Mercury has made the round trip.

Though they have nothing to do with mercury, the commercials identify it in the same way: sudden brightness, penetration, high speed, done.

This book is an investigation of the turns of mercury captured by popular culture as it enters human bodies. It begins with a heavy turn, the silver liquid turning black when swallowed to relieve inner troubles, the historic case of an eighteenth-century English actor who died after taking the advice of Dr. Quicksilver and downing a quantity of the "Jelly of Metals." Dr. Thomas Dover was the first of a string of individuals who had an unusual involvement with mercury, possibly because they were endowed with the ability to relieve themselves of the mercury that entered them more efficiently than the others to whom they recommended it. While Dover was plying his trade, the change of silvery mercury to black powder inside was isolated and identified as a chemical event inside the body. It seemed like the death of the soul.

The next turn is of gender, but continues the downward weighting. Women swallowed mercury for the same reasons as men, to clear themselves. They also sought to simulate or stimulate conception with the weight or the animus of the metal. Mercury was also called on to assist women in the labor of childbirth. By weight it brought out the fetus before birth, causing an abortion. This reputation as an influence on birth transferred to mercury's infiltration of developing children.

Men seemed to enjoy setting up atmospheres of vaporous mercury to inspire them in the practice of alchemy, chymistry and chemistry. Mercury in alchemy supposedly establishes the lasting state of the element in relation to deliberate human action, and humans have inhaled and recoiled from the poisonous fumes and believing that they inspire an immaterial essence that resembles mercury. Obscure alchemists and well-known scientists such as Tycho Brahe and Isaac Newton drank this air. The changes mercury could be made to exhibit in enclosed laboratories paralleled a spiritual-alchemical process of bodies remade by monetary enrichment. Out of this atmosphere precipitated basic discoveries of chemistry, gathered over troughs of mercury, regulated by mercury valves and measured by mercury thermometers and pressure gauges.

With the deliberate elaboration of organic mercury compounds, a new mercurial essence is invented, neither solid, liquid nor gas exclusively. It seems to be a realization of the old idea of mercury being contained in everything, as it in fact does begin to be contained in everything. Used to increase food production as a seed treatment, it also causes mass poisoning of Iraqis and kills a biochemist trying to study how it accumulates in the body. It is in bread and in fish, but the importance assigned to that varies from one horizon to another.

Scientific Researches! New Discoveries in Pneumatics!, satirical print by James Gillray, 1802.

From before the first appearance of syphilis in Europe, mercury ointments treated skin eruptions. Mercury was soon being used in liquid and vapor forms, as well as in several solid compounds to attack the syphilis virus lodged in the body. The all-penetrating qualities of the metal seem to make it able to enter the deepest recesses and pull out the poisons in sweats, purges and salivation. The object was to get mercury into the body so it and the disease would exit together. What resulted was a new turn of mercury, as the effects it had on the body — tremors, loose teeth, mental disturbances — became enmeshed with the symptoms of syphilis and difficult to disentangle. Syphilis was an organic mercury of the human body. Mercury was the price syphilis sufferers paid for freedom from the worst ravages of their disease, or so they thought.

Gross volumes of mercury and its caustic compounds were rejected as the mercury-syphilis relation matured. They were replaced by formulations that promised to carry mercury through the body without inducing mercury disease. Small quantities of finely divided mercury taken regularly were advocated by Augustin Belloste and later by John Abernethy, both surgeons practiced in removing the surface effects of infection, which they blamed on body-system failure mercury could remedy.

Belloste was forgotten but Abernethy's name was attached to small mercury pills taken regularly, also called the "blue pill" or "blue mass." These pills had a career in American popular culture both as a commonplace remedy and as a poison to be replaced by something without mercury. Abraham Lincoln took them to change his melancholy until the time of his death, which was avenged by a sometime hatter and Union soldier named Boston Corbett, who got his mercury from his trade.

Avoiding the use of mercury in medications led to another formulation of mercury, which hid it in a fruit syrup promoted as entirely vegetal and good for a wide range of afflictions. As "rob de l'Affecteur" originating in revolutionary France, it was taken up by Giraudeau de Saint Gervais, who commissioned a poem, an advertising echo of the Frascatoro's syphilis poem, to broadcast its virtues. Giraudeau's attention to attractive young women increased the volume of his sales and brought charges of indecency, which deflected the news that chemists had discovered mercury in the bottles of his healing drink. In Pennsylvania, a bookbinder named William Swaim concluded that the imported "rob" that healed him was too expensive, and began to manufacture his own version, using Giraudeau's formula but a restrained form of his advertising technique. Swaim's Panacea was a cure–all, able to lessen the ravages even of taking too much mercury for syphilis ailments.

Mercury, applied to the skin, lightens it at first. In cosmetics made and used mainly by women it takes another gender turn. Men idealize the appearance that mercury can most easily award a persistent user, and almost in the same turn caution women that they will turn ugly if they use it regularly. Cosmetics transform the skin, while face paint, which often used to contain lead, bismuth and other heavy metals, covers it. As homemade cosmetics gave way to manufactures, the mercury was again hidden.

Harriet Hubbard Ayer, who claimed to have a facial cream formula from the descendants of Madame Recamier herself, advised the use of mercury in her columns and a book, but never admitted its presence in her products. Through the advice of exemplars, women whose skin did not meet the class standards of lightness internalized the need for the face mercury could provide. Mercury has continued to be present in cosmetics, denounced, forbidden and unknown until the results of it are visible and it can be replaced by other chemicals.

Cosmetics is one area of popular endeavor where mercury is seen not to be seen. Mining is another. The colors mercury shows on the surface of the earth lead to the interior deposits. In early China the colors followed in the earth were preserved and amplified through processing into vermilion of varying degrees of fineness.

The Western mining practices mainly developed in Spain where the oldest mine was located. Distilling the mercury from its rock matrix to serve many uses became focused with time on recovering silver and gold through the amalgamation method.

Occasionally the popular culture of the miners, Moors and Gypsies in Spain, native people in Peru and Mexico or Mexicans in California, can be glimpsed in the records of their exploiters. Spanish mining methods extended to California, where a boom and bust cycle of mercury demand has controlled operations up to the present. Much mercury has been poured into the rivers of California and remains there, slowly spreading.

One demand driving mercury mining was the use of mercury to make mercury fulminate, a detonator of explosions and impeller of projectiles. After the downfall of the Soviet Union in 1990, there appeared on the armaments market a mysterious new commodity, "red mercury," the subject of intrigue and military play among existing and would-be nuclear powers. The by-product of one of the processes used to make the hydrogen bomb, red mercury was imagined and sold as the basis of small nuclear bombs and radiation weapons advocated by a cadre of experts in a highly specialized popular culture.

While red mercury eventually receded to the embarrassed downside of the international weapons race, and no longer was a reason to open defunct mines, actual mercury continued to pass round and round in its major uses. The chlor-alkali industry, which generated the two basic industrial chemicals sodium hydroxide and chlorine gas, used the greatest amount of mercury during the twentieth century, yet its process was designed to cycle not expend mercury serving as a flowing electrode. The mercury was needed to replace what sublimated or leaked from the cells into the ground and water.

Pressure increased for this industry to abandon the use of the metal, and, as it did so, great quantities of mercury became available, making recycling a substitute for mining more mercury. Health fears of mercury envisioned a cycle moving between land, air and water, giving the metal opportunities to enter human bodies, especially developing ones, at several points. Efforts to take control of this cycle by recycling mercury added to the leakage of mercury into what was popularly becoming known as the environment. Dishonest recyclers store mercury in vessels that allow it to penetrate back into the earth and then into the water, entering the new natural cycle.

Mercury persistently approaches human bodies along the curve of a cycle powered by human activities. A popular version of the environmental approach of mercury causes it to be rejected by those who did not even know it was being used in their bodies.

Being included in amalgams used to preserve teeth against decay now can be made to seem a part of a general threat of mercury contamination. A mercury removal industry gains favor in opposition to the industries long using mercury. Used to provide a cheap filling for decayed teeth gives mercury a presence that can both be rejected and sustained at the same time. Being a component in a vaccine preservative causes its known effects to be inducted into the developmental disability autism, newly conceived to explain children's difficulties in socializing and using language at the expected levels. These two mercury uses, like the old popular uses, consist of rejecting mercury as it is consumed, and consuming mercury as it is rejected. Now, however, the rejection commands the consumption.

The absent mercury limited in negotiations with industry continues to turn up in popular culture.

If this book were being done as a graphic novel, it would show a sinister silver flood filling everything inside its outlines but only leaking out in brief poisonous flashes. The environment formed by consuming mercury to control disease increasingly kept secret turned into the environment today permeated by the threat of mercury. When the Russian spy-official-turned-dissident Mikhail Litvinenko died of radiation poisoning in November 2006, Russian prosecutors claimed that dangerous levels of mercury vapor were detected in cars, apartments, summer homes and offices in London and Moscow. Mercury was the stand-in for the less digestible polonium-210.

There are a number of popular instances of mercury that don't appear in this book beyond a brief mention. The mercury bubbles prettier than soap bubbles; the automata powered by moving masses of mercury created by the ancient engineer Daedalus and referred to by Aristotle in his essay on the soul; the mercury that generates a mild electrical current moving around in a women's Japanese sex toy; the "barometric light" that appears in the air space at the end of glass tube partially filled with mercury and the fluorescent lights that result. Mercury in photographs. Mercury in motors. Mercury in children's games.

But I promise you that the mercuries that penetrate these pages will astound and heal you, will bring light to your eyes and a new taste to your mouth. And your money will never be the same.

1

◦◦◦

Silver into Black

In 1733, the celebrated actor Barton Booth died in London at the age of 52. Booth was an actor-manager of the Drury Lane Theatre, one of the three who dominated that stage. He was best known for his portrayals of nobles and kings: his performance as the Roman senator Cato in John Addison's play *Cato* was considered definitive.

During the final two days of his life, Booth came under the care of Sir Hans Sloane, who ordered him to be bled therapeutically in an attempt to reduce the febrile humors racking his body. After Booth expired, Sloane supervised the autopsy conducted by the surgeon Alexander Small. It was one of the first celebrity autopsies in what would become a long tradition. Small's findings were published in a pamphlet by an acquaintance of Booth's: "The whole tract was found to be lined with crude mercury, divided in globules about the bigness of pins' heads. The insides of the intestines were as black as your hat [so] that they would not endure the least straining without breaking into pieces." The significance of this appearance was debated for some time afterward.

It was not Booth's renown as a tragedian that impelled the consideration of his remains. The doctors were not interested in locating the anatomical correlates of his skill as they later sought the source of Einstein's genius in the distribution of neurons in his brain. It was the possibility that Booth was killed by a massive dose of mercury prescribed for him by Dr. Quicksilver, a title applied to and embraced by Dr. Thomas Dover. Heavy mercury damage was the cause of death put forward by the anonymous pamphlet and by other writings. Sloane had discontinued Booth's consumption of mercury, but the surgeon's knife disclosed a silvered black mass in the intestines. Metallic mercury and preparations of its salts were long given to end internal blockages. Here the mercury build-up seemed to doom the man.

Booth had been away from the stage for almost six years. "In the year 1727," says Theo Cibber, "early in the acting season, Booth had been seized with a violent fever, which lasted forty-six days without intermission. He was attended by Dr. Freind and Dr. Broxholm, gentlemen very eminent in their profession. They declared he was delirious but two nights and one day, notwithstanding an ill-natured false report of his being mad the whole time of his illness.... But in 1731 his illness, a most perilous stroke of fate on the theatre, returned soon after his playing King Henry VIII.... During the course of his illness his fever turned to an inveterate jaundice."

Booth went to Bath to take the waters. When that did not relieve him he went on a sea voyage to Holland hoping seasickness would release the jaundice, that is, cause him to vomit out the poison. He thought to consult Dr. Boerhaave in Holland, but the fever came back so strongly that he returned to England. "He had a succession of violent fevers, and was often tormented with the most painful cholics. Yet, during their intermission, his spirits were lively and his voice was strong.... His illness never quite forsook him, his jaundice appeared again, and a violent periodical cholic harassed him for near six months before he died, which was on Tuesday, May 8, 1733."

This account of Booth's illness is by the son of Colley Cibber, one of his comanagers at the Drury Lane Theatre. It views the fluctuations in his health in terms of Booth's readiness for the stage. There is no mention here of mercury. That dominates other pamphlets by opponents and advocates of mercury treatment who use Booth as an eminent example. The theatrical profession was not interested in such matters.

According to Dr. Daniel Turner in another contemporary pamphlet, Booth, desperately sick and hearing favorable reports of the treatments described in Thomas Dover's *The Ancient Physician's Legacy to his Country* (1733), went out and bought a copy.

In the book, Booth read what Edward Lisle wrote from Red Lyon Square on May 16 of that year: "Sir, The Benefits I have received from the taking of Crude Quicksilver, and from the Opinion I have of the Usefulness of the Medicine in all Chronical Cases, and Distempers proceeding from Obstructions, would render me unpardonable, should I refuse to let the Particulars of my Case be published in the Work you have informed me is now in the Press." Mr. Lisle described the efforts of various physicians to treat his chronic fever and their lack of success until a friend prevailed upon him to "try what Effect Crude Quicksilver would have on me." Three quarters of an ounce every morning for about twelve days and Mr. Lisle's toes began to tingle, his "secretions were all well performed" and he could eat once more. When he halted the mercury treatment and went to Bath, his symptoms returned, and only abated when he returned to mercury. He told of other remarkable recoveries, including curing a horse of glanders by giving him an ounce of mercury every morning for a month. People of Booth's own social milieu, with similar complaints, were reporting miraculous cures from consistent mercury treatment. Dover's book ended with letter after letter extolling the virtues of mercury for blockage complaints.

In the early eighteenth century, mercury preparations were common medicine for intestinal worms, syphilis and skin diseases, but Dover's prescription of drinking raw mercury to clear out disease-causing blockages was unusual.

Dover himself came to mercury late in his career, but for all his advocacy of mercury, or he would say, because of it, he survived to an advanced age. Dover's only description in the *Ancient Physician* of himself being treated has nothing to do with mercury.

While Dover was an apprentice in the house of Thomas Sydenham, he came down with smallpox. He believed he survived because of the treatment administered. He was isolated in an unheated room (in winter), stripped to the waist, and given nothing but beer to drink. The cold air absorbed the febrile heat of his body and the frequent peeing out the beer carried away the "bad humors." And of course the alcohol helped keep his mind off his own physical state.

Though mercury certainly was in the air of any medical or chemical enterprise during Dover's early practice, he would not have imbibed it in Sydenham's house. Sydenham based his treatments on the control of body heat recommended by the second century C.E. Greco-Roman physician Galen. Differing views on mercury were attributed to Galen, but Sydenham accepted his opinion that it was a poison. From his convalescence Dover also brought away a preference for opium which later, with the addition of a component from his travels in South America, became the basis for his own medicinal powder.

It was fortunate that Dover had his smallpox in the house of one of the most versatile medical men of the time. Once he had endured a smallpox infection, Dover himself had immunity and could minister to others sick with smallpox. This was before variolation — inducing immunity through grafting with infectious matter from someone else's pustule — was introduced into Britain from Turkey where it had been practiced for some time. Those infected with the pox had to rely on good attendance by others immune to the disease, and Dover was now qualified.

But it was not only an attendant's resistance to the scourge that Dover acquired in Sydenham's house. It was the "cooling" treatment itself which enabled Dover later to bring through his slaving and privateering expeditions with minimum deaths from fevers.

The cooling treatment was a vestige of the humoral system of body constitution associated with the Greek physician Galen and his followers. The body was thought to be composed of four humors, in combinations of hot and cold, wet and dry. Individual temperament, health, and illness were all described in terms of humors. Each medicine and each treatment technique was addressed to the humoral balance of that particular body under its circumstances.

The Paracelseans, followers of the sixteenth-century Swiss physician and chemist Paracelsus, rejected the humoral system and treated the body as a chemical composition. All substances entering the body were poisons to some degree, which made them able to influence the state of the body through careful administration. Paracelsean medicine called for doctors to be chemists.

The cooling method of treating fever did not at first employ mercury. It was a humoral method in search of chemical means. To Dover at least, mercury suggested itself as able to accomplish the entire method of treatment in simple internal applications. Dover progressively used mercury's cool dryness in the direction of its weight and smoothness. He ended up subscribing to an almost chemical theory of its action against fevers and inflammations.

Dover's early education at Oxford and Cambridge, and apprenticeship to Sydenham, were followed by an appointment to a hospital in the trading port of Bristol, and the development of a private practice among the merchants and traders. He invested in and profited from maritime expeditions, and finally accompanied expeditions himself as doctor and managing partner, seizing the role of captain without the unanimous consent of the crew. His own history converged with the life a better-known character when he brought the stranded Alexander Selkirk (eventually the model for Robinson Crusoe) away from Juan Fernandez Island, only to have the more skilled Selkirk elected master of the ship that Dover captained.

Dover returned to England in 1711 and stayed in London, living off his share of the loot and the stories of one of the most successful nautical forays of his time, which had included the capture and ransom of the city of Guayaquil, Ecuador, and other seizures of Spanish possessions. The only record of Dover on these expeditions and afterward is the mention of his name in the published logs of mariners and in the petitions and court documents related to the claims made on the profits of the expedition.

In 1720, when he reemerges into the historic record, he was known as "Captain Dover." According to a letter sent by Viscountess Dupplin to her aunt Abigail Harley, this "famous man in town now called a doctor" undertakes to cure the smallpox in a new way: "quicksilver and the cold bath." The Viscountess also referred to Dover with a third noun even more often associated with him. It amazes all reasonable people that various noble ladies she lists should put aside their physicians and put themselves into "such a quack's hands."

The first thing Captain Dover did to treat a smallpox infection was to "strike it all in." Kenneth Dewhurst, who quotes this letter in his biography of Dover, surmises that this means Dover attempted to halt the fever and the emergence of smallpox pustules. This was the opposite of the usual treatment, to allow the skin to break out and the fever to run its course, under the assumption that this would eject the disease elements from the body.

This is the first mention of quicksilver in association with Dover's name. But it is not clear how he was using it. Either external applications of mercury unguent were holding down the pustules or internal consumption of raw mercury was clearing out the blockages that kept the disease inside. It is clear that by 1720, Dover had come to mercury perhaps in the way that was to give him notoriety for the rest of his life and replace Captain Dover with Dr. Quicksilver.

In the passage of *The Ancient Physician* where he describes his treatment of Miss Corbett (one of the women Viscountess Dupplin refers to), Dover writes that he was summoned after the other physicians gave up, and finding Miss Corbett blind (blindness sometimes accompanies the smallpox pustules on the face) he told her mother Lady Hotham that "all colours are the same to the blind" and brought in an adept "bleeder," a black man who released such a quantity of blood from Miss Corbett that she recovered. In his mercury-soaked book Dover doesn't mention mercury in one of the cases where it was associated with his name by a contemporary.

Nor does he attribute to mercury his success controlling the fever that spread among the crewmen after they were "very much annoy'd" by the smell of the exposed bodies of "plague" victims after taking the city of Guayaquil by storm. Dover concluded that this fever could be reduced by bleeding each man, followed by having him drink large quantities of cooling and diluting liquids to quell the internal fermentation. In this brewmaster's view of disease, the blood of a sick body was becoming overripe like a moldy liquid, and the way to treat the disease was to cool and dilute the blood.

In his own account Dover says he had oil and spirit of vitriol mixed with water to dilute the acidity and gave it to the men to drink freely. Of a hundred and eighty sick, only six of seven deathly ill died, and that was only because they rashly drank strong liquors, which increased the internal fermentation. He scorned a number of remedies that learned physicians would have prescribed; it was the cooling method that saved the men.

After his return from the South Seas in 1711, and before 1720 when he was treating smallpox victims in London, Dover traveled to the continent and the Near East. There is not much information in *The Ancient Physician* about the purpose and course of this trip. The anecdotes associated with it have to do with mercury.

For those who subscribe to the received notion that mercury is a poison, Dover declares, "Let them take a Trip to Hungary, and visit the Mines where the Quicksilver is dug; they may there see Slaves working entirely naked, to prevent them stealing this precious Jelly of Metals, as it may be called; yet every Day swallow so much, that they buy a Choppin of Drink with it at Night." Dover's mentor Augustin Belloste in his *Traitez de Mercure* is not so merry about the fate of mercury miners who steal mercury by swallowing it in quantities while in the mine shafts. The mine owners make them wait several hours locked up in a room after they finish work, intent upon recovering the quicksilver that is certain to come down.

From Pliny and Dioscorides to Bernardino Ramazzini, natural historians and physicians had been visiting the mercury mines in Spain, Italy and Dalmatia, and finding the atmosphere toxic and the miners, usually slaves or convicts, hard pressed to remain alive. Yet here is Dover, rhetorically declaring to his critics that they should go off to Hungary where the naked slaves swallow the raw metal they dig up and end the day in a tavern.

The old image of happy slaves was losing credit at this time. The mines Dover was referring to are probably those at Rosenberg, also mentioned by John Hill, Dover's contemporary and a translator of Dioscorides. They were a resort of those who couldn't get their mercury from the main source, Spain or Spain's American colonies. Mercury does occur in raw metallic form in mines, but the amount available to swallow and pass through for private sale at the end of a work day was probably not very great. It would have to come from the smelters also associated with the mines.

After this excursion to Hungary, Dover lists his uses for mercury, all dependent on its weight passing through the body. In both resorting to raw mercury and its specific uses, this regimen most resembles a practice that developed in Spain and the Spanish colonies, the diagnosis of *empacho*, stomach blockage causing a variety of ill effects that mercury can remedy by forcing through. Dover makes no explicit reference to this condition and treatment, and he does not show any sign of having read the works of Spanish physicians advocating mercury to relieve blockage. Yet a trained physician like Dover who had spent time in the Spanish New World must have imbibed something of Spanish practice to set aside objections to mercury and Belloste's finer preparations to become a determined promoter of raw mercury treatments.

Juan de Barrios, who practiced in New Spain toward the end of the sixteenth century, wrote (1607) that Avicenna advised if a child cannot digest food, he must be cured. Barrios uses the language of Galen to describe digestion as "coction," grinding the mass and drawing the nutrients into the wall of the stomach. He recommends feeding the child cooling fruits such as quince and peach juice, also in line with Galenic orthodoxy, but then he pronounces mercury, not approved by Galen, a "great remedy," given in the quantity of half a chickpea (garbanzo).

Spanish doctors brought the use of mercury to the Americas, where it was absorbed into practices of native peoples, who had their own conception of indigestion and its remedies. As European physicians turned away from mercury, and maintained a posture of using it only when there was no other possibility, its use persisted in the former Spanish colonies. The popular disease concept of *empacho* and its raw mercury remedy occasionally emerges into wider notice. An episode of an American television series focused on forensic crime detection had a Latino boxer explaining the presence of mercury on his boxing gloves as some of the metal he spilled while taking it for his *empacho*. He actually has loaded his glove with the heavy mass to give it added force that kills a superior opponent.

Like Barrios and other Spanish physicians, Dover incorporated mercury into the Galenic heat control routines, and eventually he concentrated on raw mercury exclusively. He was not interested in another use of mercury and its compounds also traced back to Galen, to cause patients to salivate and sweat out their disease poisons. The mercury mass down the throat cleared it all out, he thought.

In framing his promotion of raw mercury to avoid references to Spain and Spanish mercury mines, Dover could also avoid references to the poisonous nature of the substance. He could keep the sources of mercury, probably Spain and its colonies, concealed and remote. But there was another reason to emphasize the weighty, liquid form of the metal.

One way in which Dover was making common cause with at least some other physicians practicing in London was the "dispensary controversy." The College of Physicians had voted to allow their members to give medical advice to the poor free of charge, but when the apothecaries tried to profit from filling the resultant prescriptions, the physicians set up their own dispensary to prescribe medications and fill prescriptions at cost. Physicians divided into two camps, those favoring the dispensary and those opposing it. Dover and Sir Hans Sloane were among the dispensarians.

In a passage in *The Ancient Physician* declaring the harmlessness of quick-silver — because of its soft, globular nature it goes down more easily than pointed edged compounds — Dover advises the patient to get a small crucible and "put into it the Quantity of a Pistol-bullet of Quicksilver." Any metals that have been added to the quicksilver will remain in the heated crucible while the quicksilver itself will fly off. To make his meaning clearer, Dover quotes the price of quicksilver, eight to ten shillings, compared to the price of a pound of lead, two pence.

"The Profit that arises may be one Cause of its Adulteration, and another to bring the Medicine in Disrepute." After more praise for mercury, Dover states plainly that the doctors dare not prescribe it, "for fear of disobliging the Apothecaries."

The apothecaries would be disobliged by having to supply medications they did not compound themselves. Dover is saying you can test quicksilver for purity yourself, and if it is pure it is a wonderful remedy. You don't know what you're getting when you bring your slip to the apothecary. The weight added to mercury by the addition of lead reduces its value and makes it poisonous. It does not make it a more powerful internal force against blockages. The superiority of unadulterated mercury over the products of the apothecaries, takes precedence over the weight it would acquire by the addition of lead.

In giving his instructions to purchasers of mercury Dover warns anyone heating it to detect adulteration: "But let him take particular Care not to hang his Head over it; for the Effluvia are a Poison of the most subtile Nature." Liquid quicksilver is not a poison unless something else is added, but mercury vapors are lethal. Vapors are the opposite of the weighted body, and they are not what Dr. Dover ordered.

The Spanish ships that Dover captured carried the wealth of the empire, which included iron flasks of mercury refined at mines in Spain, Peru and California. Mercury was a basic component in the amalgamation method of refining silver. Mixed with silver ore and heated together with mild acid the mercury would draw out the silver into a spongy residue which then could be melted and cast to make metallic silver. Spanish ships traveling down the coast of the colony of Peru often carried mercury from the mines in the north to the silver mines at Potosi about a thousand miles south. The mercury was in such demand for New World silver refining operations in Peru and Mexico that it sometimes had to be brought from the mines at Almaden in Spain to keep up silver production.

Dover became Dr. Quicksilver after he returned to London because he had amassed a quantity of mercury and mercury lore from his adventures, which he used to recommend himself to the urban elites already familiar with mercury as a syphilis treatment. Using other colonial ingredients, opium and ipecac, he fashioned his powder, an alternative to one of the main uses of mercury. In his hands the mercury remedy was milder than before, and it was probably this reputation that led members of the London elite like Booth to take his recommendations seriously where before they would have dismissed mercury for its deadliness.

Dover was 72 years old in 1733, a veteran of privateering expeditions and battles with the College of Physicians. His *Ancient Physician* was an attempt to revive a flagging practice of medicine by setting forth the sensational cures achieved using the remedies he advocated. He had been so desperate prior to its publication that he solicited patients from other physicians practicing in London, including Sir Hans Sloane. In a later edition of the book he included a letter from Captain Harry Colt, who, after years of declining, heard of Dover's book, "which made a great Noise in London, and was the Subject of almost every Coffee-House, and seeing several Pamphlets daily advertis'd and wrote against it by some of the [London medical] Faculty, I resolved to buy it."

Colt summoned Dover for a consultation and Dover prescribed a heavy dose of quicksilver taken daily. Booth also called in Dover and received the same prescription. It "would effectually cure him of all his complaints," as Daniel Turner later quoted Dover saying to Booth. Colt lived on, a well man, but for Barton Booth the upshot of acting on Dover's advice was death.

Dover himself lived until 1742, producing five more editions of his book, quarreling with physicians and apothecaries, and adding new testimonials with each edition, his longevity itself seeming a recommendation of his methods. But he never mentioned Barton Booth.

Other writers did, immediately after Booth's death.

Daniel Turner, a "surgeon turned physician," was developing an expertise in diseases of the skin and he eventually published the first English treatise on that specialty on the boundary between the surgeon's interior and the physician's outward signs. He seemed to be looking back at his surgical practice when he detailed Booth's autopsy in an annex, "The Case of Mr. Booth," to his critique of Dover's prescriptions *The Ancient Physician's Legacy Impartially Survey'd* (1733). Turner wrote that he learned the details of Booth's uncovered interior from his fellow surgeon, Alexander Small.

Turner's pamphlet was a general attack on Dover's successful recipe book, and an attempt to draw to himself some of the attention given to Dover. Remember that Captain Colt bought a copy of *The Ancient Physician's Legacy* because other writers were disputing its recommendations. Colt had found that the conventional treatments did not work, and was eager to try what their proponents opposed.

Turner used the case of Booth to advance his arguments against quicksilver treatment. He looked at the most striking findings of the autopsy, the discovery of large calculi, stones, in Booth's gall bladder and bile duct, and concluded that it was a long-developing obstruction of the bile duct that caused Booth's troubles and ended his life. Booth's consumption of a pile of mercury did nothing to clear out this obstruction, and, as the post-mortem found, it lodged inside him, hastening his demise.

Turner himself would not advise the use of mercury because it was poisonous and at the same time was not absorbed into the blood as Dover claimed. He declared that those who expected mercury to cause miracles in the blood may find that it ends in their breeches. He described a lady embarrassingly losing mercury which those at the gathering mistook for "brilliants" (gems) scattered on the floor.

Turner's seemingly contradictory assessment of mercury as medicine, poisonous yet unlikely to reach the blood, revolves around the importance assigned to obstruction and release in both popular and medical understanding of disease, discomfort and healing. If mercury could get into the blood, think of the wonders it would accomplish for sluggish flow.

Hippocrates in his *Aphorisms* and other texts set down the view that solids and fluids flowed into the body, were moved around and released in the form of wastes. It was possible, he thought, to receive bad substances which would damage the container; it was possible for blockages to arise in any of the conduits which made even beneficial substances bad by keeping them in one place. Blockages were due to the nature and quantity of what was consumed, and to events in the natural movement influenced by temperature, atmospheres, environment, social life, stars and divine disposition — whichever one chose to emphasize.

In devising treatments to heal disease by clearing out blockages, physicians were giving medical form to popular belief. This also provided a way to explain remedies to potential consumers. The Spanish conquerors of Mexico, for instance, found the Aztecs using herbal purges, and introduced them to the use of liquid quicksilver which was absorbed into folk medicine and continued to be used long after it was no longer advised. The softness and heavy flow of mercury made it comparatively more desirable than other purgatives people commonly used.

Dover recommended mercury for "vermicular diseases," those caused by worms, because it "opens all obstructions," to the passage of body fluids and therefore encouraging the exit of foreign bodies. It "makes a pure balsam of the blood," making mercury the only effective treatment for venereal sores, the outward manifestation of syphilis. In addition to these major uses, Dover inserts into the list of complaints around which his book is organized a number of parenthetical uses for mercury, such as treatment of scrofula, for "the iliac passion" (appendicitis) and as a fertility promoter for both men and women. He did not recommend it for fevers, and proposed other treatments for plague and smallpox. In one case of "anomalous smallpox," he even admitted that "mercury did not answer."

Dover wrote,

> he that rightly considers the State of the Animal Oeconomy, the various alterations it suffers from the Stagnation of its most viscid Juices in the smallest Canals, and how much the Impulse and Force of the circling Blood, by which Obstructions are to be removed, must be increased by along with it such Particles as the Mercurial Globuli, will perhaps see good Reason to allow, that the prudent and cautious Management of Quicksilver, may do that in some obstinate and dangerous Diseases, which we cannot promise ourselves from any other of our known Medicines whatsoever.

The impetus of mercury in the blood was analogous to its obvious weight in carrying obstructions down through the digestive system. Mercury has the additional advantage of being soft and globular, not spiny, acidic and with edges like other drugs. It goes down swiftly and easily.

All the uses Dover conceived for mercury, even its effect on the blood, had to do with its gross material impetus. The rest were the long-established uses to reduce skin rashes.

Dover was so dedicated to crude mercury weight as a treatment strategy that he cited such authorities as Belloste, who favored light mercury preparations, as supporters of mercury in the raw state, and he ignored such mercury compounds as calomel (mercurous chloride, $HgCl$) and corrosive sublimate (mercuric chloride, $HgCl2$) which themselves had a pharmaceutical history. He even recruited supporters of a medication called Aethiops mineral to his raw mercury preference.

Treatment strategies for restoring and ensuring health by cleansing the body of poisons and obstructions had been in use for the entire recorded history of medicine. The accumulated disease-causing substance can be forced out directly, by purging through the mouth, by forcing evacuation of the intestines, by increasing urine flow, clearing the rectum with enemas or by causing sweats. There was a long list of procedures and medicines to accomplish these, to which Dover emphatically added raw mercury.

Thomas Dover had made a historic contribution to the sweating (diaphoretic) remedy by compounding a powder long afterward associated with his name, a mixture of opium, ipecacuanha and other ingredients meant to make it palatable. Dover originally promoted the formulation as an analgesic to relieve the pain of gout, source of the most gnawing pain his likely patrons suffered. The opium promoted sleep and exciting dreams, the ipecacuanha profuse sweating, with the result that the consumer awoke feeling much better and wanting more. But Dover didn't prescribe his powder for Booth. He prescribed mercury, which by its heaviness would weigh down and force open the stopper.

The debate that followed in pamphlets for years after Booth's death and autopsy turned around whether the mercury did no harm and might even have benefited the dying actor, or whether it had sealed the obstruction already created by the stones in Booth's gall bladder and bile duct and added more poison to what already built up there.

A pamphleteer who signed himself only "Mercurialist" disputed that mercury could have caused Booth's death, since the description of the intestines at autopsy was not consistent with the smooth appearance when mercury destroys a patient. This would not seem to give much support to Dover since it was an admission that mercury does destroy patients. Another of Dover's defenders, a "Gentleman of Trinity College," in a pamphlet published after Booth's death, did not take the risk of mentioning Booth at all, and just upheld Dover's assertion that crude mercury taken internally cleanses the blood and blunts acids. Some drugs have spines, points or edges, Dover held, which mercury smooths over with its soft globules.

The anonymous post-mortem pamphlet writer, Turner and H. Bradley maintained that the mercury poisoned Booth; Dover, the "Mercurialist" writing after Turner's contribution, and others held for the benefits of mercury. Both sides of the controversy assigned power to mercury but differed on what it accomplished inside the body as they conceived it. Thomas Harris, a physician who had accumulated a dossier of "experiments and histories" supporting the "innocency and usefulness" of crude mercury, proclaimed its "force and energy," while Turner and a range of pamphleteers maintained the stealing, insidious nature of the substance.

Dover rejected the statements of classical authors Dioscorides, Pliny, and Galen that mercury is a poison, and he mockingly pointed out that the "Aethiops mineral" prescribed by his contemporaries was a compound of mercury and sulfur. Dioscorides had even appended the comment that "hydrargyrum" (in John Goodyer's 1655 English translation) "has a pernicious faculty, being drank, eating through the inward parts, by weight."

Dover's critics rejoined that Dover's own mentor Sydenham, whom Turner accused Dover of merely copying, was opposed to using mercury as a medication. The controversy went on for a number of years in pamphlet after pamphlet, Booth being forgotten, but many of the issues about mercury and other debates on medical treatment appearing in the discussion, including some catchphrases such as "the use and abuse of mercury," which appeared and reappeared in the voluminous literature.

Surveying this literature, the medical historian Kenneth Dewhurst concluded that the "heroic doses of oral quicksilver" promoted by Dover and his supporters were only effective psychologically, serving to comfort sufferers of gastrointestinal ailments conceived as blockages, in the period before the development of abdominal surgery. But Booth's exposed interior showed something darker.

Booth's autopsy put Sir Hans Sloane in mind of a letter he had received some time previously from Dublin physician Dr. Madden, and Sloane published the letter in the *Philosophical Transactions of The Royal Society* in 1734. "The internal Use of crude Mercury is become so frequent of late, that I believe it may produce some great Benefit to Mankind hereafter, if a careful Collection was made of all the extraordinary Cases relating to the good or bad Effects of this Practice," Madden writes. Dr. Madden also writes that he was present with another doctor and a surgeon at the opening of the body of "a Gentleman of Note in Dublin who for several years had found difficulty in going to Stool.... In order to procure a passage downward (which I suppose was a principal Complaint) he took, by the advice of a Physician, since dead, several Ounces of crude Mercury, at different times, without any Relief, and at length died." Opening the gentleman's distended abdomen released "a great Quantity of Wind," and the Stomach was empty and inflamed inside: "We observed in several Places of the small Guts, some scatter'd Grains of crude Mercury, and along with them we generally found a black gritty Powder, very like Aethiops Mineral, which was, without doubt, the Mercury changed into the Consistence."

The gentleman's interior was very much like Booth's, except here the blackness was compared to the mercury-sulfur preparation Aethiops mineral. This was the figurative name for a black sulfide of mercury made simply by rubbing mercury and sulfur together, as it could be imagined was what happened in the intestines. Alchemists and painters had learned that Aethiops mineral heated would sublimate and condense on a cooler surface as a red-orange deposit which gave its name to its peculiar color, vermilion. The silver into black into vermilion cycle achieved only with mercury, sulfur and heat had all the colors of life and death. The Aethiops mineral interior of the gut would be found in others dead of ingesting mercury.

As the examination of the dead gentleman's digestive organs progressed, the medical men discovered crude mercury and black powder in the volume of liquid excrement accumulated in the colon. Cutting the large intestine horizontally, amid other signs of inflammation, they found a body obstructing the passage downward, a small cartiliginous plumb-stone. And that is where the letter abruptly ends.

Sloane had the letter printed to provide another case parallel to Booth's postmortem still being debated in pamphlets. The mercury had not cleared the intestinal obstruction; in fact it had not made it past the colon blocked by a gastric stone, which explained the man's struggles with passing his stools. This had gone on for some time prior to his death. Dr. Madden does not speculate on the cause of death. The visible presence of mercury in the inflamed stomach and colon suggested that it had a role in hastening the man's demise rather than clearing his digestive tract as intended. This is an extraordinary case of the bad effects of taking crude mercury. It confirms Dioscorides' classical precedent together with Booth's example.

In the late sixteenth century, an interested King Charles IX of France asked the surgeon Ambroise Paré if a type of stone found in the intestines of goats, the bezoar, was an antidote to any poison that might be swallowed. Paré said there was no such thing as a universal antidote, but the king chose to make an experiment. He offered a condemned man his life if he was willing to take an unknown poison provided by an apothecary followed by some bezoar. The man died in agony, pawing the floor of his cell like a beast with blood pouring from all his openings. In the presence of witnesses Paré opened him up and found the bottom of his stomach black and dry. He then knew that the apothecary had given him sublimate of mercury.

The black powder that appears in Booth's and the unnamed gentleman's intestines after taking raw mercury and in the stomach of the unfortunate prisoner after being fed sublimate may be akin to the black "faeces" of mercury that alchemists regarded as an impurity to be removed on the way to creating "philosophical mercury."

In that same year, 1734, the Dutch physician Hermann Boerhaave, whom Booth planned to consult during his final illness, published *Some Experiments Concerning Mercury* in London. These were English translations from the Latin of letters Boerhaave was sending to the Royal Society for publication in their *Philosophical Transactions*. Boerhaave taught a generation of English doctors the importance of connecting symptoms to physical lesions rather than relying on vague humoral causes. In his mercury experiments he reported the results of performing chemical and physical actions on raw mercury, and he rigorously tested specific alchemical notions.

Simply heating mercury produced a black powder, and then heating the black powder at a higher temperature, yielded a lesser amount of metallic mercury than was originally heated. Boerhaave had identified the process that led to formation of the black powder observed in Booth's and the Dublin gentleman's interior after they swallowed quantities of mercury. Rather than entering the blood and passing down the gut as Dover and his supporters believed, mercury changed consistency in the heat of the body, with some of the metal lost to sublimation. Oxygen had not yet been named, the chemical process of oxidation was unknown, and the black substance was not yet called mercuric oxide, but it was known that mercury yielded a black powder when heated, as in the body. Sulfide, chloride and oxide each contributed a blackness where mercury ended in the gut. "In a purely metallic state, mercury, when taken into the human stomach, produces no effects except such as are owing to its mechanical properties. Nevertheless, it may become oxidized, and, by combination with some of the acids in the stomach, occasion violent disorders." This piece of information in a popular encyclopedia article on mercury written in the early nineteenth century gave a scientific description to what had already been seen in the stomachs of people who took too much mercury and died. Further research suggested that it was the oxides of other metals amalgamated with the mercury and not the mercury itself that yielded the black powder.

Considered medical advice turned against using uncontained metallic mercury to relieve obstructions in the digestive tract, yet in the 1880s an experienced forensic scientist could flatly state, "Nothing is more common than to discover traces of mercury in the stomach, bowels, liver, kidneys and other organs of a dead body." By then, there were many other ways for it to get there.

2

⚯

The Women of Smyrna

> M. le Duc, Physician, who made the tour of the Levant, says that women in
> Smyrna who want to become fat often swallow two drams of crude mercury, giv-
> ing the lie to those who consider it a poison.

Augustin Belloste reports this in the 1733 edition of his physician's guide. The
women may want to become fat to appear pregnant, or just to show an appeal-
ing plumpness. Belloste uses this as another example of how commonplace it
is to use mercury.

M. le Duc was not the first one who carried to Europe word of this practice by the women of the ancient Mediterranean port. M. Dodart, a member of
the Académie Royale des Sciences, writing in *Journal des Sçavans* in 1680
recounted the plague preventive used by a French physician in the city of
Smyrna: wearing dried toads in his armpits and groin to dry out the skin sores
while taking pills made of powdered toad. The same French physician told
Dodart that the women of Smyrna take two drams of mercury, accompanied
by superstitious ceremonies, to "become fat."

The women of Smyrna, Christians of Greek origin, were already known
to Europeans as legendary beauties much desired by the ruling Turks for their
harems. They were the subject of soft-carpeted fantasies for both men and
women. The tendency to look eastward when seeking sexually explicit dramas
was embodied in Oriental romances and in the first translation into a European language (French) of the *Arabian nights*, which began to appear in print
during the early eighteenth century. The male physicians who were reporting this practice (but no instance of its success) were casting a sly glance both
east and west and suggesting to women that this was how they might appear
voluptuous without actually being pregnant, an art which those eastern women

presumably commanded. Added to this was the thought that the sensual Anatolian males preferred well-rounded female partners.

Adding another exotic population, Thomas Dover broadened the prescription but changed its purpose. "The Indians at the Malucco Islands, and the Ladies at Smyrna, often take Quicksilver as a Remedy against Barrenness. An ounce may be taken once a Day for a Month or two, which will prove an extraordinary Remedy." Now mercury has become a cure for a woman's infertility.

A few pages later Dover quotes a letter from the merchant Samuel Jenkins who recounts the story of a Russian glass-house workman. The man spilled some mercury onto his food and later timed his wife's conceiving a child to the day he ate that food. The fertilizing force of crude mercury could apparently be transmitted from men to women. It was no longer a matter of sheer weight in the body; it seemed to spark the ability to father children as it did the appearance of conceiving them. In the course of doing this, Dover used an approximation of the Cyrillic letters spelling the Russian word for mercury, РТУТ, rtut, adding the further exoticism of the Far North to the Spice Islands and the perfumed East.

According to Dover's secondhand tale, mercury canceled out both impotence and barrenness, and helped couples blamelessly make children. This parallels his recruiting mercury as a purgative of extraordinary virtue that could be transferred from stomach to blood. The advocate of mercury by weight found that virtue extended to fertility as well.

Dover's critic Daniel Turner recognized what would happen if women swallowed quantities of crude mercury in the pursuit of comeliness: they scattered it on the ballroom floor behind them in a trail bearing laughable resemblance to shining jewels. Mercury actually would affect women the same way it affected men and animals, as a laxative. Thomas Dover, ever a promoter of swallowing mercury to clear the interior by weight, must also have known the result of a woman following his advice.

Mercury acts in the body through oppositions. It is both poison and medicine, both solid and liquid, both gravity and flight. It leapt briefly into the fecundating role because these shifting qualities matched it well with the ambiguous interior of a woman's body. An ancient Assyrian medical text explains that liquid mercury could be used to stimulate contractions during a difficult birth. This suggests that the mercury would add force to the muscles to hasten the birth, and that it could have this effect at other times too.

Since Hippocrates, the womb was thought to wander about the body influencing mood and health, which explained women's changeability. It was like other organs both men and women shared, the stomach and the bladder, in its ability to absorb fluids and become blocked, and it seemed to be directly connected to the digestive system. Yet it was becoming, in the phrase of the sixteenth-century astrologer-midwife Simon Forman, "a wordle unto itself." Using the Anglo-Norman word "matrix" for the female organ, Forman prescribed the same medicines as are used for the stomach "For medisons given to exempte the matrix or to purge the matrix and to make yt vomite out that which is in yt, muste and oughte to be of that nature and quality, that other medisons are that ar given to a man or a woman to exempte the stomake that is cloyed with humors to make him vomite vp those humores out of his stomake and soe to rid his stomake thereof." The uterus was subject to the same external influences as the stomach and could receive the same medicines for the same purpose, yet its responses were independent and utterly different from the other fluid-receiving organs. This was an attempt to formulate strategies for affecting what the uterus does, shape children, by using drugs with effects established for other organs. Any variations from experience, for Forman at least, were explained by the positions of stars and planets.

Whether the women of Smyrna were familiar with these beliefs or not, the male physicians propagating word of the practice thought that their drinking liquid mercury would enter the uterus as it did the stomach. But the uterus was different from the stomach. The mercury would weigh it down and to the exploring hand of a midwife might make it seem to contain a fetus.

This notion passed quickly through the literature, but there is no record of anyone actually trying this with mercury. Instead, another effect on the uterus of taking quantities of liquid mercury made its guarded appearance. If there already was a child in the uterus when the mercury was consumed, then mercury would cause it to be aborted by the pressure of its arrival.

Commenting on the bodily uses of raw mercury in his 1746 translation into English of Theophrastus's *History of Stones*, John Hill wrote, "It [raw mercury] first got into Use externally among the Arabians; and afterwards, but not long afterwards, got introduced into the Number of internal Medicines, from the repeated Observations of its Safety and good Effects when given to Cattle, and from the hardy Attempts of some unhappy People, who had ventured to take it down in large Quantities (in order to procure Abortion) without any ill Effect."

From pregnancy simulation to a cure for barrenness is not far, but to understand raw mercury as an abortion prescription requires accounting for its peculiar weight in the female body. "The Arabians" used it externally, but it was through cattle that its internal effect on reproduction was confirmed. Women, much less the women of Smyrna, are not explicitly mentioned; they are "some unhappy people" implied through the word "abortion," common to cattle and women.

There are records of mercury actually being used to induce premature births in cattle, and only hints that it voluntarily was used that way by humans. An instance that surfaced in the medical literature in the late nineteenth century suggests that crude mercury abortions actually were a continual belief sometimes leading to attempts. Discussing the toxicity of raw mercury, the pioneering forensic toxicologist Alexander Wynter Blyth refers to:

the case of a girl who swallowed 4½ oz. by weight of the liquid metal, for the purpose of procuring abortion — this it did not effect; but, in a few days, she suffered from a trembling and a shaking of the body and loss of muscular power. Those symptoms continued for two months, but there was no salivation and no bile marks on the gums. The case is a rare one, and a pound or more has been taken without injury.

Blyth cites this report from a note in the medical journal *Lancet* published twelve years earlier, and the only corroborative detail he can muster is an allusion to others who have taken more without injury. Alfred Swaine Taylor, in a fundamental treatise on medical jurisprudence, twice alludes to this same abortion attempt. Neither Blyth nor Taylor speculatively asks why the girl thought downing 4½ ounces of mercury would cause the fetus to be ejected, nor does Sir Duncan Gibb, who wrote the original note. They all are interested in the highly uncommon opportunity this case affords to observe the symptoms of gross mercury in the body. The attempted abortion itself was not a success. The mass of mercury is unpleasant, ineffective and harmless.

It may be that this was an opportunistic abortion attempt which seemed likely to work from the character of the materials and the idea that they would bear down softly on the womb. Given the other methods of procuring abortion, mechanical, botanical and chemical, external pressure, internal penetration, violent emetics and purgatives, liquid mercury must have appeared to be a gentler alternative to anyone who tried it without knowing of a precedent. So it was discovered again by another desperate woman with a bottle of mercury, and again it did not succeed, but that outcome was not promulgated until the young woman came to Dr. Gibb's attention.

By the early twentieth century, knowledge of abortion by liquid mercury remained sufficiently current for doctors to allude to the possibility, but not so important that they would include it among the agents for procuring abortion (liquid mercury, not the compounds). One author of a general treatise on the treatment of internal disease surveyed the prophylactic uses of raw mercury in many contexts, and discussing the occasions it should not be used, wrote, "Pregnancy is no contraindication, except that undue zeal in its use may produce abortion by irritation of the large intestine; on the other hand a proper use of the drug in many instances prevents abortion." Dr. Forchheimer doesn't describe any instances in which mercury caused an abortion by irritating the large intestine, and like most of his predecessors he found mercury prevented abortion by extinguishing infections.

Equally elliptical was the use of mercury by weight to induce therapeutic abortions that several turn-of-the-century obstetricians revealed in their writings. In cases of "incarceration of the pregnant uterus [which] cannot be relieved except by emptying the uterus," Dr. Frederick Joseph Taussig recommended that the uterus be "brought forward" and thus emptied either by the woman taking "the knee-chest posture" or "by introduction into the vagina of a colpourynter filled with one to two pound of mercury." In a book with many cross-sectional illustrations of the uterus in states of pregnancy and manipulation, this latter procedure is illustrated only by a photograph of the instruments, a pair of obstetric forceps, a bottle, a funnel and a soft bag connected to a tube, the colpourynter of the description.

In this method the woman did not take the mercury by mouth; she had it inserted into her, in a mass that was intended to force the uterus to change position and "empty its contents." This is where any mention of abortion by liquid mercury ends.

When drinking raw mercury to cause an abortion is mentioned at all in present-day literature, it is shifted again eastward (and into the past) by noting without reference that ancient Chinese women sought abortion this way. As with many other notices of abortion, it passes as a generality and a rumor, with no names attached.

The Taoist physician Sun Si-Mao (d. 695 C.E.) included in his *Thousand Gold Prescriptions* a recipe for a contraceptive pill: fry mercury with oil and take it on an empty stomach. This depended upon a stomach-uterus connection, and was likely to forestall conception because it would make the consumer too sick to be sexually available. A similar backhanded recommendation exists in the statement of a Chinese pharmacopeia that mercury is good for treating skin conditions, adding a warning to be careful since it might cause a miscarriage.

A further suggestion of the effects of drinking crude mercury on the sexual body is in the birth story of the eleventh-century Japanese Buddhist monk Joson. His father Ningai is reputed to have ceased sexual relations with his wife, who tried to poison the newborn by making him drink mercury. Joson survived, but with deformed genitals that led to lifelong celibacy. In this story there is a shadow of the effects of mercury on a child's development, a glance forward toward the effects of mercury on the children of Minamata centuries later.

The belief that raw (or lightly fried) mercury could affect the organs of conception through the stomach persisted because the tangible weight of the substance and its softness seemed likely to bear down harmlessly when taken by mouth. This is no record of experience, just a traditional supposition based on mercury's attributes and an image of the body's interior.

In Ayurvedic writings of India, mercury is the shining, potent semen of Shiva which can only be contained by the sulfur of his female consort, together making the black and the red of birth. Mercury was the basis therefore of many medicines spurring both virility and fertility, coyly described as rejuvenating. Unalloyed mercury was thought to overwhelm the sex organs and induce abortions and monsters, and it was seen as needing to be modulated by mixture with herbal ingredients.

Fertility drugs in Europe were unlikely to contain mercury, which joined other heavy metals in being used to induce abortions by weight.

Lead, another heavy metal, also was reputed to cause abortions if eaten in weighty quantity. It was sold in pharmacies in the form of lead oleate ("black stick") used to tampen bandages but also was rolled into pills and swallowed to induce an abortion. There was a minor epidemic of lead poisoning in some English counties during the 1890s as women attempted this expedient. Taking lead also was based on the belief that downward pressure in the stomach could force the uterus to expel its contents, not on any peculiar ability of lead to cause abortions. Iron had a similar reputation, and when "female pills" were advertised as containing iron it was an oblique message that taking them could terminate an unwanted pregnancy.

As early as the sixteenth century, when mercury and its compounds were used to treat the victims of syphilis, the concern was expressed that if mercury was given to a pregnant woman it might cause an abortion. In 1673, Nicolas de Blegny, surgeon to the French king, declared that the mercury cure of a woman with child was very dangerous: "For a Foetus is too weak to endure the commotions caus'd by Mercury and other remedies: Besides, that it runs the greatest risk of being render'd abortive."

Thomas Hawkes Tanner, an American syphilologist of the mid–nineteenth century, calls this an error, and has no doubt that it is the "syphilitic poison" and not the mercury that causes abortions in women known to be infected. Of thirty-seven women who had primary syphilitic sores in the past, twenty-three aborted once or oftener, or were prematurely delivered of dead children, and of the rest, seven gave birth to syphilitic children. This and other examples Tanner puts out as proof that mercury doesn't induce abortions.

Midwives and physicians, while making appeals to mercury to control the effects of syphilis and prevent abortion, were convinced that given in excess it might bring about the abortion it prevented.

> In syphilis affecting the mother, or when the father is syphilitic, there can be no question of the propriety of mild mercurialization as a means of warding off the dangers of abortion, regard being had to the fact that the careless use of [it] may of itself be the cause of abortion.

Mercury here entering the body of a pregnant woman with syphilis is part of a larger duality of mercury and syphilis in human bodies, and mercury is no longer the liquid metal swallowed. It is mixtures and compounds rubbed on the skin, breathed in steaming vapors and digested in liquids and pills.

Dr. James Hamilton, a second-generation professor of midwifery at the University of Edinburgh, recognized in an 1821 publication on the use and abuse of mercurial medications, that infants with congenital syphilis "as well as those infected by nurses," invariably died if mercury was *not* used. Mercury was the sole barrier between the developing fetus and the infections that might come from the mother or from handling by diseased nurses. Many alternatives had been tried to avoid the deleterious effects of mercury, but "it is to be hoped, that in this empire any future attempts to cure so alarming a disease as Syphilis by any other medicine than MERCURY, will be regarded with the reprobation they merit."

The debate over when and in what quantities and concentrations to administer mercury to pregnant women with syphilis had been going on for some time when a benefit of using mercury in all deliveries was discovered. A solution of bichloride of mercury injected into the vagina after birth reduced the likelihood of postpartum infections which endangered the life of the mother. The symptoms of mercury poisoning and any secondary inflammation caused by the injection were considered less dangerous than the puerperal fever that often arose and ended a life that had just given one.

Yet this procedure, much discussed in medical journals in the latter decades of the nineteenth century, was performed by birth attendants who themselves had a role in creating the conditions it solved. From the time of Simon Forman onward, men all over Europe were moving into the women's preserve of birth assistance, bringing with them, they claimed, a greater technical sophistication, or, as women asserted, a lack of finesse. The midwife Sarah Stone, for instance, in a polemic, luridly accused man-midwives of dragging the birth child out with forceps, crushing its head so its brains leaked.

Oliver Wendell Holmes observed that the physicians or midwives who had contact with a woman who had died of childbed (puerperal) fever not infrequently had attended other women similarly afflicted. At the conclusion of his paper "The Contagiousness of Puerperal Fever" (1843) he set out a series of rules for birthing practitioners to follow to avoid spreading the contagion. By 1853, in a revised version of the paper, he mentioned a physician in Vienna who had already proposed sanitary measures in a maternity hospital.

Holmes was thanked for his paper, but Ignac Semmelweis became the unwitting savior of the colleagues who disparaged him, or at least of the hospital-centered birthing system that employed them. Semmelweis asked the doctors in a Viennese birthing hospital to wash their hands with antiseptic before they went from examining the corpses of women recently deceased to visiting women about to give birth. The incredulity today over the career-killing resistance he encountered is a tribute to how completely physicians like him transformed attitudes and procedures. But the problem they solved only came into existence with the emergence of a male-dominated obstetrics profession and the lying-in hospitals where they practiced.

Before the bacterial cause of the contagion and fever was identified, substances like the bichloride of mercury (the chemically precise and less daunting new name for corrosive sublimate) became known for their ability to halt the spread and prevent the arrival of birth-associated sickness now known to be at the hands of physicians. Once bacteria were connected with illness and streptococcus species in particular were known and seen to cause childbed fever, the efficacy of mercury compounds could be measured on bacteria in cultures. Gynecologists and obstetricians became so reliant on this prop of their ability to move about hospitals without spreading contagion that, as with mercurial treatments of syphilis, they weighed its potential damage and continued to use it.

The degree of professional acceptance this had reached by the 1890s can be seen in the instructions T. Gaillard Thomas gave for assuring that a woman who has just endured a therapeutic abortion does not develop a lethal infection:

> Anesthetize the patient with ether, not chloroform, and place her on a table in the Sims position. The vagina, vulva, and anus having been thoroughly cleansed with carbolized water, take a sponge saturated with bichloride solution (1 to 2,000), and with it fill the vagina with the solution. By this means the os will be placed in a lake of the antiseptic fluid. But may not the bichloride poison the patient? Well, I have never yet met with this accident; but even if the mercury should affect her system to some extent, the dose will not be sufficient to kill her, and it is better to run this slight risk rather than expose her to the danger of septic infection.

Mild mercurialization is the price the woman pays for survival in the hospital environment, where the bichloride offsets the risk of infection created by conditions in the place. The bichloride saves the life of the mother and her newborn, but only because they are in the hospital where they acquire the infection.

On the average, giving birth in hospitals where sanitation was an established practice improved the chances of both mother and infant living past the experience. In the absence of antibiotics which could control systemic infections caused by bacterial toxins, physicians used antiseptics to cleanse and protect susceptible tissues. Their detached inspection of suffering birth mothers built a barrier against initial infection which then could be prevented from raging out of control.

Commenting on the antiseptic control of childbed infections, a writer in a compilation of medical practices current in the late nineteenth century declared, "That antiseptic has been too freely practiced there can be no question, nor can it be doubted that corrosive sublimate is a most dangerous weapon, if carelessly used. The charge upon the microbe has really been too aggressive." This author favors *aseptic* practices, heat-sterilizing instruments, gloves and surfaces, over antiseptics applied to the exposed tissues. New, milder antiseptics were being developed, but the difficulty of clearing out an infection once it had established itself made the reliably preventive bichloride the continued choice, and those who used it too freely were criticized but not regulated.

The net increase in survivorship accomplished even by the moderate use of bichloride accompanied a net increase in mercury entering women's bodies. Little attention was paid to the effects upon the children born under these conditions. The physiologist François Magendie had shown in the mid–nineteenth century that mercury kills germ cells of animals, but many doctors took this as an indication of its effectiveness which could be moderated with smaller doses. Statements as plain as "no embryo can live when exposed to the deleterious effects of mercury" and "mercury destroys the power of reproduction" were counterbalanced by the assertion that mercury is "homeopathic" to the symptoms of decay, that mercury in moderate doses could control them.

As the medical professions tried to establish what that moderate dose might be, families were learning about and using bichloride of mercury and a range of other substances to control births and thus the number of dependent children. If this took the form of abortion, of administering the mercury compound after conception, it could be called criminal abortion if discovered by legal authorities, who would hold the supplier of the caustic substance responsible. But mercury could also be used as a contraceptive. During the time of anti-syphilis invention that led to the creation of condoms, there is a record of men smearing their genitals with a mercury preparation to destroy the sperm.

For those disposed to view mercury as a way of controlling conception, an analogy could be drawn between the germs that might enter a woman's vagina and other living bodies that might be injected there, male sperm. Bichloride then can be a contraceptive. The sperm are equated with germs eliminated by antiseptics. Thus, in her 1914 pamphlet offering women the means of birth control, Margaret Sanger lists a number of solutions which could be used in a douche after intercourse to prevent pregnancy. On "bichloride," she warns the woman reader that the blue tablets obtained from the druggist are "less dangerous to have about because of the color." The white bichloride tablets also obtainable so resembled other tablets (particularly quinine) that they were more likely to be consumed by accident. "Always mix this solution thoroughly in a glass or pitcher before turning it into the bag. Never drop the tablet directly into the bag. One tablet in two quarts of water makes a splendid solution for preventive purposes." Sanger did not include the other medicinal chloride of mercury, calomel, which is less soluble in water than bichloride, and therefore would be more likely to leave a caustic residue damaging to vaginal tissue. Bichloride of mercury, or corrosive sublimate, was recommended with cautions over carbolic acid solution because the acid solution would require a prescription while the bichloride pills were readily available without a doctor's consent. Chinosol is less injurious to tissues than bichloride, and was available at a specific address in Manhattan that Sanger provided. Potassium permanganate, another soluble antiseptic, has the disadvantage of staining skin and clothing and thus revealing its use. Vinegar was used by European peasants, a salt solution can be used, as could plain water, but with the disadvantage of not reaching all the semen, which could "hide itself away in the vaginal cavity."

Sanger recommended commonly used sanitizing agents to kill the sperm before implantation into the egg took place, a use not detected by pharmacies, doctors and family members. Bichloride had been available in pill form since the 1880s, for general cleansing purposes, and Sanger was not the first to include it among contraceptives. Her counsel was part of a population-control program, on the one hand protofeminist in the attempt to put childbearing decisions in the hands of women, and on the other hand eugenic in the attempt to limit the births of children belonging to certain racial and ethnic groups.

Bichloride of mercury (not called corrosive sublimate by any of its suppliers) had been causing cases of acute mercury poisoning reported in medical journals ever since its introduction in tablet form. Sanger's pamphlet probably reduced this slightly by providing instructions.

Yet a survey of twenty-one cases of acute mercurial poisoning collected by B. I. Johnstone found three instances of women who had misused bichloride tablets in the ways Sanger warned against, one of them who douched daily for three months, another who put three tablets into a single douche.

Johnstone's purpose in publishing the cases was to examine this type of poisoning, not to condemn the use of bichloride as a contraceptive. The poisoning only took place when the chemical was used too frequently or in too great a quantity at one time. That led to a toxic accumulation of mercury that showed symptoms easily mistaken for many other conditions—nausea, loss of coordination, tremors—until the bichloride use was admitted. Then steps could be taken to clear the mercury from the body, mainly by keeping the victim alive until the body itself accomplished that.

Johnstone included the case of a man who suffered poisoning when he took the advice of a quack, and spread "blue ointment," metallic mercury in grease, on his genitals in an attempt to cure impotence. Dover's view that the metal itself induced fertility in men as in woman had survived. Mercury was being used to promote fertility at the same time mercury compounds were being used contraceptively, both leading to the same poisoning that called for the same treatment.

A few years after Johnstone's 1931 survey, an examination of a much larger number of cases of poisoning found misuse of bichloride for contraception to account for the largest proportion of acute accidental poisonings (24 out of 300). The physician who compiled the survey observed that the number of such poisonings had fallen in recent years due to the spread of information about the potentially harmful nature of bichloride and the introduction of safer means.

In 1938, the same writer, I.M. Rabinowitch, reported on a single case of a woman who poisoned herself after placing two bichloride tablets directly into her vagina without knowing their contents. She had been told that the pills would induce menstruation. It was apparent that only someone who did not know that the pills contained mercury would try to use them in such a concentration to avoid conceiving. The contraceptive quality of bichloride, no longer softened in a douche, was confused with its ability to induce, thus the attempt to restart the menses after a worrisome hiatus, by which time it was too late for contraception and too early for abortion.

The few cases of bichloride poisoning in the medical literature after the 1930s are related to abortion, not contraception, and do not point to a general if sometimes misguided use of the substance but rather to isolated desperate instances. The dialectic of mercury as promoter or stimulant of fertility against mercury as contraceptive and abortifacient was encompassed by the greater contrast, mercury as safe remedy versus mercury as poison. Belloste told the women-of-Smyrna story to demonstrate that mercury was not a poison as reputed in the early eighteenth century.

Twentieth century cases of bichloride poisoning marked a boundary between mercury controlling conception and causing illness, a line that was obliterated by the discovery of other means of contraception. In none of these reproductive uses of mercury was a seemingly obvious consequence introduced: the effect of mercury on the developing fetus. A few observed that the children of women who had used mercury or had contact with men in mercury-intensive industries were likely to be sickly. With the discovery of the effects of mercury on development, the woman's body vanished again to be replaced by the uterus and then by the fetus. The solid mass of mercury purposefully swallowed was replaced by mercury stealing into and through the body across generations.

From simulating and inducing fertility to contraception and abortion, mercury remained a body in itself. When it was used as a chemical compound it became an influence upon childbirth, first protecting it from infection then preventing it through contraception. As deliberate application of mercury and compounds for any reproductive purpose diminished, the accidental effects of mercury upon the process of birth and development took the center, and the woman's body once at the center was exiled to the periphery.

A study of workers in a French hat-making shop, where the process of firming animal fibers with mercuric nitrate caused constant exposure, gave evidence that pregnant workers, and those married to workers but not working themselves, suffered high rates of unhealthy childbearing. Among ten women nonworkers pregnant, there were two stillbirths, three infant deaths, and five sickly children while seven women who were directly exposed to the mercury suffered three miscarriages. Where both of fourteen pairs of parents were workers, there were five stillbirths, six early deaths (before five years) and three surviving in doubtful health. The rates of stillbirth and sickly children for all three groups were greater than the average for their class and period.

Most striking was the ability of the father to convey the damaging influence of mercury into his offspring. Adrien Lizé, the investigator in this study, thought that the "paternal influence" was of mercury carried in the father's clothing, on his skin and hair. He resisted any idea that the mercury passed into the pregnant mother and struck the developing fetus. It either poisoned the mother, causing her to abort, as in the cases of women's direct exposure, or it entered the lungs of the newborn, causing him to become sickly, as hatters did from breathing the atmosphere of the factory.

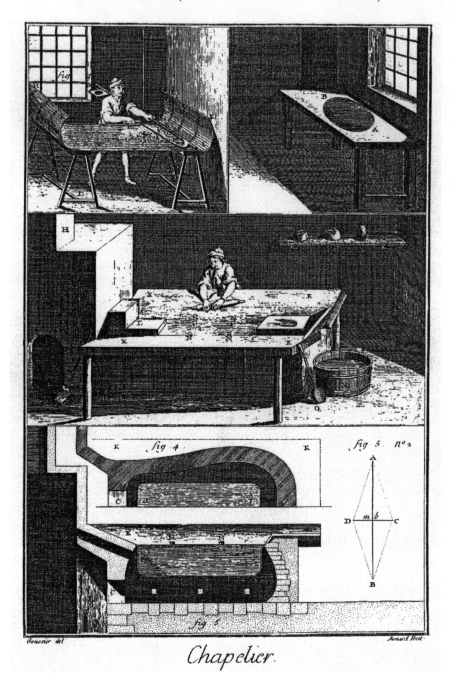

Chapelier.

Chapelerie illustration from "L'Art de Habilement" section of Diderot and D'Alembert, *L'Encyclopédie*, 1751–80.

Though it was eventually shown that the developing fetus has a greater affinity for mercury than the body that nourishes it, the actual consequences of that absorption were not apparent in places known to be saturated with mercury. There is an awakening awareness among those most concerned about the development of children that we are all immersed in a sea containing mercury in a form with an affinity for body tissues and likely to have the most long-lasting effects upon the fetus and the child.

Mercury is blamed for tremors and loss of speech among adults, but it also is the cause of birth defects and permanent learning disabilities in newborns and the young. The state and the corporate structure which releases the mercury in the course of business are apprised of the consequences for the next generation, and evade responsibility even as they plan to take greater control of women's fertility by regulating contraceptives and abortion, and setting premiums for the birth of children in dwindling populations.

The effects of organic mercury compounds, primarily methylmercury, infiltrating water and food in Minamata and Niigata, Japan, and Grassy Narrows, Canada, took a long time to bring to light because the communities affected depended upon the corporation releasing the mercury for their livelihood. The first time congenital effects of mercury were identified was in 1962, when symptoms in newborn children were equated with those of adults already known to be suffering from what came to be called Minamata disease, environmental mercury poisoning from industrial sources. Testing of customarily preserved umbilical cords confirmed that fetuses were receiving a high intrauterine dose of mercury and that was what contributed to the high rates of developmental and learning disorders observable in the Minamata area.

It was eventually recognized that consumption of seafood in which mercury had concentrated precipitated prenatal, postnatal and adult poisonings. The mercury was in the wastewater sent into local streams by the Chisso Corporation which had been using it as a catalyst in manufacturing acetaldehyde in a local plant. The process was halted in 1968 only after considerable pressure came to bear on the corporation from citizens groups. By then several thousand people were certified as having Minamata disease.

Dr. Masuzumi Harada, using analytic techniques developed in Minamata to detect mercury in the bodies of environmental poisoning victims, proved that the members of a community of native Ojibwa people who lived on the shores of a river in Ontario, a river polluted by a papermill, were also victims of Minamata disease. In Grassy Narrows there were children born with physical and cognitive deficiencies similar to those found in Minamata. The Minamata model for matching pathologies to the presence of mercury was applied to several other settings with a similar level of industrial release of mercury.

A suspicion arose in late-twentieth-century America that an organic mercury compound, thimerosal, used as a vaccine preservative, was the cause of birth defects in children of women without any other discernible contact with the metal. The set of conditions grouped under the label "autism" meant that children vaccinated against childhood diseases in growing numbers were born with learning difficulties and had to be managed more closely than other children. Parental activism succeeded in forcing the corporation producing the vaccine to reduce the thimerosol content, amid continued controversy over the validity of the belief that it affected development of children. Rather than consuming metallic mercury to cause children to form, now women were trying to repel the mercury from entering their children's forming minds, through food and preventive medications.

The women of Smyrna lost control over their own mercurial fertility. Instead of women swallowing metallic mercury to cause or fake fertility, mercury compounds were blamed for stealing into a woman's body and disrupting reproduction itself. Where previously mercury was used for abortion, it was later the reason abortions took place. If there was no identifiable source of mercury, the infertility and birth defects could be referred to dental amalgams formed from silver with the help of mercury or to vaccines given before birth or in infancy. Any and all of these phases of mercury in relation to women's bodies could be present at the same time. The general trend was for mercury to go from consumable quicksilver to furtive poison spreading into the uterus and down through the generations as the result of human action and inaction.

3

⊗≫○

Lab Work

One to whom neither a gorgeous home, nor security of occupation, nor fame, nor health appeals; for me rather my chemicals amid the smoke, soot and flame of coals blown by bellows. Stronger than Hercules, I work forever in an Augean stable, blind almost from the furnace glare, my breathing affected by the vapour of mercury....

These words, quoted in histories of chemistry, often stripped of the classical references to tasks of Hercules and the wealth of Mithradates, are a translation from the preface to *Physica subterranea* (1669) by the alchemist-economist Johann Joachim Becher, who lived for fifty years in the center of the seventeenth century. The passage celebrates work Becher actually performed, or directed others performing. The persistent quoting of these words by historians of chemistry says more about the masculine heroic image of chemistry as an evolving laboratory practice than it does about Becher himself. For all the mercury vapor to be breathed and for all the discussion of the poisonous nature of mercury vapor, no chemist made an issue of the health effects of mercury upon laboratory workers until the twentieth century when the assertion of scientific preponderance was accompanied by doubts, dissents and deaths. Becher's declaration expresses the existence of a mercury atmosphere which benefits those able to brave it.

Becher himself claimed to have transmuted lead into silver with the help of mercury, and cast a medallion in honor of his success. The phlogiston theory of chemical transformation he propounded could explain his success. His name Becher is the same as the German word *Becher* ("beaker") and in Becher's own time referred to any enclosed vessel, including an alchemical furnace, as

39

Becher himself punned in diagrams of a portable alchemical furnace which could be disassembled.

Becher was like one of the perpetual motion machines he proposed but never completed. He had scheme after scheme to improve the revenues of the courts of the Holy Roman Empire. He did not hesitate to recall that the Roman god Mercury was the patron of merchants and of thieves. When he revealed in the laboratory, the vapors of mercury were one of the trials he had to endure in order to advance commerce, but this enabled him to work in secret, cloaking his knowledge of operations in emblems and hieroglyphs to be revealed only to the initiate.

Becher set down many recipes for compounding powders and elixirs, and descriptions of working procedures, but it is not clear to what extent he did this work himself. His plan for a laboratory to be constructed called for managers to guide the work and procure the materials, and supervisors (dispensators) to divide and allocate the tasks to the laborers who would actually perform them. The laborers would be illiterate and unable to use the materials and equipment on their own projects.

Prints of alchemical and chemical laboratories from this period and later, which show workers laboring at ovens with or without the directing presence of an alchemist, confirm that Becher's plan was a formalization of an existing division of labor. Whether or not the directing alchemist breathed mercury (and other) vapors, the workers certainly did. This is a long-established pattern underlying the entire documented history of airborne-mercury exposure.

Becher's laboratory was not unlike the Manhattan Project sponsored by the U.S. government, that led to the first practical nuclear reactor and the testing of the fission bomb in 1945. General Leslie Groves, the military commander in charge of the Project, had to discourage Enrico Fermi, one of the chief scientists, from taking bets on the likelihood the detonation of the first atomic bomb would initiate a chain reaction in the atmosphere, causing a universal conflagration. Groves was concerned that the soldiers laboring on the construction of the bomb itself and who were not for the most part aware of the purpose of their efforts, would be agitated by this possibility given out by one of the scientists.

Cosimo de' Medici, in a letter he supposedly wrote to Pope Pius II (1458–64) instructing the Pope in the preparation of a panacea, told the cautionary tale of the Florentine alchemist Alexander Tarentius, who was heating sulfur with mercury in an enclosed spherical vessel for 170 days, to sublime them through the stages of transformation and create the elixir of a perfect union. While opening the glass vessel and removing the potent substance Tarentius dropped dead, as did his servant Arnelius, who tried to "control" the medicine. This lethal elixir was buried in the old sewers of Florence, a precocious contribution to environmental mercury.

Western and Chinese alchemists were aware that some of the substances they worked with in close quarters were poisonous if breathed, but this was precisely the reason for working with them. The poisonous properties were a kind of energy that would have a strong effect on the body and therefore could be tamed and purified into medicines. Not the substance itself but impurities were thought to be the cause of death. Disease symptoms in the consumer of medicines were a sign that the medicine was driving out disease properties. After listing the itches, crawling feeling, swelling feet and nausea that accompany taking an elixir (invariably containing mercury), an eighth-century Chinese treatise reassured the consumer, "These are merely proofs that the elixir is driving out the illness."

Mercury was confidence-inspiring because it caused salivation and itself visibly exited the body after its work was done. But this was only if it was put into the body in a form that conveyed its potency, which required skill to produce. The use of modified viruses to carry genetic improvements to body tissues is a strategy similar to this manipulation of mercury. Purification required heating mercury, and putting it through a cycle of sublimation and condensation in enclosed vessels from which it might escape as it became stronger. This was where the preparer, the operator, the alchemist and the chemist met deadly mercury.

"Eugenius Philalethes died as twere suddenly w[he]n he was operating strong mercurie, some of w[hic]h by chance getting up into his nose marched him off." So the Oxford antiquarian Anthony à Wood describes the death of Thomas Vaughan, who was conducting alchemical experiments at the house of a patron on April 14, 1666. The twin brother of the metaphysical poet Henry Vaughan and himself a poet and author of alchemical writings, Thomas Vaughan, like Becher, could exult in his mastery of mercury. Wood's account of the death is unique and may be more gossip than truth, but as with the Becher declaration it expresses a strain of belief about the properties of airborne mercury. Wood believed that mercury getting into the nose could kill in about the same way that soldiers in the recent civil war marched off a captured foe.

In early 1652, the American "chymist" George Starkey fell ill with "very horrid and seemingly Pestilential Symptomes," according to his associate Robert Boyle. A friend of Starkey's later told a mutual mentor that he warned Starkey that "he would ruine himself by using charcoale in places without chimneys, as also by the preparation of mercuriall and Antimonius medicines."

Starkey published a number of alchemical treatises under the name Irenaeus Philalethes, in evident correspondence with Vaughan. The Philalethes in their common name refers to the "love of forgetting" which reflected the deliberate obscurity of their writing. Like Vaughan, Starkey died fairly young, after a period of erratic behavior which his biographers have attributed to mercury exposure.

Both Starkey and Vaughan left ornately symbolic alchemical writings under their pseudonyms, but also kept detailed laboratory notebooks of their experiments. And both reported their laboratory reveries and dreams, part literary allegory and part account of genuine dreams.

Vaughan wrote a remarkable book in collaboration with his wife Rebecca, who was dead at the time.

Neither Vaughan nor Starkey recorded their response to breathing mercury and other heavy metal fumes; that information came from other writers. Their contemporary Johann Rudolf Glauber reported on his sickness, but it is not possible to determine whether this was an allegorical sickness or a real one.

Glauber was performing practical chemical experiments which he carefully recorded and published while at the same time selling his *sal mirabilis* (sodium sulfate, the chief ingredient of mineral water), a cure for all ills later packaged as "Glauber's salt." Becher again refers to the foul Augean stables in *Physica subterranea* to introduce his remarks on Glauber.

Distilling coal tar and finding use for the results in insecticides and cloth treatments, Glauber also claimed that one of his elixirs worked as a hair restoration formula, which put him in line with modern-day biogenetics research. Glauber published his *New Philosophical Furnaces* (1651) with designs for ovens capable of distilling fluids, assaying and refining metals under finely controlled heat conditions. His method of sulfuric acid production was adopted by emergent industries but his experimentation affected his health.

Planning to make a great quantity of "the [mercury] of [Mars]," as Glauber's Elizabethan translator resolves the hidden words of the text, Glauber was "seized with Sickness not long after, and continuing Bed-rid till now; my design was hindered." Toward the end of his life (1670) he complained that he had been sickened by the compounds of mercury, antimony and arsenic, and that for all his work he had made no profit.

By the end of the seventeenth century, a number of men were commenting on the results of inhaling heavy metal vapors in the course of their work, or at least others believed that they did. This was a time when writers of alchemical texts themselves performed operations which they may also have set down in forms permitting them to be reconstructed as laboratory work. But the presence of the alchemist in the laboratory was not simply a matter of inadvertent self-poisoning. The laboratory itself seems to induce a state that corresponds to the dreams and visions that alchemists often described in their veiled writings. Mercury would not have been the sole component of this atmosphere. Besides having other heavy metals, antimony, arsenic and lead and their compounds in the air, alchemists like Starkey tested opium, not explicitly on themselves, but making it part of the atmosphere around themselves.

A similar dream state amid toxic fumes has been speculated for Chinese alchemists, who used mercury in their attempts to create an elixir of immortality. It was not entirely ironic that when killed by consuming the elixir, the body of the alchemist lasted a long time, demonstrating mercury's value as a component of embalming fluid.

Mercury was of such an interest that the work of the laboratory was certain to include it and contribute to its release into the air and water. The projects of alchemy, then "chymistry," then chemistry, required the continual presence of mercury as the object, standard and means of operations. The opportunities for mercury exposure grew with time. Until early in the twentieth century, to work in chemical endeavors often was to breathe mercury.

The operators on all levels of the enterprise knew mercury fumes were poisonous, but either chose to ignore it or regarded that as a confirmation of the power and efficacy of mercury. While there is considerable variation in beliefs about consuming mercury and its salts as medicine, there is nothing but caution about the fumes. One of the aims of working with mercury was to find a way to cancel out its poisonous properties which were conceived to be distinct from its curative and generative powers.

Those who were regularly exposed to mercury as part of their work did not have a choice. Becher imagined the workers in his laboratory to be loyal and illiterate, unwilling and unable to write down the processes they carried out as part of a larger plan. The workers on the Manhattan Project did not know the long-range effects of radiation. At that time, in the 1940s, radioactive materials were roughly in the same category as mercury, thought by some to have healthful applications if taken internally as radium water. In the long run both leaders and the workers suffered the ill effects of radiation. It took much longer to know how mercury acted in this way.

A striking image of an occupational encounter with mercury vapor comes from the first century C.E. Greek physician Dioscorides, who served in the Roman army under Emperor Nero. In the 1655 translation of Dioscordes' Latin into English by John Goodyer, Dioscorides discourses on cinnabar, also called ammium, which was mined in Spain, and "in the furnace changes into a very lively and flaming colour, but it has among metals a choking smell, and therefore the workmen put bladders about their faces, that they may see but not draw in the vapours." The cinnabar was used as eye medicine, and in binding and blood stanching. Bladder-masked workers also appear in the section on mercury of the *Historia naturalis* (around 77 C.E.) by the inquisitive Roman administrator Pliny the Elder. Here the workers are protecting themselves from the pernicious dust spread in the factories baking minium, sometimes a name for cinnabar.

Both writers comment on the insinuating nature of mercury, how it penetrates most vessels made to hold it. For them it is the processed ore that issues the fumes workers want to protect themselves from. The smelters had the most saturated mercury atmosphere and the workers who were most persistently exposed to it. But other mercury atmospheres were being made.

By 1733, Thomas Dover, minimizing Pliny's and Dioscorides' warnings

about liquid mercury, was promoting the penetrative power of quicksilver remedies while warning the home tester of mercury samples against the effluvia
extending from it when heated. A growing number of occupations and practices, kept private and even secret, placed people in mercury-tainted air. The
mines and the foundry remained the place where the effects of mercury were
most appreciable. It was believed that the mercury absorbed in medicine or in
the laboratory had been "purified" and was no longer poisonous.

The work of alchemy centered on transforming mercury while inciden-
tally inhaling the vapors. If the work was entirely in the imagination, it could
be assimilated to spiritual transformations. For Becher and others, the imagi-
native work had a material correlate which could lead to health, riches and the
public good, but that involved being closed in with furnaces where mercury
was being processed. Actual work in an environment with mercury always was
ambiguous, potentially rewarding, potentially lethal, and vaguely desirable.

A library of texts praises the transformative power of mercury and its role
in enriching its users. There are hints and descriptions in the surviving writings of alchemists about what working methods they followed. Alchemy did
not simply progress into chemistry. A record of means and achievements was
retained, if not in writing, then in the teaching passed from one generation of
scientists, promoters and confidence artists to the next.

The activity within the laboratory or workshop was codified in images
that only those who became familiar with the processes could grasp, because
they referred to operations and observed transformations. When the precision
of chemistry was attained, there remained something of alchemy in chemistry's
sense of wonder, experimental freedom and the profiteering on fictions. Mercury vapor and its inhalation define both sides of the line.

Perhaps some idea of the atmosphere of the alchemist's laboratory can be
recovered from the contemporary practice of *rasayana*, "mercury method," by
Tantrists in India. At least as it is reported by wide-eyed Western commenta-
tors, the Tantric adept accustoms his body to mercury by carefully and systematically imbibing the liquid and breathing the air of its preparation. Having
achieved a mercurial body, he is prepared to take no other food and is assured
of long life and healing prowess. Quicksilver is the semen of the god Shiva,
which united with the blood (sulfur) of his *shakti*, "female consort," ostensibly gives new life. A continuing immunity to the poisonous influences of raw
mercury contributes to the physical mastery the alchemists desired.

The apparatus and the materials the alchemists used are evident. Their
aims, to achieve the philosopher's stone which would allow them to make gold
out of iron, tin and other base metals, to develop a universal solvent, and to
synthesize a cure for all diseases, seem to be an appeal to the ignorance of their
patrons: cash-laden monarchs, sick and greedy bourgeois. These aims point to
projects promising instant results.

Pliny describes the amalgamation method of purifying gold: "On being shaken in an earthen vessel with gold, it rejects all the impurities that are mixed with it ... it is poured out upon skins that have been tawed [cured], and so, exuding through them like a sort of perspiration, it leaves the gold in a state of purity behind." Pliny makes no claims for the spiritual meaning of mercury, but it is possible to see in a technique like this the code of mercury purifying body and the soul.

All the alchemists' powdering, amalgamating, sublimating and calcining materials led to some outcomes useful beyond appearances, because the experience gained by repeating the processes gave formulas and recipes and yielded new products or because a patron made it difficult to leave without something to show for his investment. Mercury lends itself well to complex processing and showing results.

The written and pictorial allegories left by alchemists and others strongly influenced by them reflect the esoterism of the practice of alchemy, symbols known only to initiates who carried the secrets of combinations and processes that would yield desired outcomes. The imagery was often that of the human body standing in for the mercury mass. A wedding, a gestation, a race, or the Passion of Christ might also describe a method for causing raw materials to merge into a more valuable shape. Material referents might be concealed when the narrative was connected to the inner values of the adept who attained the state of imagining in himself the oven fired and the vessel placed inside it.

The eighth-century C.E. Arab writer whose name, Jabir ibn Hayyan, was latinized as Geber, and many of whose alleged writings were fabricated in Latin, became the authority for the supposition that mercury is not only a substance, but a basic component of many things. Together with sulfur in varying proportions, it was seen as forming all metals, and according to a set of astrological relations, adhering differentially to metals. Mercury forms inside the earth, where a moderate heat joins the humid with the dry. It runs fluid like water but it does not adhere to or moisten what it runs over because of its dryness. This process going on inside the earth producing economically valuable ores and minerals is the subject of many alchemical writings, for instance Becher's *Physica subterranea.*

Mercury represented fluidity, coolness, lunar femininity and a long list of other attributes to counter (and join) sulfur's fixed, hot, solar masculinity (the opposite in Indian *rasayana*). Mercury of varying degrees of purity combined with sulfur of varying purity to form different substances. The marriage of the purest mercury with the purest sulfur was thought to yield the philosopher's stone, a brilliant red powder that could transmute the base metals into gold. This had both spiritual and practical significance, since mercury and sulfur actually do make a red powder, the purer the two, the closer to blood-red in color. Fused with iron or tin, mercuric sulfide (cinnabar) does give them a golden tinge. Mercury extracts gold from ore.

One of the writers under the name of Geber describes experiments which demonstrate how the observable attributes of metals are the result of the amount and type of quicksilver and sulfur, fixed or unfixed, that form them. The creaking sound that tin makes when bent can be transferred to lead, which normally doesn't creak, by washing the lead sample with mercury and then melting the lead with mercury. Geber maintains that adding the fugitive or unfixed mercury doesn't make lead into tin, but it does transfer an attribute of tin and create creaking lead. My purpose in citing this experiment is just to exemplify how Geber's conception of the components of metals promoted much heating of mercury in alchemical laboratories. George Starkey performed exacting variations on this experiment in his efforts to isolate the philosopher's mercury.

Paracelsus, the early-sixteenth-century medical alchemist and physician, declared that mercury and sulfur were joined by salt in the composition of all bodies, not just metals, as Geber maintained. Another factor entered into the foreground and created the grounds for mercury use that exceeded the existing craft and medical uses. This expanding interest in mercury was the discovery that absorbing it acted on the symptoms of syphilis, which had become epidemic in Europe with the age of overseas travel and exploitation.

Mercury fumes were used to treat syphilis because they were poisonous. The body of the syphilis patient was enclosed in a cabinet suffused with the smoke of roasting cinnabar, which they were not to breathe. This was a treatment derived from the experience of mercury miners, who were free of skin infections while dying of respiratory and nervous disorders.

Mercury also was applied externally in elemental form to eliminate the sores that were the most evident appearance of infection, or it was taken internally in the hope that it would drive out the noxious contents that had built up inside. The skin eruptions went away (which they would have, untreated) but the cumulative treatment sickened the patients, seemed to cause tremors and mental degeneration, just as likely to be the result of the progression of the venereal infection, which only took a little longer to kill the vulnerable patient. People could live for years simultaneously afflicted by syphilis and mercury, and they could live for years making and applying these treatments.

Mercury, the astrological god of the marketplace (including the sexual marketplace, which is where syphilis is acquired), should also dominate its cure. The market in mercury (the metal) led to the censorship of the writings of Paracelsus. Paracelsus authored pamphlets opposing guiac wood treatments in which a syphilis sufferer was engulfed in the astringent smoke of the burning wood. Asserting that mercury's poisonous properties were precisely what made it capable of healing, he advocated a measured internal consumption of mercury compounds, not mercury fumigations.

This advice incited a merchant family, the Fuggers, who had a monopoly on guiac wood but not on mercury, and who already had the Holy Roman Emperor so much in their debt that he lifted the ban on usury to facilitate their business practices. Paracelsus's views on mercury could only raise the price of the commodity the Fuggers did not control over the price of the guiac wood they did. Paracelsus's books on syphilis were banned, an early example of commerce and politics taking precedence over (proto-)scientific advice, but his ideas and practices circulated freely, and contributed to the emergence of a branch of alchemy dedicated to pharmaceuticals and cosmetics.

Paracelsus enjoined alchemists to make medicines, not gold, most likely knowing what gold there was in medicines. The marketplace and the state tightened mercury's poison-remedy tangle. An increasing number of people, patients and preparers, became exposed to mercury in a variety of forms as a result. If mercury was not already a constituent of all life it was becoming so.

Spagyric alchemists, practitioners of the art of "taking apart and putting together" advanced by Paracelsus, worked on the body of mercury, taking it apart and putting it back together as they have ever since. Conditions in the mines and smelters prefigured the laboratory where mercury was prepared for growing uses or studied and examined for the source of its properties. The intellectual and spiritual symbolism of mercury was an excellent distraction. Alchemists are usually shown in a crowded laboratory staring into a book. Mercury was crucial to their enterprises, the more readily acquired root of gold and well-being. It involved alchemists and alchemical laborers in an air of poisoning, utility and wonder. It was an agent that penetrated all vessels.

Mercury itself might object to the manner of its usage. The seventeenth-century Polish alchemist who used the name Michael Sendivogius wrote into his treatise a joking dialogue between the alchemist and Mercury. The alchemist, embarking on the Great Work, finds that when he places Mercury in a vessel and heats it, it is gone. He blames his wife for stealing it and beats her. He then places Mercury in an enclosed vessel and heats it, finding that it rises to the top in a steam. He thinks he is on the right track and begins to torture Mercury with all manner of alchemical processes, with no favorable result. It occurs to him to use dung in his operations, and when that fails he falls into a deep sleep. An old man advises him to seek "the Mercury of the Sages," which the alchemist does, by redoubling his excrement assaults. Falling into a fever, he encounters another apparition who suggests that he recite an incantation. Mercury does manifest, and with an assumed obsequiousness (like a surly lab worker) mocks the alchemist's pretensions and vanishes without giving in to his demands. The alchemist returns to torturing Mercury and when that brings no result is about to apply swine excrement when Mercury reappears and answers his questions in an oblique language that would amuse initiates.

Under further threat of swine feces, Mercury calls on his Mother Nature, who enjoins the alchemist not to treat her son cruelly. Nature's utterances are more cryptic than Mercury's, leading the alchemist to recognize that he knows nothing but he must not say so if he expects to get money for his experiments. If they fail, he will go to other countries where there are many greedy persons who will allow themselves to be taken in by his promises of mountains of gold.

Nature curses him and tells him that the best he can do is to give himself up to king's officers, who will quickly put an end to him and his ideas.

Sendivogius himself almost ended this way, after he was robbed of his belongings and a precious powder he received from a Scottish alchemist he rescued from the elector of Saxony, who was torturing him to get him to reveal the secret of a transmutation. This was a story spread to increase the credibility of the historical Sendivogius, who, like Glauber and Becher, was devising processes of chemical manufacture worth more than gold while promoting himself with extravagant mysteries. A later elector of Saxony imprisoned another alchemist promising gold, and was rewarded with the invention of hard-paste porcelain (Meissen, 1708).

Sendivogius seemed to take a dim view of alchemists and their claims. He was setting the wife-beating, dung-using operator against the true aspirant to philosophical mercury. The susceptibility to visions and supernatural advice, the intransigent inability to learn, may have been characteristic of the fool who tortures Mercury in his laboratory.

The canon's yeoman in Geoffrey Chaucer's *Canterbury Tales* introduces himself with a lament:

> With this Chanoun I dwelt have seven yeer,
> And with his science I am never the neer.
> Al that I hadde I have lost thereby,
> And, God woot, so hath many mo than I.
> There I was wont to be right fressh and gay
> Of clothyng and of oother good array,
> Now may I were an hose upon myn heed;
> And where my color was both fressh and reed,
> Now is it wan and of a leden hewe-

The yeoman has become impoverished and ill because of his devotion to the "slidynge science" of alchemy practiced by the canon. For all the sublimating, amalgamating and calcining "of quycksilver, yclept mercurie crude," the yeoman has nothing to show for it, "ne eek oure spirites ascencioun" ("not even uplifting our spirits"). The yeoman warns anyone occupied with these activities all night that when he goes out by day, "Men may hem know by smel of brymstoon. For al the world they stynken as a goot." The smell can infect someone a mile away. The yeoman later describes a crafty alchemist's trick of hiding a piece of silver in a coal placed in a crucible with quicksilver. When heat is applied the quicksilver evaporates and the silver melts making it look as if the alchemist has the formula for "fixing" quicksilver, making it still and therefore silver. This deceit is the only way anyone can profit from the philosophy, and it too requires vaporizing mercury. The yeoman himself has gone through his own alchemical transformation from fresh and red to leaden rather than bright and golden.

Chaucer's portrayal of the yeoman is a rare literary portrait of a working alchemist, who is imbued with the essences he releases in his futile quest for gold. He cannot even succeed as a fraud. But there were different grades of alchemists. The canon's yeoman is a "puffer," a laborer who kept the furnaces supplied with a stream of air necessary to keep the coals hot enough to sublime mercury and leave the glittering residue. His work is not unlike that in a gold or silver rendering operation where the mercury is driven off, leaving the precious metal to which it has amalgamated in the crushed ore. Except, of course, the puffer doesn't start with ore, only mercury and other ingredients which may leave a result that looks precious.

The literate who practiced alchemy, and probably employed puffers of their own, left writings that sometimes describe laboratory procedures but more often set out allegories intended to imply that the alchemists arrived at physical and metaphysical riches but cannot reveal the method directly. It is only with some scholarly penetration that the use of "operators" by alchemists and chymists has been discovered. There is almost no reference to the health effects of the atmospheres that were created by the chemical agents sent into the air and placed on the skin. It required a poet like Chaucer or an artist like Pieter Brueghel the Elder to find a moral lesson and a curious humor in the state of the people actually operating the laboratories.

Brueghel's *The Alchemist in the Kitchen* (around 1558) has the robed alchemist seated at his lecturn, reading a recipe from a book, while one assistant squeezes a bellows aimed at a few coals in a brazier, while another assistant seated at a bench before a still places a coin in a crucible. In the center of the floor a woman seated and gazing off to the side with a dazed, bemused expression shakes the neck of a flour sack to find if there is anything left, and the children, one of whom wears a cooking pot on his head, a figurative expression of poverty, crawl into the empty cupboard. Outside a window opening, other children, one of them also with a cooking pot on his head, are being led away.

The alchemist as charlatan or as impoverished obsessive seemed to be in play for Anthony à Wood as he looked in on Thomas Vaughan's death or for Johann Friedrich Becher as he told the non-alchemists he expected to read his book, "There's no disputing tastes," this is what we do, breathe mercury and yet in our laboratories we are richer than Croesus. Laboratory work was conducted with a visionary awareness of public disapproval and noxious atmosphere.

Present-day scholars have retrospectively emphasized the poisonous qualities of the fumes apart from the less readily assimilated dreams in their midst. The few cases of alchemical poisoning from the late seventeenth century mark the beginning of a transition toward treating mercury as a physical substance with pronounced effects on human health, especially when breathed. At the same time the physical progress of mercury from out of the laboratory, where the means of releasing it were perfected, into the environment, gradually extended both lab work and the atmosphere it created everywhere.

The activities of the alchemists and chemists were part of the ongoing release of mercury which could locally approach an industrial level. The laboratory and its work prefigure the creation of a general mercury environment long before scientists realized this was happening and recognized its effects in themselves. The move to organize a few prominent cases into our own mercury environment may be overinterpreting scant information to bring the past into the present and imagine the present load of mercury in the past. That this is even attempted is a product of a gradual awakening not inconsistent with the practice of lab work and alchemy becoming chemistry but remaining alchemy. Intrigue and deliberate acts of poisoning take the place of the voluntary accession to the fumes of mercury.

The sixteenth-century astronomer Tycho Brahe would seem to be a candidate for laboratory mercury poisoning. His fame was based on his pre-telescope tables of star and planet locations and movements, activity not inconsistent with spagyric (medical) alchemy in the view of his time. He perfected a method of "correcting" mercury and freeing it from its harmful nature to render it a treatment for diseases affecting the skin and blood, such as scabies and chronic venereal infection. Tycho's published formula proposes removing the impurities from mercury, both the amalgamated contaminant metals and poisonous qualities that make it a dangerous remedy for syphilis. If the written procedure is analyzed in terms of what it accomplishes chemically, it amounts to precipitating insoluble yellow mercuric sulfate, which entered the pharmacopeia as "turbith mineral."

It was not Tycho's lab work that led later investigators to suspect he had been poisoned. Tests of his hair suggest that his body absorbed mercury in a spike not long before his death. That is consistent with receiving a concentrated dose of metallic mercury, which would have induced the painful urine retention recorded in his last days. A lesser dose, also recorded in his hair, would have caused an excruciating death by provoking a surge of urine. Joshua and Anne-Lee Gilder accuse Tycho's one-time assistant, the theoretician Johannes Kepler, of administering the fatal sequence of doses so he could take possession of the long accumulated celestial data Tycho was withholding. Possessing the data freed Kepler to complete his laws of planetary motion, and win the fame and position he long sought.

Whether this intrigue happened or not, the narrative turns Tycho's astronomical-alchemical involvements into a modern poison-history-murder mystery. This same group of elements appears in a more stately form in the mercurially reconstructed life of Isaac Newton.

When Isaac Newton's body was moved a few years after his death, mercury droplets were found on the inside of his coffin. This is very seldom mentioned in biographies of Newton, yet it impressed his contemporaries as a sign of his dedication and absorption in his work, and not that he was killed by mercury or even embalmed with it.

Newton's law of universal gravitation and theory of planetary motion followed from Tycho's and Kepler's opening the sky to humanly understandable principles. As uncritical reverence for Newton was replaced by an examination of his personality, his episodes of "madness" — agitation, fury and withdrawal from society — came into focus for Newton biographers.

Newton formulated his physical theories mostly without experiment. "Hypotheses non fingo" ("I do not pretend to hypotheses"), he declared. In his alchemical "elaboratory," he did nothing but experiment. "About six weeks at spring, and six in the fall, the fire in the elaboratory scarcely went out ... the transmuting of metals being his chief design." Newton's optical experiments called for open beds of mercury to transmit and scatter light. Newton even conceived of a version of his invention, the reflecting telescope, using a spinning pool of mercury in place of the mercury mirror receiving the astral light.

The specifics of Newton's erratic behavior, his rages and insomnia, even his disturbed handwriting, have been correlated with the symptoms of mercury poisoning, which diminished when he desisted from his closeted immersion in chemical fumes. Newton's hair was tested, and was found to contain mercury. The tests were not as precise as those made of Tycho's hair, however, and may have been prejudiced by mercury in embalming fluid or progressive atmospheric contamination.

Other scientists living at the same time, and who had laboratory exposure to mercury, as well as complex medical histories, including drug consumption, were not made into cases of behavioral mercury poisoning. Robert Hooke, who recorded his ailments and his medications in a diary, did not record much conscious mercury consumption. His biography has not evolved so much as a cultural property as Newton's has, and is not subject to the fads of analysis.

It also may be that the mercury environment of the laboratory and pharmacy did not affect everyone the same way, due to different make-up, physiology and interactions with other substances in the body. Newton's life is a turning point in the recognition of how mercury acts upon individuals casually exposed. The intoxicating laboratory atmosphere is giving way to the poisonous milieu.

"Chemists boast that they have mastered the art of subduing every kind of mineral, yet they themselves do not come off scot-free from their pernicious influence," wrote Bernardino Ramazzini in the 1723 edition of his book on the diseases of workers, *De morbis artificium diatriba.* He was referring to preparers of medications and cosmetics, the forebears of the "chemists" who operated pharmacies in twentieth-century Britain, manufacturing chemists and not experimental chemists. "I used to know Carlo Lancillotti, my compatriot, a well-known chemist; he was palsied, blear-eyed, toothless, short of breath, and disgusting; the mere sight of him was enough to ruin the reputation of the medicaments, the cosmetics especially, he used to sell."

In 1683, Lancilloti had published a *Farmaceutica antimoniale* and a *Farmaceutica mercuriale* collections of recipes for treatments and beauty enhancements made primarily of antimony or mercury, and over the years he compounded quantities of them, with the result that he himself was neither healthy nor pleasant to look at.

Ramazzini focused on individual workers diseased by the materials and processes they used. His only instance of describing the effects of a factory on those living nearby singles out a chemical manufacturing operation which brought a lawsuit from the neighbors who believed that the fumes were sickening and killing them. The factory produced sublimate (mercuric chloride, used to treat syphilis) by combining metallic mercury with vitriol (hydrochloric acid). It was only the palpable smells issuing from the workshop that bothered the neighbors; no mention was made of the effect of the effluvia on water or plant life.

Ramazzini departed from his usual practice and did not suggest any remedies for the diseases of chemists. That would insult the chemists, who could produce a ready and effectual remedy for almost any disease. It also was ironic that there was no remedy for the remedies.

Ramazzini faulted mercury for the ill health suffered by miners, gilders, makers of mirrors, appliers of syphilis unctions and painters. He did not equate the symptoms with mercury across the professions, or seek out others with regular exposure to mercury to verify his observations. Mercury was by no means the only chemical hazard, nor were chemicals the only type of threat faced by workers.

In a number of ways Ramazzini's summaries were diagnostic of mercury-using industries still kept secret or not yet begun. Alchemists become chemists continued their absorption of mercury as they helped the mercurial environment expand around them.

Ramazzini's ailing countryman, also a native of the city of Modena, Carlo Lancillotti had written his books in Italian for a more local audience than Ramazzini's Latin treatise, which was eventually translated into European vernaculars. Lancillotti's books on mercury and antimony, and his *Guida Chemica* were never translated into other languages, but unlike Ramazzini's book they were illustrated. There were allegorical drawings showing personified mercury and antimony moving in a triumphal procession, and "hieroglyphic" illustrations of the preparation of the metals.

There also were practical drawings of apparatus set up to distill the fluid forms of the metals. Chapter 75 of *The Triumph of Antimony* shows a plain line drawing of "oil of antimony" being distilled from one bottle to another. At the bottom of the drawing is an illustration of the vase "called sick" ("chiamato infermo"), a container with a conical interior "like the one we use in Modena to store syrups," only here inverted, pointed end upward to store mercury "so it can't escape." The vase was used in Modena to store syrup so the foreign bodies would fall into the narrowing point and not be picked up when the syrup was taken from the top. For mercury it was the opposite; it couldn't escape the convergent vase walls above it.

Processing antimony as medicine, but containing mercury so it couldn't escape, Ramazzini was the specialist who identified the ailments of those dwelling in work environments, and Lancillotti was the creator of one of those environments. Ramazzini leaned into the past to detect the emergent poisoning in ancient and new crafts. Ramazzini took an overview, seeing the affliction of the compounding chemist Lancillotti who enclosed the mercury he used within his syrup pots and his own body, but the mercury escaped and affected people living nearby.

Ramazzini's view of Lancillotti could have been occasioned by the rivalry between physicians and pharmacists going on everywhere in Europe at that time. Ramazzini contested the implicit suggestion that long-term workers with mercury develop a resistance to its poison and could concoct their medicines from mercury in the raw state without suffering lethal effects. In proclaiming the triumph of mercury and of antimony and setting down mercury recipes, Lancillotti seemed to be asserting that mercury workers did develop immunity while benefiting from the corrosive properties he can resist. But Ramazzini gave this belief the lie.

Again mercury appears to be a risk some were willing and able to take. Not just individuals. Entire curative systems depend on such people. The Indian compounders of mercury medicine described by David Crow, a twentieth-century acupuncturist and herbalist who apprenticed himself to Indian doctors, do not themselves show signs of mercury poisoning, though Crow is quite aware of the possibilities and makes no claim of immunity for himself.

In the developing environment of mercury, unself-critical operators make mercury products that through the process of manufacture release mercury into the air and water. The producers seem insulated against the effects of the mercury while knowing it is poison. Someone not involved in making mercury drugs might be equipped to recognize this. These relations fluctuate but always surround mercury: confined, escaping, and attended to by a determined, degenerating scientist with an economic interest. Newton's developing history is a product of this environment.

The physician-chemist Boerhaave, who described his torture of mercury in letters to the Royal Society in London, reputedly kept a sealed pot of mercury heating in his laboratory for fifteen years (another version makes it a pot of lead for twenty years). On opening the pot, Boerhaave found unchanged mercury and a little black powder, which he turned back into mercury with a little grinding.

Boerhaave was testing the alchemical belief that long heating and conden-

C. 75 trionfo del Antimonio.

Figura, che dimostra come si distilla l'aceto d'Antimonio posto nella bozza .A. che destilla nel recipiente .B.

E la figura à basso dimostra come si deue esere il Vaso chiamato infermo, che è vn Vaso di vetro oue vi è nel mezzo del corpo fatto come l'ampole che vsiamo qui in Modona per li siroppi, & è con vn picciolo buco alla puta per oue si mette il Mercurio che non può più vscire

Woodcut of antimony still and "container for mercury from which it cannot escape" from *Il Trionfo di Antimonio*, by Carlo Lancillotti (1599), chapter 75.

sation of mercury accompanied by the clearing out of the black powder impurities would yield the purest mercury. Inside the earth, the alchemists claimed, constant heat turns mercury into precious metals. The purest mercury Boerhaave produced did not differ from metallic mercury; it was no more able to spontaneously transform into other metals. The story marks the end of some alchemical aspirations, but a continuation of alchemical methods and the further generation of mercury vapors from long-heated test pots. The mercury atmosphere of the chemical laboratory was replacing the mercury atmosphere of the alchemical workshop.

The isolation and identification of the element oxygen as it was recorded in the late eighteenth century was primarily a work of mercury experimentation. Oxygen had already been isolated by Sendivogius, almost a hundred years earlier, as "air of life," from heating saltpeter, and more recently as "fire air" by Scheele, from heating of "fixed" nitric acid, and probably by several others before Joseph Priestley and Antoine-Laurent Lavoisier conducted their mercury operations.

Following the advice of both Scheele and Priestley (heat "mercurius calcinatus"), Lavoisier heated crude mercury in a long-necked retort that reached up through a trough of mercury into a bell jar. Lavoisier's wife, Marie-Anne Pierette Paulze, who could read English and communicated the work of the English experimenters to Lavoisier, drew the illustrations of the apparatus accompanying Lavoisier's paper.

Red flecks formed on the surface of the heated mercury. After twelve days they ceased to form, and Lavoisier found that the aggregate weight of the solids in the retort had increased while the volume of air in the system, measured by the change in the level of the mercury at the base of the bell jar, had decreased. The air now in the system would support combustion only with difficulty. Lavoisier removed the red calx, weighed it and placed it in another retort protruding into a mercury bell jar. As the calx followed the well-known alchemical route of becoming raw mercury again the volume of gas in the bell jar increased. This was what Priestley called "dephlogisticated air": it was receptive to fire, it supported the burning of a candle and the respiration of a small animal more readily than ordinary air. Lavoisier called it "oxygen."

Others had attained a similar juggling of gases and heated solids, but Lavoisier observed quantitative constancy amid the qualitative changes. He enclosed the long-known transformations of mercury in a receptacle of mercury that would contain elusive gases. It was the culmination of the mercurial tradition of experimentation, at once grander and more definitive than the other projects that had preceded it. Rather than confining himself in a locked cabinet to savor the inspiration of mercury fumes, Lavoisier enveloped mercury itself, and demonstrated other distinct elements were combining in regular proportions to make known compounds.

Apparatus for heating mercury in a closed volume of air, illustration by Marie-Pier-rette Paulze for Lavoisier, *Traité de Chimie*.

There is no record of rages or shakes or the eccentricities associated with mercury in Lavoisier's career, and it would be churlish to suggest that his being guillotined eliminated that possibility. Henry Cavendish, perhaps the last of the wealthy, reclusive chemical experimenters, examined the composition of the atmosphere around the same time as Lavoisier's researches, and was able to estimate the proportions of gases in breathable air. He generally collected his gases over water, and did not use mercury as subject or as tool. Cavendish was extremely retiring, scarcely communicated with anyone else to the degree of not even publishing his findings. He certainly employed assistants, who have vanished into the absence of records. The laboratory he endowed at Oxford, celebrated for chemistry and physics advances, was eventually handed over to social scientists who became sick from the mercury vapors remaining, though the natural scientists working there before that did not complain.

At the end of the eighteenth century, Humphry Davy generated and breathed gases, and was affected by the gases themselves, not by any mercury used to collect or measure them. Davy was a poet first: his descriptions of his expanding perceptions after taking deep breaths of nitrous oxide ("A thrilling, extending from the chest to the extremities was almost immediately produced") are not unlike what his contemporaries wrote about opium or later experimen-talists wrote about LSD.

He evidently was continuing an alchemical tradition of imbibing artificially generated atmospheres literally as inspiration, at the same time engaging in scientific research. Davy's friend Joseph Cottle thought that Davy acted as if he had more than one life to sacrifice to his enthusiastic experimenting, and the inhalation of gases caused his lifelong "affection of the chest" and shortened his days. In his second Bakerian lecture delivered before the Royal Society in 1807, Davy spoke of the globules of the element sodium he isolated by electrolysis, burning at the moment of formation, flying through the air, "producing a beautiful effect of continued jets of fire." Davy recalled the alkhahests of the alchemists that reacted with everything they touched.

In that same year, at age twenty-nine, he fell seriously ill and had to stop working for several weeks, the result of breathing the fumes of a mineral baryta he was attempting to analyze by electrolytic decomposition, or of breathing the foul air of Newgate prison where he was making a study to improve the ventilation, or simply due to fatigue and excitement as one of his doctors thought. Davy's was the life and nearly the death of the sensuous chemist, but neither in the visions and tremors of life nor in the threat of death did it involve mercury in any significant way. His chief innovation, which brought him a knighthood and a fortune (largely through marriage), was a lantern which miners could use without risking an explosion of underground gases. These were the tin mines of Davy's native Cornwall and the coal mines of the Midlands, not the mercury mines of the continent.

After the vapors of heated mercury dissipated, and the transformations of mercury were confined to the interior of vessels, the solid body of mercury remained. Newly developing assessments of the nature of matter, including the matter of the human body, came to depend on this solidity.

Augustin Belloste, whom Thomas Dover quoted, cited, paraphrased and misunderstood, wrote in his *Traitez de Mercure* (1733) that mercury is so firm and forceful that it can undo the knots of tumors in the flesh of the body when carried along with the flow. This flow was soon to be known as the circulation of blood and lymph, and the passage of electrical charges through the nerves. There was ancient support for this concept of mercury, and it now was becoming integrated with measuring ideas of matter that set aside sensations and physical qualities. It may have been the old mercury fed into the body, but its action began to be explained in terms of mass and force, atoms, molecules and rate of flow.

At the beginning of the long section on mercury in his 1675 *Cours de chymie*, the most influential chemical and pharmaceutical preparation manual of the seventeenth and eighteenth centuries, Nicolas Lemery declares that this "prodigy among metals" is very powerful because it takes off when put to the fire. The pores of the substance are so compact that fire can't enter them and it carries them away only by its speed. Lemery rejected the symbolic formulations and gold-making of the alchemists in favor of a practical formulary backed

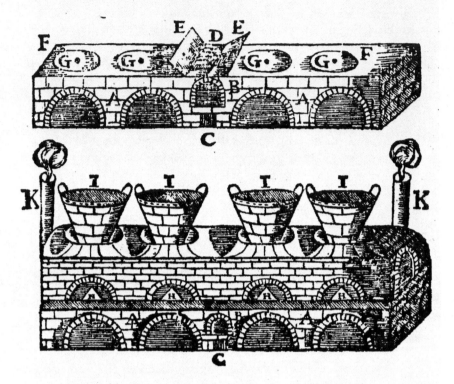

CAPITULO XII.

Como se han de beneficiar los metales por cocimiento.

MOlidos, y cernidos los metales con la mayor sutileza que se pudiere, si todavia tocada la harina entre los dedos se sintiere aspereza de relabe gruesso, se eche en tinas, birques, ò bateas, con agua suficiente, y se menee muy bien, y con un breve descanso se apartará lo sutil de lo mal molido, que se assentara en el fondo. El agua en la lama se eche en los fondos, ò calderas grandes, à que algo antes se les havrá comenzado à dar fuego, con una, ò dos botijas de agua clara, segun su capacidad, y con el Azogue necessario, conforme la riqueza del metal, aunque nunca se ha de echar menos del que fuere suficiente à cubrir todo el suelo de la caldera, para que por ninguna parte pueda assen-

Engraving of a furnace for rendering mercury from ore, from Arte de los Metales, by Albaro Alonso Barba (1770), chapter 6.

by theory. The mercury of this formulary was a weighty liquid integral in its mass.

As mercury takes flight bodily with heat, it otherwise remains solid but not hard. The theoretical characterization of mercury substantiates this and sustains the intuitive sense of mercury as a solid fluid. This mercury resistant to fire privileges the mercury of scientific instruments and apparatus and the driving fluid untangling the body's knots.

This mercury does not evaporate at room temperature. As Belloste wrote, the heat of the body does not cause crude mercury traveling inside it to vaporize and assume its poisonous form. Its instrumental and medical uses are in concord with the way its substance is now imagined.

Mercury's flight when heated was confirmation of its weight and solidity. That mercury evaporated at room temperature was counterintuitive for the "sensuous chemist" who breathed, touched and tasted her way through chemicals, and it remained counterintuitive for the "new" chemist, who preferred to weight measure and test properties. It therefore took a long time for even the most pragmatic chemists to accept that mercury evaporates at room temperature. The 1756 edition of Lemery's *Cours de Chimie*, edited by Theodor Baron, as critical of the loose, unmeasured assumptions that Lemery made as Lemery's original was critical of alchemy, still maintained the massiveness of crude mercury.

Quicksilver's weight and luster were so emphasized that the centuries of observing its condensation inside containers and opened graves did not lead to generalizations about its volatility at room temperature. Its solidity and the dramatic changes it underwent when heated continued to define its body.

It was not until after Michael Faraday measured the evaporation rate of mercury at different temperatures and reported his results to the Royal Society that William Burnett, M.D., could speculate convincingly on the causes of a maritime disaster thirteen years earlier.

In 1810, a Spanish cargo ship transporting mercury to Peru to be used to extract silver and gold was wrecked on an exposed shoal. The mercury was stored in leather sacks closed in wooden boxes, but only the sacks were salvaged and piled below decks on the English man-of-war *Triumph* and a smaller sloop. Rotting from contact with sea water, a number of the sacks broke and a quantity of mercury flowed over the boards while the crew worked, ate and slept. It spilled over the area where their biscuit rations were stored.

Severe salivation, mouth ulcers and tremors afflicted the crew and later a relief crew. Most recovered after they left the ship. A writer in an Edinburgh medical journal suggested effluvia from the interaction of mercury and leather were the cause, but William Burnett, in 1810 a medical official with the Mediterranean fleet, concluded in his article published in 1823 that breathing mercury vapor induced the outbreak. At the beginning of his account, Burnett wrote that the experience of miners, of mercury in barometers and of Michael Faraday's recently published researches established that mercury could become a vapor without heating.

It required observations on the volatile nature of mercury to equate the presence of the metal with the appearance of certain symptoms in those who only breathed the surrounding air. The reaction of bodies to mercury-based syphilis treatments was well-known, especially in the fleet, and perhaps this was one of the reasons for taking so long to make the connection.

Faraday's own use of mercury straddled the boundary between flighty, changing, alchemical mercury and ponderous, forceful, instrumental mercury. He had begun as Humphry Davy's assistant, and inherited Davy's flair for public demonstrations of scientific discoveries and deriving useful (and profitable) inventions from scientific principles. But Faraday was not given to flamboyant inhaling of gases, and he did not accept a knighthood or the presidency of the Royal Society when they were offered to him. In 1821, among other material properties, he investigated "the vaporization of mercury at common temperature," as his student and biographer John Tyndall referred to it, "a subject which he would return to later." Faraday had placed a leaf of gold foil across the mouth of a bottle containing raw mercury, and showed that the gold amalgamated with mercury that can only have reached it as a vapor at room temperature.

On Christmas Day of that year, working by himself in the basement of the Royal Institution, Faraday induced mechanical motion through electrical current. The basis for his claim to have invented the electric motor, this demonstration places a circular magnet at the center of an open pool of metallic mercury in a flat dish. A thin wire attached to both poles of a battery extends from above, its tip in the mercury, moving in a circular motion around the magnet. Faraday illustrated that this is a principle of the relationship between electricity and magnetism by including a second vessel of mercury, a wire connected to the battery fixed in the center, and a magnet left free in the vessel to revolve around the wire.

In two years Faraday showed that if the magnet was moved manually about the wire not attached to a battery, current was generated in the wire.

In the public lectures and experiments that were published as *The Chemical History of a Candle* after the last time he delivered and performed them (Christmas 1860), Faraday made little mention of mercury and he only used free mercury in a marginal way in his experiments. After it served as the basis for his most original contribution to technology, he abandoned it to sealed instruments.

Mercury continued to be a substance processed and experimented upon in the laboratory, and its weight and apparently neutral fluidity recommended it for many other uses. Its physical properties encountered the variables-temperature and pressure-needing measurement. It expanded regularly with the increase of heat and became the substance of thermometers. It resisted compression by changes in pressure and became the substance of gauges measuring atmospheric, gaseous and eventually blood pressure. It did not absorb gases that passed through it and became the substance of troughs over which gases were collected in bottles for study.

Mercury had turned from one of the fundamental components of all matter to one of the fundamental components of its study. Open and enclosed vessels of mercury, often heated for various experimental purposes, were inevitable in chemical laboratories by the beginning of the nineteenth century, and in the industries fabricating scientific instruments. As mercury disappeared from some laboratory and industrial uses, it appeared in others and remained in the air. Gold rushes, thermometer making and electrolysis joined hat and mirror-making. World production, transport and consumption of mercury increased during the nineteenth century.

Looking back from his own mercury affliction, the early twentieth-century chemist Alfred Stock thought that Michael Faraday must have suffered mercury poisoning. He did not mention any of his other predecessors in the laboratory as suffering exposure but fixed on Faraday perhaps because of the mercury vapor measurements. For a brief while Stock's speculation was repeated in the science press, but did not enter biographies of Faraday as Newton's "madness" entered Newton biography. It is surprising how few scientists of this period expressed or were described by contemporaries as exhibiting the signs of mercury. Perhaps Becher's bravado prevailed.

The venue of the low continual dose of the laboratory, confined to a small number of people, specialists and amateurs, had expanded into the regular consumption of medicines and dental amalgams containing small amounts of mercury and in some geographic areas to exposure to the industrial release of mercury and compounds.

Alfred Stock was well situated to recognize the presence of the inorganic mercury environment that had suffused chemical laboratories for centuries with varying realization of its effects. Stock's studies of the chemical bonding of metals, and for that matter of the hydride bonding of specific metals such as boron, were not primarily focused on mercury but employed it as a laboratory agent. The concepts he articulated would later have considerable application to the action of mercury in the human body, though he did not make this link himself.

In 1916, in the course of articulating a nomenclature for inorganic compounds, Stock described a type of chemical bond he called a "ligand," in which a metal atom is associated with a non-metal atom or group of atoms. The term did not come into general use until the 1950s, when it was used to describe how heavy metals like mercury can become attached to organic compounds.

Stock also gave more technical specificity to the idea of the chelate, which decades later would become an important concept in explaining the passage of mercury through the human body. His examination and synthesis of boron hydrides (boranes) would be useful in the development of rocket fuels by former Nazi scientists working in the United States during the 1960s.

Stock came to awareness of the effects of mercury through his participation in a controversy related to dental amalgams. Since the mid–nineteenth century, mercury was used to liquefy and set corrosion-resistant metals to fill cavities in teeth corroded by bacteria (see chapter 12). The amalgam fillings had the great advantage of resisting further corrosion in the active environment of the mouth while providing adequate weight and substance to the teeth. As dentistry professionalized, many dentists adopted mercury amalgams as a technique allowing them to claim success against the tooth decay caused by an increasingly sugary diet. But the growing use of amalgams generated an opposition who claimed that mercury poisoned dentists and patients more than it prevented decay.

The applicable skill Stock brought to this controversy was chemical analysis. Stock found an elevated level of mercury in the urine of dentists and dental patients whose teeth were filled with mercury-silver and with the less expensive mercury-copper amalgams. This assay was the result of fine analysis achieved by the development of ever more sensitive balance scales. It also was nationalistic. French practitioners promoted the use of amalgams, and it was France that had repelled the attack of Germany in the recent war. Stock was able to link the presence of dental amalgams, elevated levels of body mercury with the symptoms of mercury poisoning only in a few anecdotal cases. He theorized that metallic mercury vapors released by saliva and mechanical action in the mouth entered the respiratory system and the blood stream.

Stock was primed by his part in the amalgam controversy to reflect on his own illness and that of his laboratory colleagues as they began to work more with mercury in research unrelated to the substance itself.

When in 1926 Stock wrote of the effects of mercury vapor on laboratory personnel, himself included, he chronicled a slow and painful realization. He had unthinkingly inhaled mercury fumes from the time he was a child setting up a laboratory at home. Only his eagerness to warn all those who had to deal with metallic mercury moved him to report his personal problems. Science requires that the experimenter control the materials of experimentation.

Stock's chemical work consisted of placing volatile substances in a closed vessel over a mercury tub and evacuating the air using a mercury pump and mercury valves, then measuring the resulting changes in vapor pressure using a mercury pressure gauge (manometer). He had been breathing airborne mercury for twenty-five years.

"With me," Stock wrote, "the situation began with slight intermittent headaches and mild drowsiness," which increased gradually over the years to constant nervous restlessness and "jitteriness." This progressed to a constant headache, vertigo, cold-like symptoms, strong saliva flow, mental weariness, distributed body pains, bladder and intestinal disorders, loosening of teeth and most distressing to him, loss of memory. Stock's coworkers also were affected with many of the same disorders and most evident to all of them was the deficit in intellectual functions. "Soon after all of us in the laboratory had found out what was wrong with us, we sat down together to put down on paper a completed piece of work where we had to do a lot of mathematics. None of us was able to add up columns of ten to twenty multi-digit numbers without making mistakes."

Stock found himself becoming unsociable; his humor turning "rusty."

He addressed the growing illness with a number of measures, including stays in the mountains and cocaine treatment of the nose, but these brought no relief at all or at best temporary remission. Students and assistants who left the laboratory recovered from their illness after a few years, but that at first did not give Stock and those who continued working there any hints about the cause. He discovered later, after mercury was known to be the cause and he could correlate it with other cases of mercury poisoning, that the symptoms come and go as if the poison remains buried in body organs, and reemerges unprovoked. Serious exposure in the past can lead to more severe symptoms on later exposure. The many mercury apparatuses and the chance spills of mercury, the shutting off of the ventilation system to save on electricity, and the large rooms with unmoving air could serve to increase the amount of mercury in the air to be breathed.

It was only after a combination of these conditions produced symptoms of acute mercury poisoning in Stock and two other researchers working under the same conditions that the experienced poison researcher Louis Lewin was consulted and diagnosed mercury poisoning.

The laboratory took steps to eliminate pockets of spilled mercury, to enclose open vessels and do all work with mercury under ventilation hoods. Chemical abatement did not work: sulfur powder, zinc dust or tin flags did not absorb appreciable amounts of mercury when spread about. The laboratory workers just had to endure the cold of leaving the windows open during the winter to allow air flow.

The colleagues who left the laboratory recovered the fastest, but even for them it took 1-2 years away from the mercury to regain their well-being. Stock himself, who continued to work in the laboratory and took measures to clear the air and eliminate or cover open pockets of mercury, was the longest in recovering. He still had relapses of headaches, drowsiness and mild mouth inflammations, but at the time of the writing of the article he expected he would fully recover. Twenty years of mercury built up in the body would take a long time to excrete.

Stock wrote at the beginning of his article that normally he would hesitate to publicize his personal problems which usually wouldn't concern others, but that he was motivated by a wish to warn those who work with metallic mercury about the frightening events that had ruined his life. The scientist's heroic indifference to the personal consequences of his experiments was placed behind the need to warn other scientists. Stock's warning was part of a trend toward improving laboratory safety, not only by controlling the use of obviously corrosive and explosive materials, but by containing invasive chemicals, as well.

Inspired by Stock, a few other chemists reported their physical reactions to the mercury on the loose in the laboratory. Becher's bravado was being replaced by measured caution in experimental science, making the transition to science fiction.

The physicist Otto Robert Frisch recalled in his memoirs that while working in the physics department of the University of Berlin in the late 1920s he was assigned to develop a device that could detect the mercury spilled about the laboratory from past experiments. The poisonous vapor was cause for concern. However, Frisch resignedly continues, the instrument he and his colleague assembled detected mercury and many other chemicals at the same time. He does not say what was done about the mercury, but his reminiscence marks a rising awareness of the problem loose mercury posed for laboratory workers contemporary with Stock's publications.

What eventually happened to the laboratory mercury atmosphere can be seen from the warnings that began to appear in instructional manuals and experiment books, and the reactions to any manifestation of elemental mercury in teaching and research environments. To take one example, in 1988 the U.S. Centers for Disease Control reported mercury exposure in a Connecticut high school laboratory. The details of time, persons and place were not specific, but the circumstances were given precisely.

A high school chemistry class was to conduct an experiment illustrating sublimation of metals from compounds. They were to heat silver oxide to release the silver metal, then weigh the separate components to recognize mass balance. Silver oxide was not available and mercuric oxide was substituted. The students heated the oxide in crucibles under ventilation hoods, which, however, were not working. As the experiment progressed, the mercury did not appear in the amount predicted by chemical law. The mercury had entered the air and was breathed by the students and instructor in the enclosed laboratory. Blood tests showed a dangerously elevated mercury blood level in some, requiring almost a year to recover. The case became an instructive instance repeated in textbooks on toxic exposure.

Using mercury did illustrate mass balance after all, but by extension into the biology of the experimenters. The silver merely would have been visible and weighed; the mercury was in the blood.

Becher's bravado had been deflated. Rather than an airborne force the alchemist drew upon to his advantage and at his peril, mercury was enclosed and watched but still left pools about the laboratory, sickening some who worked there. Mercury suffused the laboratory and therefore opened the possibility that its symptomatic presence is environmental. Mercury was no longer something a person could decide to take in or breathe. It was in the air we breathe, the water we drink.

Never was the knowledge that mercury is a poison absent from laboratory workers' understanding, but it was a component of the laboratory atmosphere to inspire the workers and to be overcome. In Stock's time, caution gained the upper hand over the triumphalist mode. As chemistry extended to the analysis of blood, drinking water, food and air, the realm of mercury was found beyond the laboratory.

The controversy about the use of mercury started as laboratory workers became aware that the means of research was affecting their own lives and the lives of those in the vicinity, while the work went on just the same, for profit, glory, the good of the state, and so on. The alchemist locked away in his steaming laboratory obtained inspiration and reputation by cultivating a mercurial (and arsenical and sulfurous) atmosphere, while at the same time knowing it was poisonous. The chemist put aside the fluidity and changeability of mercury and locked it away in glass, using its solidity and permanence as a standard. But mercury escaped these restraints and went up into the air and down into the flooring. A capacity to understand where it was going lagged behind the accumulation.

4

⸺∞⸺

Bread and Fish

In early 2007 there was good news for fish eaters. The selenium contained in the flesh of commonly consumed fish counteracts the mercury concentrated there. It's safe to eat as much fish as you want without fearing the mercury poisoning for decades associated with seafood. One toxic metal will protect you from the other. Except, one brief notice snidely remarked, for pilot whale meat, which in any event is unlikely to be available.

Since 1970, the public in Europe and North America has been presented with imagery depicting the dangers of mercury in food. After recalls and prohibitions, the news of fish and other varieties of seafood has settled into a pattern of alerts and reassurances. Yes, there is mercury in the fish; no, it won't harm you (or your children). Except that swordfish has more mercury than tuna. And do not fish here in this river, this lake, this bay.

Small notices that the product contains mercury may be posted near the fresh fish department in supermarkets, but not on cans of processed fish. The sellers in open-air fish markets don't post these notices. Stories of mercury concentrations in seafood do appear occasionally in newspapers. The amount of mercury in airborne emissions is the subject of negotiations between government regulators and coal-burning industries. Warnings to treat as hazardous waste also appear on the packaging of some batteries and fluorescent lights, because they contain what now is a new mercury.

The mercury of this rhythm of warning and acceptance is different from the mercury confined to the atmosphere and vessels of the laboratory, the mine and the workshop. Laboratory and factory workers encountered mercury in an enclosed space. The mercury they worked with was imagined and transformed in the context of that limited encounter. A mercury that could be imagined and worked spreading in the living world had to have a form more suited to living creatures. It is not the artisanal mercury of the alchemists, but a corporate, governmental mercury released into nature and human bodies that is feared today.

That mercury known, feared and never seen, is the result of two streams merging in popular lore: organic mercury compounds used as seed treatments which through bread and to a lesser extent through wild birds got into humans; and inorganic (and organic) mercury compounds released into water and transformed into new organic mercury by bacteria, then entering fish and the animals that eat them, including humans. The seed mercury set up the model for damage by this new organic mercury.

A few people in industrialized countries were harmed by the mercury that entered flour and meat from seed treatments. This was followed by epidemics of mercury poisoning among people in several countries more dependent on agriculture. Then some glaring cases of mercury reaching people through the fish they consumed spurred the analysis of mercury in sea life, and spawned a pervasive fear.

At first, organic mercury, compounds of mercury containing carbon, was one of many organometallics elaborated by chemists according to a pattern of chemical invention. One type of organic mercury, mercury fulminate, was found to be an explosive, and was treated with caution after initial blow-ups. Another discovered to be a poison in the laboratory entered the wider world as a fungicide. The movement of this mercury from laboratory and factory made mercury environmental — environmental mercury. The creation of this new mercury began slowly, but then it sped quickly, as social and political conditions favored it.

"The apparatus was demolished by an explosion, and an arsenic flame several feet high arose, covering the surrounding objects with a black layer of foul-smelling arsenic." Robert Wilhelm Bunsen described what happened when a droplet of an organic arsenic compound, cacodyl oxide, fell on a heated part of the distilling tube. An explosion had already taken part of the sight of one of Bunsen's eyes. He had to breathe through glass tubes while he was working with the choking substances. But his studies showed that cacodyl was a radical that could combine with elements to form a series of unique compounds.

"Cacodyl" means "bad-smelling substance"; it also means $C_4H_{12}As_2$. Establishing its existence experimentally marked a transition from the era in which chemicals were named for their physical properties— hydrargyrum, quicksilver — to the present when they are formed of proportions of typical components: elements, radicals. Sensory impressions and material actions are buried in names. Cacodyl is a chemical radical which causes some compounds containing it to stink and explode. The sensuous chemist is giving way to the chemical accountant.

Bunsen's English student Edward Frankland showed that there was a range of organic compounds formed of metals and groups of carbon and hydrogen (methyl, ethyl, butyl and so on). Frankland formed the compounds by sealing a sample of a metal in a glass tube with the relevant alcohol and exposing it to heat and/or light. Like earlier chemists, Frankland inhaled chemical vapors to learn their physiological effects, not mercury, but (like Davy) ether and chloroform intoxicated him, and like Bunsen he narrowly escaped injury when a glass tube exploded as the gas generated by his experiment met the mercury that was to measure it. A fragment of the glass struck the laboratory assistant below the eye.

Zinc ethyl, zinc methyl and the rest of the various metal series could be formed in glass-enclosed reactions. Mercury came late in Frankland's collection of "organic bodies containing metals," and was made to form mercury ethide and mercury methide. The synthesis of methylmercury iodide was a slow process requiring patience rather than daring. Frankland's purpose was to examine systematically the reactions that led to characterizing an entire species of what he called "organometallic compounds" and beyond that to a theory of chemical valency.

This elaboration of chemical combinations in a series was the common practice of nineteenth-century chemistry. It was a process of charting interactions of known chemical units to learn the conditions of synthesis and the properties of the result, and to test the theory that groups of elements, and in particular combinations of carbon and hydrogen, could act as radicals in joining others to make compounds with varying degrees of stability. What alchemists may have accidentally hit upon, the chemists derived by systematic experiment.

What may accidentally have killed and injured the alchemists also killed and injured the chemists, but the chemists learned what would repeat those conditions and how to control them. When they generated a new compound, however, filling in a space in their charts, the chemists had no way of knowing except by experiences like Bunsen's what the compound might do to the experimenter and the surroundings. Both effects could be sudden or gradual.

Alice Hamilton in her text on industrial toxicology commented that laboratories using mercury are notorious for their carelessness. Yet a twenty-year study of a hospital and academic community with many laboratories uncovered few examples of mercury poisoning. Perhaps metallic mercury with its many uses was so frequently spilled and so infrequently punished by apparent illness that it became a casual standard, a kind of perpetuation of the alchemist's mercury atmosphere.

The great variation in individual sensitivity to mercury and modes of reaction in part account for the differences reported between neutral chemicals and poisons. Alchemists and chemists turned out to be experimenters who could survive the atmosphere of their research to the point of benefiting from it. But new chemicals were always being generated, and they reached the body of the laboratory technician first.

The "strong mercury" that Anthony à Wood says "marched off" Thomas Vaughan may have been an organic preparation which in his brief life Vaughan had not yet encountered. Heat speeds up the formation of organic mercury compounds, and the widespread belief that heated mercury could kill anyone breathing it might express experiences of precipitously forming carbon-hydrogen-mercury compounds. The "effluvia" that sickened the crew of the HMS *Triumph* may have been the result of mercury reacting with tanning compounds in the leather bags stored in the overheated hold.

Frankland's generation of chemists used mercury as a tool and less often as a subject of their synthesis projects. When Frankland was asked to teach a group of farmers basic chemistry to assist them with their work, the supplies he listed did not include mercury as a substance, but as a medium for gas collection, for measuring pressure and to serve as a standard for density comparison. Frankland made some of the first accurate analyses of the chemical contents of drinking water, which did not, at that time, include mercury.

The cautious tabular development of organic metal compounds was arbitrarily repeated by exploratory researchers who did not know what they were producing. The first reported accident that allowed doctors to observe the effects of an organic mercury compound on the human body occurred in a laboratory at the Royal Institution in London, initially reported to be supervised by Frankland. A German, Dr. Carl Ulrich, was admitted to St. Bartholomew's Hospital on February 3, 1865, with slurred speech and paralysis of arms and legs, which developed into a coma and death on February 13. A man who had worked in the same laboratory, the 23-year old T. Sloper, was admitted on March 25 with similar symptoms, and lingered for a year before dying. Another assistant in the same laboratory breathed the fumes, became ill but survived.

The events were reported in the *Chemistry News*, and later in *St. Barts Hospital Notes*, but they received an almost Dickensian treatment in an article in the English-language Paris journal *Cosmos*. According to the article, Frankland forced his assistant Mr. C. U. (Ulrich) to labor for three months at generating a large amount of methylmercury. "In consequence, the poor young man became poisoned ... paralysis of the limbs, deafness, inflammation of the gums, scarcely able to stand, very imperfect vision, indistinct speech ... followed by intermittent delirium ... he died on 14 February!"

The second assistant (Sloper), the article said "has become a virtual idiot, recognizing no one."

The author of the *Cosmos* article, T. L. Phipson, a chemist rival of Frankland's, was using the poisonings to attack Frankland in order to aggrandize himself, but as Frankland and several of his colleagues quickly pointed out, Frankland did not have a laboratory at St. Bartholomew's Hospital at the time. The two poisoned men were under the supervision of Professor William Odling, who was conducting research through assistants into the reactions of sodium-mercury amalgams with methyl iodide.

One of Ulrich's friends revealed that Ulrich told him he had broken open a sealed glass tube containing methide of mercury and both he and Sloper had breathed the fumes: not a surprising accident. This evidence of the power of dimethyl mercury led to a series of tests on animals and humans to determine its potential as a syphilis remedy. It might be able to deliver mercury to the source of the syphilis "virus" (not yet known to be bacteria). The course of dimethyl mercury poisoning resembled a speeded up progression of syphilis. Dogs injected with a weak (1 percent) solution of dimethyl mercury in alcohol did not survive long. The tests were discontinued.

The methylmercury deaths became absorbed into the cautionary lore of organic mercury and passed down in a part-oral, part-written tradition among laboratory workers, as previous mercury operational beliefs had been.

Since then there have been a few recorded deaths of people who inhaled dimethyl mercury fumes: stenographers working in a Calgary, Alberta warehouse where a mass of treated seed was stored, a Czech chemist who synthesized a quantity of dimethyl mercury, knowing its chemistry but not its properties. An organic mercury atmosphere did not exist in most laboratories as a metallic mercury atmosphere once did. There would have been far more deaths if it had. Organic mercury exposure moved from a laboratory occasion to an occupational exposure that bridged laboratory and farm, from an enclosed cabinet to the soil itself. Organic mercury compounds used as fungicides became one of the components of mechanized agriculture.

The progression from occupational to environmental exposure, and from inorganic to organic mercury is through seeds treated with organic mercury compounds to retard the growth of fungi that might kill the developing plant. As prepared seed-based agriculture expanded worldwide, it became imperative to develop a means of increasing the productivity of large plantings. It was found that seed shaken with a fine dust containing an organic mercury compound would resist the growth of ruinous fungal blight when newly planted. By 1913, commercially distributed grain seed was being washed with a dilute organic mercury bath, ethyl, methyl or dimethyl mercury. This eliminated the need to apply the treatment in the field, but it created seed that was not what it seemed.

The same process of chemical elaboration that Frankland originated in his organometallic researches was used by technicians for the chemical industry to derive numerous variants of mercury and other heavy metal-based fungicides from the ethyl and dimethyl models. It was an effort to make dry compounds that could be uniformly distributed over seed without caking or clotting, were lethal to fungi but not the seed or sprouting plants, and of course were unique and patentable.

In 1929, E.I. du Pont de Nemours Corporation trademarked Granosan, a "seed disinfectant for treating small grains." The trademark registration did not state the chemical composition of Granosan, which was later written as

N-(ethylmercuri)-p-toluenesulfonanilide, or similar writing of the formula. It was an organic compound of mercury based on linking ethylmercury with the organic solvent toluene. Tests showed that in low concentrations it had the same fungus-suppressing qualities as ethylmercury.

Granosan and other trademarked anti-fungals made it possible for American agricultural enterprises to export seed grain. Where previously large quantities of grain in bags would decay into foul-smelling uselessness, now it could be shipped far away to contribute to increasing crop yields in areas where grain agriculture was limited by climatic conditions. And the chemicals themselves could be sold abroad to improve the growth of crops indigenous to an area, or introduced and susceptible to local pests.

When, for instance, agronomist Francisco Banda examined the "agro-economic potential of Ecuador" in a 1937 manifesto, he cited Granosan as an agent that could raise the "generative potential" ("*poder generativo*") of certain crops by protecting the weaker, more productive shoots from damps. The social and economic elites of a number of countries trying to build agriculture to feed populations and enter an international export market found antifungals designed for distribution a positive adjunct to seeds bred for the locale and pesticides to reduce loss at maturity. Forward-looking, and exploitative, agrobusinesses in many places were helped into existence by the seed treatments.

These chemicals, salubrious as they were for food plants, were not harmless to the humans who handled them.

The majority of the forty-five cases of organic mercury toxicity P. Lesley Bidstrup drew from the medical literature to illustrate her 1964 study of mercury poisoning are the consequence of antifungal seed treatment. These included laborers and laboratory technicians in the factory making the seed dressings, packers, inspectors and sellers of the preparation, and farm laborers who applied the dressings before planting.

One young farmer did not follow the instructions on the dressing package and breathed the dust as he applied it to the seeds, resulting in acute prickling pains and a cough which faded in eight days after symptomatic treatment. Another farmer was enveloped in dust when he opened a container of Germisan (phenyl mercury pyrocatechin) and besides tiredness and shortness of breath suffered exacerbation of existing kidney damage. One of the laborers in the factory after four months exposure to methyl mercury iodide began to exhibit exaggerated reflexes and explosive speech which doctors at first thought was hysteria until another worker in the factory came down with the same symptoms. The man affected first was permanently disabled. A laboratory assistant ate treated seed and had violent diarrhea and nausea, from which he recovered after two days.

The one assistant who ate the seed clearly was uninformed at first, then was well warned for the future. The application of mercury to seed created an environment which could compromise the health of anyone along a line of production and use established by agricultural enterprise. As the treatment became a routine component of the seed provided to farmers, the environment that produced the chemicals and treated the seed traveled with the seed.

As in all cases of human-mercury involvement, some individuals were more severely affected than others. Despite wearing gloves, goggles and dust masks as they treated masses of seed with alkylmercurial compounds, four out of sixteen workers after two months showed cognitive and emotional effects of mercury poisoning. One who developed blisters on his arms was transferred to work with inorganic mercury compounds before other symptoms developed, but the other three went on working and developed gait and speech difficulties which an examining physician deemed permanent. His recommendation that organic mercury seed treatments be banned was ignored. In 1954, fourteen years later, when one of these workers died of pneumonia, his autopsy showed brain damage characteristic of mercury poisoning. The pathology results were used later to identify a similar cause in the deaths of the Minamata victims. There is no telling how the other workers were affected, not to mention countless others who had contact with the seed.

If factory and laboratory workers with organic mercury were poisoned, how much more likely was it for agricultural workers who did not know what they were handling? If a farmer or a farm laborer became sick because of exposure to mercury compounds on the seed he was distributing or planting, it was deemed not because the mercury was poisonous, but because he or she wasn't following the instructions. But those who ate food products made from contaminated seed did not even have the instructions. The case of a Swedish family with two children whose developmental disability was clearly linked to eating food containing flour made from mercury treated seed appeared in a pediatrics journal in 1952. That instance was not well known enough to serve as a warning.

The organic mercury compound in this case was Panogen, trademarked by an American corporation in 1942 and used to treat seed exported from the United States, as well as produced by subsidiaries in industrial countries like Sweden. Panogen — like Granosan and several others, now a defunct trademark — was 2-methoxymethylmercuri acetate, and according to its U.S. trademark registration had a range of uses to protect common materials: "seed disinfectant and impregnation for wood, textiles and other porous stuffs to protect them against moisture, rot, mould, insects and fire."

Investigators only knew that the members of the Huckleby family of Alamogordo, New Mexico, were suffering from "Minamata disease" because one of them had read about the symptoms exhibited by Japanese fishing families exposed to industrial effluent through the fish they caught and ate, and matched them to the unknown at hand. Yet it hadn't done any good that American physicians had attended a conference in Sweden on the transmission of organic mercury to humans eating treated seed. Reaction to the discovery that mercury was the cause and attempts to ban mercury seed treatments caused the seed to be sold abroad, to Iraq, where both Swedish and American scientists studied the consequent epidemic of poisonings. This was the scientific and medical knowledge. How popular culture invented organic mercury can only be traced from the outlines of events.

A sequence of events culminating in mass poisonings in 1970 marks the maturation of organic mercury. The events follow one another, but the participants in one were not conscious of the others, though knowledge would have clarified their situation. A scientific view in retrospect can visualize the general trend in these events. The popular view departed from the scientific, and proceeded under its own momentum.

The Minamata poisoning was concurrent with a few human poisonings outside Japan and a large-scale wildlife die-off in Sweden. There followed incidents of human debility and death due to treated-seed consumption in a number of countries. Disabling of several children in a farm family in an American town happened at the same time as a catastrophic epidemic in Iraq. There was no overview of these events, though one sometimes explained another. Bans and prohibitions were declared, and the information made public was ambiguous, quantifying the mercury present in the environment that made it seem pervasive, inescapable yet negligible.

Entire populations of farmers were placed under threat by not knowing the instructions for using the treated seed. As the technology of treating seed with organic mercury, the organic mercury compounds, and the seed itself, spread outside the laboratories, factories and farms of Europe and America, cautionary packaging did not accompany it, or could not be read. A few children in industrialized Sweden were permanently damaged eating food derived from treated grain. Consider starving people who, whatever their knowledge of mercury compounds had great need of bread. The seed itself was food for starving people long before the extended process of making bread could be completed.

The practice of eating seed grain before planting it was something governments have been trying to discourage since ancient times. Some ancient cities in Mesopotamia, present-day Iraq, and in Egypt, were built around temples which also were granaries from which seed was distributed for planting and in times of need. Papyrus receipts survive from Hellenistic Egypt which show the amount of seed given to farmer of royal lands at the time of planting, with the expectation that the same amount would be returned (with interest) at harvest. This was to insure that the seed was not eaten. Some African oral literature turns around the dangers of eating seed after bread has been the usual food. Peasants in India, Russia and Mexico all have related stories of the balance between need and planting, to hold the seed for the future while hunger gnaws.

In 1962 there were four deaths after thirty-four cases of poisoning in West Pakistan. In 1966, starving Guatemalan peasants given treated seed to plant ate it instead: forty-five of them fell ill and twenty died, it was believed, of encephalitis brought on by the mercury poisoning. Two died of seventy people known to have eaten treated seed in Russia. In Ghana, desperate people eating maize treated with Panogen at a state farm died by the dozens. This occurred in 1964, but was not reported in the news media at the time or in the scientific literature until 1976.

All these events except for the Ghana poisonings were mentioned and grouped with the Minamata poisonings at hearings of a U.S. Senate Subcommittee in 1970, on the "effects of mercury on man and the environment." What prompted these hearings and the subsequent legislative and bureaucratic action was a homegrown American family poisoning that did not result in deaths, but in photogenic damage to children.

Ernest Huckleby, who supplemented his work as a janitor for Alamogordo, New Mexico, schools with pig farming for food and profit, was given an opportunity to collect sweepings from an agricultural seed depot in Texico, Texas, around 200 miles from his home. Five years later, in 1975, a federal judge turned down a petition by Huckleby's attorneys to sue the federal government because its agents at the depot did not warn him that mercury-treated seed would cause illness in humans who ate its products. The judge agreed with the defense, that Huckleby had been warned, but he added the seed to garbage he cooked to make a mash to feed his pigs, thinking that the cooking would banish the poison. Iraqi farmers and merchants had already taken — and were again taking — a similar approach.

Huckleby, his pregnant wife and three of his seven children who ate bacon and ham from hogs that had been fed the mash developed coordination and vision disturbances. Two of the children became disoriented and went blind, as did the newborn infant Mrs. Huckleby was carrying when she ate the meat. The lawsuit against the federal government failed, but the following year three corporate defendants, the producer of the seed treatment, the distributor and the warehouser all settled out of court for an undisclosed sum of money which the attorneys said would support the Huckleby children for life.

It was not immediately clear to local physicians what afflicted the children when they began to lose balance and slur their speech. Alamogordo was the closest populated area to the site of the first nuclear test in 1945 (at Los Alamos, about 60 miles away), and nuclear-weapons research continued in the area. It had a larger complement of scientists and technicians than other communities of comparable size. The physicians referred the case to the Centers for Disease Control (CDC), thinking that it must be a contagion that should be identified before it became epidemic.

None of the Hucklebys' other five children were seriously affected, and the two parents and an older daughter recovered. The Panogen on the seed fed to the pigs eaten by the family was only identified as the cause after a physician at the CDC recalled reading about similar symptoms of the Minamata disease caused by mercury in fish consumed by children and adults. It was this connection between two separate types of organic mercury and two distinct media of poisoning, fish and pig meat, that created organic mercury as a public issue.

The Huckleby story was a national news item in 1970. Large urban newspapers followed the discovery of the disease once mercury was identified as the cause and stayed with the story until the settlement agreement with the corporations in 1976. Photographs of 13-year-old Amos Huckleby on crutches made the threat of poison in food vividly immediate. That the Hucklebys were African Americans and among the rural poor whom this industrial chemical could now reach stole into the popular awareness. Generally the people who suffered mercury poisoning were those who made food out of seed that was a component of industrialized agriculture and no longer potentially food in itself.

Where mercury previously had been regulated among other chemicals used for specific purposes, it now was something national authorities at least needed to make a show of keeping out of the food supply. Late in 1970, one of the first official acts of the newly formed Environmental Protection Agency in the United States was to ban alkylmercury (ethyl and methylmercury) seed treatments. The Swedish national agricultural authority had already done the same in 1966, while keeping less toxic mercury treatments in use. Both countries continued to export treated seeds and the treating chemicals themselves.

The Department of the Interior addressed the presence of mercury in bay and lake waters, and in the fish and shellfish gathered there. But the Department of Agriculture, at the time charged with enforcing the Federal Insecticide, Fungicide and Rodenticide Act, backed down after agribusiness leaders resisted their gesture of blocking shipments of treated seed, and allowed companies to sell stock on hand.

In 1971, the first legislative proposal since 1938 expand to the scope of the federal Food and Drug Administration was made. The Toxic Substances Control Act would make the FDA responsible for a range of substances beyond drugs, insecticides and food additives. Facing determined resistance from industries using substances judged toxic by a growing number of research studies, the TSCA did not become law until 1976, paralleling the eventual settlement of the Hucklebys' lawsuit against the three corporations.

In 1969, raw mercury use by the electrical equipment industry — a great variety of uses from valves and meters to gyroscopes and lighting — exceeded the amount used in manufacturing processes, primarily the chlor-alkali industry, for the first time. There actually was an increase of mercury in motion, both in variety and quantity of manufacturing processes and consumption. The year 1970 saw the establishment of the Occupational Safety and Health Administration which was charged with investigating work conditions likely to lead to accidents and illness. None of these laws and bureaucratic formations referred exclusively to mercury fungicide poisonings. All are part of an atmosphere from which mercury precipitated as a major threat to life and environment.

During 1970 in response to the Huckleby poisonings, Senate mercury pollution hearings were held, and the EPA soon issued the first and only national recall of canned fish (albacore tuna) due to mercury. In that year there also was a ban in Ontario, on the sale of perch and pickerel taken across the border from Lake St. Clair, Michigan; 634 separate fish kills in which 23 million fish died in 45 states (up 34 percent from the previous year); and a ban on fishing along a length of the Wabigoon-English-Winnipeg River system in Ontario and Manitoba (including the Grassy Narrows Reserve).

Charles Hyder, a physicist at the National Aeronautics and Space Administration Space Flight Center in Albuquerque, New Mexico, announced in late 1970 that gases released by burning coal at the large regional power plant at Four Corners were putting appreciable amounts of mercury into the atmosphere. This was broadcasting mercury pollution over a far wider area than that of mercury precipitated into waters where it underwent chemical transformation and entered animals living in the water. Hyder testified at Senate hearings the following year, but there was no legislative action on this mercury source for a long time.

After the Hucklebys came to national attention early in 1970, the cascade of mercury concerns, even if unrelated to each other, were grouped together as environmental. They seemed to be responses to the underlying anxiety about the possibility of contamination by radioactive materials and a rising sensitivity to the safety of even the most basic foods. In 1969 there had been a scare that breast milk was carrying the pesticide DDT because dairy farms used it to keep down insect pests. Alamogordo and the Hucklebys located and personified these fears.

The 1970 Senate hearings cited the Hucklebys and Minamata (neither by name) and a several seed poisonings, including one in Iraq.

The number of people who died in Iraq in 1956 from eating bread made from milled methylmercury-treated wheat seed is unknown. The cause of death was recorded, but no measures were taken to prevent it from happening again. In 1961, 321 individuals in Iraq were sickened by the consumption of ethylmercury-treated seed, and thirty-five of them are known to have died. The farmers had been informed that the seed was coated with fungicide and was not to be eaten or fed to animals, but they believed they could wash the poison away.

Iraqi doctors who examined the victims of these outbreaks recommended that the seed be dyed a striking color both to warn people that it was not edible and to keep opportunists from hoarding the seed and trying to cash it in by making bread.

This advice was followed and the drought-resistant wheat seed the Iraqi government purchased from subsidiaries of the multinational agribusiness Cargill was dyed pink. Alkylmercury compounds were banned for use as fungicides in the United States in 1970, but existing stock could be exported. After a drought decimated crops in 1971, the Iraqi government ordered a quantity of this wheat seed and distributed it to farmers between September and December of that year. The first poisoning cases arrived at hospitals in late December.

The Iraqi farmers received hundreds of bags of treated seeds with indecipherable writing and symbols too late in the season to plant. Drought conditions made it unlikely that the seeds would sprout. The optimum use of the seed was to grind it into flour and bake it into unleavened bread, to make it last a little longer. Some of the farmers thought that if they washed the dye away, the chemicals would go as well. They tested its safety by feeding it to chickens and then to livestock, which did not immediately show any change in behavior indicative of poisoning. By the time the cattle did begin to act disoriented some of the seed had already been made into bread. The cattle were sent to slaughterhouses, and the bread was sold in quantity. That those who ate it first did not develop symptoms encouraged others. The bread was eaten by an estimated 50,000 men, women and children; 6,530 were hospitalized and 459 died.

The severity of the poisonings was magnified by the response of Saddam Hussein's government. When the lethal results of eating even processed seed grain became clear, those hoarding it were threatened with penalties. Sale of meat from sick animals was banned. Army squadrons began executing people found in possession of seed. Some farmers dumped it into the irrigation channels and waterways, where the mercury coating entered the water and the fish, or where the seed was eaten by migratory birds, which then became feeble and easier for the starving people to capture. The mercury entered people through several of the possible routes.

In a fugitive glimpse provided by Khidr Hamza, a physicist who fled Iraq to avoid working on Saddam Hussein's bomb projects, Iraq health officials were so ill-prepared for the mercury poisoning that they had to call on chemists and physicists in the better-funded military projects to measure the mercury concentration in water and body tissues.

In September 1974, the World Health Organization (WHO) held a conference in Baghdad to discuss "intoxication due to alkylmercury treated seed." A number of the Iraqi doctors who had seen the victims of the poisoning presented papers on the clinical course and the epidemiology of the disorder from 1971 to 1973.

The overwhelming emphasis of the conference was on the direct effects of mercury accidentally consumed as in any mass poisoning. Several of the papers calculated the dose of mercury compound as measured in blood and hair in relation to the severity of symptoms (dose-response relationship), and others examined the geographical distribution of the symptoms and tabulated their frequency in relation to the amount and type of seed consumed in that area. There was no account of the Iraqi government efforts to curb hoarding of the seed, and only one brief complaint by one of the conference organizers that the greed of some of the farmers had led to the recent disaster as it had to past ones.

During the years after the conference, Iraqi physicians completed studies of the long-term consequences of organic mercury consumption for individuals and groups. They also observed that they were unable to collect data on a wide scale soon enough to present accurately representative findings. The estimates of morbidity and mortality were based on hospital admissions. Having had some training in Europe or America, they published papers in English, French and German medical and chemistry journals and, in a sign of an emerging Cold War relation, Soviet journals. But the beginning of the devastating Iraq-Iran war in 1980 curtailed active research activities and increased Iraq's impoverishment as national revenues were diverted to military purposes.

One of the declared intentions in organizing the 1974 WHO conference was to generate knowledge to prevent further outbreaks of this magnitude. The writers were aware of previous mercury-seed poisonings in Iraq and elsewhere, as well as of organic mercury epidemics not caused by eating treated seed, especially the industrial pollution at Minamata, Japan. British and American experts contributed clinical expertise. Two Brazilian scientists authored a paper on a program successfully limiting the use of organomercury fungicide.

The alkylmercurials in all cases were manufactured outside of the countries where epidemics of poisoning took place, but the corporations that produced the chemicals and sold the treated seed were not named. The generic names of the treatments, Granosan, Panogen, and others, were not used in the literature.

It was noticed that the alkylmercury seed dressings had more serious effects than phenylmercury acetate, also widely used for seed. There were government bans on using ethyl and methyl mercury compounds, but not on phenylmercury.

Swedish scientists also took part in the conference. The author of the one paper on environmental aspects of the seed treatment was Arne Jernelov. He found that the feathers of birds that were captured closer to the granaries where the treated seed was stored had a greater concentration of mercury than the feathers of birds found at a greater distance. Jernelov was an expert on the presence of mercury in the food chain. His work with the evidence of bird feathers had contributed to the discovery that whatever form mercury took when it entered the environment, it eventually accumulated in living tissue as methyl mercury. He warned in 1969 that the mercury being found in fish tissues would disappear only after there was no more mercury in the waterways.

People, the intended beneficiaries, were the chief casualties of treated seeds. Other victims were predatory and seed-eating birds. In the 1950s, hawks and kestrels were seen to shudder and waver in Swedish fields, and then die (around the same time the cats were dancing and dying at Minamata). Other species of birds were simply disappearing from their habitats and nesting sites, and among those that remained were birds whose eggs rotted in the nests or whose nestlings died. Of birds found both in rural areas and in cities, the rural birds seemed more affected, and their disorders were correlated with the planting season.

Researchers surmised that the birds were suffering from the neurological effects of mercury concentrated from rodent prey that had eaten fungicide-treated seed. The researchers were able to support this belief by mercury concentration analysis of the birds' feathers. Taking advantage of over a century of bird specimens preserved in museums, they showed that the sudden increase in the concentration of mercury in the feathers coincided with the introduction of anti-fungal seed treatments in the early twentieth century, and their increased use after the end of the Second World War.

The Swedish government was impelled to act after news of high mercury concentrations limited the sales of eggs and dairy products exported to other European countries. Reduction in the use of alkylmercury compounds as antifungals and adoption of other compounds, including other organic mercurials, led to a marked decrease in mercury levels and the return of most bird populations to their prior size. After 1970, the high concentrations of the heavy metal in urban birds was due to industrial pollution.

Seeds as a source of mercury explained the concentration of the metal found in the internal organs of the erratic raptors. For the sake of comparison, the researchers analyzed the mercury levels in aquatic birds that ate only fish. There was no source of organic mercury in their food, yet the fish-eating birds also showed an elevated level of mercury, as did the fish they ate. Predatory saltwater animals such as shark and marine mammals, and fresh water predators such as bass all showed a level of mercury accumulation that could only be explained by their position in the food chain. There had to be a source of organic mercury in the water itself.

The bacteria that exist in all environments either are able to use the chemical elements they encounter as part of their physiological processes, or they have ways of rejecting them. Different species of bacteria have different needs and tolerances, and they live where those needs and tolerances can be observed. There are no known species of bacteria that can use mercury metabolically as some can use sulfur. But many can continue to carry out their life functions in the presence of increasing concentrations of mercury brought about by industrial disposal into water. Perhaps they evolved in a natural world where amounts of mercury and other heavy metals would appear, not in sufficient quantities to drive selection of the types that could use them but enough to pose a challenge that could be met most easily by elimination. A gene that prejudices bacterial physiology toward the elimination of mercury was selected in exposed populations. Different types of bacteria vary in the ways they accomplish this, but it all results in methylation.

Elimination calls for making the extraneous substance harmless to the life processes of the bacteria, or at least likely to leave. Mercury can promote damaging oxidation by drawing oxygen into reactions with normal chemistry. These reactions need to be neutralized. This is accomplished by rendering them organic, in the case of mercury affixing to their electrostatically threatening atoms methyl (CH_3) molecules that make them positively charged ions free in the surrounding water.

Methylated mercury is preferentially drawn out of bacteria, and drawn into larger organisms because it now has the profile of an organic molecule. The larger organisms eliminate mercury as well, but more slowly. If there is enough mercury being passed along this way, then at any one time the larger organisms, and especially the ones that eat others, will contain concentrations of mercury greater than others in the surrounding water. Mercury bioaccumulates in aquatic predators, and in those who prey upon them. The cats dancing in the streets of Minamata, the birds twisting in the Swedish fields, the palsied fishers and their disabled children were the end consumers of the aquatic scavengers and predators who built up the most mercury.

There are species of bacteria that demethylate mercury compounds and render metallic mercury, which disappears, then sublimates or forms new compounds. There is potential for bacterial remediation of water polluted by methylated mercury.

Humans had synthesized methyl mercury as a chemical exercise and discovered its toxic properties, occasionally poisoning themselves by accident. Now industrial and agricultural discharges of mercury compounds into waters were known to be turned into methylmercury transported to humans through food and water, and accumulating in our tissues. Industrial residues and scientific knowledge were substantiated by the slow realization that Minamata and similar situations meant mercury wastes were being processed to enter our bodies without our knowing.

The release of alkylmercury in the form of seed treatments simply joined and concentrated a process of mercury methylation already going on. People eating bread from treated seed, eating animals who had eaten the seed, or who had eaten other animals who fed upon the seed all accumulated organic mercury in their tissues.

Iraq fit into the larger sphere of mercury contamination traced through local ecologies. When reporting on the Iraq outbreak in 1971, the *New York Times* also commented on the spread of organic mercury from seed to water and fish and gamebirds in Canada, which was then thought to be the source of the seed sent to Iraq.

Even before the World Health Organization conference in Baghdad in 1974, scientists were incorporating knowledge about the Iraq poisoning with what they knew about the Minamata and Niigata poisonings and others into a picture of how methylmercury could originate in industry, move and accumulate in the natural environment and in human bodies. In a pharmacological biochemistry group colloquium on "mercury intoxication" in 1971, P. Lesley

Bidstrup pointed out that since bichloride of mercury has "become less popular as an agent of homicide and suicide, acute systemic mercury poisoning is seldom seen." Neither the Minamata nor the Huckleby poisonings yielded information about organic mercury in bodily tissues. They only yielded accounts of symptoms, timing and individual differences.

Individual, inorganic and organic mercury poisoning, investigated by police authorities, has been succeeded by environmental poisoning of masses of people by organic mercury compounds investigated by public health authorities. Occupational mercury poisoning by a growing list of complex organic compounds continues, and the products of the industries in which these poisonings take place join the available mercury released into air and water. The organic mercury can be manufactured by humans or by bacteria from mercury compounds humans have released.

The discovery of environmental organic mercury poisoning by concentration in animal and human tissue raised concerns about its extent. During the 1970s and 1980s, studies were undertaken of populations who depended upon seafood for their diet. The aim was to quantify the extent of their exposure, determine if their general health was affected, and determine if methylmercury constituted a global health threat.

The World Health Organization's "Environmental Health Criteria 101" (1990) took stock of research into methylmercury's effects on human well-being from Minamata and Iraq onward, and stated that the "general population does not face a significant health risk from methylmercury." It was not much of a qualification of that statement for them to add that groups with a high fish consumption faced the small possibility of neurological damage to adults if their blood and hair mercury levels exceeded a certain standard.

A much more pronounced concern was the risk to the fetus. The threshold of neurological damage in the offspring was quantified at 70 milligrams of mercury per gram of maternal hair, yielding a 30 percent chance of neurological damage. The authors of the criteria referred to the data from years of study of the children born to Iraqi mothers who ate bread made of treated seed when they stated that 10–20 milligrams/gram created a five percent risk of neurological impairment.

They urged psychological and behavioral testing of children who had been exposed to minimal amounts of methylmercury while still in the uterus. The global danger dissipated, and a more subtle eagerness for knowledge developed. The consequences of methylmercury contact for development might be far-reaching, yet difficult to detect.

Preferential attraction of mercury to the fetus was confirmed with Minamata. The poisoning left heartbreaking images of congenital deformity. The children born in the aftermath of the Iraq consumption of treated seed did not show outward defects. The doctors studying their progress found that they often were slower in acquiring life skills, and appeared more susceptible to accident and disease. The Iraq data for decades afterward were reinterpreted in conjunction with new discoveries about the insinuation of methylmercury into the central nervous system. The 1990 call for more measurement of psychological and behavioral development of children was in response to knowing that mercury also was a latent cause of defects not directly connected with it.

The evident ills caused by mercury as by any other pathogen could be addressed clinically, but the permanent damage caused by uterine, infant and childhood exposure demanded measures to keep mercury from invading the developing body in the first place. It called for government regulation of industrial mercury release in whatever form that took.

The mercury content of a single strand of hair from the mother was graphed against the frequency of retarded walking in the offspring and it was found that the disability increased in direct proportion to the concentration of mercury. American and European environmental and public health agencies used this information to set the reference dose for maximum mercury exposure through food.

The Environmental Protection Agency, for instance, ascertained through studies of fish-consuming populations that 1.0 micrograms of mercury per kilogram of body weight was the most a child could absorb without disabling effects. They then divided this by 10, to give the standard, 0.1 micrograms. The dose differs from one public health agency to another: the United States Food and Drug Agency sets it at 0.4 micrograms and the World Health Organization at 1.6 micrograms.

The long-term effects of the Iraq epidemic confirmed what already was observed in the other instances of methylmercury absorption. The amount of mercury that reached the brain determined the degree to which the individual showed "mercury" symptoms, and it could only reach the brain in a certain form produced by manufacturing enterprise and biomethylation. There were individual differences in the outcome based on everything from form of mercury encountered (the toxicity of ethylmercury was different, eliminated from the body faster but at a greater brain blood ratio, than that of methylmercury) and the precise circumstances of contact, to genetics and health history. Any condition of organic mercury exposure was an environment within the larger environment that set human cognitive and motor functions against the influence of organic mercury.

The Iraqi children affected by mercury poisoning, and their mothers, were included in the American laboratory environment to provide standards that would apply to American children, at least as far as ingested mercury was concerned. This marked a change in the mercury environment of the world as a whole, the expansion of a pattern of mercury delivery to the human brain that included the brain's own study of the delivery.

Why did this environment extend noticeably to Iraq? The arrival of mercury in a form that could affect children through their own mothers was one aspect of globalization. Organic mercury was not produced in Iraq, and no one would have absorbed it if it hadn't entered from the outside. Like a ball rolling down an incline, mercury could achieve a physical momentum of its own once it entered a human food system, but contrary to weight, it rolled upwards into the top predators, sharks, eagles and humans.

At the same time, public health warnings about the mercury content of fish were extended particularly to pregnant women. Mercury was apparently as widespread as the oceans, lakes and rivers, and their yield, and as invasive and harmful as ever. This was the second stream of organic mercury, literally a liquid, though even less tangible than the mercury of the seeds. It was industrial waste from industries that used mercury compounds to suppress fungi that might ruin the product (papermaking) and industries where it was used as an electrode (chlor-alkali, see chapter 12) or as a catalyst (for instance, acetylene manufacture, as by the Chisso Corporation).

Industrial waste containing organic and inorganic mercury was taken up by the fish that lived in the waters where the waste was dumped either directly or after intermediary processing by bacteria. Then it was taken up by the people who ate the fish. Minamata and Grassy Narrows were its only manifestations in clusters of sick people and deformed children. Afterward this mercury was measure and threat, negotiation and notice, with a few scattered instances of human physical response that could be traced to its presence.

This waterborne mercury exists mainly as quantity in a body. The amount of mercury lost annually by industry, the number of parts of mercury per million in the body of a fish, and the amount of time it takes for a body to eliminate mercury are the key amounts. Scientists differ on which measures are significant and how, but the popular culture dimension is their bearing on the health of those who consume seafood.

This was played out when the Japanese public had it confirmed that Minamata disease was caused by mercury absorbed from seafood, and that people were affected in several other maritime communities. In July 1973, after years of protest by victims and their supporters, the Chisso Corporation signed an agreement promising compensation for old and new victims of the condition. This constituted an acceptance of responsibility by the corporation, but it also undermined consumer confidence in fish as a food. Sales of fish in Japan's large markets fell, and red meat sales increased. An order that government officials eat fish daily followed by a list of recommended weekly limits of specific fish did not restore the former consumer routines entirely.

The sufferings of those affected at Minamata had been before the public; they were made yet more vivid by the publication of Eugene Smith's photographs in 1973. But it was the corporation's concession after concealing for years the link between its own production and the effects of a seafood diet that placed the issue in the marketplace. The government attempted to assert control by dictating numbers and limits, implying that there were alternatives to rejecting fish entirely. This did establish a safe area of fish consumption, but one under constant threat of being altered by revelations of fact and rumors. The Chisso Corporation itself went bankrupt, leaving other mercury-using companies, and the fishing industry, with the ever-negotiated mercury it had helped to create.

This was an international mercury. The scientists who studied the Minamata cases published papers and attended conferences, as did the activists and even the victims. Japanese physicians were, for instance, involved in the efforts to make papermaking and chlor-alkali companies accountable for the symptoms suffered by native peoples at the Grassy Narrows Reserve in Canada. The fungicide-based epidemics became part of the background for this broader continuing arrival of mercury through water and its food products.

After initial scares and market upsets, mercury in fish is a substance of time. A case of poisoning by fish is reported or a new set of statistics is made known, there are meetings and administrative statements, followed by refutation through other cases and other research reports.

Varieties of fish are still caught, bought and eaten, but under threat. The existing organic mercury environment is formed of steady consumption of mercury-bearing food, shot through with outcries of the damage done to individuals, especially to children.

It was known by the mid–nineteenth century that fish and other aquatic creatures could not survive even in a very diluted solution of mercury compounds, especially of mercuric iodide. Experiments were performed to test the conjecture that metallic mercury too would harm marine life. One physiologist placed a number of cyprinus fish in a cask of water with liquid mercury at the bottom, keeping them separate from the mercury by a layer of mesh. All of the fish were dead within 50 days due to the influence of mercury vapors. Mercury-caused fish kills were therefore to be expected. It was against experience that fish would remain alive absorbing mercury and communicating it to the tissues of the humans who eat them. The mercury itself could be abated and remediated, but could the consumption of fish?

In March 2004, two U.S. federal agencies, the Food and Drug Administration (FDA) and the Environmental Protection Agency (EPA), issued a joint advisory on mercury in fish for women who are or could become pregnant, plus nursing mothers and young children. After years of differing and sometimes contradictory cautions they straightforwardly told these people not to eat shark, swordfish, king mackerel or tilefish because of their high mercury content. They listed five varieties of seafood lower in mercury: shrimp, canned light tuna, salmon, pollock and catfish, which could be eaten up to twelve ounces (two average meals) per week, and albacore tuna at half this rate. Regarding local catches, people were instructed to check any posted information but if none was available, to eat up to six ounces a week, then to avoid other fish that week. Instructions said to give young children smaller portions than these. Others were warned not to confine their diets to these fish.

For several years the FDA has maintained a Website giving the mercury concentration in parts per million (ppm) in different varieties of fish, and as the years passed these remained the same, based on data collected in 1990 and earlier. The FDA "action level" dose of mercury for an adult was set at 0.5 ppm in 1969, before the publicity surrounding the Huckleby poisonings, and it remained at that level until 1979, when pressure from the fishing and canning industries caused it to be raised to 1.0 ppm. As indicated earlier, these levels varied from one federal and international agency to another. Whatever the "action level," there was no action.

The 2004 FDA-EPA joint advisory consolidated federal mercury in fish policy. By emphasizing ounces per week to be eaten by vulnerable populations over parts per million in the fish itself, the advisory placed the burden of mercury control on the consumer rather than on the industry. The amount of fish consumed was the consumer's option, not the responsibility of the fishing and processing industries. They could continue to sell swordfish, tilefish and tuna; any consequences were the fault of those who bought and ate them in greater quantity than recommended.

The counterpoise to this pro-business strategy was to personalize its effects. An August 2005 article in *The Wall Street Journal* began with the story of a San Francisco boy, formerly bright and active, who began losing energy and focus. Blood tests showed that the boy's blood mercury level was nearly twice the EPA's maximum. He was diagnosed with mercury poisoning. The parents only made the connection to fish consumption after they read a newspaper article on adults with similar concentration problems associated with eating swordfish, tuna steaks and other fish in restaurants. They were pleased that their son had chosen to eat tuna rather than junk food. Once the high amount of tuna was dropped from his diet he began to return to his old energetic self. The federal advisory came after the parents had made their discovery, and they realized that the federal agencies had known for years what they had to find out through their son's malaise.

The March 2004 federal advisory began with a paragraph on the health benefits of fish and shellfish which "contain high-quality protein and other essential nutrients, are low in saturated fat and contain omega-3 fatty acids." A "healthy diet" strong in fish, if it included regular servings of swordfish or tuna, was a prelude to the signs of mercury poisoning in some people. The health benefits did not counteract the dangers of overindulgence in the chief health food. Government food-safety monitors simultaneously declaring the positive qualities of fish and setting limits revived and magnified the uncertainties that had existed since the seventies.

They had begun making these dissonant recommendations in 1970, after an upstate New York chemistry professor purchased a can of tuna at a supermarket and tested its contents for mercury. The figure of 0.75 ppm came as a surprise, because tuna do not feed near the shore where they might pick up mercury from industrial effluent. The FDA confirmed the tuna safe to eat, yet recalled 921,000 cans before they reached the supermarkets that year, and millions more the following year, and then only 843 cases in 1973. Testing of this recalled tuna did not give high numbers, and there were no more recalls.

There were no reported instances of people suffering mercurialism from eating tuna, but people following low-fat diets centered around swordfish in a few cases developed unexplained lethargy, headaches, tremors and blurred vision that were readily explained when the high mercury content of the fish was made known. The symptoms went away when the weight watchers changed their diets. Tremors and disorientation ceased when they stopped eating the fish.

In 2004 the federal agencies were again issuing warnings, this time to specific groups about specific fish, and a few children who had seemingly been becoming autistic reverted to their former sharpness when tuna was removed from their diet. Was there something the government was trying to keep from the public? Attention shifted from government instructions on how much fish should be eaten to the quantity of mercury in fish.

The presence of mercury in substances has been detectable since time immemorial. It was just a matter of heating a sample in an enclosed container and watching for droplets of mercury on the less heated wall. Mercury was derived from its ores in smelters by crushing and heating the ore and collecting the condensed vapor. This method could be adapted to assay samples for the proportion of mercury in the entire sample. Determining the chemical form of mercury in a sample and the quantity of that chemical in the sample was much more difficult. Determining the amount and kind of mercury in an organic compound was not accurately accomplished until the advent of mass spectroscopy and special adaptations for instant analysis of mercury compounds and mixtures. After, that analysis of mercury in plant and animal tissue required further invention which did not always lead to repeatable results.

When the editorial staff of the *Chicago Tribune* set out to perform their own survey of mercury in canned seafood, they turned to one of the few non-governmental laboratories in the country capable of making the analyses. Revelations of government concealments matched with physical consequences are always newsworthy. The lead of the article reporting the results of the tests was that government and industry fail to protect consumers as Americans buy more fish than ever. Eighteen samples of eight different kinds of fish were randomly collected from markets large and small in the Chicago area and sent to the laboratory at Rutgers University in New Jersey for testing. The results showed that mercury levels in the fish previously tested by government labs were at least as high as the government tests showed. Two species not the subject of any government warnings, orange roughy and walleye, also had high levels of mercury.

The *Tribune* article emphasized the arbitrariness of mercury content in pieces of fish known to concentrate mercury. One filet of orange roughy or one can of tuna may have a great deal more mercury than the identical one next to it. Swordfish again came out with the highest mercury content. In general, there is more mercury in fish than consumers recognize.

Different sources of fish come under the regulation of different state and federal agencies. The Department of Agriculture holds importers to standards that the FDA doesn't impose. Local authorities regulate fish locally caught. In the end it is up to the individual to be aware of the dangers posed and adjust fish intake accordingly. The *Tribune* reporters told another story of a child who regularly ate tuna, and only recovered from listlessness after that diet was limited.

They recognized that the federal authorities would not decree another recall of tuna or other fish products because of the effect on fishing and canning enterprises. It is incumbent on the government to disseminate accurate information on the content of fish and give consumers an opportunity to make informed choices about their food. But they were not doing that, and the newspaper stepped in to rectify that deficiency. At the end of the article the reporters quoted a toxicologist who said that people can't be expected to research mercury content of fish and keep a diary of what they've eaten. But that's what it has come down to, she concludes.

Only consumer choice is there to meet the threat of organic mercury reaching through the food chain to uninformed families. The newspaper intervenes where the government protectors have slackened due to politics. In the end you need to know what you might eat can do to you and those you feed. Negotiation is always going on between the guardians of business as usual which allows the mercury to leak in, and those who want consumers to be fully cognizant of what their food contains.

To other fish-eating populations, the American struggle over mercury in fish seems to be overblown. The effects of the mercury concentration are less serious than the Americans claim, they think, and by limiting their fish consumption they may be missing key nutrients.

A British study reported in early 2007 measured the effects of maternal seafood consumption during pregnancy on neurodevelopmental outcomes in childhood. The researchers found that women who ate at least 340 grams of seafood per week during pregnancy gave birth to children with higher intelligence, greater sociability and better "physical performance" than those whose mothers ate less or no seafood. The difference may be due to the rich omega-3 fatty acid content of fish, known to stimulate nerve growth. The 340-gram downward limit for benefits was also, they admitted, the maximum amount of seafood the FDA and EPA said a pregnant woman should eat before facing damage to herself and the fetus brought on by the mercury in the fish. The British authors of the study disagreed with the American advice. Not eating fish caused greater harm than eating it ever could.

Mercury has made a simple food choice progressively more trenchant. A transatlantic disagreement generates conflicting advice to pregnant mothers. One nation's popular culture assigns mercury a different impact than another's. The Americans seem determined to point to the approaching mercury, then withdraw from it.

What is approaching through the water is also approaching through the air, the same mercury to be held back by negotiation. In this case it is the cap and trade system introduced by the EPA in 2005 to allow coal-burning companies that exceed the maximum emissions of mercury to trade for emissions credits earned by less polluting companies. As with the state of information about mercury in fish, this system confirms a state of anxiety about a shadowy toxin bearing down on everyone who breathes. Mercury in the air falls into the water where it reaches living creatures. The government sets up a system of negotiation among businesses that seems to control mercury, and is an acknowledgment of its presence.

The cap and trade system is opposed by environmentalists. Regulating mercury emissions by industry, they contend, does not take into account the actual distribution of the metal in different waterscapes around the country. The distribution of mercury over the land is irregular because of variable factors such as climate, tree cover and previous pollution (legacy mercury). More mercury may precipitate from the air in some locales than in others, and conditions will cause it to concentrate and spread without reference to emission quantities from any one source.

Business interests and their government representatives try to keep the debate on airborne mercury confined to the credits and debits of the trade system, to avoid even considering a ban on emissions, especially those created by burning coal to replace oil in power generation.

Mercury in the air is harmful because it ends up in the water and in water-dwelling creatures. Every once in a while it leaks into a case which is resolved by changing the numbers. The child's tuna diet or the dieter's swordfish meals are reduced, and the hand of mercury draws back from the throat of humanity once more. Very rarely it comes into a human body in a way that illustrates its ineluctability. Like the old laboratory mercury it mostly stays in the atmosphere, winking on occasion, more agonized and numerical than previous popular mercuries, but then suddenly it kills.

It is not usual for a professor of chemistry at a major university to do her own laboratory work. Usually such a professor has applied for and received a grant for a project which is then carried out by supervised students. She or he has a laboratory provided by the institution for the purposes of research and training of students, and can undertake projects likely to result in papers submitted to scientific journals. Chemical studies with industrial and, most particularly, pharmaceutical implications are welcome for all parties. The tradition of chemistry that examines the nature of a compound in its relations with other compounds is still alive.

Karen Wetterhahn was a specialist in the biological action of heavy metals, most particularly chromium and its role in cancer. She had applied for and received in 1995 a National Institute of Environmental Health Sciences grant of seven million dollars to study the effects of heavy-metal contamination on human biology. A research sabbatical at a colleague's laboratory in 1997 led her to become interested in the molecular biology of contaminant mercury compounds, and she planned a study of the effects of mercury on animal tissue. It was (and is) a matter of some urgency, as environmental mercury poisoning is being linked to autism and other unexplained conditions.

The first step in such a study would be to establish a chemical standard through nuclear magnetic resonance spectroscopy. This would give her a printed pattern of mercury data against which samples of specimens could be compared to reveal the metal's presence and its associations. The standard was a compound through which the spectrograph's light beam could pass, indicating a concentration of mercury without registering irregularities. A fluid compound was better for this purpose than a solution of a solid. Wetterhahn tried a solution of mercuric chloride but was not satisfied with the reading and instead she ordered the much more dangerous dimethyl mercury from a chemical supplier. She thus unintentionally repeated the sequence of mercury poisons over time. Dimethyl mercury succeeded bichloride.

The dimethyl mercury arrived in a sealed glass ampoule, packed in a box well-cushioned against breakage. A colleague of Wetterhahn's cooled the ampoule in ice water to reduce the internal vapor pressure, placed it within a shielded fume hood, then scored and broke off the glass top. He then left the room to allow Wetterhahn to complete the sampling. She drew a measured quantity of the dimethyl mercury from the ampoule into a thin glass sample tube, which she put aside. Then she transferred the remaining liquid to a screw-top bottle using a pipette, a glass tube that is dipped into a liquid, a finger pressed at the open end of the tube holding the liquid inside until it is released by lifting the finger.

During this procedure Wetterhahn dropped a little dimethyl mercury onto her hand covered with a latex surgical glove. After all the liquid was transferred she closed the receiving bottle, labeled it KEW8/14/97 and set it aside in a holding container as a record of this particular sample. She pulled off one glove over the other to form a ball which she left under the vapor hood to be disposed of as hazardous material.

Wetterhahn completed her initial spectroscopic study, finding that the results given by the dimethyl mercury standard compared well with the mercuric chloride solution, and that it may not have been necessary to work with dimethyl after all.

After about three months, however, the condition of her health began to impinge on her research and teaching. Her speech became slurred, her hearing and vision impaired, and she started walking into door jambs, signs which she herself identified as possibly linked to cumulative heavy-metal poisoning. Samples of blood and tissue showed an elevated level of mercury. She then recalled the dimethyl mercury spill onto her gloved hand.

Her neurologist prescribed chelation therapy, which introduces into the body chemical agents that attract mercury ions and clear them from tissue where they have become lodged. Her condition worsened. Before falling into the coma that led to her death, she asked her colleagues to find what could be done to protect other researchers from this condition.

The results of her autopsy were reported in the *New England Journal of Medicine* (1998).

There was extensive atrophy of cerebral tissue and loss of neurons. The mercury content of the brain was about 6 times that of the blood, and there was a concentration of mercury in the liver and kidney cortex.

The damage to particular areas and cellular types of brain tissue mirrors the symptoms Karen Wetterhahn progressively exhibited. Mercury was in the brain by preference to any other organ, and most concentrated in tissue found only in the brain. The mercury had left the blood and traveled upward, the opposite of its use to force body contents downward by weight in earlier times.

Augustin Belloste and Thomas Dover's claim that it would enter the blood and contribute to the circulation was once again disproven. The mercury did enter the blood, and left as soon as it reached the brain. Chelation therapy, which depends on circulating chemicals reaching the concentrations of mercury and carrying them away, could not clear brain tissue because the blood-brain barrier, while admitting mercury ions, could not admit and then release the chelate molecules in the necessary quantities.

In the aftermath of Karen Wetterhahn's death, chemist Tom Clarkson of the University of Rochester in New York, where her blood had been sent for analysis, urged his colleagues to adopt a different standard chemical for calibration. Clarkson had been one of the participants in the 1974 WHO conference on the Iraq epidemic, and he had participated in several of the subsequent research programs to collect and analyze the Iraq data. Some years after Wetterhahn's death, Clarkson was one of the authors of a paper on silent latent periods in methylmercury poisoning, a paper that cited both Wetterhahn's case and the Iraqi epidemic to exemplify the ability of the poison to go undetected until the damage is done.

Wetterhahn's Dartmouth colleagues, conducting tests on how the poison might have been delivered, discovered that the latex of gloves readily passes dimethyl mercury to the skin inside the glove, which then passes it to the circulatory system. They learned that none of the standard laboratory gloves alone would protect the hand from the invading molecules and in order to be safe, a researcher would have to wear double layer of gloves, one laminated and the other thick, to keep dimethyl mercury from quickly entering the body.

In August 1997, *Chemical and Engineering News* reported that the federal agency OSHA had fined Dartmouth College for not providing adequate personal protection, leading to Karen Wetterhahn's death. The fine was, of course, a warning to provide protection in the future now that the liabilities of working with methylmercury were better known. No one knew prior to this accident. Neither AlfaAesar, the chemical supplier, nor Organometallic, the manufacturer of the dimethyl mercury Wetterhahn used, had advised using gloves able to block an organic mercury compound spilled on the glove from entering the circulatory system. They changed their printed guidelines and the safety practices used by their own employees.

Dimethyl mercury was well known to be highly poisonous, but its precise action and the degree of toxicity were not well known. Those previously poisoned had been exposed over a period of time and by inhalation. Wetterhahn was unique in having received one dose through the skin while all access routes — eyes, mouth, nose — were shielded. It was considered that the mercury might have built up from long-term exposure. All the members of the chemistry department, the students and staff who worked in the laboratory and Wetterhahn's family were tested for blood mercury concentrations and none was found to have an elevated level. That one incident with dimethyl was unique to Karen Wetterhahn.

How could so little dimethyl mercury do so much damage? Another element of the poisoning that was learned in this instance was that mercury ions originating in a small sample, conveyed to cellular sites, could cause outwardly visible behavioral symptoms leading to death.

A twenty-three-year-old laborer in a chemical factory making antifungal treatments for seeds absorbed quantities of inorganic mercury compounds for eighteen months as well as methylmercury phosphate and nitrate for four months. As Hunter, Bomford and Russell described him in a 1940 paper, he became permanently disabled, ataxic, his field of vision measurably constricted, and unable to stand unaided, speak clearly or "care for himself." The autopsy after his death fifteen years later showed cerebellar cortical atrophy involving the granular-cell layer of the neocerebellum and bilateral cortical atrophy of the area striate, a symptomatology and a necrology similar to that of Karen Wetterhahn but building up over a much longer period of time. Apart from the differences of their two bodies and states of health, the difference between the factory worker and the laboratory worker was the type of chemical they absorbed. The factory worker received inorganic and organic compounds. Wetterhahn received only that one dose, but it was dimethyl mercury.

Other cases of factory, farm and laboratory exposure to methylmercury led to temporary or permanent disability, and rarely death within as little as ten months. Wetterhahn's was the only occasion in which such a small amount of organic mercury passed through barriers and caused death in a short period of time. In most of these cases the compound was not pure but an elaborated preparation of organic mercury for agricultural or industrial purposes. The mercury impaired the same bodily faculties but did not kill the recipient.

The body excretes mercury as it receives it, and there is a "normal level" of mercury in humans that does no harm and may be a necessary trace element. Mercury does damage when it arrives in concentrations too high to excrete before it begins to have effects on vital processes.

Swallowed in quantity it can denature proteins in the stomach and intestines before it makes its way out. Using mercury by weight as Barton Booth did, rather than by chemical action, risked this gastrointestinal damage.

The form in which mercury arrives in the body more than the quantity in which it arrives decides what its effects will be. Organic mercury, that is, mercury ions which have formed compounds with carbon groups, can deliver great concentrations of mercury ions to where they can affect life processes in relatively small amounts. Mercury is a "soft acid" that forms ligands, electrostatic metal bonds, with inorganic atoms and organic molecules. Mercury loves sulfur where it occurs, and where sulfur is part of organic molecules such as enzymes, mercury forms ligands that disrupt the action of the molecule by introducing a metal ion.

When methyl (or dimethyl) mercury arrives in the blood, entering through the skin, by inhalation through the lungs or ingestion, it often forms a ligand with the amino acid cysteine. Cysteine contains a sulfur atom against which the mercury-methyl group positions itself in an electrostatic bond. In that form it resembles another amino acid, methionone. This ligand is able to pass through the blood-brain barrier because the endothelial cells that serve as the gatekeepers act upon what appears to be "methionone" to produce "glutathionone." Once inside the cells of the brain it is hydrolyzed back to what appears to be methionone. This is how mercury enters the brain, but still does not explain why it accumulates in some areas of the brain. Perhaps it replaces one of the amino acids that becomes depleted.

Having passed into the blood and into the brain in this form, individual mercury atoms are spread where they can have maximum effect on body processes.

The greatest concentration of mercury on the planet is in the ore cinnabar, fundamentally mercuric sulfide, HgS. The thiol group of enzymes that operate in the brain are built around sulfur atoms. With mercury linking electrostatically to those sulfur atoms, the enzyme cannot function as a site for reactions necessary to maintain the life of the cells. When these mercury-sulfur congregates reach the cellular lipids, they denature the protein, electrostatically causing the chains that form it to collapse, much as mercury causes hair to curl and grow limp by making the long collagen chains buckle. Long-abandoned methods of using mercury to firm the furs used in hat production and to make hair curling formulas are very generally analogous to what organic mercury compounds do in brain and nerve tissue.

Hair samples from a long-dead person can be analyzed to detect accumulated mercury, and determine long afterward if the hair's owner ingested mercury medications. But the rising tide of organic mercury in the environment may bias this sample and make it impossible to determine how much mercury was ingested and how much filtered in from air and water and attached itself to the hair.

The distance between Becher's exultant cry of heroic stolidity amid laboratory poisons and Wetterhahn's death is the accumulation of all the theory and knowledge that could have prevented that death and now will prevent others. But now no one, least of all experimenters, is declaring invulnerability to mercury. Yet the degree of vulnerability in the general population through food resources is much studied and debated. In 1990 the World Health Organization declared methylmercury not to be a threat to the health of human populations, but the continuing struggle to set industrial mercury emissions levels and have them enforced, especially with the increased use of coal to power electricity generation, suggests that not everyone is convinced.

Mercury deliberately consumed in the atmosphere of the laboratory became mercury accidentally absorbed from artificial conditions recreated in the laboratory to study the human absorption of mercury. The disease syphilis was one of the longest-running popular culture systems made up of the interplay between deliberate consumption and actual assimilation of mercury by humans. Before it ever was known to be caused by bacteria, syphilis was an organic mercury system that remained in the body until the mercury could be replaced.

5

———— ⊗⊗⊗ ————

Syphilis, Mercury, Syphilis

Syphilis sufferers martyred themselves with mercury. The early rash, the joint pains, the fevers, called for the penance of applying the metal forcibly to the diseased body with rubs and fumigation to drive out poison and stench.

In 1519, Ulrich von Hutten wrote his essay *On the Wondrous Healing Power of Guaiac Wood and the Healing of the French Disease.* The thirty-one-year-old knight of the Holy Roman Empire had picked up the disease on his wanderings about Central Europe as he marshaled Germanic opposition to the Roman Church with his writings. Hutten gave a long list of alternatives to mercury which he himself tried in rubs and sweating inside a closed room. Myrrh, mastic, white lead, laurel, alum, Armenian "soundearth," cinnabar (not an alternative to mercury), mennige (a lead mineral), coral, copper ash, and/or rust were mixed with aromatic oils and animal fats in various combinations and rubbed on the body several times a day.

This, he wrote, is what the treatment was like:

> The sick person is placed in a sealed, over-heated chamber for twenty, or as long as thirty days, or even longer. He is thoroughly rubbed, and then laid on a bed in the room covered in several layers of sheets. Soon after the second rubbing the sick person began to feel very weak, so forceful was the action of the rubbing that it carried the poison of the sickness from the body vessels into the intestines and the brain from which it flows out of the throat and mouth with such force that the teeth fell out if the mouth wasn't carefully bound.... It stank in the sick room, and this treatment was so severe that many sick people would sooner die than undertake such a cure.... From this description can readily be seen what I endured with this sickness, that I went through eleven cures like this. With such a great danger, such ghastly martyrdoms, I bore the burden for nine years back and forth from one medicine to another which were said to help.

One factor that seems to unite all the medicines Hutten was trying: to instill into his body the penetrating power of a strong and pleasant aroma. The regimen he believed did help was fumigation with the aromatic wood guiac (or guaiac), imported from the Spanish colonies in the New World on merchant ships.

The year 1519, when Hutten wrote this piece, was also the year that Charles V, Duke of Burgundy and King of Spain, used a large sum of money, loaned to him by the banking family the Fuggers, to out-bribe Francis I of France and become Holy Roman Emperor. One benefit the Fuggers obtained was a monopoly on the import of guiac wood from the Spanish colonies. Hutten was promoting it as a less noxious alternative to mercury as a treatment for the "French disease," not necessarily because he was a friend of the Fuggers but because it temporarily gave him relief or at least a better smell than that of mercury. Since the French disease apparently came from the New World, a plant from the same climate should heal it.

Hutten was not himself successful in obtaining the favor of the Emperor, or the health the "holy wood" seemed to promise. Rejected by his fellow Humanists — Erasmus would not receive him because he reputedly smelled so bad — he was taken in by the Zurich reformer Ulrich Zwingli and died at age thirty-five isolated on an island in Lake Lucerne.

Theophrastus Bombastus von Hohenheim, who called himself Paracelsus, took the time to write a brief essay on Hutten and the foolishness of thinking that wood could save anyone from the ravages of the disease. He continued his attack against the pretense of a vegetable cure in a longer treatise and, under growing threat from those who benefited from sale of healing services and medications in a book on the origins and causes of syphilis (1529).

Paracelsus proclaimed the essence of the disease to be mercurial. This was not good news for the many doctors, fumigators and massagers who delivered quicksilver and its compounds to suffering bodies. Superficially applying forms of mercury only created a temporary distraction from the initial skin disease, while the syphilitic poison reached far deeper into the body. Paracelsus was the enemy of the mercurializers, who sold quick results at the cost of long-term poisoning. Paracelsus taught that measured doses of mercury given internally over a period of time were more likely to reach the rooted venom. He had to go into hiding to escape his sometimes violent critics; his book on syphilis was not published as a whole until after his death. He was the only writer on mercury in syphilis who had seen mercury come out of the mines and witnessed the ill health of the miners. He worked for a time as a physician in Vilach, where the Fuggers operated mercury mines.

After the Fuggers gained control of the Almaden mine in Spain, and became merchants of mercury as well as guiac, they nearly cornered the market in syphilis treatments. By then Paracelsus was dead, though the cause is unknown.

Guiac says to Mercury, in a 1527 dialogue by Jacques de Bethencourt, "I have an answer to all that. In the first place, my Fast cures illnesses you have prolonged by the poison of rubbing repeated ten times. Your Purgatory has never cured anyone and is fitting only to engender illnesses yet more detestable than the pox of which you pretend to be the sovereign remedy." Guiac is in agreement with Paracelsus: mercury causes the pox. Both Mercury and Guiac boast a heavenly if not divine origin and each confronts the other with its failures. At the end of their debate they submit to the judge, who rules in favor of Mercury just because its nature is opposed to the body and heals by the Hippocratic principle of contraries.

Jacques de Bethencourt's 1527 *Nouvel Carême de Penitence et Purgatoire d'Expiation*, the French translation of its Latin title meaning *New Penitential Fast and Expiatory Purgatory*, again uses religious language to describe the treatment of the disorder which he still calls *"morbus Gallicus,"* "the French disease." Treatment with guiac fumigations requires that the patient refrain from eating solid food, as was a common practice in seasonal and weekly Christian devotional fasts. Treatment with mercury rubs and pills puts the patient through torment similar to that of purgatory, where sullied sinners are severely cleansed before they ascend to heaven.

The dialogue finishes Bethencourt's brief treatise on the disease in which he, in tandem with (but not aware of) Paracelsus, displays a surprisingly modern knowledge of its nature and course. The disease is contagious only when the skin lesions appear at the beginning; contagion is by contact and predominantly "venereal" (Bethencourt is the first writer to use this word, referring to the goddess Venus, patroness of sexual activity). There are later stages, disorders of the bones, stomach, teeth and blood which are caused by the venereal poison, though they do not seem directly related to the first signs. The poison loses its potency with time.

Bethencourt's decision in favor of the overbearing Mercury reflects a historic preference. Mercury's contest with the tropical wood also reflects the state of mercury in its predominance, always placed in opposition to another remedy. The other remedy might bid to replace Mercury, or it may work cooperatively. For Bethencourt there is no other successful approach and, as Mercury announces summing up the case, "my Purgatory is the most active and powerful medication that can be set against venereal disease, and it keeps to the precepts of Hippocrates and Galen." Guiac's argument of "new remedies for new diseases" will be repeated many times in the centuries that follow, as the new French (Spanish, Neapolitan, English, German, Russian, etc.) disease becomes an old disease never entirely cured by mercury alone.

Frascatoro, writing his medical poem section by section until 1530, invented a myth of origin and a name that made the French disease "syphilis," not the result of any one nation's degeneracy and lewdness. Frascatoro also considered mercury and later guiac possible treatments, all of which slowly spread to the rest of the world together with the disease. Syphilis became a health condition to be addressed by healers and studied by doctors, and it remained a form of politics involving mercury.

Mercury is a chemical element and syphilis is a disease caused by the bacterium *Treponema pallidum*. Their commingling is a long project of the human body. Before syphilis was named, mercury was being rubbed into the skin surface as a healing unction, while recognized as a poison for both surgeon and patient. Theodoric of Cervia, thirteenth-century Italian bishop and surgeon, commented on the variety of genital sores healed by mercury-in-fat rubs, and he mentioned the resultant salivation. Theodoric also described mercury fumigations. Some of what Theodoric and other medieval writers were addressing with mercury may have been skin conditions caused by bacteria of the same genus as the syphilis bacteria. "The French disease" was not just syphilis but a cultural construct, including a skin condition that was grouped with other diseases as syphilis, on and off.

The association between mercury and syphilis remained deep and intimate. The same process of observation and classification that identified and named the chemical elements and the species of bacteria also assisted in keeping mercury and syphilis together, perpetuating a conjunction that persisted as its original elements acquired independent existence. Other diseases— gonorrhea, genital herpes, non-syphilitic chancre — were separated from syphilis. One metaphor partakes of all the cures: a down-bearing weight, strong fumes, a sweet aromatic pill or a syrup like a virgin body again. Syphilis, its stages, states and counterparts, is a living body of mercury, a project that precedes our contemporary organic mercury, and recedes as it arrives.

By the late nineteenth century, after hundreds of years struggling with the disease (and spreading it throughout the world), Europeans were still dependent upon mercury to curtail its worst ravages, even at the price of being slowly and continually poisoned. The theory that syphilis and mercury poisoning were one and the same, and could not be separated, was convenient for those who found relief in mercury medications and those who supplied the medications.

Ulcers rose on the skin and in the mouth after the victim was imbued with mercury ointment and wrapped in blankets, fumigated with mercury vapors or fed pills and syrups composed of drugs inducing salivation, sweating and frequent urination. The ulcers and sweats were the poison exiting the body and dwelling within it; they were the result of the infection itself and the mercury used to force it out. Mercury concentrated in the body to the point that the body poured it out, carrying the poison with it, was a treatment for syphilis but also itself an affliction that had to be treated. The sore watery mouth and the skin eruptions were the explosion of health that caused ill health.

The role of mercury in the treatment of disease was ambiguous, and its application ambivalent, from before there was syphilis. The tenth century Persian medical writer Rhazes, who considered himself the Muslim Hippocrates, introduced formulas for mercury unctions to be applied to skin diseases and he introduced them with an element of caution. When he fed mercury to his pet ape, all that resulted was a stomach ache.

During the late fifteenth century explosion of the great pox in Europe, doctors adopted Rhazes' formulas but not always his cautions when trying to reduce the chancres and rashes appearing first with infection. The ability of mercury ointment to clear skin eruptions like scabies caused it to be applied to the chancres that often signal the beginning of a syphilis infection and the rashes that often follow. If mercury rubs seemed to make the disease disappear, then the cosmetic success became medical success and new formulas were devised and promulgated. Mercury's compounds are strong diuretics, causing urine flow at the same time as characteristic salivation. It was assumed that the mercury in the compounds could penetrate the interior and run out, carrying the poison lodged there. When the disease seemed to embed itself in the body and reappear in many different places, it was pursued by fumigations and oral doses of mercury and its salts.

The "law of contagion" dictated that a transmissible infection manifested itself first at the point of entry: venereal syphilis on the genitals, nursing syphilis of infants on the mouth that sucked the nipple. Applications of mercury could address all of these and make them seem to go away. Syphilis seemed to vanish superficially as the bacteria invaded bones, organs, blood vessels, spinal cord and brain over a period of time.

The use of mercury supported successful individual treatment specialists and their formulas. There was a persistent belief that the poisonous nature of mercury was moderated by skillful administration. Many different treatment regimens developed, often repeating the same beliefs about the nature of the body and the action of the drug in different social and political contexts. A complex pharmacy worked metallic mercury into many different forms, each new for a while.

At the same time, the superficial success of mercury treatments helped sustain the syphilis epidemic, because the erasure of superficial symptoms did not eliminate the disease and allowed infectious individuals to sport freely while infectious and decay quietly afterward. A corresponding mercurial disease arose as more mercury was consumed. Mercury grew more popular, chased by the ancient cautions against its use in a dialectical combination with syphilis. Mercury is always used on the skin; it is always accompanied and opposed by other substances.

In the writings of individuals, and in individuals through time, syphilis became submerged in mercury, but then there was a turn away from mercury toward something else.

Frascatoro moved from promoting mercury, amid other substances, to rejecting them in favor of guiac wood, to a reasoned inclusion of all of them. Two hundred years later, Daniel Turner recommended mercury ointments for skin diseases, especially syphilis, but rejected fumigations and massive internal doses. The Portuguese surgeon Duarte Madeira Arrais in 1642 counseled the moderate use of mercury and calomel (mercurous chloride), among several other concoctions. This book was republished in 1715 with a commentary by Francisco de Fonseca Henriques, who scorned Madeira's wariness and gave far greater credence to mercury.

Benvenuto Cellini did not even try the mercury the doctors urged upon him when he recognized the signs of syphilis after a brief liaison with a young woman. He dedicated himself to guiac wood fumigations and, pronouncing himself cured, went off hunting. He survived several poisoning attempts, including powdered diamonds placed in his food, before late in life he signed a life contract to lease a farm from a local landowner. Regaled with a meal by the landowner's wife, he fell deathly ill on the way home. A doctor told him his stomach had been corroded. It was *sollimato* (sublimate of mercury), worked into the meal by the wife, a known poisoner. Cellini declared, however, that he suffered no further syphilis symptoms after that, though he did not go so far as admit that guiac did not cure him entirely or that mercury might have helped him earlier.

Jacques Casanova's encounters with mercury during the mid–18th century continued the opportunistic play of alchemical mercury from before syphilis appeared: he increased the mass of mercury by adulterating it with lead and bismuth and he observed, he thought, transmutations of base metals into gold. For the most part the use of the word "mercury" in Casanova's *Memoirs* implies the presence of syphilis without naming it outright. Mercury in Bethencourt's dialogue boasts to the skeptical Guiac that he can cure all of the ills that plague people, but in Casanova's narrative mercury has only one use.

Casanova tells of saving the life of a Venetian senator, and winning a reputation as a doctor, when he removed the plasters that a surgeon had placed on the senator's chest to hold in the mercury ointment he had copiously applied. "That impure and always injurious metal" made a hollow in Casanova's brain when a doctor recognized certain symptoms and sacrificed him to the god Mercury. Yet the unfortunate Count Lamberg was "treated mercurially for a disease that was not venereal, and this treatment not only killed him but took away his good name." The count was then thought by society to be suffering from syphilis. There would be no other reason for all that mercury.

Mercury had evidently won the debate with guiac, even with the recognition that mercury was poisonous. Yet guiac remained, in part as an alternative to mercury and in part as a treatment for it.

Also in the early eighteenth century Ramazzini's medical survey of occupational illness made mercury out to be a poison that crept into the artisan's body. "At present, those who anoint with mercurial ointment persons afflicted with *lues Gallica* belong to the lowest class of surgeons who belong to the business for the money to be made." No better class of surgeon would want to do this. Mercury invades the bodies of the surgeon applicators even when they wore leather gloves. Leather was also used to strain and clarify mercury: it is no great surprise that surgeons' hands become palsied. There is collateral damage. The wife of a man being rubbed with mercury ointment developed sores in her throat just by breathing the atmosphere.

A decoction of guiac could be taken to diminish the palsy and vertigo resulting from mercury poisoning (hydragyrosis). For syphilis itself, Ramazzini approved of mercury's ability to be one element in the total cure when engaged with guiac in what he described as a military campaign. "First guiac engages the enemy *Gallicus morbus* with a skirmish, and weakens it; next mercury comes to closer quarters; finally, guiac comes in again to kill the enemy and finish off the stragglers." Ramazzini thus repeats the early history of the two remedies in a single metaphor. Military analogies are never very far from the discussion of syphilis treatments because the military is never very far from needing them, and from needing treatments for the mercury.

The Portuguese seaborne empire carried syphilis bacteria to the colonies in India, and by 1550 the ayurvedic physician Bhavamisra was describing "*firanga*," "the Frankish disease" in his Sanskrit compilation *Bhavaprakasa*. That terminology was not exclusively aimed at the French but referred to all the foreigners who attacked eastern cities during the Crusades and after.

Ayurveda employs both vegetable and mineral medicines, among which mercury preparations have always been prominent, but Bhavamisra did not adopt European mercury treatments. Instead he put forward an extract of the leaves of the imported vine sarsaparilla for the treatment of the imported disease. For reasons related to the Ayurvedic apportionment of remedies according to the origins of the disease, he independently replicated the studied European avoidance of mercury for the treatment of syphilis.

In the recommendations of doctor after doctor mercury taken in different forms was counterbalanced and its own ravages contained by other substances, usually vegetable in nature. That dialectical combination became the nature of mercury-syphilis.

To follow Dr. John Profily's *Easy and Exact Method of Curing the Venereal Disease in All its Different Appearances* (1748), the patient progressively rubbed herself with mercurial ointment starting from the foot and ankle upward, each day another section of the body, wrapping it in cloths and remaining in a warm room all the time. At the end of the seventh day, the patient supposedly began to spit out "a thick, tenacious, viscid, putrid Substance" in great quantities. The spitting was to continue for twenty days, watered by daily consumption of ptisan, a barley-water solution, and the mercury rub was repeated if the spitting diminished or stopped prematurely. The ulcerated mouth and swollen tongue caused by the treatment were relieved with a spirit of salt and honey, and the body washed with oil of sweet almond and brandy as the venereal lesions disappeared and the sweet-smelling patient returned to society. The mercury had traveled through the body, taking up the syphilitic poison as it went, exiting in the copious salivation that the wrapped-up unguent certainly induced. All of this was done in private.

If mercury is poisonous, the solution is to find exactly the right dosage and timing, not give it up entirely.

During the latter years of eighteenth century, syphilitic inmates of the Bicêtre asylum in Paris were being subjected to the *grandes remèdes*, a topical application of mercury in lard, accompanied by oral ingestion of corrosive sublimate (mercuric chloride) which caused eruptions in the mouth, nausea, vomiting, problems with eyesight and ulcerations of the digestive tract. The patient was purged and bled, both before and after the course of drugs, and was supposedly then free of corrupting influences, which included the mercury treatment.

The *grandes remèdes* at the Bicêtre transacted in a publicly funded institution for poor people what Dr. Profily's technique promised to accomplish for literate bourgeois secretly and in private. Syphilis treatment of impoverished women became public policy where there was not yet a public-health system because of fears that the spread of syphilis from prostitutes would lower the birth rate and threaten the nation with debilitating disease and depopulation. For the same reason the military always was in the forefront of syphilis treatments.

At the same time, however, "the secret malady" was kept secret by the middle and upper classes, but in a publicly secret way. Lower-class female prostitutes could be locked up and forcibly mercurialized, while the men who infected them and their wives carried the disease at infectious stages. The syphilitic poison, no longer infectious and genuinely secret, made its way through everyone's internal organs. Discussion of venereal matters was coded.

There were benefits to be gained by anyone who could project a simple, discreet and effective method for syphilis cure. In 1766 Dr. J. J. von Plenck, an eminent Viennese physician, published in Latin (all his other writings were in German), his *New and Easy Secret Method of Administering Quicksilver to Venereal Disease Sufferers.* This was soon translated into German, Dutch, English, French, Spanish, Italian and Portuguese, and probably was an inspiration for the "rob" that Boyveau Laffecteur began promoting at the same time, as well as a number of other pamphlets and medicines with similar titles.

But von Plenck's method was a mercury delivery system, and did not take into account the already existing counterpoise between mercury and other drugs aimed at treating the secret malady.

Within the nineteenth-century world of self-prepared medicines, there was Dr. Elisha Smith's Anti-Mercurial Syrup. This was not a secret remedy. Its formula was published by Benjamin Colby of Milford, New Hampshire, in his 1846 *Guide to Health*:

Take of sarsaparilla (Smilax)	2 lbs.
guiac chips (G.officinalis)	1 lb.
blue flag (Iris varicolor)	6 oz.
prickly ash bark (Xanthoxylum)	3 oz.
liquorice (Glycorrhiza)	4 oz.
stramonium seeds (Datura)*	? oz.

*This article we always reject from the compound, for reasons well known to Thomsonians.

Boil in two of three waters, until the strength is obtained, forming two gallons of the decoction; to which is to be added, when cold, one and a half gallon of molasses and two ounces of the oil of sassafras; the whole is to be shaken together and bottled for use. This compound is highly recommended by Dr. Smith of New York, for cancerous, scrofulous, and all other humors and taints, particularly for those forms of disease produced by mercury that everywhere exhibit themselves, and venereal.

The followers of Samuel Thomson, who rejected the principle of medicine by poison practiced since Paracelsus, do not include the heart stimulant Datura. What is most striking about the list of ingredients is the heavy dose of guiac combined with the sarsaparilla panacea and other medicinal flavorings certain to make it a strong but not unpleasant-smelling concoction.

Dr. Smith's syrup is slyly composed like many syphilis remedies that only indirectly disclose their purpose. It is drunk to manage "those forms of disease produced by mercury" which are likely to have appeared because of mercury used to heal syphilis, "and venereal," as the formula hastily tacks on at the end. The anti-mercurial syrup presupposes that the user already has taken mercury, which will work against syphilis, and supplies the usual vegetable components of syphilis treatment which will also cover the mercury smell.

Guiac turned out to be ineffective against syphilis. At least not obviously toxic, what it did about the mercury was obscure its smell. It did not do for syphilis what another tropical wood, cinchona, did for malaria. There are records of people downing quantities of the anti-mercurial syrup together with Swaim's Panacea and other sweet, good-smelling, and alcoholic solutions to assure themselves that those sores weren't syphilis.

In 1811, Andrew Mathias, an eminent London physician, identified "mercurial disease" as a condition resulting from the mercury *replacing* the syphilis "virus" it was supposed to expel:

I therefore give the title of mercurial disease to that effect produced by mercury, when it excites a specific state of diseased irritation in the habit, suppressing the further progress of the venereal virus, but not removing it; changing the pains, sores and ulcerations in the body into pains and ulcerations of its own specific nature; exciting new excoriations, eruptions, and ulcers in fresh parts, with pains, nodes, and various other affections of the tendons, periosteum, bones, &c.

Mathias believed that the syphilis would remain at bay as long as mercury was administered and would surge back if it was withdrawn. But as long as mercury compounds were the medicine, the mercurial disease would continue to ravage the body in its replacement of syphilis. Elemental mercury in finely divided form was the best compromise between syphilis and the mercurial disease. It held down the syphilis and produced minimal symptoms of its own. Knowing that mercury caused its own "disease," Mathias believed that its curative power was so great that a compromise had to be reached to continue feeding it to patients. Mercury could clear the initial sores but then should be stopped before the mercurial disease sets in.

Many of Mathias's contemporaries recognized mercurial disease but they were unwilling to take the risk or surrender the revenues that withholding mercury from patients would entail. And physicians might not be able to prevent determined syphilis sufferers from taking it on their own.

Mercurial disease soon became one of the conditions listed among those treated by panaceas which included the symptoms of syphilis in their range of healing powers. The stigma of admitting to syphilis and its signs made mercurial disease another covering label for venereal disease. The long-standing practice of being prescribed or spontaneously taking mercury for syphilis encouraged the idea of common symptoms between the disease and heavy metal poisoning: it was difficult both for physicians and lay people to tell them apart. Mercury got into the body of a syphilitic early and had many ways to remain there.

As the long-term effects of syphilis on the body were identified — its association with heart attacks because of breaches of the aorta, seen at autopsy; its implication in personality changes and dementia — these elements of syphilis also were transferred to mercurial disease. The identification of a microbe, a bacterium, in fluid taken from chancres did not end the association of mercury and syphilis symptoms, because it did not end the necessary association of mercury with syphilis treatment.

Rothstein writes,

> The mouth feels unusually hot, and is sometimes sensible of a coppery or metallic taste; the gums are swollen, red and tender; ulcers make their appearance and spread in all directions; the saliva is thick and stringy and has that peculiar, offensive odor characteristic of mercurial disease; the tongue is swollen and stiff; and there is some fever, with derangement of the secretions. The disease progressing, it destroys every part that it touches, until the lips, the cheeks, and even the bones have been eaten away before death comes to the sufferer's relief.

These symptoms of mercurial disease, not entirely identical with those of syphilis, were not observed independently of syphilis as the very persistent nature of syphilis became known. The effects of medical treatment could not be distinguished from the disease being treated. It was a challenge which seen in retrospect resembles deciphering the nature of retroviruses to be able to forestall Human ImmunoVirus. Was much of what we are calling syphilis actually mercury poisoning? Can we separate the two the better to define both? Learning the true nature of syphilis depended on this. The alternative would be to withhold mercury treatment from people showing the first signs of syphilis. That was done, but only after the contribution of mercury became better known.

Mercurial disease may have benefited the medicine marketers, but posed a dual dilemma for the medical profession. Were doctors prescribing a drug that caused the disease they were prescribing it for? If that was true, was it ethical to continue this treatment? How to find out without withholding a treatment known to work?

As medical record-keeping improved and individuals could be followed through time, cases collected and compared across space, it seemed the initial chancre, rash and joint pain were followed years later by other episodes. They might not be distinguished from the results of former or continuing mercury treatment. When the damage to the aorta leading eventually to fatal heart attacks was linked to syphilis in 1847, the question arose: was this the result of so much mercury entering the circulatory system? As the ultimate mental degeneration of some syphilis patients became noticeable and correlated with brain damage observed in autopsy, how could it be known whether or not this was the result of mercury poisoning?

Defining mercury poisoning in differential diagnosis with syphilis became a project of medicine. "Researches into the relationship between constitutional mercurialism and constitutional syphilis," was how Adolf Kussmaul named his 1861 examination of the question. Mercury poisoning brings about certain inherent, "constitutional" body effects and so does syphilis. Are they the same thing? Or is what we are calling syphilis actually mercury poisoning? Is there a constitutional mercurialism to match constitutional syphilis?

In his autobiography published at the end of his career Kussmaul remarked that he was fortunate to have lived as a child of the nineteenth century. No century, he wrote, had made greater advances penetrating the secrets of nature and improving the general welfare. No century had more decisively "broken the chains of slavery" throughout the world.

Kussmaul's strong sense of historical progress guided his research into mercury. At the beginning of his book he identified three periods in the development of an understanding of constitutional mercurialism:

(1) The Greek and Roman doctors knew little more than that mercury is a poison.
(2) Some of the oldest writers on venereal diseases ... offer us countless cases of what is experienced in the aftermath of vapor and rubbing mercury treatments as well as washing with sublimate of mercury.
(3) In Simon's history of inunction cures one can read how 18th century doctors took precautions to overcome the disadvantages of mercury in extensive treat-

ments, and more and more reached the firm conclusion that it [mercury] in many but not in all cases brings about healing.

The historical development that Kussmaul saw behind him is also displayed in an array of recent and contemporary observations of the relations between mercury and syphilis. Where people are exposed to mercury, either deliberately consuming it or through occupational exposure, its consumption is also associated with syphilis. Kussmaul's intention was to examine cases in which the two, constitutional mercurialism and constitutional syphilis, might be present but could be distinguished from each other.

The cases he described of workers in the mirror-plating shops (*Beleger*) of Fürth and Erlangen, in central Bavaria near Nuremburg, were an opportunity to observe a population intensively exposed to mercury, some of whom also were medicated for syphilis.

Jewish migrants from St. Petersburg in Russia had brought a version of the "secret" Venetian mirror-making technique to Fürth, which had the largest Jewish population in South Germany. At the time of Kussmaul's study, there were thirty-four shops with between 174 and 212 workers, men and women. Several other physicians in the area had already published in medical journals case studies of mirror workers' mercury poisoning, and Kussmaul epitomized them in his book. Kussmaul quoted a description of the work conditions written by his colleague at Würzburg, Heinrich Aldinger, who published an inaugural dissertation on the subject:

> The plating shops are for the most part very large rooms in which the windows remain open the whole year round. In the depths of winter they are not heated....
> Each plater has a table before him, on which lies a finely polished marble slab the same size as the glass to be plated, and around which runs a deep groove to catch the mercury runoff. This marble slab will be covered with a sheet of tinfoil over which the mercury will be poured so that it amalgamates with the tin; over this foil anything accumulated is rubbed. A flawless and cleaned pane of Wischerin glass is lowered over the foil as the excess mercury drains off, and accumulates in a vessel placed below. The plated glass is brought to another table where felt-covered stones are placed on it to press out any mercury that has not amalgamated.
> More dangerous than these labors in the plating room is the distillation of the cast off mercury joined with tin, although it happens outside, in iron retorts, and although the workers stand aside and now and again agitate the mass. (I add to this that in Erlangen sweeping up the dust in the plating room, from which mercury later will be recovered, is equally dangerous as the plating operation itself. Also the mirror packers succumb to mercurialism, but less frequently and in less serious forms.)

Aldinger adds details on the variable effects of the mercury on the population of workers.

Some people who do not work in the plating rooms but just pass through on occasion get sick while others can work there for fifteen years without show-

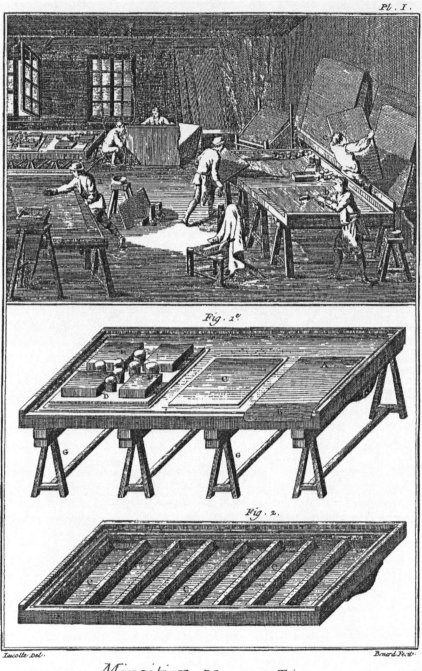

Pl. I.

Fig. 1.ᵉ

Fig. 2.

Lucotte Del.   Benard Fecit.

Miroitier, Metteur au Teint.

Mirror-maker illustration from "L'Art du Verre" section of Diderot and D'Alembert,
L'Encyclopédie, 1751–80.

ing any symptoms. Spanish mercury was more damaging than that from Idria, with the mercury from the near Rhine falling somewhere in between the two. The hotter times of the year were the most likely to send people to the hospital with mercury symptoms.

Taking an overview of the numerous researches, Kussmaul identified two large groups of symptoms—digestive system infections and damage to nerve operations, with many additional disease manifestations. His own position in the clinic at Erlangen situated him to examine the presence of these symptoms in cases which he arranged in logical groupings. What resulted was the most thorough clinical description of the symptoms of mercury poisoning achieved by that date.

Kussmaul did not examine the context, the social history of the Beleger or even the work procedures. He is occupied with the observable effects which could be attributed to mercury exposure and contrasted with the effects of syphilis. His unstated aim was broadly preventive. By disaggregating mercury from syphilis he could identify a disease cause which the owners of the workshops could be persuaded or legally forced to protect their workers from. The social-class stigma attached to syphilis could no longer be used to explain the workers' symptoms actually due to mercury.

The differential diagnosis of mercury poisoning from syphilis was both socially and politically motivated. The mirror workers formed a population under constant exposure to mercury whose cases could be followed. Examining them could begin to answer the ethical and scientific questions arising from the entanglement of mercury and syphilis.

The history Kussmaul had built came to a point in the long list of cases gradually separating strains of illness in which the workers are involved. Like other ambitious, exacting physicians of his time, he was becoming an industrial hygienist, using the force of medical logic to define a condition by linking outward body signs with the work environment, rather than the "moral state" of the workers. But Kussmaul also had the larger environment in mind. There was some evidence that mercury had spread from the Beleger into the homes of the workers and was beginning to affect those who never set foot in the shops.

The relationship between constitutional mercurialism and constitutional syphilis was an environmental effect and not simply conditioned by a working-class tendency to develop syphilis and take mercury-based drugs while suffering occupational exposure. Mercurialism and syphilis were two distinct conditions. Kussmaul found that tuberculosis, with its own distinct symptoms, occurred in those suffering from mercury exposure more often than syphilis did.

The cases from Fürth are based on sanitation police reports, but those from Erlangen are more detailed, based on Kussmaul's own examinations. "A survey of persons who at some time in their lives were sickened by occupational mercury and were physically examined by me in the 1860 and 1861" is the heading of the first major grouping of cases, and it is further subdivided into several categories of greater and lesser severity, each with its own set of cases. "Persons who had occupational contact with mercury, and early once or more times suffered from severe forms of mercurialism." "Persons, who later exposed to occupational mercury suffered from mercurialism or now suffer from it." Duration and frequency of exposure formed the chief division of cases for Kussmaul.

"Persons who suffer from occupational mercurialism and syphilis" formed a separate section of cases, followed by "deceased persons who suffered from occupational mercurialism and in whom I discovered complications."

Among those with early, severe forms of mercurialism was Case 37:

Friedrich M., 55 years old. Single. Laid mirrors from 1830 to 1850 with two breaks of 1½ to 2 years.

1823. Epileptic seizure.

1850. Tremor. Since M. only had tooth pain during the beginning of his mirror-work, at its end in 1850, after he had long uninterruptedly endured the influence of quicksilver, suddenly was afflicted with violent tremors. Which came unanticipated, without shivers or light shakes before them, only the appetite was diminished long before. The shakes were so hard that he had to be restrained, his speech was slurred, he was unable to leave his bed. Few headaches. Poor sleep, with frightful dreams. No loss of hair.

1856. Gonorrhoea and orchitis dextra.

1858. Epileptic seizure.

August 1860. Epileptic seizure. M. was certain that he only suffered three of these seizures in his life, the last of which was subject of a polyclinic examination. There are grounds to accept his declaration.

Oct. 1860. Well proportioned strong man of rather florid aspect. Recently suffered often from nausea and headaches. Thick head and beard hair. Teeth all firmly in place. Mouth and throat secretions normal, only the uvula lengthened and thickened. Lymph flow, liver and the like normal. Penis and scrotum nothing unusual. M. does not suffer from joint pain, rheumatism or the like.

Father died at 41 years of age from nerve fever. Mother, 51 years old, from hernia. 2 brothers 58 and 61 years old still living, 1 died at 54 from apoplexy, 3 sisters died in childhood.

Overview of Case 37

Examination confirms: 1) the undiminished and sudden appearance of a stark case of tremor, as with almost every symptom well known among the mirror-layers, is felt after years of work with quicksilver; 2) epilepsy, which during 37 years occurred three times with two intervals of 35 and 2 years. *As long as he worked in the mirror shop, he didn't have any epileptic seizures.* [italicized in the original]

Examining the cases of two women mirror workers (67 and 68) who had secondary syphilis, Kussmaul concludes, "Both women had in secondary syphilis mouth and throat sores and breiten condylomen and later were in the tremor condition of occupational mercurialism, one of them to the point of convulsions. Physical examination uncovered no remains of syphilis or traces of characteristic damages in either."

In the extensive review of cases which follows, Kussmaul gives the most complete examination-based analysis of the symptoms of mercury poisoning any writer has offered. Only then does he proceed to develop the relationship between the physical effects of mercury and the disease it is most often employed to treat, and which he can trace through individual cases where both are discernible in distinct stages. Kussmaul does not stop at the old observation that the symptoms of syphilis are caused by mercury treatments. For him the symptoms of syphilis and those of mercury poisoning are interrelated, the mercury giving appearances of syphilis while holding it at bay. His study differentiates constitutional mercurialism from constitutional syphilis rather than charting their resemblance to each other, as Mathias did. Kussmaul does define mercury poisoning, but as a phenomenon inextricable from syphilis at a time when syphilis was becoming defined in greater detail. His clinical definition differed from that of others trying to isolate the disease even when they recognized mercury had a role in it.

There had long been an opinion among doctors given the opportunity to examine multiple cases of syphilis that mercury had a role in the symptoms attributed to the disease.

This was an observation advanced by the promoters of plant-based medicines who had taken issue with the mainstream medical mercurialists. *Mercury Stark Naked*, shouted the title of a 1797 tract by Isaac Swainson, the proprietor of Velnos's Vegetable Syrup, *A Series of Letters Addressed to Dr. Beddoes; Stripping that Poisonous Mineral of its Medical Pretentions; and Showing That it Perpetuates, Increases, and Multiplies all Diseases for which it is Administered*. Like his younger American counterpart William Swaim, Swainson expended a number of pamphlets trying to disprove the accusation that his syrup contained mercury.

The English surgeon David McLoughlin, who was not seeking to sell a nostrum, in 1864 published a pamphlet in which he claimed that syphilis did not exist as a constitutional disease. Referring to the practice of army and naval surgeons of treating with mercury every ulcer appearing on the genitals of the enlisted men under their care, McLoughlin argued that if only they made a scientific record of their observations they would recognize the cause and effect relationship between treatment and disease. They would recognize that "syphilis" was an adjunct of the regimen used to treat it.

Members of a parliamentary committee of medical men formed to inquire into the nature of venereal disease took notice of McLoughlin's claims, and totally dismissed them during their subsequent hearings. The existence of a syphilis "virus" independent of mercury applications was too much of a vested interest for the medical profession, and the superficial efficacy of mercury against the ulcers and rashes of syphilis's first appearance was too valuable for doctors to accept views like McLoughlin's. The committee's conclusion was that syphilis was a deep-seated constitutional poison and that the effects of mercury itself were secondary to the relief brought by its application. As always, there was a great deal of reliance on the belief that such categories of people as "prostitutes" and "foreigners" were more syphilis-prone than the men of "our" community, and the perpetuation of the disease in a large collective body like the armed forces was due to their habitual and professional contact with these outsiders. Sex between men and between women was not even considered.

A corollary of this conclusion was that the syphilis virus was ineluctable and inextricable from the bodies of those who carried it. Mercury could only bring superficial relief and cause superficial effects of its own. This is what led some doctors to seek ways to attack the inner virus while using mercury only to control the outward symptoms. By analogy with the one successful treatment of an infectious disease, the use of vaccination to prevent smallpox, several European physicians attempted to forestall the development of syphilis by injecting infectious matter into chancres, the initial skin sores that develop soon after infection with the disease. Some claimed success in reducing the skin eruptions and other symptoms, and even undertook trials of the syphilization (deliberate administration of infectious matter) method, using prostitutes as the subjects. By the end of the 1850s, the lack of success of the method was apparent and plans for large scale syphilization in France, for instance, did not go forward.

Kussmaul did not comment on either the rejection of constitutional syphilis or making it into an essence. He did not address the medical or ethical issues created by syphilization and similar procedures. Instead he defined the common poisonous nature of both mercury and syphilis, and distinguished them from each other.

His clinical examination and case history examination of the mirror workers showed him that a suite of symptoms were always associated with mercury whether or not the individual had a history of syphilis or any other disease. And he found that certain variables affected the presence and degree of identifiable symptom suites. Workers who brushed their teeth regularly and did not eat or drink in the work rooms were less likely to come down with the symptoms; alcoholics were more susceptible, pregnant women less, and younger people were more susceptible than older ones. Finally, there were unexplained individual differences:

> Some persons have worked in the mirror shop 10, 20, 30, 40 years, one man the greater part of his life up to age 76, without getting sick (Aldinger); others were unaffected by the severe form of mercurialism after they handled the metal for years and held it in their own hands [compare cases 37 and 46]; others immediately after one or two weeks at work in the mirror shop came down with stomatitis [mouth abscess], ptyalism [strong salivation], headache, and light shakes.

Kussmaul saw stages in worker mercurialism, beginning with erethism, a phase of hypersensitivity that includes stomatitis, saliva flow, stomach upsets and diarrhea, followed by the development of tremors and what he called the terminal stage, where the nervous system became involved. Those who worked a long time in the rooms could develop a "habitual" mercury poisoning in which the early symptoms remained at a middle level of intensity, and no new symptoms appeared. Those who left the work after developing symptoms could retain them for a period of time. For some, however, the penetration of the mercury into their organic being led to an intensification of the early symptoms into terminal conditions, stomatitis in the form of abscesses, loss of teeth and so on.

After a long review of the appearances of mercury poisoning Kussmaul turns again to syphilis:

> We need to use the word "poison" in its broadest sense, to call both mercurialism and syphilis "poison diseases" [*Giftkrankheiten*]. If we make the distinction, as it is only fitting, between poison in the strict sense (venenum) and infectious material, then only mercurialism is a poison disease, and syphilis is an infectious disease.... *Mercurialism and syphilis are at base different diseases.* But in fact different diseases can resemble each other in many appearances and outcomes.

Kussmaul then asked three questions: 1. What are the common antecedents of both mercury and syphilis? 2. Which afflictions of the organs appear identical for both? 3. In which order does this happen?

The answers placed a medical observer in a framework to tell mercurialism from syphilis in specific cases, and they advanced Kussmaul's view that the mercurial environment of the shops held back syphilis while inducing mercurialism to varying degrees, exchanging mercurial symptoms for syphilitic ones. Syphilis could confer an immunity to other afflictions while mercurialism cannot, yet mercurialism often accompanied a lessening of shared symptoms. The two were at base different diseases, but they established a complex interrelationship in human bodies exposed to both. "In the same bodies mercury and syphilis can stand side by side."

Treatment of syphilis by mercury could never resolve syphilis entirely because that resulted in the symptom complex Kussmaul described. More mercury just intensified mutual and contrasting symptoms. Another treatment must enter to bring about improvement. Kussmaul believed potassium iodide (Jodkalium) in conjunction with mercury could cure syphilis, and he offered several case studies to illustrate that.

> If I openly said that the influence of mercury on syphilis has been grossly overstated, it came to me naturally not in the sense of taking the pain in stride like an [Ulrich von] Hutten of bygone times, when the management of mercury treatment was in the hands of the boldest empirical physicians. I have the present in view when the use of quicksilver in syphilis is kept within such strict limits and

governed by rational rules. If every renowned non-doctor [*Nicht-arzt*] in his venereal recollections has experienced well and thoroughly the frightful aspect of the
effects of mercury, which today destroys the bodies and souls of quicksilverwork-
ers, that he could leave for posterity a remarkable, harrowing picture of these sufferings, our celebrated present-day syphilologists seldom study mercurialism in its
worse forms; they must go to the mines, shops and factories, where quicksilver is
extracted and worked, if they would learn the ravages of quicksilver.

I used "mercury" and "quicksilver" to translate Kussmaul's "*mercur*" and
"*quecksilber*" respectively. Mercury used to treat syphilis has been contained
to the degree that doctors who specialize in its use cannot witness its ravages.
The mines and factories can offer an index of mercury exposure no longer available to physicians cautiously dosing patients. Looking at the health of the workers in these places, so different from the elite patients usually presenting
themselves to the doctors, could enable the syphilologist to know what was
mercury poisoning and what was syphilis, and adjust treatments accordingly.

It seemed that in some cases working in a mercury environment could
replace medical mercury and grant some respite from syphilis and possibly
other diseases and conditions. The growing number of recorded and published
case histories allowed Kussmaul and other physicians to envision the details of
disease, treatment and exposure. But the mercury dosage through work was
much in excess of what was found helpful in private treatment. Syphilis was
common to all classes and both genders; refinement of mercury treatment separated classes and genders.

The use of mercury in treating syphilis declined as the course of syphilis
and the effects of mercury became better known. Kussmaul's conclusions were
part of the finer knowledge of when and how mercury ointments could most
advantageously be applied by professional applicators, and which other poisons
could be administered for a fuller cure. The low doses already advocated by
some writers became routine and for the urban middle classes institutional-
ized in proprietary medicines. As late as the 1920s, as a new non-mercurial
remedy was becoming available, "the Aachen method," a system of sulfur-bath
immersions and massages with 37.5 percent mercury ointment that originated
in the German spa, was spreading in Europe and America.

In separating the consequences of absorbing mercury from the symptoms
of syphilis, Kussmaul developed a new type of clinical reasoning that was to
mature in the further search for an alternative to mercury. Somehow mercury
not only diluted the syphilis poison; it enhanced the ability of organs to hold
off disease. The long quest for a mercury replacement had simply focused on
finding or claiming to find a less toxic remedy. That formed the advertising
strategy of the patent medicine cures of many ills, including syphilis. Any poison could replace mercury but might not affect syphilis. Kussmaul's work suggested that there was a differential between syphilis and mercury that could be
widened. A genuine remedy would have to be a poison resembling syphilis as

mercury did. If a poison itself, it would have to be better than mercury at opposing syphilis poison without intensifying symptoms identical with syphilis.

There were many mercury-dosage programs devised by doctors making claims that this exact sequence of administrations surely would root out the syphilis. It was not possible to prove any of these wrong.

One of these refined treatment programs was a revival of the fumigation technique under the title of "mercurial vapor bath." Fumigation never was completely abandoned; practitioners continually reinvented it, combining it with other techniques such as inunction and bathing. A Bristol, England, surgeon named Samuel William Langston Parker wrote a mercurial vapor bath manual that went through a number of British and American editions between 1845 and 1874, successively citing more endorsements from colleagues and more successful treatments.

> The bath should be administered in the following way: the patient is placed on a chair, on the seat of which should be a thin cushion; he should be covered over with an oiled cloth, or india-rubber cape, lined with flannel, or a blanket. The coverings should be made tight, so as to prevent the escape of the vapour, unless it is intended that the patient should breathe it, which, under some circumstances, is better; under the chair is placed a small copper tin bath, holding from a pint to a quart of water, and a stand, supporting a tinned iron plate, on which is placed the preparation to be used; under each of these is a large porcelain spirit lamp.

The preparation heated on the plate as the water steamed was a sulfate, oxide, iodide or chloride of mercury. Parker noted that 5–10 minutes of exposure to the vapors should be sufficient to achieve invariably successful results with syphilis patients. The amount of time, the intensity of the heat and the type and quantity of the preparation could be changed to suit a patient's needs.

Parker explicitly rejected internal medication with mercury. He believed that the steam carried the mercury into the skin first causing it to slough off superficial lesions, then drove it into the body where it forced out the syphilis virus. At a time when steam was powering railroads, boats, and heavy industrial machinery, Parker though it could power mercury too. As a surgeon he was relieved to have a treatment that would eliminate the surface lesions of primary and secondary syphilis without his having to touch them with the scalpel. He was not the first surgeon to look to mercury for this help; two of the earlier surgeon mercurialists, seen in the next chapter, before steam power, looked to the weight of mercury instead.

Thousands of patients were helped by the vapor bath, Parker claimed. He did not admit, as Henry Lee, another surgeon who proposed the same treatment did, that the mercurial vapor bath was less effective for some individuals than for others. His optimism reflects the early beliefs that steam power was a positive force of social transformation. A Boston physician, John Foye, prefaced his reprinting of Parker's and Lee's booklets with his own booklet

Mercurial Vapour Bath; Foye's Fumigating Apparatus (1874).

illustrating his design for a metal housing where the vapor-bath patient could be placed for the duration of the treatment.

Over the decades that Parker's manual was in print, the mercurial vapor bath was recommended in a number of other medical treatises and textbooks, primarily as a treatment for syphilis and similar skin conditions, but also for internal discomforts, including those associated with pregnancy. Some of the recommendations were qualified, as in Silas Durkee's observation that the perspiration of the clad patient in the vapor bath would prevent the mercury from penetrating the skin, making the treatment valid only for superficial lesions.

There was little criticism of the method, but also apart from Parker's own reported cases, little testimony of its success. It seemed to be advocated without actually being extensively adopted. It was a way of imagining a syphilis treatment that "does away with the evils attributable to mercury treatments whilst it possesses all these advantages," as Parker himself wrote.

The mercurial vapor bath remained on the books, but quietly evaporated as a treatment during the early twentieth century. The evils attributable to mercury could be eliminated from the syphilis complex by eliminating the mercury.

Paul Ehrlich applied his painstakingly developed knowledge of staining tissues for study under the microscope to the search for chemicals that attached themselves to specific bacteria inside the tissues. Ehrlich was a medical doctor, but his vision of health and illness was that of a chemist. He made studies of oxygen utilization in living tissue by developing dyes that changed color in accordance with oxygen absorption. He theorized that cells decoyed invading bacteria away from themselves by casting off replica molecules of their surface chemicals (side chains) to which the bacteria attached themselves. Ehrlich's medical chemistry was a play of attraction and distraction.

It was a play Ehrlich could quantify. By measuring the degree of attachment achieved by differing concentrations and quantities of vaccine, Ehrlich helped make genuinely preventive the diphtheria antitoxin discovered by his colleague von Behring. Testing a series of organic arsenic compounds on animals infected by the trypanosome that causes sleeping sickness, Ehrlich determined which preparation was least likely to kill the victim cured. In this research Ehrlich combined the serial synthesis of organic arsenic compounds originated by Bunsen with the animal testing practices of Robert Koch, in whose laboratory he worked.

Ehrlich turned his attention to syphilis after Hoffman, a physician, and Schaudinn, a parasitologist, in 1905 identified the microbe present in the infectious early soft lesions of the disease. As in Ehrlich's own work, this required a combination of skills: Hoffman extracted infectious matter from a patient's chancre and sent it to Schaudinn, who was a specialist in detecting through the microscope presence of invasive parasites in animal tissue.

The treponema that causes syphilis had not yet been made to grow in culture: treatment would have to be observed in animal models. Ehrlich asked Sahachiro Hata, who had succeeded in transferring syphilis infection to rabbits, to test some of the organic arsenic compounds that had proven ineffective against trypanosomes. Hata found that the compound numbered 606 reduced skin lesions and restored general health in infected animals after a course of injections. Human case studies were encouraging. In 1909, Salvarsan, the trade name Ehrlich invented to label the compound arsphenamine, was released as a "magic bullet" aimed at syphilis.

We might have our weapons forged by the best smith, Kussmaul himself wrote, but we will never triumph over such a fierce enemy as syphilis without understanding the means of healing the disease itself provides. Ehrlich had in mind the bullet of folklore that always reaches the mark it is aimed at. But his own weapons analogy made Kussmaul's ironic. Salvarsan proved to be a measure of debatable effectiveness that like mercury came back to worsen the disease.

Salvarsan was supplied by the manufacturer as a powder in a sealed container that a physician had to open and dissolve in alcohol then dilute in water and administer to a patient by injection, or intravenously, over a period of weeks. Its administration was a form of chemotherapy. Soon after its introduction there were announcements of its miraculous effectiveness, and declarations that like other drugs in the past it would replace mercury and make its further use unnecessary.

Yet it does seem to have replaced mercury precisely. Its use entailed imbuing the body of the patient with a caustic substance with its own considerable side effects. The doctors who used Salvarsan had a vested interest in keeping control over its use: it was a continuation of the extended small-dose mercury regimens that had developed against the self-medication and patent medicines that were often the cheaper, favored resort. For the first few years after Salvarsan's release, Ehrlich and his associates dominated its distribution and the training of its applicators.

This displeased those in the medical profession who could not satisfy the perceived need that news about the remedy encouraged. And of course naturopathic and homeopathic doctors, who rejected all use of undiluted poisons, openly declared their opposition.

Comparisons of mercury with compound 606, or Salvarsan, began to appear in the professional literature, especially examining the ability of the new medication to abate what were recognized as the later symptoms of the disease, the ocular and mental disturbances for instance. Practitioners were not willing to relinquish raw mercury and mercury compounds entirely, and tended to include Salvarsan in existing mercury regimens or mercury in stages of Salvarsan administration.

From the very beginning of 606's introduction, however, the public discourse in newspapers and journals maintained the same discretion that had characterized all such discussion of venereal disease since the eighteenth century. Ehrlich himself initiated this by announcing in the press that the new treatment was aimed at a "blood disease" that had long been the scourge of humankind, and associating his trypanosomiasis cure, an organic arsenic compound of which 606 was one of the trial stages, with the blood disease. Both cures were bundled into the same tropical disease concerns that had expanded since Columbus's arrival back in Spain with infected sailors and abducted islanders. Syphilis was assimilated into the colonialist psychology of conquest, illness and guilt, together with all the other blood diseases acquired in the tropics, and it was healed by wonder drugs brought from the tropics, or now synthesized in the laboratory and mass produced by factories.

In the public announcements of Salvarsan, the professional discussions (and conflicts) of the physicians intersected with guarded public wording of venereal disease references. Certain cues evoked a tacit understanding. "The usefulness of this remedy is not alone to cure the disease for which it has been tested," ends the October 5, 1910, report of the arrival of a doctor in New York with a supply of 606, "but also to prevent the development in later years of serious affections of the mind and nervous system as well as locomotor ataxia and other forms of paralysis." This was as far as anyone could go in describing late syphilis without using the word "syphilis."

The word "Salvarsan" was constructed from the Latin prefix "salv-" plus "ars(enic)" plus the "-n" suffix that designates drug (aspir-in, chlorac-in); "salvation by arsenic" was understood to be the expected outcome. As with mercury, arsenic was a known poison but was now scientifically recruited in a word.

This grave optimism was maintained until Salvarsan was replaced by better treatments. The 1940 MGM film *Dr. Ehrlich's Magic Bullet*, a well-crafted historical drama, manages to avoid any explicit mention of syphilis and that a Japanese experimenter had a key role in identifying and testing the remedy, all the while making cinema out of the German doctor's struggles with skeptics of this own profession.

Commenting on "the present status of Ehrlich's remedy," William J. Robinson, M.D. declares that as a rule he did not discuss technical medical problems or the virtues and defects of medicinal agents in the general press. But the publicity surrounding 606, rechristened Salvarsan, had caused it to become prematurely popular. People of such poor general health that a dose of Salvarsan would be like a shot of cyanide or a well-placed bullet were petitioning for treatment, and the perfectly healthy were asking for medication "just in case." The latest news from the clinics in Germany where patients have been treated with Salvarsan told of relapses, though there was not enough evidence to reach conclusions at that stage. Mercury and potassium iodide in addition to, or instead of, 606, seemed to produce more stable results. "Mercury and the iodides have not yet lost their raison d'etre, and will probably retain it for some time to come," Robinson concluded.

United States Army assistant surgeon Captain Henry J. Nichols was working in Paul Ehrlich's laboratory at the time 606 was identified. In his 1907 annual
report, United States Surgeon General O'Reilly estimated that venereal infections in the armed services caused a loss equal to an entire year of service of
eleven full companies of infantry. The 1909 figure of over eleven venereally
debilitated soldiers per thousand stationed in the continental United States was
already very high. Among American troops in the occupied Philippines in 1910,
the infection rate was measured at over 275 per thousand active duty soldiers.
Syphilis and gonorrhea were the major cause for the rejection of recruits. This
information was good reason for a military doctor like Captain Nichols to pay
close attention to compound 606, which he brought to America for testing.

The United States Army had previously made do with the same topical
applications and injections of mercury and potassium iodide that served elsewhere. Nichols noted that one military surgeon was injecting syphilis patients
with doses of "gray oil," a mixture of mercury with vegetable oil, which created its own subcutaneous infections.

The intramuscular injection of Salvarsan also caused swelling and pain that
itself called for treatment, and intravenous administration of the drug caused
severe nausea, headache, fever, and vomiting. And the Salvarsan series wasn't
consistently effective in reducing primary syphilis symptoms. Captain Nichols
initiated treatment of a patient with primary syphilis lesions with an intravenous injection of Salvarsan followed by a month of mercury inunction, then
another Salvarsan injection and another month of inunction. Secondary and
tertiary syphilis required yet more aggressive and prolonged Salvarsan and mercury. Despite the severe side effects of the Salvarsan, this combination of the
drug with mercury became the common resort. It was found that it yielded a
72 percent negative Wassermann test result in those who tested positive before
the treatment began.

Salvarsan quickly replaced guiac as the support and opponent of mercury
in syphilis treatment. Ehrlich's 1914 introduction of arsenic compound 914,
which he named Neosalvarsan answered the calls for a less lethal treatment. This
powder was soluble in water and did not require the initial dissolution in alcohol that induced the severe skin reactions characteristic of Salvarsan injections.
But it didn't have the cure rate of Salvarsan. Hostilities during the First World
War cut off supplies of Salvarsan imported into the United States from the
enemy country of Germany and gave rise to legislation that allowed the Federal Trade Commission to issue licenses for the domestic production of Salvarsan and Neosalvarsan.

The assimilation of Salvarsan into medical practice produced over a shorter
time the same considerations that had long developed with mercury. Initially
it was thought that Salvarsan could be the *sterilisans magna*, the substance
able to purify the body of bacteria in one strong coup. The clinical study of
sudden deaths following Salvarsan injections led to the advice that it be given

in a number of small doses spread over time. Writing of the early attempts to find a Salvarsan regimen, New Jersey physician Henry T. Wallhauser gave the example of an apparently healthy woman with a hand lesions who received a single dose of Salvarsan, passed into a coma and died ten days later. An autopsy revealed syphilitic damage to the meninges (outer layer of the brain) and bleeding encephalitis, none of which was previously apparent. Wallhauser concluded that the Salvarsan had fatally inflamed already damaged tissue while targeting the syphilis bacteria infesting the tissue. This parallels the tendency of mercury to produce symptoms like those of the syphilis lesions it heals. Salvarsan took the place of mercury all too well.

Injected Salvarsan and topical mercury continued to be used in tandem until the introduction of penicillin for syphilis in the mid 1940s eliminated both of them. The antibacterial action of the penicillium mold had been discovered several times before Alexander Fleming found it reducing laboratory colonies of staphylococcus bacteria in 1928, but it was not available in quantities and in a form sufficient for the treatment of a disease like syphilis until almost two decades later. The knowledge that penicillin was effective against syphilis did not immediately cause its universal replacement of mercury for that purpose. Mercury remained the cheaper medication, and was used for the immediate relief of populations of patients who could not afford any better.

A tragic reminder of this slow succession of treatments was the Tuskegee Study of Untreated Syphilis in the Negro Male, which went on using a population of African-American men in Alabama from 1932 until 1972. The study was planned and conducted by the United States Public Health Service with the collaboration of the Tuskegee Institute for Men, a college founded by the pioneering educator Booker T. Washington. Six hundred men were enlisted for the study, three hundred and one of whom were known to be infected with late-stage syphilis.

There already was a history of studies in which treatment was deliberately denied to people known to be infected with syphilis but none of them spanned the years in which Salvarsan and then penicillin were available. An excuse later made, that mercury and arsphenamine were dangerous medications that the researchers withheld to the benefit of the study subjects, did not apply to penicillin, which would have eased and prolonged the lives even of late-term syphilis sufferers. The same pairing that existed between mercury and guiac, or mercury and Salvarsan, a dialectical imbalance over time, could not exist with mercury and penicillin, which did not exact the same penance.

6

Little Blue Pills

There was no difficulty getting mercury into the body during mercury's long coexistence with syphilis. The difficulty was getting it to stay long enough to permeate the body and carry with it all the damaging poisons, including itself, as it drained out. Rubs, fumigations, raw mercury and mercury compounds drunk or swallowed had unpleasant effects, were not very discreet, and did not accomplish as much as it was believed they could. The search continued for a way to deliver mercury that would employ its weighty clearing essence without the disadvantages of its corrosive potential.

W. Ellis, "farmer, at Little Gaddesden, near Hempstead, Hertfordshire," in *The Country Housewife's Family Companion* (1750), after giving instructions on fruit preservation and improvement of grains and directions on fattening hogs, in his section "of cheap, approved and experienced medicines and remedies," proclaimed the virtues of mercury water. His neighbor Richard Hanowell had paid a famous London practitioner in physic five pounds for bottles of a liquor which was supposed to heal the running sores about his head caused by the King's-evil (scrofula). The costly remedy did not work. Ellis lent (didn't give) Hanowell a pound of quicksilver, and advised him to make quicksilver water and drink it regularly. The sores disappeared, leaving skin so sound that he could pinch it without breaking it. Hanowell and Ellis exchanged a series of letters on the virtues of quicksilver water, "the best cure in the whole world for the Pox, King's-Evil, Gout, Rheumatism, Scurvy, &c., &c."

In one of the letters Hanowell writes,

> a pound of quicksilver, which costs about four shillings and sixpence, or five shillings, I think will serve many years, boiled or rather simmered in any quantity of water, in an iron pot, or a glazed earthen pot, for no other metal will do, for a space of five or six hours or more ... it is a water that will not corrupt in bottles for

a long time, if ever: for it destroys all kind of animalcula, and resists and destroys all manner of acidity and fermentation in the water it is boiled in ... and certainly the most minute and divisible and I am persuaded, all the particles of the effluvia that mix with the water are perfectly and minutely globular, and fitted by such a form and smoothness to enter and pass in the circulation thro' the imperceptible vascular system.

Giving a mangy horse this water to drink, and regular sponge baths, was supposed to purify the horse's blood and make the mange disappear. Hanowell cured a pointer dog covered with universal mange.

This recipe for a mercury water, save the cost of expending mercury as it did, did not accomplish much more than reducing mange, and the recipe did not spread far and wide.

In France, a line of experimentation among pharmacists tested the ability of boiling water to absorb the active properties of mercury through contact. Water was known to absorb gases and mercury vaporized even at low temperatures. The mercury, however, was shown not to lose any of its mass by contact with the water in a sealed vessel. In 1838, Paton reproduced the water preparations of mercury recommended by his predecessors and did not find that any of them contained mercury. Mercury water was no longer pursued.

If mercury could not communicate its properties by association to something as palatable as water, perhaps it could be transformed into a medicine able to spread comfortably through the body after being swallowed.

The potential for this was already evident from the ancient mixture of metallic mercury with lard or grease to be rubbed on skin as a treatment for eczema and rashes. When mixed with oily substances, mercury subdivided into myriad shining points visible in the transparent medium. This encouraged the belief that it entered the skin and infiltrated the interior of the body. The same could be accomplished with a dry medium, the mercury ground or levigated with a powder, for instance with chalk, until it disappeared, its weight and tone added to the powder. This was called "killing" or "extinguishing" the mercury. If this powder itself was medicinal, then its healing was likely to be carried deep into the body by its penetrative mercury contents.

Numerous mixtures of raw mercury with purgatives were invented and tried. If the mercury transferred the purge into the body, then the subsequent eruption of noxious elements would be complete and fully cleansing. The finer the mercury, the more likely it was to reach everywhere the venom was harbored. A truly refined mercury medication had a potential for discrete self-administration, but first the doctors and chemists had to provide the formula and the picture of how it worked. The formula they would try to keep secret while projecting the picture of tiny mercury globules passing through the viscera.

Augustin Belloste wrote,

When crude mercury is taken by mouth in pills, although its parts are very much divided and very minute, in spite of the purgatives with which it is mixed, it communicates itself very promptly to the liquids, it swims in a fluid, and it is in a perpetual movement, and so it can't be sublimed: the warmth of the body serves as a pump for it, animates it, augments its movement, and causes it to penetrate everywhere. It only leaves the liquids with which it is compounded to gain the organs of elimination.

Belloste was a military surgeon seeing service during the late sixteenth-century wars of Savoy, and his conception of the action of mercury in the body is a military surgeon's conception. Belloste thought that globular forceful mercury smoothed the sharp points of the acids that damaged body tissue the same way that a skillful surgeon trimmed away the inflammation that could cause a wound to grow foul. Thomas Dover advanced a similar view, derived from Belloste, but he assumed that Belloste meant mercury in a single massive body, which he didn't.

The *Traitez de Mercure* was published as an annex to Belloste's surgical text *Chirurgien d'Hôpital* in which he describes many of his practices designed to moderate the violent treatment accorded war wounds. Since Ambroise Paré in the sixteenth century stopped the pouring of boiling oil on battlefield wounds, surgeons had been devising treatments that diminished trauma. Belloste did not make notable contributions to the development of surgical technique, but he did set down in writing minor innovations such as washing wounds carefully and in stages to encourage the natural suppuration of flesh or exfoliation of bone.

The *Traitez de Mercure* does not include any military examples. All the treatments and testimonials it contains are from urban nobility and rich bourgeois, not soldiers or farmers. The book is a product of Belloste's later career, when he had become well-known for the treatments he describes, and for being called in when other physicians were not having any success. The book's hallmark is in the imagery of edges and points it uses to advance the use of crude mercury. A military surgeon is writing only for his colleagues; the advocate of a medicinal treatment is writing for consumers.

Belloste claimed that "our mercury" ("*notre mercure*") was unique and original with him, that it did not have a classical precedent. The penetrating, weighty quality of this mercury was much written about before Belloste, but mainly as a property needing to be controlled and not as a medicinal strength.

Belloste compared crude mercury to "little pearls very fine and solid that destroy the weak points of the acids" as they followed a gentle but firm course through the body. The imagery he used seems ancestral to the animated pictures later used by drug promoters to make clear to the general public the direct and soothingly physical ways their products will relax the skin or the belly. Belloste promoted the smoothness of mercury as a solution to the pain caused by irregularities invisible inside the body.

Mercury was thought to enter the moving (not yet known to be circulating) fluids of the body in a finely divided mass, softly unraveling visible knots of fleshlike tumors that otherwise would have to be removed surgically and undoing invisible obstructions to the flow of fluids the same way that crude mercury pushed out the contents of the bowels and mouth through ejection and salivation. This was the translation of the oral and intestinal action of mercury into an imaginary mechanics of the entire body system, making the liquid metal a surgeon's fluid tool.

Belloste distinguished his mercury from the mercury applied to the body in an unguent or suffused about the body in fumigation. He wrote that mercury entering the blood vessels through the skin had the effect of a "dike" on the blood flow, the shock causing the blood to back up and creating a more serious obstruction than the illness for which the mercury was applied. The mercury then returned to the nerves of the skin from the inside and entered the nerve fibers, with paralysis the result. Promoters of vegetable medications argued that all mineral ingredients had this obstructive effect, and that the more gentle plant derivatives moved smoothly through the body as Belloste claimed subdivided mercury did.

Belloste here was explaining one of the possible outcomes of a syphilis infection as the result of rogue mercury improperly introduced into the body. He does not mention syphilis at all, but it would be obvious to anyone having reason to read his treatise that he was referring to the typical unguent and vapor (perfume) treatments in force for syphilis sufferers. He also explains the mouth and throat sores (which might be the result of either syphilis or mercury) and the excessive salivation that often accompanied taking raw mercury orally as the result of mercury shaking loose the pointed acids that accompany infections. In other words sores and salivation are signs of the particular efficacy of mercury.

The obviously destructive properties of corrosive sublimate, calomel and other mercury salts is the result of the heat that raw mercury has absorbed to produce them. The heat of the body itself, Belloste repeatedly emphasized, was not sufficient to turn mercury into its deadly vapor form, or into an inflammatory compound. He thus dismissed the experience of syphilis and skin disease treatments in order to support his imagery of a gentle, coursing raw mercury further liberated to treat the body's tightened tissues and blocked passages in the form of a pill.

Belloste wrote that he believed, though he had never seen the experiment performed, that a person holding a finger in a pool of raw mercury would whiten a coin held in his or her mouth. The penetrative power of the substance is that great, that infinitely divisible. This was Belloste's persuasive strategy, to hold up striking pictures of what he had not seen.

Having dismissed the damaging aspects of mercury treatments and affirmed the smooth, healing subtlety of plain mercury, Belloste promoted the even greater efficacy of the pill formed of raw mercury in a minute quantity joined with a purgative. His formulation, which he never gives explicitly, concentrates all the virtues of mercury while discarding the disadvantageous forms and applications. The demulcent force of mercury overcoming pointed acids and thick blockages is an image easily grasped within and outside the context of Belloste's own time.

Belloste claimed that his formulation of mercury pills was original with him, but recipes for pills formed of small quantities of crude mercury combined with binders and purgatives had been included in pharmacopeias for some time. What was original with Belloste, and what lasted after his name had fallen away from the pills, was a vision of them as a vehicle for introducing mercury into the body which did not have the disadvantages of unguents and fumigations and even of quantities of crude mercury, which Belloste did advocate.

Belloste's ideas about the particulate fluidity of mercury in the body were among many similar notions circulating at the time, all of them attempts to harness mercury's weight to clear out the body of obstructions and poisons. Professional pharmacists were trying to conceptualize mercury combining with the body as a result of their initiating the combination with other substances they ground with mercury in the mortar.

Paul-Jacques Malouin, professor of medicine at the Collège de France and of chemistry at the Jardin de Plantes in Paris, wrote in his *Chimie médicinale* (1750):

> Mercury is more or less effective as it is more or less divided. To use it effectively, it is necessary to divide it and it is necessary that the substance used to divide the parts of mercury be able to elude the action of the first digestion, lest the mercury reassemble itself in globules. In the end, mercury acts above all by its weight and extreme divisibility; it amalgamates so to speak with the lymph and the humors, divides them by its weight and penetrates into the smallest vessels and by the minuteness of its parts separated by the heat of the body.

And, Malouin adds, not only does it not harm the teeth, it cleans them.

Thomas Dover, writing while Belloste's books were still in print, issued under the imprint of his widow in Paris, did not mention the pills but projected the treatment by crude mercury in quantity as a way to blunt the points of bodily acids. The disadvantages of massive mercury readily gave way to the advantages of pills subdividing yet further in the body fluids reaching all the places that a flood of mercury would bypass.

Belloste cast mercury in a form which translated its penetrating power into saturation of the real and imaginary motions of the body. He did not give cases of pills working; his remarkable cures still come from the heavy emissions forced out by crude mercury. While this is dramatic evidence of relieving material obstructions, the quantity of fecal matter Belloste described pouring out of crude mercury users contrasted almost comically with the much subtler treatment by pill. Pills distributed the relief felt after a heavy purge. Taken in a series they produced a series of mild purges and a general clearing of the body, including the skin. The negative symptoms of mercury consumption were like the milder symptoms of the disease it was supposed to address. Pills reduced the symptoms further.

Belloste's pills in particular gained a reputation for being a secret formula. One of the reasons Belloste published his treatise was to advertise both raw mercury and pills which included it as the main ingredient, all available from Belloste himself and his successors. The account of the pills' action is specific enough to take advantage of the virtues of mercury while not revealing the other ingredients that made them so effective. Different formulas of ingredients and proportions were revealed over the years, differing from each other in the details but in general incorporating raw mercury, a purgative and a sweetener.

Diderot and d'Alembert's *Encyclopédie des Arts et Métiers* (*Encyclopedia of Arts and Trades*) published from 1750 onward, in its section on mercury declares that the contents of Belloste's pills are unknown, but are thought to resemble strongly the contents of mercury pills listed in the Pharmacopeia of Paris: "[T]ake an ounce of mercury restored from cinnabar, two gros powdered sugar, jalap resin and powdered rhubarb, a half-ounce of each; grind the mercury with the sugar thoroughly in an iron or marble mortar, a little water and a part of scammony, then add the jalap resin, the rest of the scammony and the rhubarb; mix completely beating a very long time, make a mass." The sugar gave flavor and the jalap, rhubarb and scammony had purgative qualities.

Anthelme Richerand, a prominent surgeon and physiologist of the early nineteenth century, treated the novelist Stendhal with mercury washes and Belloste's pills, which Stendhal wrote were compounded of mercury, aloes and scammony, purgative plant derivatives.

Belloste's pills survived as a lingering reputation of mercury combined with vegetable purgatives and flavoring, consumed in small amounts to treat rheumatism.

A 16-page pamphlet, *An Analysis of Belloste's Pills,* appeared in London around 1733, under the authorship of a Belloste with a different first name. It is largely a translation of parts of the *Traitez de Mercure* referring to the pills, and apparently was produced to promote sales of the pills from some source claiming to have the original formula, which was not given in the book.

Formulations like those of Belloste's pills were among the mercury remedies apothecaries offered throughout Europe, but they did not reemerge in the medical literature until the early nineteenth century, again being advanced by a surgeon.

John Abernethy seems to have been two different people. The one you read about looking up his name today was an early nineteenth-century surgeon, a follower of the great John Hunter, a professor of anatomy and surgery at Saint Bartholomew's Hospital in London, who gave popular lectures and was the subject of anecdotes emphasizing his abruptness and stinginess. The other John Abernethy, execrated as much as he was admired in the nineteenth century but recovered only with research today, treated all diseases by giving the blue pill.

At the beginning of his career as surgeon and lecturer, John Abernethy performed physiological experiments. In one of them he placed his hand in a trough of mercury beneath a jar to determine what gases were released by the skin. Abernethy kept his hand submerged for a total of sixteen hours, one hour at a time, and found through analysis that the accumulated gas was about two thirds "carbonic air" and one third "nitrogenous air." He did not mention any health effects of mercury exposure, nor did his biographers blame his eccentricities or death (in 1831) on mercury poisoning. Perhaps he possessed a constitution extraordinarily tolerant of mercury.

He lay the groundwork for use of the mercury pill in an early publication, *Surgical Observations on the Constitutional Origin and Treatment of Local Diseases* (1809), which was included in all subsequent compilations of his lectures and writings.

Abernethy declared that the work of the surgeon, operating on diseased flesh in distinct locations of the body, and the work of the physician, treating illness with medicines generally administered, are compatible with each other. He found that the local irritations he observed as a surgeon were reflected in a disorder of digestion he could attend to as a physician. By the same token, he saw that poor digestion brings about a constitutional disorder that manifests as local diseases, both physical and mental. The substance of this constitutional disruption he believed, was the bile carried by the blood from the liver to the rest of the body, inducing the local diseases. Abernethy called this state "biliousness."

He illustrated the constitutional origins of local disease with cases from his medical practice. "To display how much hepatic irritation may affect the sensorium and consequently the whole nervous system," he offers Case 2. A gentleman came to consult him about a lump on his shin. It had troubled him for over a year, and he had not slept for three months. He wanted to undergo a course of mercury, though his doctors did not think his disease was venereal. His tongue was furred, his appetite was moderate but his digestion did not seem bad.

Abernethy had him take "five grains of the pilul. hydrarg" [small mercury pills] every second night, and watch his stools to see if there was any change. After a week the man came to Abernethy and the lump that had so bothered him was gone, and for the first time in months he had been able to sleep. He thought that the pills were a "most wonderful compound of opium" because none of the other opium preparations he took had any effect. The pills themselves had no perceptible effect, but his stools had changed color from "black as your hat" to "the colour of a ripe Seville orange."

Cases like this one, Abernethy continues, show how liver disorders disturb the senses by disordering other organs concerned with digestion. "And they further shew that unirritating and undebilitating doses of mercury have, probably by their local action in the bowels, a great influence in correcting secretion of the bile, and by this means of relieving hepatic irritation."

The man came to Abernethy with what appeared to be a surgical problem, a lump on his shin that troubled him greatly, and as a surgeon Abernethy saw that there was no lump there. He then recommended a dose of mercury far less drastic than the dose the man was planning to take for syphilis he did not have. The mercury, not heavy enough to cause other irritations, acted upon secretion of the bile. The man no longer thought he had a lump, and he was able to sleep.

Decaying wounds, aching joints, blurry vision, skin rashes, downcast moods all had to have their beginnings in the constitutional effects of "biliousness." To the frustration and amusement of his colleagues, Abernethy never defined exactly what biliousness was.

He did, however, propose a treatment. By control of diet, exercise and the taking of small quantities of mercury in the form of pills followed by a mild purgative, the individual could alter constitutional biliousness and raise the quality of his or her general health. Abernethy's colleagues joked that biliousness was anything that could be treated with mercury.

In giving his fellow doctors a single cause and a connection between the cause and felt discomforts—indigestion, stomach upset, queasiness—Abernethy set a pattern that others would follow. By suggesting blue pills as the alterative of choice, he provided a simple, accessible solution to that root of all problems. You could feel the pills as they went down. They caused no immediate physical reaction, yet they entered the bowels and regulated bile secretion by the liver. The pills were taken in the evening, followed the next morning by a drink of "black draught," a purgative made a mercury compound.

A five- or three-grain pill taken in the evening was far less mercury than what would be absorbed in inunctions or calomel consumption for syphilis treatment. And certainly the reaction was less discomfiting. One of the standards that Abernethy suggested for mercury pills was that the quantity of mercury delivered fall short of causing salivation. For patients like the gentleman of Case 2, fearing that they might have syphilis, imagining that their persistent lumps and aches were venereal in origin, a light course of mercury put the metal into the body addressed only to digestive issues. Abernethy compiled cases of diseases resembling syphilis into a book and he featured the inability of heavy mercury applications to resolve these cases. This was the phenomenological underpinning of his mercury pill treatment portrayed as bile adjustment: fear of possible syphilis allayed by mercury. Mercury lite for syphilis lite.

Abernethy's harshest critics couldn't resist his system. They did try to replace the mercury with other medications. John Elliotson, a younger contemporary of Abernethy, declared that even if Abernethy lived a hundred years and did good all the time, he would not overcome the mischief he caused by his blue pills. Yet Elliotson offered to replace blue pills with colocynth, bitter lemon, a purgative so powerful that his patients accused him of poisoning them.

Elliotson was an exemplar of the new medical professional in the nineteenth century. He abandoned the knee breeches and silk stockings of the past in favor of trousers and a beard, and he lost his job as professor of medicine because of his enthusiasm for mesmerism. Abernethy and his followers had created a medicine of continual slight relief that patients could take into their own hands. Elliotson's mesmerism/hypnotism of course had its future too, but only in the hands of experts and not as a way of easing surgery, as Elliotson claimed.

Abernethy and the blue pill made their way into a great many medical handbooks and treatises on a range of diseases and conditions during the middle years of the nineteenth century. The writers fell on a line between wholehearted embrace of the blue pill treatment to great wariness and outright rejection. Even the strongest supporters had their reservations, when they saw they might lose control of the medication. George Hamilton Bell, an Edinburgh-trained physician who practiced in colonial India for a number of years, dedicated his treatise on diseases of the liver (1833) to Abernethy. Bell was so convinced by the advantages of mercury ("we need not restrict ourselves to any one formula") that he describes himself forcing different preparations (he gave the formulas) on a patient with griping pains in the abdomen who was pleading with him to stop the mercury. Later in the book, however, he advised a patient who had been dosing himself with blue pill to leave off lest he poison himself.

James Johnson, another medical doctor writing on disease in tropical climates, includes blue pills with herbal medications as a remedy for the "most indescribably disagreeable sensations" produced by acrid biliary secretions reaching the duodenum. Johnson himself can attest that this suite of medications helped to keep the irritation in check and corrects "the vitiated state of biliary secretion." He found that Abernethy was correct in his prescriptions, but not so correct he that would rely solely on the blue pill to end his misery.

What Abernethy had that Belloste, a century earlier, did not have, was a growing popular medical literature to disseminate his remedy, his theory abbreviated to the word "biliousness." Blue pill "is the favourite remedy of that celebrated, but eccentric man, Mr. Abernethy, whose recommendation of it has been the principal cause of its high repute in the present day," Thomas John Graham informed the readers of his manual of "domestic medicine," a home-care book alphabetically organized by treatment and condition. Graham found the blue pill without advantage for complaints where the stomach is very irritable from a primary disease, but that it would work wonders for stomach conditions caused by disorders in other organs.

The "Abernethy Medicines," begins an entry in an encyclopedia of recipes for practical use,

> originally consisted of a three-grain mercurial pill, administered over-night, followed by an aromatized black draught in the morning. Finding, however, that when frequently taken they produced salivation, which proved injurious to their sale, the proprietor lessened the quantity of blue pill, and added a proportionate weight of compound extract of colocynth.

All is forgiven between Abernethy and Elliotson in the expediency of a popular formula.

George G. Sigmond, a specialist in materia medica, also attributed the popularity of the pills to Abernethy. Writing in his 1850 compilation of mercury treatments, Sigmond extolled Abernethy's clear and accurate knowledge of the principles of science. Abernethy did not have the learning of other medical men, and he did not encumber his writings with phrases from the Greek or try to erect artificial systems. "He watched the powers of Nature; he recalled the surgeon to the path of physic, he showed to him the effect of local disorders upon the constitution, and the reciprocal operations of constitutional disorders upon local diseases." Like any good surgeon Abernethy concentrated upon the effect of the diseased body part ("local diseases") upon the whole. Abernethy's object was "to excite, by means of medicine, a more copious and healthy secretion."

Abernethy's method of exciting secretions when it came to mercury was to limit the dosage. Sigmond wrote that he avoided the mistake of increasing the quantity of mercury given when a benefit became perceptible. "In small doses the biliary secretion is corrected, and the digestive organs are placed in a healthier condition; larger quantities exert an influence on the whole constitution, and alter the state of the nervous system."

Sigmond wrote that five grains of the "blue pill" taken at night would not irritate the bowels, but that generally three grains were sufficient. The mouth could be affected, but this was the result of the "badness" of the pill resulting from sulfuric acid in the rose conserve used as one of the ingredients. The blue pill could replace calomel, mercurous chloride, taken as a remedy, where the calomel was too irritating.

With all the benefits the blue pill conferred on the state of health, the digestive system and therefore the skin and the operations of the mind, "it is liable to be followed with too sanguine expectations ... its abuse is as formidable a cause of disease as its proper employment is certain of being a source of health." Mercury was both a remedy and a poison.

Sigmond had already reviewed the disasters resulting from consumption of mercury in massive doses, Barton Booth's death among them, and this treatment by volume he clearly rejected. What he did find in Abernethy's formulation of the blue pill was a moderate intake of mercury which had wide constitutional effects as long as it remained moderate but which had severe local effects if it became excessive. This mercury environment was one of controlled dosage.

Sigmond did speculate upon the pill's action, attributing it to the ability of mercury to enhance the electrical storage of the body so evidently affected by outside factors such as the weather, and hence the mood of the person which could be gloomy (warm, humid weather, discharged electricity) or cheerful (temperate, dry weather, stored electricity). Sigmond updated Abernethy's ideas to refer to Faraday's well-known electrical experiments with mercury. This allowed him to maintain that the pills varied in their effects depending on exterior factors. The objective for Abernethy and Sigmond, and those who knowingly or unknowingly took their advice, was an ordinary health maintained amid the vicissitudes of mood and climate.

The little blue pills defined the dosage regime that balanced between benefit and harm. There was no idea of main action and side effects, only a shifting set of outcomes dependent upon dosage. The size of the blue pills described an environment of mercury consumption: they were large enough to deliver mercury for positive outcomes and small enough to permit excess with resulting negative outcomes to be measured as a quantity of pills. Mercury could be used or abused in this form, creating a line across which health and illness are interchangeable. Internal consumption of mercury is measured in blue pills.

A.P.W. Philip, a physician and Fellow of the Royal Society practicing in Washington, D.C., spelled out the relative value of different forms of mercury in greater detail. Philip had no doubt about the medicinal force of mercury itself, which he saw influenced the action of the extreme parts of the nerve and blood systems more powerfully than any other medicine. Its injurious effects came from the same cause.

Of the four mercurials that he reviewed, Philip found the blue pill the most convenient and effective, and generally lighter on the stomach than another preparation closer to raw mercury. He supported Abernethy's plan of using mercury in smaller doses given more frequently. All agents affecting the living body were stimulants in low doses and sedatives in larger doses, he thought. The object was to find that dose of mercury that suited the constitution of the individual being treated and that exercised in that individual's constitution the array of stimulant and sedative effects needed to cause improvement. Philip quantified the stimulant-sedative effects of mercury in terms of blue pill dosage:

> Mercury is one of those agents in which the stimulant and sedative effects are so nearly balanced that neither predominates so much as to obtain for it either appellation, but it observes the same law as all other agents capable of affecting the living animal body.... Is there a dose, then, so small as to produce little or no sedative effect, and yet capable of the stimulant effect on which we have reason to believe the beneficial tendency of this medicine always depends?

Philip's experience was that the dosage ranged between half a grain of blue pill, the largest dose, to an eighth part of a grain, the smallest dose from which much good could arise. Individual constitutions might respond to a lower dosage given over longer intervals. "By these doses, given at such intervals, we can in most constitutions, and for a considerable length of time, in some for an unlimited, obtain the stimulant without the sedative effect of the medicine, which ought to be the great object in the employment of mercury."

Neither Sigmond nor Philip referred to Belloste's pill; the ingredients of the pill fixed by Abernethy had become an assumed standard left to the compounding pharmacist. The amount and timing of dosage were organized according to a schedule appropriate to the individual constitution and the disease being treated. This placed the use of the pill in the hands of the prescribing physician, who had his own theories on how the systems of the body operate. But it also gave the apothecary an opportunity to sell a preparation with known components that fit into the treatment programs of physicians and self-prescribing individuals.

In the blue pill, mercury had become rationalized as an internal remedy and fixed as a standard of internal mercury consumption. Its weighty mass was contained in a pill, which also could be called a "blue mass." It was a heavy pill which could penetrate the finest channels of the body, into mood and temper itself. The charge of mercury clearing out the stomach Belloste adapted into a clearing out of the body's fine network. In the hands of its later advocates, this produced an internal mercury atmosphere through a continual small dosage of pills never very large in size. This mercury did not reappear anywhere; it was absorbed by the body.

At least for the consumer, there was no question that mercury entered the stomach, blood and nerves beneficially as a pill where in other forms it was poison. The blue pill did much to make raw mercury into a threat while establishing the idea of a regular dosage needed to perpetuate health. The violent cures of sweats and salivation, of purges and defecation, were past; the steady beat of life went on with the help of pills.

All of the traditions of mercury use for drugs — Arabic, Indian, Chinese, Tibetan — developed small pills composed to have digestive and mental effects. The pills answered to culturally specific conceptions of body states that would in turn respond to medication. Pills were made of active ingredients and symbolic ingredients, with mercury remaining one of the most conspicuous elements in both categories.

There had to be some immediate result from taking the pill, a taste and a shift of feeling, which was the work of ingredients, often derived from plants. As hereditary and initiatory pharmacy was set down in recipe books and taught in schools, the mystique surrounding the making of pills became encapsulated in names emphasizing an identifying attribute of the pill: color, shape, smell, resemblance to other objects, such as jewels. This enclosed mystique was passed on to pills manufactured and mass-produced. Their packaging projected an appearance of being hand-assembled by an expert steeped in tradition.

Tibetan pill-making, derived from both Chinese and Indian sources, evolved the preparation of mercury to make "black pills" (*rin-chen ril-nag*) useful in the treatment of nerve illnesses and healing bone fractures. Mercury also was combined with long lists of components to yield "jewel-pills" or "precious medicines" that incorporated or at least resembled gold, silver, gems, pearls, seashells or coral (rarities in Tibet). Tibetan pharmacies in northern India, Germany and America sold a packaged pill, *Dschu-mar 2 (Jewel Pill 25)*, accompanied by a brochure in Tibetan and English explaining that the late seventeenth-century physician-monk Tenzin Phuntsok saved himself from an unspecified deadly illness by devising and taking the pill. The pills themselves were tiny grain-like blue jewels. The ingredients and the metaphors surrounding their use were very different from those of European and American mercury pill traditions, but the physical form of small-dose mercury had assumed a similar shape.

Apart from a few scattered references, it is not possible to know how these low-dose mercury pills were used and what effects they had on their consumers in Europe, China, India or Tibet. There is a sense of eternity about them: when they enter the period of print they are projected backward to early scholars and religious figures, and they are not openly evaluated. There is no present-day news to report their effects.

The blue pill standardized the consumption of mercury in nineteenth century America in a manner opposed to proprietary medicines. Its use can be traced through references in newspapers, advertising and pharmaceutical manuals. It became the common knowledge which purveyors of new remedies could address.

The makers of Gouraud's Italian Medicated Soap announced in an advertisement in the *New York Daily Times* of June 25, 1853 (page 7) that mercurial ointment induced salivation as readily as quicksilver taken internally in the form of blue pill. And so their soap applied to the skin also reached the seat of diseases "by absorption." They did not claim or deny that the soap contained mercury; they only suggested that the soap was as good as blue pills in delivering its anti-inflammatory to the body.

"Do not believe," reads a column ad in the *New York Daily Times* of April 12, 1856 (page 5),

> You are positively obliged to resort to calomel or blue pill for bilious attacks, headache or giddiness which Spring brings in its train. DR. SANDFORD'S INVIGORATOR removes these difficulties without debilitating your system or preventing attention to business.

Here the advertised medication would calm attacks on stability originating in the stomach while allowing the consumer to continue with business, which calomel and blue pill apparently did not allow. Treating the ills of the body required keeping it in the busy flow of the city. Making offers in the same densely packed column are a dyeing establishment, several purveyors of cod-liver oil, a seller of trees and shrubs, an ice-house, a cough candy, a phrenologist and a dealer in gas fittings. A casual reader would be looking over the life of the city.

"Radway's Regulators" is a product that appeared in an announcement in early 1856 that occupies most of one of these newspaper columns and attempts to incorporate the variety of the surrounding columns. According to the copy, coughs, rheumatism, and headaches are local manifestations of blockage which can be released through mild regulation. The drastic measures of cod-liver oil, blue pill and other emetics and purgatives are not needed to restore health.

The image of constricted flow of fluids that Belloste evoked to promote crude mercury and milder pills could be used to sell yet milder pills of unknown composition. The blue pill, which began the trend toward subtler, more sustained medication, was itself opposed by "regulators" and "relaxants." The stream of fluids Belloste wanted to drive forcibly with mercury was now mildly managed to avoid the initial impact of the medication's arrival.

Dr. C. G. Wittstein's handbook of "secret remedies" (1871), which reveals the ingredients of many extravagantly named nostrums of the period, and contrasts the monetary value of a sample with its price, analyzes Radway's Renovating Resolvent as a vinous tincture of ginger and cardamon sweetened with sugar, and Radway's Ready Relief, besides a compound of "r" alliterations, an ethereal tincture of capsicum, with alcohol and camphor, the ingredients of considerably less value than what was charged for the medication. These alternatives to blue pill were strong, hot-flavored mildly alcoholic concoctions with sugar that would eventually become throat lozenges and cough syrups. Opposing mineral and metal pills made of mercury, arsenic and antimony with unfamiliar vegetable heat promised to revivify and regulate the sluggish, flaccid fluids of the body, an imagined interior best activated by peppery flavoring and the heady mist of spirits.

In some advertisements the rejection of mercurials, antimoniacals and arsenicals, strong metal drugs, became explicit, and part of a campaign against allopathic medicine. Allopathic medicine treated a condition by attempting to overwhelm symptoms with the opposite sensation, cold applied to inflammation, weight forced into stilled passages. The homeopathic approach called for highly diluted herbal mixtures with effects the same as the disease treated, to initiate a healing response in the body. Belloste would seem to be an extreme allopath in his crude mercury advocacy, but his mercury pills reduced the amount of mercury almost to a homeopathic level. This possible vegetable action of a mineral made the blue pill a necessary target of the mild-vegetable-medicine promoters. The old battle between those favoring mineral remedies and those favoring vegetable remedies, the Paracelsans and the herbalists, is joined again in the accusations against mercury.

Belloste is never mentioned in the American advertising, but Abernethy is. The copy for "Holloway's Pills," an advertisement printed several times in 1856, reads, "Abernethy's insidious remedy, blue pill, pervades the system with a mineral poison, while HOLLOWAY'S great medicine composed exclusively of vegetable extracts regulates every internal function, and leaves no sting behind."

In a revelation by a "spirit rapper" at a meeting of the "faculty," the shade of Dr. Abernethy recommends Leslie's Aromatic Stomach Bitters. The venerable inventor of the blue pill speaks beyond the grave in favor of a vegetable digestive more comforting than mercury.

The blue pill had become the prevalent medication with side effects well enough known to the general public that it was the mineral exemplar for advertisers of alternatives to attack and for anyone planning an expedition, a war or a home to include. The inventory of medical supplies for the Lewis and Clark Expedition (1801–8) included Glauber salts, laudanum, purgatives and mercurial ointment but no blue pills. They also brought Dr. Rush's Bilious Pills formulated by Dr. Benjamin Rush for the treatment of venereal disease. These were a mixture of diarrhoeic jalap and sweat-inducing calomel that cleared body passages all at once and not by soft permeation as blue pill supposedly did.

During the American Civil War, quartermasters routinely stocked quantities of the pills, pleaded for more and reputedly gave them out at every opportunity. "Blue pill" was the Union soldiers' nickname for a bullet, its weight and deadliness recalling the medication. The Boston preacher George H. Hepworth, who served as a chaplain in the Union army, portrayed the soldier's response to receiving a dose of blue pills. "But what are three blue pills to an ounce of lead? To be sure, in the aggregate, blue pills have killed more than the lead. But the particular three will do no harm; for the cunning dog, who knows his own disease, the moment the nurse's back is turned, quietly disposes of the hoard by throwing it out the window."

"Do you value the blue-pills of your father?" asks a medical metaphor-laden political essay. "Then vote for WOOD." Blue pills were an established part of tradition that New York mayor Fernando Wood's supporters hoped would sustain him at the polls.

Yet most descriptions of the use of the blue pill and its consequences, like the advertisements, do not praise the medication. "Too free use of mercury" had long been a condition itself calling for detoxification, or at least for time spent steeping in Hanna's Chemical Vapor Baths, which seem to be a pleasing answer to harsh mineral fumigations for unmentioned syphilis as Gouraud's Italian Medicated Soap vegetally answered mineral inunctions for the same condition.

"Blue pill" was the mercury taken with consequences, and it was the mercury to be cured.

In an 1852 essay on "Pesterments—Not Troubles," an anonymous author reflects on the less serious problems of life and offers as a routine solution, "Take a blue pill to-night, and a Seidlitz in the morning." Get an additional hour of sleep, work the bile out of your eyes "and the gloomy aspect of things will marvelously change." It is a measure of how routine medication has shifted that Seidlitz powders were still commercially available as late as the 1950s, but nothing was known of the blue pill.

Job Wort, the "Blighted Being" of a farce that premiered at the Broadway Theatre, in Manhattan on Thanksgiving night 1854, contracts with an apothecary to end his life with notoriety rather than live without fame. But then Job discovers that the lady who blighted his heart actually loves him and that he is the heir to a fortune left by a deceased relative. He wants to live, but suspects everyone being in league with the apothecary to slip him something lethal. A friend has intervened, however, and substituted a dose of blue pill "instead of a more active poison." Job lives, with only a slight upset.

A doctor testified during the inquest into the death of John W. Williams, a Westchester farmer, that calomel mixed with chloride in the man's stomach might have produced the corrosive sublimate and acid that perforated the walls of the lower digestive tract and caused his death. Morphine and blue pills also had been administered, but the stronger mercury compounds caused the chemical reactions that led to the man's death. Yet the verdict of the coroner's jury was that the corrosive sublimate was deliberately given by some party or parties unknown (the farmer's abused wife?) to poison him. The blue pill was just a bystander in this gastric drama.

By 1885 when a Parisian woman reported in the *London Daily Dispatch* told the police officer who apprehended her, "Tu me fais l'effet d'une pillule" ("You have the effect of a pill on me" or "You're a pill"), the reporter speculated that if she meant a blue pill she would have been treated with greater contempt. A blue pill does not cure; it causes a bellyache, but no more than that.

In a column printed on July 18, 1865, in the aftermath of President Abraham Lincoln's assassination, a correspondent recalled his visit to Mrs. Lincoln "before she left for Chicago." He wrote that he told her that he always expected that "the slavery" would poison Lincoln as it had Presidents Harrison and Taylor. The idea appeared new to her, but then she recalled that Lincoln had been very ill for several days "from the effects of a dose of blue pills taken shortly before his second inaugural."

Lincoln had been ill, and required a dose of his usual medicine, blue pills; Mrs. Lincoln sent to a drug store and gave them to Lincoln before going to bed at night. He was even more ill the following morning, looking deathly pale, and was unable to rise from bed to conduct pressing business. Blue pills had never affected him that way before; he and she concluded that the attendant at the drug store did not know how to compound the pills, and resolved never to order them from that establishment again.

The correspondent described a similar pallor of Union army officers living in a boarding house in Georgia. Many of the officers died, but the woman who told the correspondent about the happenings never learned the conclusions of an investigation. The correspondent believed that "those fiends" had infiltrated an unknown poison into the officers through their boarding house meals, and into Lincoln through his blue pills. The assassinations are not over, he fearfully wrote.

The blue pills were the medium for the poison, not the poison itself. Lincoln routinely took blue pills when he was not feeling well, but the pills he wife obtained from a drugstore where a known conspirator (it was later learned) had worked must have contained the same venom used to poison Union officers in the occupied South. The older explanations, that slaves working as kitchen help deliberately poisoned Lincoln as they had earlier masters, including presidents, or that the drug preparer did not assemble the pill ingredients correctly, gave way to the conspiracy theme born of the assassination and assassination attempts.

Lincoln's use of blue pills, not unusual for the time, has recently undergone a revision similar to the retrospective mercury poisoning found in the careers of Isaac Newton and other experimenters.

During his early years as an attorney and local politician in Illinois, a much-reported research study maintains, Lincoln consumed the pills to overcome his depression. He traded the melancholy mental state for a perpetually upset stomach, and, historians believe, a tendency to violent rages. There is no record of what motivated his decision to stop taking the pills. The even-tempered, judicious Lincoln who led the nation through the Civil War was not absorbing mercury. Only someone focused on mercury causation would see that leadership style resulting from no longer taking the little blue pills. Lincoln's presidency was not the result of single material causes, or their absence.

There also is the evidence cited by Dolores Hayden that Lincoln admitted to a law partner and later biographer that a sexual adventure infected him with syphilis, and that he later infected his wife, Mary Todd. That may be so, and many of the takers of blue pills may have been similarly afflicted.

The severity of Lincoln's depression is suggested by the therapy chosen to cancel it out. It was recognized that the pills were poisonous. "Properly managed, they are gentle in their operation, and certain to afford relief, but they may be converted into most dangerous weapons," wrote Sigmond.

The pills' small size limited the dosage to a set of effects that overwhelmed melancholy with other bodily conditions. Compare this with an herbal treatment for depression, an infusion of the herb wormwood. This is one of the bitterest tastes that still can be considered bitter. The negative flavor value shocks the routine of depression and replaces it with an immediate sensation that has to be assimilated. Wormwood is not poisonous. Opium, which Lincoln occasionally used, was taken to relieve pain, and is a poison to which the consumer builds a tolerance.

The little blue pills also were gradually tolerated in the greater doses needed to produce the uplifting reaction in the body. No one claimed, however, that mercury was addictive. In small doses it was maintained as long as the recognizable effects were desirable. Contrary to the historians' theory, Lincoln clearly was still consuming the pills regularly after he became the even-tempered leader of the Union, and could even be acknowledged taking them after he became "the Nation's Martyr."

Lincoln's controlled self-medication with mercury can be contrasted with the practices of his younger contemporary, Boston Corbett. Corbett was an English immigrant who had a conversion experience in Boston and vowed to become "a soldier for the Lord." He enlisted in the Union Army repeatedly, and was in the squadron selected to pursue Lincoln's assassin, John Wilkes Booth. Having spotted the cornered Booth in a barn that was set on fire, Corbett shot him, in self-defense, he claimed, and was acquitted in the subsequent court-martial.

Both before that event and after, Corbett exhibited mood swings and committed sudden acts of violence. Soon after his conversion in Boston he castrated himself with a pair of scissors, then went through his day before eventually visiting a hospital. After the war he waved a gun at a group of men who questioned his story of Booth's death. Having moved to the Kansas territory, he lived in a hole in the ground and stockpiled guns, but also managed to have himself appointed assistant doorkeeper of the legislature. He was committed to an asylum after he produced a gun in the legislature building, he said because he heard the assembly's opening prayer mocked. He escaped from the asylum on horseback, and headed toward Mexico never to be heard from again.

Even Corbett's own contemporaries blamed his temperament on the mercury he imbibed practicing his trade of hatter, which he left and returned to intermittently throughout his life. It would seem that Corbett kept himself mercurialized through his sometime occupation. He had worked in a Troy, New York, hat shop not long before moving to Boston and having his conversion experience, and he found work in hat factories wherever he went. It is not known if he ever resorted to blue pills or calomel. There were many hatters who went through life without exhibiting behavior like Corbett's, and a few patrio-religious fanatics who never had such exposure to mercury.

By attaching himself to sacred causes, Corbett procured public accommodations to his threats of violence. His life is an example of how frontier society could accept and employ someone with a mental disorder, whatever may have caused it. If mercury had a role in his disorder then, he was not controlling it through the medium of the pills as Lincoln did, but by occupational exposure while exercising the one work skill he possessed.

Occupational exposure had existed for a long time, but the blue pills, a way of modulating mercury intake, were a recent development. Hatters traditionally had no choice but to absorb mercury and permanently exhibit the symptoms. The "Mad Hatter" title could be applied to frantic individuals who were not hatters. Lewis Carroll's character by that name is an evocation of a recognized type (and of an individual).

Corbett exercised his occupational mercurialism in a way generally similar to the consumption of blue pills, though not as fine-tuned. He was not replacing depression with mercury effects as Lincoln was; he was negotiating his own tendencies around whatever impetus occasional mercury gave him. In Kansas, far from hat factories, he was still mad in his way.

Lincoln and Corbett are related to each other by arbitrary events and by personal choices some of which involve assimilating mercury. Politics and religion formed the public matrix of their relations which mercury enters as an element allowing a further interpretation of their behavior. For many people this information is not available. Simply the existence and use of the blue pill associated with its effects suggests an environment, but the details of its participants are lacking because the blue pill existed to suppress outward appearances otherwise expressed through religion and politics. It was used to erase evidence of its use. It took a long time for historians to recognize that someone in the public eye, Lincoln, used it.

The concept of a medication's side effects becomes separated from its main action when the role of the side effects in the main action is suppressed. The blue pill and its mercury contents were an artifact of this distinction. Mercury may have had a great many forms and purposes. Enclosing it in a small pill was aimed at producing defined symptoms which mercury

Sgt. Boston Corbett, photograph from glass negative by unknown photographer, 1860–70. Courtesy of Library of Congress Prints and Photographs Division.

could produce. Melancholy became depression which could be superseded by a blue-pill stomachache.

The possible poisoning of President Lincoln through (not by) his usual medication recalls that a medication was defined by long experience.

And long experience with a drug could be the result of habit, which with blue pill was being recognized as not that beneficial. Harry Campbell instances "an individual to high living and a sedentary life ... suffering from a sluggish liver and constipation" who felt better each time after he took a blue pill at night and Epsom salts the morning after "all unconscious that he is doing himself lasting harm.... *What impresses him is the immediate benefit he immediately derives from the medicine.*" Campbell does not say what that harm might be; he recommends diet and exercise to help the liver work more efficiently. It was understood by his readers that regular doses of blue pill were damaging, all the more so because the temporary relief they brought could be repeated time after time.

Campbell was also concerned that the blue pill might give the immediate relief it was supposed to. The commonest variation in the effect of a usual medication was the result of adulteration, not with the intent to poison, but only to dilute the concentration of a component for greater profit from the same amount. Remedies long taken with specific expectations were diminishing in intensity. The salubrious sweat or the copious salivation they once produced now was a glow or a spit:

> The analysis of a specimen of blue pill, largely imported into this City awhile ago, showed that it contained one-fifth the proper proportion of mercury, and on heating it on a shovel, instead of two percent of ash remaining, as from the genuine, it gave 29 per cent. Prussian blue gave it the proper color, and earthy clay its weight and bulk.... The mercury and chalk mixture, one of the mildest and most manageable of mercurials, is frequently from the bad quality of the chalk used, and by faulty preparation made an absolute poison to the infants to whom it is administered. Blue pill and calomel not unfrequently are so prepared that instead of their mild and legitimate effects, we have salivation and horrible disease.

This column in the *New York Times* at first appears to be a protest against adulteration, citing the dangers of well-known medicines made by quacks. It turns into an advertisement for Dr. Squibb's preparations now becoming known throughout the city. Doctors actually found that if they used medicines in doses established by their own long experience they were overmedicating, that is, they had become accustomed to using adulterated medicines of diminished potency. Squibb had set up a standard which conforms to the formulas set down in books. The days when even honest pharmacists made remedies according to their own standards were giving way to name brands.

Focusing on adulteration, whether poisonous or diluting, reflected a growing drive to standardize drugs. The old named medication couldn't be trusted to act as it always had. Brands, measured doses and the corporations that owned them emerged from the reputable preparations of individual pharmacists who, like Squibb in the article just quoted, can provide safeguards against counterfeits and thus assure the right dosage. Of course, Squibb also became a name brand and a corporation.

Pharmacy schools, professional training and licensing criteria, legislated purity and ingredient safety requirements and government testing laboratories all were part of devising, encoding and trying to enforce standards. This led to a complex mesh of control, liability and healing that only intensified with the discovery of new chemical remedies and proposed remedies.

The blue pill was taken up into this developing drug regime only to the extent that it could be incorporated as a traditional medicine with known properties. By the early twentieth century it was fading from the public record. It was included in the first United States Pharmacopeia, but no company tried to sell a branded blue pill. By the early twentieth century, advertisers promoting new medicines stopped even using it as a foil to the greater virtues of their proprietary products.

The laboratory exercise manual assembled by L. D. Havenhill for the Pharmaceutical Laboratory of the University of Kansas in 1913 (according to the U.S. Pharmacopeia and the National Formulary), contains recipes for making iron, lead, zinc, opium, and cod liver oil medications, as well as a number of fruit syrups and lemon juice, but there is no antimony or arsenic and only one use of mercury, Massa Hydragyri, Mass of Mercury:

Mercury	33 gm.
Glycyrrhiza, in No. 60 powder	10 gm.
Althaea, in No. 60 powder	15 gm.
Glycerin	9 gm.
Honey of Rose	33 gm.
To make	**100 gm.**

Triturate the mercury with the Honey of Rose until it is extinguished and globules of mercury are no longer visible under a lens magnifying at least two diameters. Then add the Glycerin, then the Glycyrrhiza, and Althaea gradually, and continue the trituration until the mass is homogeneous. Keep the product in well-closed containers.

Research: What are the synonyms for the Mass?
[written in pencil below] —
Blue Mass.

The prescribed preparation was almost a visual image of mercury globules vanishing by fine mixing into the slightly acidic sweetness of honey that had absorbed rose oil from petals. A taste of licorice (glycyrrhiza powder fine enough to pass through a number 60 sieve) was bound with the honey with the powder of marshmallow root (althaea) of the same texture, and a small amount of glycerin to assure smoothness. The mass had to be placed in a stoppered bottle for the same reason Carlo Lancillotti advised chemists to store their mercury in inverted syrup containers, to keep the mercury contents from sublimating. The mercury was held inside the mass inside the container.

Since 1820, when it was first issued, the U.S. Pharmacopeia, the privately compiled and periodically revised listing of accepted drug formulas, had listed "blue pill" and "blue mass" as names for the same mercury preparation. When the University of Kansas manual was used by a pharmacy student, who carefully noted the reduced portions in a column of blanks alongside the portions adding up to 100 grams, the answer to the question "What is a synonym for Mass of Mercury?" was not "Blue pill."

Forgetting of blue pill had proceeded to such a point by 1913 that there were a number of deaths in New York State of people who swallowed white pills containing bichloride of mercury (a common antiseptic) thinking they were quinine pills (also colored white) or some other medicine. Pharmacists planned a statewide conference, and an amendment to the Sanitary Code was considered: bichloride of mercury pills must be colored blue and clearly labeled "poison."

There was no mention of "blue pill" as a phrase in public records for many decades, and when the phrase came to be commonly recognized again it was just as a description of a pill with a patented name which does not contain mercury at all.

7

‒‒‒∞∞∞‒‒‒

Rob de Laffecteur

A man saving the life of a suicidal friend by substituting a blue pill for the poison makes a different sense when "blue pill" refers to a trademarked male sexual enhancer, and that could change again if another blue pill gains prominence. A self-reported witticism of the mid–nineteenth-century physician Philippe Ricord would make no sense at all even by the middle of the twentieth century.

Ricord was taking part in salon banter about the social credentials of a doctor, Giraudeau de Saint-Gervais. "He's the son of a miller from the town of Saint-Gervais," said one of the men. "What do you think, my dear Ricord," another doctor present asked him, "Does the Giraudeau family belong to the nobility?" "Yes, certainly," Ricord replied, "to the nobility of *Rob*."

At the very least this story tells us how the word "rob" was pronounced — the same as the French and English word "*robe.*" There were two ways to gain (as opposed to inherit) noble rank under French kings from the time of Louis XIV onward — through military accomplishment (*noblesse de l'épée*, nobility of the sword) and through administrative staying-power (*noblesse de la robe*, nobility of the gown). Ricord's pun was to substitute an anti-syphilis medication for the robe of the noble in answering the question about the social status of the doctor being discussed.

Dispensing that medication was how Giraudeau earned his peculiarly medical claim to high standing. As Paris society knew, Giraudeau had obtained the warrant (*marque*) to sell his syphilis cure under the name of Boyveau-Laffecteur, a Paris tradition since 1778.

For such a glittering, lively fluid, mercury has its secrets. Mercury penetrates everywhere, and the story of rob de Laffecteur is an account of its veiled entrance into the body, as it carried its suppliers upward in the body politic.

As with the blue pill, rob de Laffecteur was a name that entailed a manner of preparation and a use, but unlike the blue pill, which refined weighty crude mercury into a finely divided, colored, aromatic convenience, rob de Laffecteur hid its mercury under an exotic name, and it was mainly for treating syphilis. The presence of mercury in rob de Laffecteur enclosed in syrup a game of syphilis and other games in which syphilis and mercury were involved.

Gerard van Swieten, a Dutch physician employed in the eighteenth-century Austrian court, spent his lifetime composing a commentary on the *Aphorisms* of his mentor Boerhaave. He sketched the stages of infection with syphilis, and became an advocate of a treatment of syphilis that limited the amount of mercury given to the amount that would show an effect on the patient. To control the mouth sores and drastic salivation that came from swallowing corrosive sublimate in pills and powders, he dissolved it in alcohol and added flavoring agents to cover the horrid taste. Van Swieten's liquor was a milder delivery of mercury than rubs and fumigations, and it didn't require a chemist to make it. Its use spread under van Swieten's and other names.

It was a model for other liquid preparations of mercury compounds to pass them bearably into the interior of the body without damaging the tissues on the way.

Anatomists and physiologists had observed the specifically vascular penetrativeness of mercury into animal and human bodies. From the late eighteenth century onward, injections of mercury were used to prepare specimens showing the outlines of the vessels in silver. It was injected into living animals, particularly dogs, who were then dissected to learn where it had gone. Thomas Beddoes, attempting to determine the source of nodules found in the lungs of those who had suffered from consumption, injected liquid mercury into puppies and found that it had formed the center of nodules in their lungs. This confirmed his hypothesis that the noxious agent that produced the nodules in the lungs of consumption victims must have entered from the outside. Entering the body, mercury would infiltrate the tissues. A liquid swallowed would make that easier than fumigations and unctions.

The need to create a palatable mercury for syphilis treatment was addressed by a great variety of experimenters, physicians and entrepreneurs drawing upon emergent industrial chemistry, herbalism and culinary arts to produce liquors and syrups that could be consumed immediately upon purchase and without the assistance of a professional applicator. Alongside the finely divided mercury of the blue pill, these medications were a way to introduce mercury into the body without feeling the force of entry.

Mercury-inclusive mixtures, designed to conceal the mercury from the consumer's body, might also conceal it entirely. Drawing upon the salubrious effects of mercury while ignoring the sweats and abscesses signaling its presence, the makers of nostrums sought the right compound in the right medium to achieve their ends. A dynamic formula of mercury-not-mercury would become the next entrance of the metal into the body.

The Bordeaux physician Isaac Bellet (or Belet) introduced another mercury compound in another liquid medium. Bellet was best known for his letters to prominent physicians on the question of maternal imagination, the Hippocratic contention that a pregnant woman's reactions might impress a material reminder of her experience on her newborn. He also wrote studies of Roman history and served as royal inspector of French mineral waters. Late in his career, in the 1760s, he introduced into the urban venereal-disease-remedies market a "syrop mercuriel" made by mixing mercuric nitrate with a thick sugar syrup.

Mercuric nitrate already was used in liniments to cause venereal sores to slough away, but its chief use at this time and after was as secretage. Dousing certain types of animal fur — rabbit and beaver — with a mercuric-nitrate solution caused the barbed sheaths of the hairs to rise from the shaft and interlock, creating a felt that could then be molded into hats. This was the secret that ceased to be one when the Catholic French king revoked the Edict of Nantes in 1685 and drove the Protestant Huguenots, many of whom were skilled fur dressers and hat makers, out of France and to England and the colonies in America. *Alice in Wonderland*'s Mad Hatter, and the Troy, New York, shops where Boston Corbett picked up his mercury were byproducts of this forced migration.

The family name Bellet was a Huguenot name, and it may just be that the syrop mercuriel was a distillation of secretage. Certainly the hatters were mad (palsied) but also free of the worst ravages of venereal disease. The syrup had the cachet of its association with secretage and lively hatters, but that was not the reason it was a "secret remedy" (*"remède secrète"*).

For much of the century, the French government and its allied professional classes were trying to suppress the "secret remedies" that proliferated in the cities and out into the countryside. These were liquids, rubs, powders and pills often named after their originator, based both on tradition and invention, all pushed into view with street cries and pamphlets containing testimonials and the address where they might be purchased. The ingredients were known and unknown, their results backed by public tests and word of mouth. The development of analytic chemistry and clinical tests were in part spurred by the attempts to identify and validate or invalidate secret remedies. Syphilis was one of the diseases addressed and mercury compounds were among the ingredients.

Jacques Horne, a military physician and consultant to aristocrats, commissioned in the early 1760s to test the potency of various mercury preparations in the treatment of syphilis, determined that a syrup containing corrosive sublimate (mercuric chloride) restored the health of syphilis sufferers without relapse. At the request of the government, Horne eventually composed a multivolume study of the mercury cures of patients under his care during the decade from 1776–86.

Horne's conclusions were attacked in print by Bellet, who advanced mercuric nitrate against corrosive sublimate in what may have been religious polemic (Protestant versus Catholic) in the form of medical controversy. Augustin Roux, a member of the Paris faculty of medicine, defended Horne's conclusions, and a pamphlet exchange continued into the 1770s.

In 1778, the year of Bellet's death, the French Crown made another attempt to co-opt the makers of secret remedies by granting the *Société Royale de Médecine* the authority to issue warrants (*brevets*) to select makers of drugs. A warrant entailed the right to sell the medicines through agents and to distribute them around the city and country. This approval could set a remedy apart from many other untried pretenders. One of the remedies they granted a warrant was rob de Laffecteur.

In 1764, he later claimed, a Paris physician named Pierre Boyveau confected a syrupy, vegetal, non-mercurial, potable treatment for syphilis. Before submitting it for endorsement, Boyveau formed a commercial partnership with his father-in-law, the marquis de Marcilly, and recruited a Ministry of War employee named Denis Laffecteur to attach his name to the partnership. In the competitive field of syphilis remedies (and of course in Old Regime society) names mattered. Aristocrats did not want their names associated with commercial enterprises, Laffecteur's name sounded as if it might accomplish something, and his employment in the Ministry of War was a connection to the always promising military market for syphilis cures.

In December 1777 Pierre Boyveau Laffecteur presented himself to M. Berthier, intendant of the Paris region, and declared that the rob de Laffecteur was the sole remedy for venereal diseases. For the time Boyveau was handling the promotion and using Laffecteur's name. Later, there would be a break.

The word "*rob*" had been used in French, English and Spanish for some time for a confiture made by boiling the juice of a fruit or vegetable to thicken it, then adding clarifying agents and perhaps some sugar to give it the consistency of honey. The most frequently prepared rob was *rob de sureau*, elderberry rob, recommended by the medical school of Salerno as a mild sudorific and purgative. When Galland needed to translate the Arabic word "*rubb*" in his 1704–17 rendition in French of part of *The Arabian Nights*, he chose the French word "*rob.*" The passage compares the charms of a woman to a sweet syrup, but Galland's readers probably tasted something a little more astringent in their rob.

Boyveau, in calling his syrup a rob, completed an act of formulation that began with van Swieten's liquor that dissolved corrosive sublimate in alcohol and Belet's syrup which incorporated mercuric nitrate. Boyveau's rob de Laffecteur referred to the purgative qualities of elderberry and similar robs but it was not supposed to contain mercury. It had effects similar to the mercury remedies and the known vegetable ones.

According to Boyveau-Laffecteur's 1777 petition to the intendant, this entirely vegetable composition of Laffecteur's own invention unfailingly cured young and old, men and women, without endangering the patient through the administration of mercury. Laffecteur asked the intendant to allow him to test the remedy on soldiers. The rob de Laffecteur's action, Laffecteur explained in a brochure printed in 1784 and describing this test, did not alter any of the animal functions, but reestablished them after they had become entangled with the syphilitic poison (*virus*).

The three soldiers in the troupe of pioneers barracked at Saint-Denis who received the rob de Laffecteur were healed to the satisfaction of Laffecteur, but Dr. Poisonnier-Desperrieres, assigned to monitor the test, had reservations. Laffecteur himself gamely admits in his brochure that the doctor suggested he repeat the trial with a larger number of subjects.

Laffecteur then obtained the authorization of the lieutenant general of the police to treat all the sick people he might want at the Bicêtre asylum. With a commission of twelve doctors in attendance, Laffecteur treated twelve subjects, three of whom were severely ill with syphilis symptoms. The rapid recovery of the patients lifted Laffecteur to considerable prominence over the crowded field of syphilis specialists, who then tried to cast doubt on the composition of his rob de Laffecteur.

Syphilis can't be cured without mercury, the critics said. Two authoritative chemists charged with analyzing rob de Laffecteur affirmed that they found no trace of mercury, but hedged their conclusion, saying that there was no guarantee it was entirely without mercury, that some bit might have escaped their investigation. It was noticed that those who used rob de Laffecteur salivated copiously as they would under mercury treatment. A formula for rob de Laffecteur that later passed into pharmacopeias from military sources made it out to be made up primarily of sarsaparilla, honey and sugar, with small amounts of sesame and rose. Franz Swediaur, who commented on rob de Laffecteur from medical experience in his treatise on venereal diseases, said that from the physical reactions of patients he was sure it contained not only mercury, but mercury in its most lethal form, corrosive sublimate, soluble mercuric chloride. "It is amazing," he wrote, "that under a government enlightened and humane, the sale and administration of a drug like corrosive sublimate is allowed."

Laffecteur counterattacked the doubters in their home base. He gave the formula for rob de Laffecteur to the *Société Royale de Médecine* and asked for their authorization to promote it. They issued a warrant to the state council, for reasons evident in the order (*arrêt*) that the council promulgated on September 12, 1778. Boyveau Laffecteur was granted permission to "sell and distribute in all of France, the anti-syphilitic Rob, with the charge that he deliver it for the treatment of venereal diseases only under the supervision of professionals (*gens de l'art*)."

This privilege would be the economic identity of the rob de Laffecteur bought, sold, and disputed in lawsuits as the monarchy fell, the republic was formed, Napoleon became First Consul and then Emperor, the monarchy was restored, and then the empire again, until the privilege was vacated by the courts under the second empire in 1866.

Laffecteur obtained the stamp of the authorities, civil and military. He secured the collusion of the medical profession by sponsoring trials presided over by eminent doctors and by requiring a written prescription for the sale of his thick, aromatic syrup. He had printed, distributed and posted on walls and buildings copies of the official orders, and he planted articles in journals.

In the *Gazette de Santé* of October 15, 1778, a seemingly disinterested piece began, "As long as the venereal disease has existed in Europe, the means to combat its frightening effects have been ceaselessly sought." Since the beginning, sweat-causing woods and mercury have been the treatments of choice, with mercury the most powerful. But mercury had its inconveniences. From there, Laffecteur declared that his remedy, proven to be without a trace of metal, had withstood public trials to become the happiest response to this scourge of humanity. A thick syrup, rather, a rob, with a "not disagreeable taste," this cure was available upon application with a ticket signed by a doctor at the sieur Laffecteur, rue de Rondi.

Laffecteur's system of authoritative publicity spread the name "rob de Laffecteur" throughout France. Cities were swelling with populations of former peasants who became literate and learned of rob de Laffecteur almost as soon as they learned of syphilis and mercury. Laffecteur's genius was to focus the (fraudulent) vegetable opposition to mercury treatments on his rob de Laffecteur, and call all of France to witness through the same currents of publication and enlistment of key supporters that soon launched a larger political revolution throughout the country.

In 1785 he begins a pamphlet written in defense of his *"rob anti-syphilitique,"*

> When I gave an account in 1779 of the efforts I had made until then, to make my remedy known and prove that one could cure venereal diseases without mercury, I did it because the greatest number of those in the healing arts cast doubt upon the existence of the means to which I pretended.

"Had I come from abroad claiming miraculous results," he continued, "there would be reason to question my claims. Under the very eyes of doctors and surgeons of Paris I have healed the sick...."

> I have not wanted to quarrel with anyone, however Mr. Andrieux, in a notice he distributes, to proclaim the incalculable merit of a mercurial powder of the Chevalier de Gouderneau ... dares to assert that he has healed the sick I have fruitlessly treated for entire years, which I defy him to prove, and offer to demonstrate is false, proposing to him to have singled out twenty or thirty of the most severely infected, the despair of the Hospital, the least susceptible to healing by known mercury methods, in fact incurables; he will treat half of them with the powders and no other help, while I will treat the other half with my remedy.

Laffecteur soon was addressing the citizen representatives of the convention that formed the ruling body of state following the overthrow of the monarchy, offering them his anti-syphilitic rob de Laffecteur at cost for use on incurables in hospitals, military and civilian, agreeing to receive no compensation at all for those not healed by his hands. Despite the encouragement of Laffecteur's supporters, the minister of war gave an evasive answer to the offer, and the best he could manage was to obtain an order from the Committee of Public Safety, some of these same supporters, permitting him to export bottles of the syrup from the Republic.

While he was reviving the rob de Laffecteur franchise in the following years, Giraudeau exhibited a copy of a decree from the revolutionary Committee of Public Safety allowing the marquis de Marcilly to remain in Paris to administer the application of the invaluable remedy in public hospitals. An aristocrat would not have been allowed to remain in the city alive unless he was making a signal contribution to the revolution, thus the great worth of the rob de Laffecteur was implied. But this paper of Giraudeau's was only a copy.

Boyveau had an eye to the growing overseas market for syphilis treatments and to the value of sophisticated literary advertising, which had the potential to expand support for his product by recruiting elites. Before the revolution, he commissioned a hack poet to write an ode to the rob de Laffecteur. But in 1793, with the execution of the king and queen, Boyveau-Laffecteur and Laffecteur split up, and afterward quarreled with each other over the 1771 warrant and the merits of rob Boyveau-Laffecteur against rob Laffecteur.

With the next century rob de Laffecteur continued to be sold, and there were further proclamations from its two proprietors. Other pretenders appeared, Boyveau's partner Hoffman and a Bordeaux rob-maker named Gouzil, who claimed that he purchased the formula from the marquis de Marcilly, who Gouzil said had obtained it from an Arab, a chain of transmission in keeping with the Arabic origins of the word.

Chemical tests involving the rob de Laffecteur began to appear in the chemistry and pharmacy journals and proceedings of the pharmacists' association. As in later periods, mercury content of specimens posed a challenge that chemists attempted to meet with new equipment and improved analytic techniques. Henry, chief of the central pharmacy of Paris hospitals, noted in an 1811 article that metallic mercury was found in the rob de Laffecteur bottles, and thus it must be contained in the rob itself. At first the researchers simply established that it was not possible to use standard reagent tests to demonstrate the presence or absence of mercury salts in the rob de Laffecteur. Corrosive sublimate was known to be highly soluble in ether, and one chemist, Tapis, persistently asserted that he had extracted corrosive sublimate from the rob de Laffecteur using ether, while others firmly contested his claim.

This debate continued, but obviously the tests would not have been initiated if it wasn't already known that the rob de Laffecteur did contain mercury artfully concealed in a vegetable matrix. It was just a question how it was hidden there. Henry and Guibourt, in their *Traité de Pharmacie*, with bland irony advised the sick to invert the bottles and shake them before taking each dose of the syrup in order to redissolve the mercury.

Rob de Laffecteur's most energetic supplier emerges into the record in a criminal proceeding. Dr. Giraudeau de Saint-Gervais in May 1829 was accused of illegally selling a secret remedy. The expert panel of a physician and two pharmacists who reported to the judicial tribunal stated that contrary to the law Giraudeau was guilty of publishing an incomplete formula for his drug, and included indecent phrasing in his brochures of "advice for victims of love." The pharmacists were especially annoyed that Giraudeau deposited his bottles with them for delivery to patients only upon presentation of a prescription from a physician. "Although he speaks of his disinterest and philanthropy, analysis by experts shows that he is selling for 6 and 12 francs robs that cost him 24 sous." With 60 sous to the franc that was a considerable profit margin.

The experts also concluded that the rob de Laffecteur prepared in their presence did contain the ingredients according to formula, but in portions too small to have significant medicinal activity. And the doses were never indicated on the bottle. Giraudeau was fined 600 francs.

In 1831, however, "le rob de Boyveau Laffecteur" joined "les pillules de Belloste" as two of the six officially listed secret remedies that could be sold in the capital.

Over the intervening years Giraudeau managed his practice and distribution of rob de Laffecteur at home and to the French colonies in the Americas, Polynesia and Africa by both supplying the medication and offering advice to those made ill by taking it.

Giraudeau was acting much in the same way as his predecessor, and seeking the same licenses. He did eventually purchase the rights to both rob Laffecteur and rob Boyveau-Laffecteur. The pharmacists were better organized than during Laffecteur's initiatives, and had formed an alliance with the physicians that he could not subvert. The language of his advertising brochures and the contents of his preparation itself were scrutinized, analyzed, priced and condemned. Yet Giraudeau's sales did continue. Like Laffecteur, he made an appeal for prestige by hiring a literary man to put the claims of rob de Laffecteur in verse.

Giraudeau's notes to the four parts of Auguste-Marseille Barthélémy's poem "Syphilis" (1851) included testimonials from named physicians and the minutes of a meeting of the Belgian Academy of Medicine at which the doctors declared themselves in favor of the rob de Laffecteur. The poem itself is not occupied with bare-faced advertising; it appropriates for rob de Laffecteur a tradition that had begun with the name "syphilis" itself.

Girolamo Frascatoro's Latin poem *Syphilidis sive de Morbo Gallico* (1510–30) at first attributed the malady, which he called "of Syphilis" and "the French disease" in the same title, to the French soldiers besieged in Naples in 1495.

Having captured the city on behalf of Charles VIII of France, they were attacked by forces loyal to the king of Naples and the Holy Roman Emperor, including some Spanish troops. Frascatoro, a citizen of Verona allied with Naples against the French, supported Maximilian I, the Holy Roman Emperor who controlled Spain, and his poem was a combination of medical discourse and political propaganda meant to pin the disease on the French, who themselves tended to call it "the Neapolitan disease." Venereal diseases always seem to be the fault of the enemy. In inventing the word "syphilis," Frascatoro made the disease a medical entity potentially apart from national slanders.

Barthélémy, born under the Republic in 1796 and named after the first city of the Revolution, wanted to imitate Frascatoro's Vergilian style while casting aside French blame for the contagion. Like Frascatoro, Barthélémy in the first part of his poem describes syphilis the disease without copying Frascatoro's story of a cursed hunter and a vengeful Greek god to explain its origins:

> These pustulous bandages, the clots of decay
> Swollen with a dark blood, and a rotten humor,
> When you see naked in flesh and bone,
> The imprints of illness, of flame and iron,
> Believe me your knees will weaken in fear....

The second part of Frascatoro's poem celebrates the discovery of mercury. A pitying goddess conducts the afflicted hunter underground, away from the sun god's punishment where mercury found in the earth heals him. Barthélémy has neither myth nor praise for mercury:

> But this art, so often the slave of a system,
> Combats the illness with an extreme remedy,
> And a fervent votary of the liquid metal
> Infuses it into the body it kills while saving,
> Misfortune to him who claims such assistance!

The third part of Barthélémy's epic offers the remedy, rob de Laffecteur. Frascatoro's offers a remedy too, not rob de Laffecteur, which had not been formulated in his time, but guiac wood. Some years after completing the second part of his poem, Frascatoro learned of this miraculous cure imported into Europe from the New World, which his patron Charles VII, the Holy Roman Emperor, had granted in monopoly to his chief creditors, the Fuggers banking family. Barthélémy, too, vigorously set out the virtues of this aromatic fumigant brought from afar to heal the syphilis sufferer.

But the rob that Barthélémy extols moves in the opposite direction:

> On the banks of la Plata crowned with green trees,
> On African sands, on the isles of Oceania,
> It is invoked; it hears the cry of agony,
> And in a brief space, to the mournful sufferer,
> The traveling steam-boat brings health.

In his French meter, Barthélémy uses the English phrase "steam-boat" to evoke the fastest means of international delivery. Rob de Laffecteur answers the anguished calls of the sick the world over and as the peroration of the poem puts it, like the Nile seen from the heights of the pyramids it reaches the ends of the earth, an imperishable and regenerating river.

Barthélémy's poem reflected the mercury-denying, vegetable-remedy-affirming past of syphilis treatment begun in Frascutoro's poem that named the disease "syphilis." But that poem also reflected the future of rob de Laffecteur, which Laffecteur had anticipated with his export license. By the latter part of the nineteenth century, rob de Laffecteur had disappeared from use in France, but it still was being sent in great quantities to the Americas. Frascatoro's political-economic change of loyalty from mercury to the ineffective guiac wood was perpetuated in the avowedly non-mercury but actually mercury-containing vegetable rob de Laffecteur.

Rob de Laffecteur was effective to the extent that it contained mercury and did not admit it. It was one more product that the European colonial powers could provide to their nationals abroad to meet the disease their political, economic and sexual conquests helped spread. The novelist Alphonse Daudet was taking rob de Laffecteur for his syphilis in Paris during the 1830s; the painter Paul Gauguin was taking it for his syphilis which he brought from Paris to Tahiti during the 1870s.

Giraudeau himself authored a "practical guide to curing oneself without mercury syphilitic illnesses and afflictions arising from the accumulation of blood and humors due to the use of *rob* Boyveau" (1850). The patient can cure himself or herself without the help of a doctor or pharmacist, without the mercury they prescribe and supply. The cure also applied to the illness *caused* by using rob de Laffecteur. What Giraudeau was supplying had no mercury and acted as mercury always (assertedly) had to clear out blood blockages built up from the mercury of rob de Laffecteur and other treatments. This gesture of pushing a secretly mercury-containing medicine to heal the ravages of syphilis and mercury had already communicated itself to other enterprising drug makers outside of France.

Another device which Giraudeau used was ostensibly to address himself to the female population and include a section on "maladies des femmes" in his book. For a woman to be known to have syphilis was likely to get her labeled a prostitute, even though she may have acquired the disease from a philandering husband, and so Giraudeau couched his advice to women in obscure and moralizing language. Appended to his most detailed treatise on venereal disease and catalog of treatments (1858) was a "hygienic and moral essay on prostitution." In the guise of commenting on the issues surrounding the legalization of prostitution, Giraudeau described the prostitute's life at one remove only from the naturalist works of Emile Zola soon to appear. Even this circumspect wording, added to a few illustrations of female anatomy touched by the disease, earned Giraudeau's books condemnation as indecent. Giraudeau's

Lithograph, "Cures Effected by Dr. Giraudeau de Saint-Gervais," including abuse of mercury, from his *Traité des Maladies Syphilitiques* (1858).

brochures contain indecent phrases, and the heads of families brought them to the attention of the police as monitors of morality and public decency, but that didn't prevent Giraudeau from distributing them in profusion.

By introducing an element of pornography, not a rare strategy in medical writings for the lay audience, Giraudeau aimed to attract readers to his book and his medication. Brunin Labiniau, a Brussels pharmacist who in 1851 published an extended brief in his lawsuit attempting to prevent the counterfeiting of rob de Laffecteur was volubly angered by the use of obscenity to advertise the fakes, which points to a more extensive and no doubt ephemeral use of pictures and prose making explicit references to women's sexual anatomy. The hidden mercury and the exposed body reappeared wherever rob de Laffecteur was sold.

In 1811, a New York doctor began to sell his own sarsaparilla syrup which he labeled rob de Laffecteur. The tart sweetness of sarsaparilla backed by the heat of sassafras was in itself a new medicinal flavor. Bottled syrups containing the extract of the tropical vine proliferated as patent medicines for a long list of conditions, including syphilis. Their organized sale became the basis for enterprises producing extensive print advertising, sponsoring their own contests, almanacs, games and toys for their customers.

A Philadelphia doctor named Berger prescribed "Rob of l'Affecteur" to a patient suffering from protracted and irregular use of mercury. The recovery of the man where other means had failed created a demand for the rob which was discouraged by the high price of the import from France. One of the consulting doctors, McNevis, published a recipe for the rob in a medical journal, praising it as a medication for a range of ills, including the mercurial disease. Several Philadelphia doctors began to make and prescribe the rob, replacing marsh reed grass in the original recipe with sassafras bark or guiac shavings in order to reduce the nauseating effect of repeated consumption.

Dr. N. J. Quackinboss successfully treated an upstate New York bookbinder, William Swaim, with doses of rob de Laffecteur, and on his demand shared the McNevis article with him. Swaim understood that mercury was an essential unwritten ingredient, and moving to Philadelphia where there was a market for the rob, began to manufacture an imitation. He called his own concoction, which he began selling in 1820, Swaim's Panacea, and in the title of a wellbound treatise (1824) announced that it was "a recent discovery for the cure of scrofula or king's evil, mercurial and liver disease, deep seated syphilis, rheumatism and all disorders arising from a contaminated and impure state of the blood." There followed pages of bombastic proclamations and specific case histories and testimonials illustrating the miraculous curative powers of his medicine.

Swaim espoused the same view of disease as a corrupt condition of the blood that was the basis for many treatments of diseases, similar to the rationale Belloste, Abernethy and Simonds had used to advocate finely divided mercury. Swaim's innovation in rob de Laffecteur merchandising was to claim that his cure-all could also relieve mercurial disease, which was the result of taking mercury to treat syphilis, while treating the interior cause of syphilis itself. By "deep-seated syphilis" Swaim was referring to a constellation of symptoms that began to appear some time after the initial skin rash that mercury salves seemed to banish.

Syphilis did not always cause later symptoms, and some of those infected might well believe they had banished it entirely after the chancres were quelled, but then the reappearance of sores about the body, joint pain, an unsteady walk, visual disturbances and urinary complaints marked a progression that had been going on all the while and which mercury taken externally and internally did not erase. Swaim's syphilis market was people who had already mercurialized themselves to the point of a distinct illness in an attempt to clear out the syphilis, and were desperate for an effective medication that contained no mercury.

He was therefore determined to prove against all criticism that his Panacea's healing properties were not due in any measure to mercury. As vigorous a promoter as his French counterpart, Swaim obtained testimonials from grateful consumers, and from doctors, including Dr. Nathaniel Chapman, an eminent Philadelphia practitioner and professor at the University of Pennsylvania who eventually became first president of the American Medical Association. Dr. William Gibson, one of Chapman's colleagues, displayed to students in the medical school lecture hall two frightfully ulcerated patients that Swaim's Panacea had allegedly restored to health. One of the doctors at the Philadelphia Alms House Infirmary became Swaim's merchandising agent in Europe.

Swaim priced his twelve-ounce bottles at three dollars, less than half the price of the equivalent-volume bottle imported from France. It was the high price of the imports that first resolved Swaim to seek out the formula and create his own. Rather than secure the support of doctors by making it a prescription drug as Giraudeau did, he enlisted the medical profession as sales agents, eliminating the doctor and the pharmacist, or rather combining them in a single point of sale. At the beginnings of organized medical and pharmaceutical professions, a businessman was offering doctors extra earnings within the precincts of their expertise.

Individual doctors took advantage of the offer, but the organized profession rose up against Swaim and other untrained and unlicensed quacks. The Medical Society of the City of New York formed a Committee on Quack Remedies. In a report they issued in 1827, the committee members granted that that Swaim's Panacea, like other sarsaparilla medicines, had some value in treating the later conditions of syphilis, but they deplored Swaim's sweeping claims that the Panacea could relieve cancer, scrofula, rheumatism, gout, hepatitis and the early stages of syphilis, all of them largely unaffected by sarsaparilla. Giraudeau's assertions of the healing power of his rob de Laffecteur grew progressively more expansive as well, even advertising that it could prevent cholera when the disease first arrived in Paris in 1827.

Swaim's dazzling appropriation of sarsaparilla syrup remedies already used by doctors for an extravagant list of maladies tended to undermine the authority of the healing art by creating unreasonable expectations among those made gullible by their own need for relief. A few partial cures announced by well-meaning doctors and it might seem that Swaim's really was a panacea, a cure-all, for which the doctors, not Swaim, would be held responsible if their treatments did not live up to the hopes created by Swaim's announcements.

Roy Porter's observation that the discourse of medicine is a dialogue between physician and patient while the discourse of a quack is a persuasive monologue applies to Swaim's enterprise quite neatly. The medical profession was quite concerned that Swaim's monologue would not only overwhelm but even subsume their commerce with patients.

Not long after the New York committee's declaration, the Philadelphia Medical Society's committee on quack medicines warned the Society's members that the miraculous cures Swaim claimed for his Panacea were either the result of natural recovery or they led to further illness and death. The committee revealed that the symptoms displayed by some patients consuming the syrup could only be traced to corrosive sublimate of mercury.

Among the cases doctors on the Philadelphia committee recorded was that of Mr. K., a professional document copier (scrivener) who was suffering from dyspepsia, and received from Swaim the predictable prescription of a bottle of Panacea. Swaim explained the eruption that appeared on the man's back and shoulders as "the medicine driving the disease out through his skin." After more bottles of Swaim's, the man began to salivate profusely, and the skin disturbance spread over the surface of his body to the point that three months and more Panacea later he sought a doctor's opinion. But it was too late; Mr K. died of "terminal dropsy." Another of the doctors was called to aid a man hemorrhaging so copiously from ulcers in his mouth that he was in danger of suffocating. This victim had followed the advice of friends and taken three or four bottles of Swaim's Panacea for his rheumatic pains. He salivated heavily and his jaw sloughed off skin, leading to the bleeding, which killed him when it relapsed.

The irregularity of the symptoms' appearance among Panacea users suggested that the mercury compound was mixed in some batches by unscrupulous sellers eager for the strong physical reaction that corrosive sublimate promised. The Philadelphia committee implied that the Panacea, which they also held up as poorly mixed, already contained mercury which individual distributors augmented. They concluded that without mercury Swaim's syrup was worthless, and with mercury it was a threat.

As did Giraudeau, Swaim, his agents and imitators made an effort to include women among their users. They did not label it a specific for "female complaints" as did other tonics on the market. Instead they combined an imagery of syphilis with women's cosmetic use of mercury to produce an ephemeral statement of the hidden nature of both syphilis and mercury. In the process, they showed that the secret malady and the secret remedy were now advertising secrets, that is, advertised as secret.

A hand-colored lithograph that the London branch of Swaim's company produced in the 1830s for distribution to stores where the Panacea was sold depicts "Nancy Linton." According to the caption it is a "Faithful Representation of her Actual Appearance & Condition after having been Cured by the use of Swaim's Panacea." What she has been cured of is not immediately apparent from the accompanying picture. An emaciated young woman is seated at a tea table, her right hand resting on a goblet set next to a bottle on the table. Nancy Linton has a silk shawl draped over bare shoulders exposed by her low-cut gown. The surprise of the picture is her legs, emerging knees-forward from a skirt. The knees are knobby and the skin of the legs looks dehydrated, exposing the shafts of bone. The woman is clearly alive, well and happily drinking the elixir that has preserved her and granted her a fine complexion, leaving the unattractive parts hidden where no one will see them.

Swaim published pamphlets entitled "The Case of Nancy Linton, illustrative of the efficacy of Swaim's Panacea"(1827) in which he gives details of her life and miseries, then trumpets the miraculous cure of the young woman's scrofula when she began imbibing his Panacea. The publication and the lithograph were the mass-marketing projection of the display of the healed sick in medical schools and later in traveling medicine shows of which Swaim was one of the pioneers. According to one of the pamphlets, Nancy Linton lived in Charlestown Township, Chester County, Pennsylvania, a specific person from a known place, but with little other biography beyond her disease and its cure by Swaim's. Her case joined many others in the compilations of cures Swaim began to publish in 1827, and was referred to in his advertising for some time after that. She was the only person who merited a hand-colored lithograph.

To show the benefits of Swaim's Panacea in one picture designed to draw in a casual viewer, the artist has transgressed the social boundary and revealed a polite woman's legs. But they are not smooth and alluring as they might be in a print of a nymph or a prostitute. They are diseased: few people would have enough medical experience to know that the particular condition was scrofula.

Nancy Linton's image accidentally mirrors a drawing circulated with many variations from the time of the beginnings of the syphilis epidemic in Europe to the anti-syphilis campaigns of the early twentieth century. A young man is gazing amorously at an apparently beautiful young woman whose face is a mask over a skull, or whose body discloses in some place a pattern of ulcers. It is a warning to young men not to frequent prostitutes and, in the broader historic context, it is a sign that the venereal diseases have become feminized, that is, located in women and not in the men who carry the infection between casual, sometimes forced sexual encounters.

In the case of Swaim's imagery of Nancy Linton, there is a connection not

Frontispice de BELIN et DESCHAMPS
pour *Syphilis*, poème publicitaire
de BARTHÉLEMY, à la gloire du « Rob de Laffecteur »

Engraving by Belin and Deschamps, frontispiece of the "publicity poem" "Syphilis" (1851), by Auguste-Marseille Barthelemy.

so much to syphilis—Nancy Linton would not have agreed to show that—but to the secret tradition of cosmetic mercury use. Swaim vigorously denied that his Panacea contained mercury, and he put it forward as a cure for everything, including syphilis, more likely to be held at bay by mercury than by sarsaparilla.

By taking the syrup regularly, the lithograph implies, a woman will recover and retain her soft skin and attractive features whatever she might be concealing beneath her clothes. Swaim and his fellow patent-medicine vendors always had to find convincing before-and-after cases, but without mass production photography or photolithography, just being invented in these years, they could not distribute images of the same person before and after treatment. In the early medical school exhibits, the doctors displayed different people with the same ghastly disease, one before and the other after a course of the elixir. Nancy Linton gave Swaim the opportunity to show before and after in the same person, as "during," implying that as long as a diseased person drinks the medication at least their face will shine, and there is no need to know what disease they have.

Morleigh, a British visitor "seeking his estate" in the American West during the late 1830s, happened upon a copy of one of Swaim's publications and was arrested by the portrait of the "skeleton in bride's dress, grinning horribly.... If this lady is cured, thought I, it would be very advisable for her to stay at home. Faugh! The very portrait made me ill." Morleigh tossed the book away, but later, thinking twice about it, obtained another copy and devoured it "like a shark." This initial revulsion followed by eagerness may also be how the medicine itself affected its consumers.

The makers of later sarsaparilla formulations with claims as broad as Swaim's followed his lead in using clever before-and-after advertising. Trade cards for Scovill's Sarsaparilla with a scrofulous young woman's bowed head visible opened up to show the same young woman beaming with health after accepting her stylish friend's bottle of Scovill's. Scovill's did not contain mercury; the joy of its users was due to the high alcohol content.

Swaim's prosperity in the face of ridicule and condemnation allowed him to take another forward step in popular medicine and open a bathhouse and spa admitting both men and women.

On January 27, 1857, however, a paragraph appeared in the New York and Philadelphia newspapers among the notices of medical consultations and treatises:

> The Academy of Medicine was established to put down quacks and quackeries and their nostrums, yet it elects as its President the author of the following caitiff certificate, which is circulated by the thousands upon thousands on the bottles of the nostrum in every corner of the globe. Who are the quacks now? "I have repeatedly used SWAIM'S PANACEA, both in the Hospital and in private practice, and have always found it to be a valuable medicine in chronic, syphilitic and scrofulous complaints, and in obstinate cutaneous affections.   VALENTINE MOTT, M.D."

This might be dismissed as sour grapes by the loser of the election, or just another sign of the ongoing rough courtship between the organized medical profession and patent medicine marketers.

In May of the following year, the annual meeting of the American Medical Association in Washington, D.C. convened in strife among speakers as some in the Philadelphia contingent wanted the chair censured because he had "violated the code of ethics by recommending a nostrum vendor." The response was that "Swaim's Panacea was a nostrum that got its immense sale and popularity on the strength of the recommendation of some of our Philadelphia brethren. When they repented and confessed, they were forgiven. [Applause and hisses.]"

Association with Swaim had become an accusation some doctors leveled against others. It was a taint always ready to be exposed. Yet the following year, an advertisement briefly appeared in the same columns declaring that "Swaim's Celebrated Panacea was introduced by the elite of the Medical Faculty fifty years ago" and that it clears the "morbile" matter built up in the blood during the cold season. "It is pleasant to the taste, contains no mercurial ingredients, and is very efficacious in scrofula and kindred diseases." The medical controversy over professional endorsement had, at least for the advertiser, been absorbed into the medicine itself, which remained a blood purifier capable of a Hippocratic springtime clearing out of the blood.

William Swaim had been shrewd recruiting Philadelphia doctors to endorse his nostrum, and thus fit his enterprise into an existing medical information and distribution network. The negative reports and denunciations, some from these very doctors, took a long time to affect Swaim's fortunes. Philadelphia also was the center for the education of medical professionals south of New York, and from there word of Swaim's Panacea spread with trainees heading south, either returning to a southern home with new skills or seeking opportunities in the slave-holding states.

Swaim's Panacea was advertised as "for Negroes who are confined in large numbers in planatations in hot climates," and it was widely adopted by plantation owners as a cure-all for the illnesses and injuries of their human property. Dr. Nathaniel Chapman of Philadelphia authored a widely circulated paragraph condemning doctors practicing in the South for administering calomel so freely that it caused ghastly deformities in the recipients: "Want of science, abuse of that noxious drug calomel in the Southern states."

Daniel Drake, the author of a series of books assessing doctors and their practices, responded to Chapman's criticisms by pointing out that most of the calomel was in the form of Swaim's Panacea, which Chapman himself had approved years earlier. Furthermore, Drake added, these doctors were just using calomel and other articles as they were taught when they went to school in Philadelphia.

Drake objected to Chapman's description of the destructive effects of calomel: "Take a man who has never had syphilis, and let him be drugged with calomel till you are tired, and he will not have perforations of the cranium, nor ulcerations of the nasal bones, nor nocturnal pains, nor any of the thousand and one afflictions that are ascribed to it." It was syphilis, and not calomel (Swaim's Panacea) that caused the decay and misery. On the brink of the Civil War, the battle over the condition of the slaves was being joined on all fronts, but it left Swaim popular.

Swaim's son, Dr. James Swaim, and then his grandson, Samuel Swaim Stewart, also one of the first American manufacturers of the banjo, maintained the business by keeping up appearances.

The proprietors of Swaim's name and Panacea relied on the past endorsements that later caused professional trouble for the doctors who made them. In advertising, only the vintage of the endorsements matters. They make no mention of syphilis and the only mention of mercury is to deny its presence, a formula which kept the unmentionable syphilis secret and the secret ingredient mentioned. The pleasant taste is a result of sugar and sarsaparilla, which was in the process of becoming sasparilla, a flavoring for soft drinks. There never was a soft drink with a hidden mercury flavor.

The 1860 edition of *Gunn's Domestic Medicine, or Poor Man's Friend* placed Swaim's panacea in its historical lineage:

> The French method of curing pox, is by use or administration of Van Swieten's liquor, as they call it, or *anti-syphilitic rob:* for this medicine and the manner of preparing it, look under that head. The rob was used in the London hospitals, until it was superseded and thrown out of use by Swaim's panacea: for the method of preparing which, see under that head. Both these medical preparations are used with advantage in secondary symptoms, by which I mean what I have said before, in cases where the disease has become constitutional, and is attended with ulcers, sores, blotches, &c.

In the first edition of *Gunn's Domestic Medicine* (1830), Dr. John C. Gunn of Knoxville, Tennessee, stated that Swaim's panacea was once an "invaluable remedy" sold at an extravagant price of five dollars a bottle. But in due time it sank into a dignified retirement, "being nothing more than an old friend with a new face: its principal and component part being the same as the French medicine called Rob Syphilitique, which is *Corrosive Sublimate.*"

Gunn then provided a recipe for making Swaim's Medicine, which called for boiling together in water, sarsaparilla, marsh reed grass, borage flowers, senna, rose leaves, sassafras and wintergreen, thickening the strained fluid with sugar and honey, then mixing in corrosive sublimate. Gunn added that the preparation of the rob de Laffecteur was identical but simpler, and the long list of ingredients added nothing to its efficacy treating the secondary stages of syphilis.

The recipe for Swaim's Panacea was printed in all 69 editions of Gunn's medical advice manual, the last being in 1920, and with it the assurance that massive amounts of therapeutic mercury could be swallowed because it would be sweated and salivated back out before the metal could be absorbed. Gunn also recognized that some individuals had a "prejudice" against it which could not be removed no matter how much was taken.

Gunn's book was written to provide uncomplicated cures and preventives for people living in the western and southern states of the United States. Despite its subtitle, *Poor Man's Friend,* it probably was used primarily by tradespeople, artisans and mothers of small children.

And though it was a "frontier" manual, from the first edition Gunn referred to European medical issues. Approving of the role of licensing and inspection of prostitutes in lowering the rate of venereal infection in France, he proposed that a similar system be adopted by his home state of Tennessee. While he was providing the plainly mercurial formula for Swaim's and the rob de Laffecteur to his readers, the promoters of both remedies in Europe and the urban north-east of America were engaged in campaigns to deny any mercury content. Gunn declared the corrosive sublimate remedies were best for secondary stages of syphilis, but in newspaper advertising syphilis was listed last or not at all among the diseases it could heal.

This was the wider construction of hidden mercury in the societies where its use was valued and denied. Hidden mercury for hidden syphilis.

The rob concealed in Swaim's concealed mercury became a historical subject, a word in the past, while Swaim's Panacea became glass bottles prized by collectors, but no longer containing anything invisible.

The rob de Laffecteur and its successors existed in a social milieu somewhere between individually compounded and mass-produced medicines, along a boundary between knowing precisely what is in the syrup you were swallowing and taking a risk, trusting a promoter, having faith it would improve your health whatever it might be. This is not a historical boundary but one always present. It runs across what is consumed and the body that it is consuming it. It only happens to be rendered briefly visible in the rob de Laffecteur, with its ancient Oriental name announcing a secret.

This open-secret mercury is the primary mode of medicinal mercury to this day. It is both in contrast to and dependent upon the old-heavy-liquid quicksilver swallowed to clear blockages by force. Its emergence can be seen, for instance, in Giraudeau de Saint-Gervais' survey of mercury remedies for syphilitic maladies beginning with the silvery liquid itself and proceeding through fumigations and unguents until it reached the virtues of no mercury at all followed by a great variety of mercury compounds and mixtures. There is mercury after no mercury. Mercury is rejected and manifestly present in many different forms. It is a poison but now, try this flavorsome formulation.

8

The Lightening Skin

The longest continuing use of mercury for which there is tangible evidence is cinnabar coloring in tattoos. The sixth–fifth century B.C.E. remains of nomadic chiefs entombed in mounds (*kurgan*) of the south Ural mountain region include skin tattooed with cinnabar. In the aftermath of World War II, Veterans Administration dermatologists observed the many complications suffered by servicemen whose tattoos had areas of cinnabar red. One sailor could precipitate a rash in another part of his body just by scratching the cinnabar area of the tattoo on his arm.

There is probably no single tradition connecting these two instances and the many others in between. The attractiveness of cinnabar's color guides it onto and into the skin of humans. Cinnabar, for a Persian word (*zinn-jafr*, the blood of the dragon), later vermilion, is mercuric sulfide that occurs naturally, it was powdered and mixed with water or other fluids to apply to people and objects. The more mercury, the finer the powder and the more delicate the layer of coloration it created where applied.

As a chemical compound, cinnabar is limited to mercury and sulfur in fixed proportions, but like other mercury compounds it has the physical property of accepting more mercury in ionic bonds. The increase in powdery penetrative masking ability as the mercury increases with respect to the sulfur makes the compound a cosmetic cosmological.

Ancient burials in China, the Mayan area of Mesoamerica, Peru and Neolithic Spain were spread with cinnabar dust. The mineral was mined locally or traded from distances. Its use to adorn the dead and their chambers is often taken to be symbolic of a vital essence, a redness of life that will last. Cinnabar and its colors last in the dark because its mercury kills anything that might cause the bones and dried skin to decay. Exposed to light, thin layers of cinnabar become the chemically identical, but electrochemically different metacinnabar, which is black. Metacinnabar also forestalls decay, but it isn't as lively to look at as cinnabar.

Use for the dead reflects use by the living. Mercury compounds vitalize living skin by covering it with color and lightness and clearing away eruptions and rashes. Like the skin of the dead, living skin becomes permanent in its brightness with mercury treatment. Cinnabar is only one mineral used to make rouge, but it was among the longest-used until recent qualms about the mercury it contained. A contemporary revival of mineral make-up does not include cinnabar-vermilion rouges. This is as much due to their mercury contents as to the excessive fineness of well-ground materials, which outline facial wrinkles.

The skin, the body's largest organ, meets mercury visibly. It is tempting to place mercury there, to see it balanced at the entrance to the body, showing its colors.

Anyone who has handled metallic mercury, and there are ever fewer with that experience, knows how easily it is absorbed into the skin. If allowed to roll in the palm of your hand, it breaks up into globules caught in the ridges of the surface and disappears except for an area of comparative brightness. Rubbed on an area of the skin it forms an ephemeral shining region which sinks away as it amalgamates with the skin's surface oils and is received into the pores, leaving a grayish patch.

This was the reassuring marvel of mercury-grease liniment for those with skin conditions and then for syphilis sufferers, to receive a shot of silver into their paling bodies and more specifically into their wilting sexual organs which were then cleared of coincidental surface infections, at least, by the mercury's anti-bacterial action. Mercury could be spread by itself as a skin adornment or worn in the skin as an amulet. It must have been noticed that where it was rubbed the skin grew lighter.

The compounds of lead, arsenic, bismuth and a number of other metals could be used to paint the skin white; serve as skin whiteners in place of chalk, rice and flour; and cover areas roughened by smallpox and other diseases disrupting the ideal uniformity of the skin. Metallic mercury and its compounds not only color the surface; they depigment skin by inhibiting the formation of the pigment melanin in the basal layer beneath the epidermis.

Ancient Greek men covered their faces with white lead paint and then added mercury rouge to create a startling mask. Deposits of lead and mercury have been found in decorated cosmetics boxes recovered from Greek archaeological sites. The white make-up of shrewd, cunning characters in the traditional Chinese music drama included (black) calomel in vegetable binders.

Melanin breaks down on exposure to light and must constantly be synthesized in the skin to prevent light from inducing mutations in skin cells that can lead to breakages, infections and cancer. When the skin is open, the light entering can also cause mercury and other heavy metals used in skin-lightening treatments to oxidize and deposit dark salts, yielding discolorations which call for more skin-lightening treatments.

Cinnabar and vermilion stood out as skin colorants because mercury ions from the mercuric sulfide entered the basal layer and reduced melanin production, leaving a lighter base for the color to shine. Native Americans traded over hundreds of miles to gain cinnabar for that effect. The facial skin of a recently discovered Peruvian (Moche) mummy of a female is covered with powdered cinnabar, which may have been to lighten, redden and preserve it in life as in death.

Other mercury compounds, mercuric iodide and mercurous sulfide, transport mercury into the skin cells. Taken internally as raw metal or as a salt, mercury travels through the bloodstream to the surface of the skin where it constricts the capillaries to cause a pallor that can be taken for lightening. Mercury seems to do from the inside what it does when applied to the skin surface. The effect is rapid but temporary and if continued, poisonous.

The absorption only confirmed the metal's affinity for living flesh, as for bright metals like gold and silver which it joins and makes fluid. This metaphor of mercurial assimilation was valid only when mercury was used occasionally. It was for people who had the option of applying mercury voluntarily in an answer to a need to feel refined, brightened and energized by assimilating its visible brilliance. A few might think that more was better, or administer it to themselves in such an extreme way that it sickened them. But the majority of mercury users did not play the poison game. They wanted the lift of a little light inside them and clear skins outside. It could go on this way for years.

Mercury's coloring and depigmenting prowess promised some control over skin color itself, and the social statuses it signifies. Race, social class, gender, age and health are all projected by skin color and texture in one context or another. Many of the words used to designate these categories, such as "fair," and "blanc," refer to skin appearances. Cosmetics, medicines and other treatments of this skin-based social order often use mercury to make a new life. As always with mercury entering the body, the improved surface covers an endangered interior.

There are references to the use of mercury in cosmetics by the Romans. The regular shipment of containers of quicksilver to Rome for this purpose was what attracted Pliny's attention to the Soroposa (Almaden?) mine in Spain. Cosmetic use, by nature and purpose ephemeral, does not leave as reliable archaeological evidence as, for instance, embalming preparations do.

According to medieval Arabic texts and their Latin "translations," Cleopatra was a skilled chemist and physician who authored a number of treatises, including one on cosmetics. Later compilers of recipes for body care attributed some of them to Cleopatra. She typified women who were repositories of traditions that included cooking, gardening, healing and beautification secrets passed on from one generation to another. These concealed traditions emerge into written records with a famous name attached to them. Cleopatra reputedly authored a gynecology treatise addressed to her daughter. Mercury sometimes fit in among her recommendations.

There were occasional manuscripts authored by specific named noblewomen divulging their skin-care secrets all innocent of precedent. "Books of secrets" printed from the mid–sixteenth century onward included skin lighteners and whiteners among their formulas. The celebrity beauty tips that have lined the shelves of American, European and Indian bookstores for decades are the descendants of these publications. Today there is less likelihood that mercury will be recommended.

As the formulary literature expanded over the years, mercury played roles that retained the ancient juxtaposition of the funerary with the cosmetic. Carolus Ludovicus de Maets, a chemistry professor at Leyden, in 1675–76 held a "secret chemical college" which left a written record of techniques of embalming corpses, whitening the skin and curing all diseases using mercury and cinnabar. Funerary, cosmetic and healing usages were only then beginning to separate.

Cosmetics were an enhancement of natural beauty; paints were artifice, theatrical makeup and revivification of the dead. Cosmetics often were made from herbs and vegetable ingredients; makeup included heavy metals like lead, arsenic and bismuth. When put on the skin the heavy metals could enter the bloodstream and damage internal organs. Paint used as a cosmetic remained effective only if the right dosage could be maintained.

Cosmetics and paints were treasures shared among practitioners. They exemplified a property of a material that the chemist had skillfully brought for the purpose of beautification. Those who used these substances were familiar with the techniques and refinements visible in each other while leaving anyone outside of this practice in the role of an observer who could accept the made-up face as "natural" or reject it as diseased and contrary to nature. Users of skin treatments, addressed as women but by no means exclusively women, have been warned for centuries not to damage their appearance with artifice. Lead, bismuth, arsenic and of course mercury, among the bases of mixtures used to paint faces white and bleach skin, were the object of denunciations and warnings that they were deadly, or at least had unpleasant side-effects.

After centuries of being formulated as a cosmetic and separately condemned as a menace to health, these two aspects of mercury meet in the same pronouncements. Thereafter mercury on the skin is a struggle between beauty and ugliness, and a merging of beauty and death. But what is beauty and who should be beautiful and who should decide who is beautiful? Humans are arrogant to try to improve upon what the divine has created, and they raised the mask of deceit to cover flaws. Mercury, which can accomplish beauty, ugliness and death, is an excellent point for that discussion.

Mona Lampiada, an older woman, breaks in to the *Dialogue on the Beauties of Women* (1548) by Agnolo Firenzuola to complain that young women use "waters and powders" that women previously used only to cover pimples and moles, to paint their entire faces as if they were covering a wall with plaster. It wears them out and makes them seem to grow old before their time, and destroys their teeth, making them appear to be wearing a carnival mask the year round. Mona didn't place the blame on mercury in particular; her disdain was for face paint used to excess. Mercury was implicitly present in the loosening of the teeth and the corruption of the skin.

The old denunciation of vanities had acquired an explicitly physical dimension. The Spanish humanist Juan Luis Vives in his *Instruction of a Christian Woman* (1541) made a grave emblem of a woman who has used ceruse (a lead compound) and quicksilver: face turning old, breath stinking, teeth rotting, an evil air surrounding the entire body, everything a woman would not want to be.

The "invective" of the sixteenth-century Spanish physician of Jewish ancestry, Andres de Laguna, aimed directly at women who "painted themselves with *solimán* [corrosive sublimate]." Laguna proclaimed that this practice tainted offspring like the original sin of Christian dogma, a hereditary blight upon humans for disobeying God's command and partaking of the forbidden fruit. The children of women who used makeup would lose their teeth one by one before they could even walk, through no fault of their own but because of a vain mother. Laguna used the intergenerational "penetration" of mercury to make a medical case against self-adornment in general.

In Elizabeth Arnold's 1616 English translation of de Laguna's Spanish,

> The excellencie of this Mercurie Sublimate is such that the women who often paint themselves with it, though they be very young, they presently turn old with wrinkled and withered faces like an Ape, and before age can come upon them, they tremble (poor wretches) as if they were sicke of the staggers, reeling, and full of quick-silver, and so they are.

Laguna used the threat of premature aging and resemblance to an ape as he did that of tainted birth, to address women's fears in particular. He added a disgusting illness, the staggers (diarrhea), and finished by comparing a woman who had used mercury to a dumb toy jerking about with mercury in the cavities of its form.

Arnold's translation was printed as an appendix to the *Treatise against Painting and Tincturing of Men and Women*, by Thomas Tuke, an English divine who attracted women followers with his call to renounce face painting and hair dyeing. "And dost thou think it lawfull," he asks, "for thee to make showes of sauor and beauty, or of another complexion and temper, than thou art of, by thy daubing, painting and borrowing?" Tuke's own treatise, dense with citations from scripture and classics, never gets as specific about the ravages of sublimate on tender young skin as his Spanish and Italian predecessors. A staunch Royalist Protestant himself, Tuke was willing to add to his text the words of a Spanish Catholic physician to a pope in a translation by a woman, to give his own words substance.

Recipes for mercury-based face paints and powders, as well as the mercury and the cosmetics themselves, were being imported into England from France, Spain and Italy during the sixteenth and seventeenth centuries, and they were accompanied by written attacks on the use of those cosmetics translated into English. Richard Haydocke's translation (1598) of *A Tracte Containing the Artes of Curious Paintinge, Caruinge & Buildinge* by Paolo Lomazzo includes instructions on using mercury compounds in painting pictures of the human face, and for painting the face itself. Lomazzo was a painter, but loss of sight at an early age forced him to give up that trade. He took to writing instructional treatises on the materials and techniques of the arts.

Surgeons call sublimate "corrosive," wrote Lomazzo, because it burned the flesh where it touched, causing great pain. The women who used it regularly had black teeth that stuck out of their gums "like a Spanish mule." It gave them an offensive breath, scorched their faces, and aged them, causing their husbands to seek out other wives. Using an already aged and worn imagery, Lomazzo and his translator tried to induce anxieties in women that would encourage them both to avoid using and to use sublimate.

This contradiction paralleled the contradiction developing during the sixteenth century in the popular use of mercury to treat syphilis. It cleared the skin but it loosened the teeth. England's Queen Elizabeth I was reputedly so ravaged by facial applications of mercury and lead compounds that she ordered all mirrors removed from the palace. Earlier in life, however, she was Cynthia, celebrated in Ben Jonson's 1601 play *The Fountain of Self-Love; or, Cynthia's Revels*, where Cupid says to Mercury (Act I, Scene 1, lines 17–19): "Alas, your palms (Iupiter knows) they are as tender as the foot of a foundred nagge, or a ladies face new mercuried, the'ile touch nothing." The mercury compound the ladies used to decorate their skin was as fragile as the injured foot of a workhorse which can't touch the ground. Touching the skin would spoil the illusion of smoothness. The mercuried face is just a made-up face out of reach. No special property of mercury was evoked. It was so common a treatment that it was the same as any dainty cosmetic application. In the Palinodia (Act V, Scene V), the Chorus repeats the refrain "Good Mercury defend us" amid numerous statements of problematic persons and conditions that "good Mercury" might improve, including "a wrinkled face."

Mercury was a routine ingredient of cosmetics at the time: it appeared in formularies and recipe-books, occasionally as a word for cosmetics in general and for the command to look at but not touch the made-up face.

Many of the formulas for cosmetics containing mercury, for instance those in Lancillotti's *Guida chemica*, straightforwardly included mercury in the list of ingredients, with no comment on the possible outcomes of using the preparation repeatedly. Inherent in some cosmetic-making instructions were warnings and animadversions about using quicksilver and its compounds. The earlier anti-mercury charges were unqualified denunciations aimed to dissuade literate aristocrats from self-adornment. As use of mercury spread to the forming middle classes, the diatribes were accompanied by recipes, and vice versa.

Giovanni Battista della Porta's *Magia naturalis* (*Natural Magic, 1558–89*) submitted to his readers a recipe for a face paint that included both crude mercury and *sollimato* (soluble mercuric chloride or corrosive sublimate) mixed with binders and pressed into black cakes. Some women were hesitant to use this, he wrote, thinking it might damage their teeth, but, he returned, the beauty that came from transferring the silver water of mercury to the skin was worth the inconvenience. While others were inveighing against sublimate cosmetics, or plainly writing down formulas, della Porta was anticipating the terms of mass popular use of mercury cosmetics. Not exactly the same as medicines which worked because they were poison, mercury cosmetics made the skin glow. What else mattered?

This set the limiting function of deliberate mercury use on the skin: more mercury forever approached greater beauty limited by damage. Cinnabar (mercuric sulfide) could be used as rouge to give the appearance of vital good health to the cheeks and lips of the living and to preserve the skin of the dead. *Sollimato* lightened the skin with an unnatural glow as it caused interior damage. The ambiguity of sublimate on the face and in the body was an emerging international tradition that della Porta only began to express.

The invasion of Britain by continental mercury cosmetics during the seventeenth and eighteenth centuries induced a negative entrepreneurial reaction among the natives. "Curious fine white for the face and neck, entirely without mercury or any hurtful thing in it," a seventeenth-century London woman purveyor of facials trumpeted her wares. The only references to mercury in all the handbills and pamphlets put out by English quacks during these centuries deny its presence and accuse competitors of using it. A quack giving his address as Plough Yard in Fetter-Lane, at the Green Door and Two Golden Spikes, broadcast this warning to those who would come seeking his counsel:

> Beware of Quacks, Mercury and all such Foes
> Lest need ye require a supplemental Nose!

Respectable doctors, quacks, disguised aristocrats all entered the lead- and mercury-free cosmetics business. The ugliness of mercurial beauty became an entrenched literary trope:

> When Mercury her tresses mows
> To think of black-lead combs is vain,
> No painting can restore a brow
> Nor will the teeth return again.

This is the least obscure reference to mercury in Jonathan Swift's 1720 poem *The Progress of Beauty*. Here, as in his other writings, Swift makes light of women's artifice: the former belle can't comb her hair black with lead and paint her face white to make up for the hair and teeth already gone due to mercury. That is the progress, the outcome, of beauty induced by mercury. Swift displays the age-old emblem of decaying mercuried beauty with a sigh resembling the regrets of aging.

A few decades earlier in Japan, another poet-novelist, Ihara Saikaku, had portrayed the compulsiveness of mercury applications. A woman whose skin was already clean and light covered her face with two hundred layers of mercury paste. "Two hundred" simply means a lot, an awful lot. Mercury powder imported into Japan from China had slowly made its way from the upper classes to the urban elites and finally to the peasantry. Saikaku was observing the excess as the tradespeople tried to catch up with the aristocrats in personal adornment.

In China, where the powder was manufactured, its cosmetic associations remained close to the funerary. The immortality of decay-free death through mercury elixirs extended to beauty, and there was little comment on the immediate consequences of mercury use.

Hsiao Shih, an alchemical immortal, courted Lung Yu, the "virtuous and beautiful" daughter of the Duke of Chin in seventh century B.C.E. China. Since high antiquity, the chronicler Ma Kao writes, lead was used as face paint. Hsiao Shih heated mercury, which flew up at the finish of his flute music, making "flying cloud cinnabar," which he offered to Lung Yu to paint her face. Later, Hsiao carried her off with him to the land of the immortals. He had given her the beauty of the well-preserved entombed dead.

The female protagonist of the eighteenth-century erotic novel *Trails of Immortals in the Green Wild*, a prostitute who is managed by her parents, literally needs to save face after they discover she has been giving her earnings to a poor young scholar to help him pass the state examinations. She swallows a quantity of her mercury face powder, her agonized death the prelude to permanent beauty. Jin Zhongher has been using every day an adornment she knows is lethal, and which will make her immortal in the mind of her lover. He leads her only figuratively to the land of the immortals. Cosmetics are the elixir of women and, in a few guarded instances, of gay men as well.

These two examples set almost a thousand years apart identify a persistent pattern: the male influenced the female to act upon herself with mercury, with a result that he both admired and deplored. Outside of China, women using face paint and cosmetics are reminded of their liabilities by the men who enjoyed them. The male agent brought attention to the immediate effects of using an ultimately disfiguring substance for temporary improvement of appearance while at the same time being a member of the sex that recommends and supplies the mercury, and expects the appearance its use produces.

A number of different roles are available in this interchange, purveyors, pre-scribers, users and critics of mercury on the face.

The women of Smyrna also painted their faces with sublimate, but when that gained the notice of a European visitor the commentary was censure: "The Greek women at Smyrna make great use of paint, which odious custom has also got footing among the Franks. This paint, which is called sulama, imparts a beautiful redness to the cheeks and gives the skin a remarkable gloss." The Ger-man traveler Egidius von Egmont, who wrote this passage in his account of a trip to the Near East, recommended chewing on a clove, then exhaling near a face that has this look. The skin will turn yellow, he writes. "But this is not the only bad consequence attending the practice, for, a considerable amount of mercury making a part of this paint, the teeth of those who use it soon suffer remarkably — and thus, for a false, they lose a real beauty."

"Sulama" was the Turkish version of the Italian *sollimato*, the name for corrosive sublimate in its cosmetic uses. The formula della Porta detailed, and its promise of silvery loveliness, had become widely adopted in the Mediter-ranean world. The beauty of the women of Smyrna, already artificial with mer-cury plumping, now was questioned by the vanity-of-cosmetics argument that had always challenged the use of facial paint whatever its composition. At the time von Egmont was writing, this criticism, largely directed at women, was

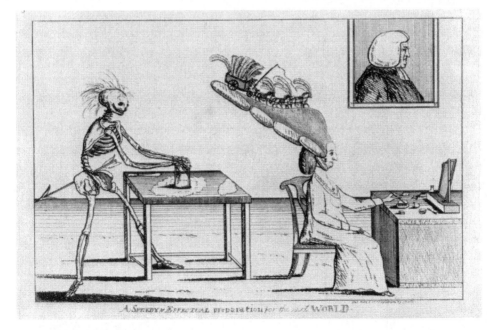

A Speedy and Effectual Preparation for the Next World, print by Matthew Darly, 1777. Courtesy of Library of Congress.

becoming scientific, that is, more likely to be referred to the health effects of using cosmetics than just to complaints about its vanity. The ugliness of yellow skin where there was a healthy blush is succeeded by the permanent effects of mercury poisoning, rotting teeth and a sunken face.

Women will "lose their teeth, develop bad breath, or have an overabundant flow of saliva," Antoine Le Camus cautioned, regarding the application of mercury-based facials. Le Camus was a physician and poet who authored the oriental romance *Abdeker, ou l'art de conserver la beauté* (*Abdeker, or The Art of Conserving Beauty*), (1754), supposedly translated from the Arabic, as *The Arabian Nights* recently had been. Le Camus also was at the forefront of a movement among physicians to give advice to the rising bourgeoisie on their personal appearance. While discouraging mercurial make-up, Le Camus had his own cosmetics to offer, as well as counsel on manners and deportment. Always the rejection of artificial beauty aids included the promotion of other, improved, beauty aids more in keeping with a newer (younger, more attractive) appearance and body, into which mercury again crept. The formula books and cosmetics instructional manuals that had long included mercury recipes acknowledged the denunciation of mercury by doctors and moralists opposed to cosmetics. Beauty was an aspect of health like others, both enhanced and threatened by mercury.

The secretage process of felting animal furs for hats was adapted, both in its name and use of the mercuric nitrate ingredient, to hair curling and dyeing for urban women in France and America. David Garrison Brinton and George H. Napheys, physicians and authors of an 1870 guide on how to cultivate personal beauty "in accordance with the laws of health," described the hair treatment and warned of its potentials effects, voicing their disapproval and stiffly refusing to give the formulas to anyone who might want to try this method. Medical authority was extending itself to govern looks managed, for better or worse, with chemicals taken from industry heedless of their consequences.

The mercury balance of health and beauty was also centered around the teeth, which would pay for the temporary advantage gained by applying mercury formulas to skin or hair. For a period in the late eighteenth to early nineteenth century, Russian women as described by Samuel Collins, English physician to the tsars, had the practice of whitening their teeth with mercury powder, but then, faced with tooth decay, tried to compensate by blackening all their teeth, which against the rouged cheeks and artificially teased hair made them into a hideous spectacle. Collins did not recognize, as other writers did, that the women entered into this cycle of self-destructive beautification through mercury to add the veneer of wealth to their existing looks. A contest of class superiority had recruited the skin effects achieved by mercury to its other adornments.

Use of cosmetics always was a personal choice subject to social pressures, to conform to a style and to make an appearance available to onlookers, potential mates, and purchasers of the cosmetics. Face-paint tended to give way to face lightening and face clearing of blemishes as preserving racial identity became a factor in cosmetic use and cosmetics were manufactured for this purpose. Then wearing a clear face became a spousal and a collective duty. Perfection of the skin and especially facial skin might mean removing skin and body from the damages of everyday existence. The perfect skin could be achieved in social separation, finally that of death.

The Chinese tradition of mercury use was not isolated from the European-American one, anticipating a global complex.

The tension that always existed between life and the lifelike death created by cosmetics found its essence in chemical beautification treatments. A short story by the American author Nathaniel Hawthorne, "The Birth-Mark" (1843) has a great scientist determined to remove the small, red, hand-shaped birthmark from the face of his otherwise flawless wife. Mercury or other cosmetics are not mentioned or even referred to, but when, after other efforts fail, the experimenter gives her a goblet of clear liquid to drink, the perfection of the wife's face through the disappearance of the blemish and the death of the wife seem perfectly suited to the history of mercury cosmetics. A male technician gives a female the means and/or the motive to remove a mark at a lethal cost. Hawthorne doesn't turn to necrophilia as others of his time did; he ends his story with a moralistic line about the dangers of science. He draws back from the conclusion that truly unblemished skin can only exist in death.

Hawthorne didn't go as far in fiction as the British anatomist Robert Knox did in reality. Knox paid "resurrection men" Burke and Hare for fresh corpses to be used in training dissections, assuming they had procured them by robbing graves and not by murdering their victims as they actually did. The body of one young woman was such a picture of female form that Knox refrained from cutting it immediately, and, after having posed it for a sketch artist's views, kept it in a barrel of whisky for several months, until the cadaver was in as bad a condition as others arriving. Knox was convinced that the white race was the pinnacle of human beauty and that young women were the very finest. Promotion of this aesthetic of race, skin and death, while officially rejected and publicly condemned, reappears in pulp fiction, news stories and horror films to this day.

An enduring yet imperiled beauty was the responsibility of the woman in a struggle to maintain racial integrity by attracting virile mates. Women were expected to embrace this struggle in their own design of personal appearance and like Hawthorne's Georgiana might accept death to achieve male approval as long as it did not entail disfigurement. Corsets and electrolysis treatments joined mineral and herbal chemistries as some of the ambiguous mechanisms of self-improvement and self-abnegation.

John V. Shoemaker, a lecturer in dermatology at a Philadelphia, Pennsylvania, medical school in the late nineteenth century, published a *Practical Trea-*

tise of Skin Diseases (1890) in which mercury taken orally, applied as ointment and injected are the only means described of controlling secondary syphilis. He did not make gender distinctions in its use. In the same year, however, he published *Heredity, Health and Personal Beauty,* which adapted Darwinism to beauty culture, primarily for women.

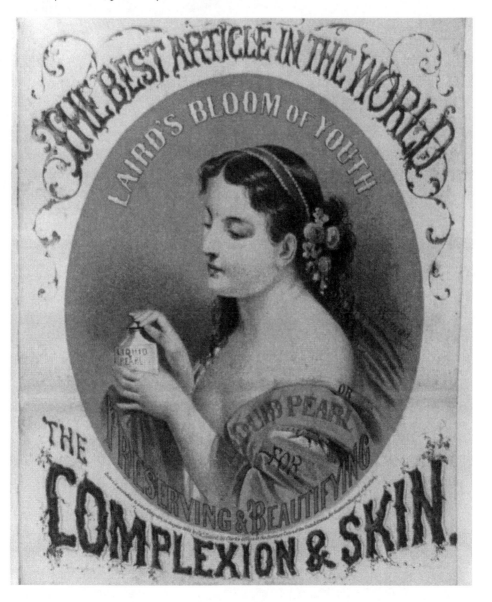

Laird's Bloom of Youth trade card. Courtesy of Library of Congress.

Shoemaker contended that women's greater attractiveness was the result of sexual selection driven by male choice of mates and women being protected from the ravages of heavy work. Shoemaker shows a class bias: few women actually were protected from hard labor. Sustaining this attractiveness, and thus preserving the integrity of female pulchritude (and class standing), demanded that women attend to their appearance healthfully. Shoemaker opposed altering the figure with corsets and stays, which confined the bosom and restricted breathing. He supported "taking the air" and bathing frequently using medicated soaps, for which he gave formulas. As he also made clear in his book on skin disease that he did not support the use of cosmetics, but at the same time was resigned to their inevitable appeal. Hair dye which was primarily silver nitrate cannot be good for the user but it as going to be used just the same, so Shoemaker gave the formula. Where he saw mercury as the only worthwhile treatment for syphilis in later stages, he did not introduce cautions about its poisonous nature. He only called the treating physician's attention to the differences in the response of individuals. He did not distinguish mercury-based cosmetics from others in his condemnation of cosmetics, but he did call mercury into use several times in the preservation of beauty.

A combination of cacao butter, castor oil, ammoniated mercury and oil of roses was "highly recommended, for removal of pigment spots that sometimes appear during pregnancy." Bichloride of mercury in a solution could remove warts and reduce the irritation of insect bites. Yellow oxide of mercury mixed with other ingredients soothed inflamed eyelids. Shoemaker is introduced mercury as a medical cosmetic applied to treat specific conditions of the skin which might reduce the woman's appeal, even during pregnancy. Turning aside elective cosmetics made to whiten faces and redden cheeks, he offered mercury, without demurring, to remove blemishes and clear the skin.

Addressing medical professionals in another book, Shoemaker also declared that bichloride of mercury injections during and after birth had reduced the death rate in maternity hospitals. The truth of this statement concealed the conditions in those hospitals. For a woman surviving childbirth, using bichloride to remove skin blemishes was a small matter.

Obviously not all women could afford to present themselves in this healthful state of appeal, and Shoemaker's enjoinders were for women of the class who could be protected from heavy labor. This lovely mercuriated complexion belonged to women of a social class and a race. The women were maintaining a *white* skin, free of blemishes and tanning. Shoemaker himself dismissed people of non-white races as not capable of the beauty of whites, which in turn was another motive for whites to retain their hereditary whiteness. The "white devil" image of Shakespeare's time is forgotten, at least by this physician.

Shoemaker was listed among the medical men acknowledged in the preface of *Harriet Hubbard Ayer's Book: A Complete and Authentic Treatise on the Laws of Health and Beauty* (1899). Mrs. Ayer doesn't need to identify her book's intended audience: it is clearly women with white skin that they wish to maintain in a suitable manner. Ayer offers advice similar to Shoemaker's but keyed to the specifics of women's expected self-image. Thin arms need to be augmented with "Skin Food," for which she gives the formula, and then whitened with a lotion made of glycerin, hydrochloric acid, rose water, bichloride of mercury crystals, distilled water and alcohol. The quantities and manner of preparation are given: women can make the lotion themselves or have it prepared by a pharmacist.

Ayer includes a face bleach, a formula for removing skin stains around the neck left by a tight or starchy collar, a hair wash (to remove parasites), a scar eraser and a tincture to apply to "granulated eyelids," all of them including a mercury compound as the chief active ingredient. She also follows each mercury formula with a warning along these lines: "It must be recognized that bichloride of mercury is a *dangerous poison*, and while perfectly proper to use as an *external* lotion, as we advised, should be kept out of the reach of children and ignorant persons." She does not identify the "ignorant persons" anywhere in the book, but it would seem to be anyone who does not share the secrets of mercury. The old cosmetic mercury is still accompanied by cautions but now it is only for external appearances not for internal consumption. The world of syphilis treatments, where bichloride was still being taken internally, is remote from Ayer's view.

To all appearances, this book was like the beauty manuals with recipes that had been authored by women since Cleopatra and which male professionals had only usurped within the previous few hundred years. There was a subtext. In 1886, Harriet Hubbard Ayer began the manufacture of beauty products under her own name. A Chicago socialite in flight from her faithless and abusive husband, she had become known in New York society as an advisor to wives of wealthy men seeking to display their fortune through the purchase of furniture and furnishings. She claimed to be in possession of the formulas for face creams and skin treatments passed down in the family of the salon hostess Madame Recamier (who had also lent her name to a type of sofa on which early-nineteenth-century beauties can be seen reclining in portrait paintings).

Rather than just mix up the formulas for personal use and selective distribution as previous women entrepreneurs had done, Ayer invented a trademark, the Recamier line of Harriet Hubbard Ayer products. Initial success led to a battle for control of the company with the main investor, her daughter's father-in-law. She was incarcerated in a hospital for the insane soon after the verdict in the lawsuit was made public. After her release over a year later she reinvented herself again and became a columnist for Joseph Pulitzer's *New York World* newspaper. The column offered stern, even dowdy, advice to women on the "laws of beauty" that eventually was collected into her book. It also included attacks on the New York Lunacy Act that had permitted her business opponents to have her (and many other "intractable" women) declared insane and incompetent to manage their own property.

Analyses of Recamier products by medical societies and state health boards showed that they contained mercury compounds. Writing of Ayer's Recamier Soap in his compilation of these and many other studies of "secret nostrums," Charles Wilmot Oleson wrote, "And what are they? Cheap, ordinary preparations known from time immemorial, and condemned by physicians on account of the corrosive sublimate — a deadly poison — which most of them contain." No one has suggested that Ayer was driven mad by the mercury she imbibed while making or using her own beauty treatments. Yet her legacy contains all the elements of women using mercury for beauty, accepting and resisting the control of men.

A young woman using a bichloride of mercury solution to erase her facial pimples began to tremble and went to see the doctor, who mentioned her case in his book on mental disease. It was unlikely she would have knowingly put something containing corrosive sublimate on her face, yet when mercury cosmetics are exposed that is what they are found to contain. The diagnosis of lunacy and the resultant confinement was by no means limited to women who had used mercury cosmetics. It did give a few physicians the opportunity to observe the connection.

Ayer's Recamier product was a standardized manufactured object stamped with a label and available to any woman at a price affordable to all classes but which yielded a sizeable markup for each item sold (another concern of Oleson's). Ayer's fitting reputation as an independent woman entrepreneur and early feminist (for her campaign against the Lunacy Acts) has obscured the contents of her products and recommendations. The criticism from male professionals was confined to studies issued by state health departments and cases reported in medical journals.

Mercury preparations for internal consumption, whether the mercury was disclosed or not, greatly diminished in availability by the time the first Pure Food and Drug Act was passed by the United States Congress and signed into law in 1906. Around the same time the denial of mercury, which had been a mainstay of advertising, also disappeared. Mercury remained an antiseptic and decontaminant in the form of "bichloride" (not "corrosive sublimate") tablets and eventually in the organic compounds mercurochrome and merthiolate, for external application.

Cosmetics were not regulated by the Pure Food and Drug Act, and would not be for decades. Their advertising also dropped references to and denial of mercury contents, but they did not lose the mercury. They avoided any reference at all to contents in favor of emphasizing the benefits of their use.

The Sears, Roebuck catalogue of 1908 offered among powders and lotions (no drugs were offered) White Lily Face Wash at $.45 a bottle. "The market is full of injurious complexion preparations," the advertising announced, "Many, in fact most of these preparations contain lead," is as far as any of the cosmetics descriptions goes in identifying ingredients. That the washes and powder are mineral negative is more distinguishing than what they actually do contain. The growing rural customer base of the catalogues were included in the urban cosmetics market.

The American Medical Association formed a Bureau of Investigation that examined and revealed the composition of medications, alcohol, tobacco and drug habit cures, "female weakness" cures, cancer and obesity cures, cosmetics and medical devices, and published brief notices in the Association's journal, later gathering them into inexpensive pamphlets. It was a publicity campaign against entrepreneurs making unfounded claims about products that consumers could not themselves easily analyze before purchasing and using.

The multivolume compilation of articles on drugs, tonics and elixirs that the Bureau published contains little reference to mercury and compounds. The brief pamphlet on "cosmetic nostrums" is another matter. It begins by stating that the "Pure Food and Drugs Law" had done much to protect the public from adulterated food and drugs by requiring the seller to tell the truth on the label and give the presence and amount of "certain potentially harmful ingredients." Cosmetics were not regulated but, the pamphlet states, "It is highly creditable to the many concerns that make cosmetics that so few of them have taken advantage of this lack of legal control." The exceptions were the producers of hair dyes and hair removers, and of some of the so-called skin bleaches or "freckle removers." The slow-acting skin bleaches were practically harmless, but the freckle removers had as their active ingredient "caustic poisons."

The Bureau's listing contained eight of these freckle-specific compounds, and a number more which included freckles among the skin conditions they supposedly erased (see Appendix C), each of them on analysis shown to contain either ammoniated mercury or corrosive sublimate as a major ingredient. Ayer's Recamier Cream, Balm, and Moth and Freckle Lotion were analyzed by the Massachusetts State Board of Health in 1902, and the face cream by the New Hampshire state chemists in 1918. The AMA's own laboratory confirmed the ammoniated mercury contents of the face cream in 1927. Obviously these analyses did nothing to change the injurious composition of the Ayer's cosmetics, nor did they draw attention to her book, which set out mercury formulas with the appropriate cautions.

The Bureau had slightly more success in the case of Berry's Freckle Ointment. This ointment was marketed by Dr. C. H. Berry Co., Chicago and New York. It was sold under the claim that it "positively removes freckles and tan" and under the further claim that "there is positively nothing injurious in any of our preparations."

The Bureau reported:

When analyzed by the government chemists, Berry's Freckle Ointment was reporter [*sic*] to contain:

    Ammoniated mercury....................12 per cent.

    Zinc oxid................................0.7 percent.

As ammoniated mercury is a caustic poison, the statement that there was "positively nothing injurious" in the ointment constituted misbranding. No one appearing as claimant when the case came on for hearing, the court found the product misbranded as alleged and entered decrees condemning and forfeiting the 180 jars that had been seized and ordered their complete destruction by the United State Marshal. (Notice of Judgment No. 1376, issued May 17, 1912.)

[A specimen of "C. H. Berry's Freckle Ointment," purchased and examined in the A.M.A. Chemical Laboratory in April 1927, showed the presence of ammoniated mercury.]

The Bureau reproduced the label of their specimen bottle alongside this entry. A clear-faced young woman gazes out from the center oval.

Given this history of legal action and continued mercury contents, all that the authors of the pamphlet can do is wag their collective finger at those hoping to free their skin of moth, tan, freckles, pimples, blackheads, oiliness and aging by applying a face bleach: "What else it does is left to the seeker after beauty to learn by experience."

Stillman's Freckle Cream was the proprietary formula of a large family pharmacy in Aurora, Illinois. By the late nineteenth century it was being mass-produced and distributed nationwide. It was analyzed in the "1001 Tests" of household products Dr. Harvey Wiley conducted for the Hearst newspapers, later gathered into a book by that name (1916). Wiley and the Indiana state

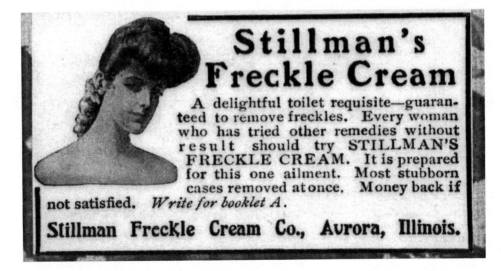

Stillman's Freckle Cream (1904), newspaper advertisement.

chemists independently found that Stillman's contained a strong concentration of ammoniated mercury, which like corrosive sublimate was likely to remove the freckle by destroying melanocytes and basal cells of the skin where applied.

Where most of the other freckle treatments exposed by laboratory work as mercurials vanished from the newspapers and pharmacy shelves, Stillman's was successfully marketed overseas, to populations with the same social anxieties about unsightly blemishes. Sid Kaufman, a member of the Abraham Lincoln Brigade formed by Americans and Europeans fighting for the socialists in the Spanish Civil War 1937–39, wrote in his journal that a young woman he encountered while trying to escape Spain asked him to send her a jar of Stillman's Freckle Cream, which due to the war was no longer imported from America. Kaufman wondered why she valued the skin treatment so highly. He thought that the Stillman Company would value the testimonial and send her a ton of the cream, but he did not want to compromise her security by sending her anything from America to Franco's Spain. In 1948 the *New York Times* advertising news reported that Stillman's Peruvian distributor had selected a new agent to handle the advertising of their local product *Crema la Belleza Aurora*.

Both Stillman's and Crema la Belleza appear occasionally in English and Spanish references. Mary, the protagonist of Jean Kerr's 1961 Broadway comedy *Mary, Mary* says while bantering with the actor Dirk that she secretly ordered Stillman's Freckle Cream and applied it until her facial skin began to peel, which she then passed off as the results of tanning. Alfonso Gonzalez Ortega uses the diminishing verbiage and references to "whiteness" in Crema la Belleza Aurora ads in Costa Rican newspapers to exemplify the turn from a print to a visual culture between 1950 and 1960. Advertisements in English-language newspapers and magazines in the Philippines during this same period matched Crema la Belleza Aurora with Stillman's Freckle Cream for their often multilingual readers.

After Stillman's Freckle Cream went out of production in America, its name and composition were taken up by small manufacturers in India, and it is still possible to buy on the Internet containers with the same characteristic labeling that was used in the 1920s and was displayed in the Bureau of Investigations pamphlet. It is sometimes

Cover from a boxed container of Stillman's Freckle Cream purchased online, 2007.

recommended in chat room exchanges about skin treatments as the most effective skin lightener. And there always is a response that it may contain harmful ingredients (never specified) or that those wanting to use it should be proud of their already beautiful dark skin and not give in to social pressure to be white.

I purchased a container from an online seller who carries several "South Asian" cosmetics. The Stillman name appears with the trademark-registered sign but the product is not listed with the U.S. Patent Office's trademark registry. On the box it is stated that the product is made "by arrangement with the Stillman Company, America," though there is no Stillman Company to be found in national or local databases, and the name and location of the producer is not visible. The ingredients are not disclosed on packaging or on the printed insert, which is in English and Arabic. The only instructions, also continued from Stillman's advertising, are to put the cream on the face before going to bed at night and wash it off in the morning.

Insert from a boxed container of Stillman's Freckle Cream purchased online, 2007.

Dr. T. Felix Gouraud and his trademark successors sold Gouraud's Oriental Cream, a skin beautifier, for over a hundred years, from 1839, without being deterred by announcements from state boards of health and the AMA Bureau of Investigation that it was just a cheap mixture of calomel and water. It was still being advertised in the movie fandom magazine *Photoplay* in 1940, aimed at women who wanted to look like movie stars in stills from films. An outburst of journalistic exposures and the cosmetics extension of the Food and Drug Act eventually ended it.

Harriet Hubbard Ayer's name decisively displaced Madame Recamier's in the cosmetics industry. For a time in the 1950s the Ideal Toy Company sold a Harriet Hubbard Ayer doll that came with a make-up kit containing Ayer cosmetics. The doll itself did not resemble Mrs. Ayer, except for the perfect skin. By then her name was a thing of the past, and the mercury had moved on as well.

Mercury compounds dominated the explicitly anti-freckle applications, and no other chemistry was used in them. Other types of unwanted skin colorations called for other destructive chemistries. For instance Anti-Mole, composed of 50 percent nitric and 25 percent glacial acetic acid, was certain to destroy any mole it reached.

Mercury compounds were one of the categories of active ingredients in face bleaches, skin whiteners and less specifically named preparations. Perry's Moth and Freckle Lotion addressed itself in addition to moth, a smooth darkened area of facial skin. Manufactured in New York and sold around the country, Perry's in some advertisements depicted the speckled "before use" face of a young woman. Palmer's Skin Whitener, which contained ammoniated mercury when analyzed in 1918, also was marketed in African-American newspapers and magazines as a means to erase the color of race. It continues to this day with the same name but different contents.

Only occasional cases reported in medical journals connected named cosmetics with mercury poisoning in patients. Had the manufacturers arrived at formulas that cleared and lightened skin but fell just short of causing mercury poisoning, or were women injured by the creams and lotions hesitant to report the damage? The chemical analyses performed by academic and government laboratories revealed the content of the cosmetics where there was limited testimony about their effects.

The decade that followed the American Medical Association's 1928 compilation of analyses of cosmetics was marked by attempts to give those analyses political weight. By the 1930s the popular fund of stories of the damage done to women who used certain cosmetics encouraged legislative proposals in America to extend the Food and Drug Act to include public oversight of cosmetics. The extended national debate exposed these stories in journalistic accounts with titles like "American Chamber of Horrors." Resistance by manufacturers delayed passage of the bill, which was signed into law in 1938. Only a few of the cosmetics names targeted in the 1928 compilation lasted past the early 1940s, and those that did had altered contents.

Hydroquinone, an organic chemical used primarily as a toner in photography, gradually replaced mercury in skin-lightening formulations. Mercury had been a critical element in the daguerreotype, and an important component of toners for the paper-based photography that followed. Its role in photography diminished as hydroquinone remained important. The movie-star stills and advertisements of the 1930s and after reflected a softly graded look also advanced by hydroquinone in skin toners. Eventually the cosmetics monitors would force limitations on the proportion of caustic hydroquinone in over-the-counter face creams sold in America, but it has not been banned as mercury has.

The ideal of whiteness and the mercury that had cosmetically and photographically supported it was sustained in other quarters.

The clear skin displayed in drawings and photographs is free of distracting blemishes, free of any hint of unclean darkness. The floating equation of class, race and beauty in cosmetics marketing proposed a mercurial body tending inward from the skin, hair and teeth. The sexual skin is one layer that could be governed by mercury, as women were commercially encouraged and medically discouraged from using mercury products to procure marketable beauty. Harriet Hubbard Ayer's hidden mercury formulas for idealized whiteness gave way to Stillman's clearing away freckles, with hidden mercury formulas as a progressive lightening (or whitening) of any skin. If beauty is lightness of skin, then the racially distinct skin is another layer ready to be engaged by hidden and emerging mercury cosmetics industries.

Benjamin Rush, Philadelphia physician and signer of the United States Declaration of Independence, was as likely to supply mercury and its compounds as a purgative, as was any physician of his time. He also advocated using mercury to solve a social problem only slightly evidenced in the document he signed, the integration of current and former slaves into emergent American society, as if skin color were the only barrier to their acceptance. Rush thought that dark skin was a disease associated with leprosy, which often darkens the complexion of victims, and his cure for the disease and concurrent blackness was to bathe the Africans with bleaching mercury soap.

This plan did not have vocal supporters, but its appearance is an instance of confusing disease with racial difference not so uncommon in American and other histories. As a doctor Rush must have observed the skin-lightening effects of mercury unguents applied to syphilis sufferers and conjectured that this would solve both leprosy and negritude.

The social problem of race was projected into a medical problem that could be addressed with the existing technology of mercury. If those with darker skin were induced to internalize a need for a whiter appearance then they would accept that their existing skin needed to be "improved" before they could be at the same level as those already white. This creates a market driven by social forces referring back to a skin color hierarchy. Those with white skins seemed to be superior just by asserting it, which was something that anyone could do with a little makeup.

African Americans were as susceptible as whites to the attractions of face paint and skin-lighteners, and as likely to criticize those using them. There was the added pressure of color-based socioeconomic inequality that might be reduced by "passing" for white. Chemical applications to change skin color marked that boundary as shifting and negotiated.

In her social history of America's beauty culture, Kathy Peiss speculates that African-American women appearing in white face powder were parodying white elites, not just copying them. That suggests that the face was a surface those more conscious of the artifice could tint to their purposes. Peiss wants to make it clear that women were not just the victims of an emergent corporate culture. Cosmetics developed from recipes and practices intimately shared among women.

Nadinola skin bleach and Nadine face powder (from the National Toilette Company of Paris, Tennessee) were marketed in mass-circulation women's magazines in the United States during the 1920s as a way for the women applying these products to resemble Southern belles with flawless skin. That Nadinola contained 10 percent ammoniated mercury made it the object of complaint by users, censure by the medical profession, and investigation by the federal Food and Drug Administration. The producers of the cream reduced the percentage of mercury to 1.5 percent by 1937, claiming that this reduced the number of complaints, but not the effectiveness of the bleach.

Nadinola was sold to women of a range of skin colors as something that could submerge that variety in a uniformly light loveliness. Gouraud's Oriental Cream, with its heavy calomel concentration, belonged to an earlier phase of mercury skin treatment that excluded both tanning and naturally darker skin, and was only offered in the colors "White, Flesh and Rachel." The color "Rachel" admitted to an expanding market segment that Jewish women might be part of the skin lightening club, but suggested that they might want to lighten their skin in the appropriate tone.

Early twentieth-century cosmetics advertising sometimes included tan with freckles and moth as a skin conditions needing a lightener. Whites began to accept as attractive the tanned body, the product of outdoor recreation, and to use lotions that would allow them to remain in the sun long enough to achieve a darkness they would reject in a person of another race. As long as the socially and legally defined barrier between the races was maintained, tanning was no threat to the social order. But it was one more indicator of the provisional nature of that barrier, which could increase the vehemence asserting it.

Black No More is the name of another mercury-compound skin lightener, and of a satirical novel (1931) by journalist George Schuyler. In the novel, Dr.

Junius Crookman, an Aframerican physician, goes to Germany and comes back with a machine he says will turn blacks white. Based on a speeding-up of the whitening skin disease vitiligo (here whiteness and not blackness is the disease effect), the machine transforms Max Disher into a white man, with white skin and white facial features, who proclaims that he will no longer need hair straightener and will have no more expenditures for skin whitener. Disher mingles with upper-class whites and founds a proto-fascist league of whites, while blacks turned white are elected to the national government. Dr. Crookman becomes surgeon-general. But even as they are enjoying their newfound whiteness, fashion intervenes and skin tints begin to become popular.

Schuyler ridiculed the pretensions of those who think that becoming white is the only way up in society, and who seek a shortcut through technology.

It was also possible to make cosmetics that enhanced the inherent beauty of skin of any color without reference to social class. Madam C. J. Walker (her preferred mode of address) made her fortune mass-producing cosmetics for black working women. Madam Walker's first success was hair rinses for women who had lost hair due to consuming mercury-containing patent medicines and poor general care. She refused to make skin bleaches. That only came about after her death, when her company introduced Tan-Off to compete in the drugstore trade. Treating black skin as a tan also was a trope Madam Walker herself would not have tolerated. Cosmetics had a give in the direction of mercury no matter who was using them.

Mercury's lightening, luster-giving properties, potential for darkening and poisonous, carcinogenic properties on the stage of success and acceptance led to the present international cosmetics arena.

The burgeoning urban areas of Nigeria, sub–Saharan Africa's most populous country, were a good market for mercury soaps and hydroquinone creams imported from Britain, the European power with the strongest colonial ties to the country. A ban on mercury soaps by the European Economic Community in 1976 and by Nigeria itself in 1982 did not halt their import.

A mercury soap does not treat skin darkness as a disease, but much more simply as a dirtiness that can be washed away to reveal the underlying lightness. Mercuric iodide, or mercurous chloride (calomel), light compounds, are readily distributed among the fatty molecules of soap, and coexist with the alkali that makes the soap body. The evenly distributed mercury seems to magnify the decoagulant property of soap that clears that skin of oil and the sullying contents it has absorbed.

Mercury penetrates the skin, disrupts the melanocytes while clogging the surface capillaries, briefly wipes out the staphylococcus and other bacteria normally on the skin, and makes the skin susceptible to infection when the oils and bacteria return. Mercury also can enter the blood stream if absorbed in sufficient quantity, and tending downward it can bring about the typical kidney damage of mercurialism, crossing into the placenta it can cause miscarriages and stillbirths. These were the reasons for the 1976–82 bans, but the cleansing idea of skin-lightening soap sustained demand. By attracting mercury ions, melanin blocks the absorption of mercury as it registers the bleaching effects, which means that the darker the skin the greater quantity and higher concentration of mercury required for a lightening effect, and the more mercury likely to be absorbed by the user.

In January 1988, Nigeria lowered import duties on cosmetics, opening "black Africa's largest cosmetics market" to freer imports. Internal businesses operating behind the tariff wall had to face greater competition from American and European firms. This made mercury soaps less expensive. In February 1988, the Nigerian Health Ministry reiterated the mercury soap ban, and in July the British trade authorities halted the export of mercury soaps and placed restrictions on the percentage of hydroquinone in skin creams.

Export may have been halted but production wasn't, and therefore export continued, because mercury soaps made in Britain and other European countries had their best market in Africa. W&E Products of Lancashire operated a plant where mercuric iodide was added to saponifying slaughterhouse waste to make bars wrapped for sale overseas. Female workers in the plant experienced miscarriages, and one gave birth to an infant who soon died and was shown to be without kidneys. Through the efforts of a local member of the European Parliament this contemporary occupational mercury poisoning became the subject of a 1988 BBC documentary and legal action against the plant owners. They settled out of court.

Taking advantage of a loan from the Irish Development Administration, W&E Products moved their factory to the small town of Arklow, Republic of Ireland, where the need for employment offset qualms about the health consequences for adults and children. Activists pursued the company, posting notice on the Internet of the plant's continued operation, and the owners changed the name again, to Killarney Enterprises, and simply refused to give information to inquirers. Their soaps and creams continued to make their way to the African market under a number of names.

Individual countries and the European Union made the sale of mercury soaps and skin creams illegal, but did not restrict their production and export. Health warnings and bans by government agencies in Nigeria, Kenya, Tanzania, Zimbabwe and South Africa did not halt their availability in stores. Lists of brands containing mercury circulated by health offices also helped advertise those brands.

The African subsidiary that controlled the Tura medicated soap brand, TURA International, Limited, tried to prevent counterfeiting of their product by "unscrupulous pretenders" in Nigeria. Using sophisticated packaging machinery from Europe, and slashing prices by 50 percent, the company offered motorbikes, generators and televisions to the wholesalers who purchased the greatest quantities of the soap, and a premium gift of soap or skin-toning cream to consumers who returned specially marked packages. African producers were copying the wraps and labeling of the brand so effectively that brand proprietors had to devise strategies to circumvent them.

The penetration of mercury skin products into African life was quantified by a survey of blood-mercury levels in people living near Lake Victoria. The scientists conducting the survey were trying to correlate the levels of mercury in people with those in the lake water and the fish caught there. What they found was a greater concentration of the element than could be predicted from food alone, and had to be explained by the use of soaps and skin creams containing mercury. Absorption of mercury through skin products supplements its absorption from environmental sources. Mercury soaps and creams followed those under cultural pressure to look whiter wherever they might be. Banned from export from Europe, they had become available in small "ethnic" shops catering to African, Near Eastern and South Asian, and in America, Mexican and Latin American migrants, who even within their own communities would be encouraged to adopt the ideal of a lighter complexion. The pressure to have light-colored skin could coexist with a recognition of the beauty of skin colors other than white, and the cosmetics to enhance them.

Urbanized populations with a range of skin colors have assimilated mercury-based skin-lightening products in a pattern of clandestine acceptance and public denial similar to the other patterns of mercury consumption and rejection. Saudi Arabian society, which requires women to appear in public with most of the body covered and out of view, affluent and with international connections, contains encouragements for women to lighten what can be seen.

An analysis of forty skin creams available for purchase in Saudi stores found that thirty of them had mercury content in concentrations ranging from 0.09 to 5650 parts per million (ppm). Last Fade Cream (The Secret of Seaweed) imported from Thailand had 0.69 ppm mercury; Ginseng (Extra Pearl Cream), of unknown provenance, contained 594.50 ppm; and ALFA (Extra Pearl Cream), also unknown but listed elsewhere as a Killarney Enterprises label, was at 1319 ppm. Drula (bleaching wax) from Germany had no detectable mercury and Tibet Snow from Pakistan had 0.39 ppm.

The colors of the creams, also reported by the investigators, were generally a shiny white or yellow with a few of the products showing pinks and oranges. The color was no predictor of mercury content, which was not indicated on the packaging. Typical of cosmetics, the color of the creams reflected the intentions of the user more than it reflected the chemical composition of the product.

The actual use of skin-whitening soaps and creams only emerged through a study of the available stock of soaps and creams or of specific cases that came to medical attention and were written up in journals. A "whitened-face" woman who appeared at a clinic in Jakarta, Indonesia, for treatment of back pain turned out to have nephrotic syndrome caused by elevated levels of mercury in her kidneys. She was a Filipino maid employed by a wealthy Indonesian family, and she left the country before the doctors could begin chelation therapy to rid her of the mercury. She only appeared for a moment, like a face suddenly illuminated in a crowd.

"Ghost!" the children cried when a young woman who used a skin-lightening cream came to the Thai restaurant where she worked, until the manager fired her. The cream had made her face into a mottled flush of pink and brown. The Thai authorities, trying to curb the sale of face, hand, armpit, and nipple lightening creams with their skin-damaging ingredients often including mercury, published a list of seventy brands to avoid.

The U.S. Food and Drug Administration had identified mercury as a drug, and therefore any substance of human consumption containing mercury was subject to rules governing drugs. That made mercury-containing cosmetics illegal, which coincidentally was a term applied to some of the people who were using them, migrants from the south who had come to do menial work more remunerative than what was available in their own countries.

America's own African-American population had since Benjamin Rush's time been addressed by the advertisers of nostrums to "improve" their skin to whiteness for the sake of improving their chances economically and socially. The entertainer Michael Jackson during a career from childhood onward transformed his voice, his facial features and his skin color to end up perhaps an excessively distinctive figure. Jackson's skin color went from dark to a glistening ivory, a change he claimed was the result of a disease, in what may have been a deliberate jibe at the blackness-as-illness fallacy. In making an example of himself, however, Jackson also seemed to demonstrate that people of great wealth could show any skin desired. Few others could afford this irony.

The majority of others were left with their skin and the cosmetics and the warnings of doctors and public health officials that the ingredients of the cosmetics are dangerous. "Whitening Skin Can Be Deadly," Dr. S. Allen Counter titled an article on his international researches into high rates of mercury poisoning. He found that most of the reported mercury-poisoning cases were in lower-latitude nations, and most of the patients who gave clinical evidence of mercury poisoning were women. In the United States, most of the cases were in the states of Texas, Arizona and California, which border Mexico. Dr. Counter conjectured that patients reporting to clinics with mercury-induced disease "believe that the health risks associated with bleaching their skins are outweighed by the rewarding sociocultural return."

Counter interviewed a Latin American woman who told him outright that whiter-skinned women are considered more attractive by many Latino men, as whiter-skinned men are considered attractive by women. He could not say that they knew the true risks of using the creams, but then, it was necessary to make an equally strong effort to convince light-skinned people that tanning their skin is risky.

Cases of mercury poisoning correlated with use of imported skin-lightening creams prompt city and state public health agencies to warn doctors and hospitals that specific named products are to be avoided. The poor and often illegal immigrants are most likely to use the cheap, illegal creams (soaps have fallen out of the picture) and least likely to be within reach of health warnings and a health care. It is only the odd cases that attract the attention of clinicians and are used by public agencies as publicity for problems they are addressing. When the health issues of the immigrant underclass intersect with the fears and interdictions of official medicine, they can win notice.

A 15-year-old boy with chronic shakes and acute weight loss was passed from a physician in Piedras Negras, Texas, whose prescription did no good, to his mother's Mexican herbal remedies and injections of B-complex vitamins, to a specialist in San Antonio, who tested the boy's urine and found the mercury levels to be twenty times normal. The boy was treated for mercury poisoning and returned home.

When a nurse in the boy's home town of Eagle Pass, Texas, found his mercury levels still elevated weeks after he stopped using the beauty cream, a team from the Texas Department of Health Office of Border Health searched the boy's house using a mercury vapor detector. Pillow cases and bed sheets showed high readings, and a jar of acne cream near the bed was higher still.

The source of the mercury was *Crema de Belleza-Manning*, a beauty cream manufactured in Mexico that lists calomel among the ingredients. The boy was mixing the beauty cream with his acne medication to lessen the irritation. The soothing and healthful beauty cream with its skin-lightening effects appealed to an adolescent already being medicated for a skin condition. Department of Health agents "fanned out" seeking containers of the beauty cream in beauty salons, flea markets and ethnic stores. Notices were issued through physicians and the Spanish-language press. Mexican authorities cooperated and halted production of the cream in laboratories south of the border, but some stock remained, and renamed versions began to appear. The boy recovered his health.

Skin-color anxiety was combined with commercially promoted teenage anxiety in the same bedside jar. The boy first had acne medication then invented his mixture to overcome the irritation of its application. The results brought him into the health-care system and the discovery of mercury made it a public-health issue, which is why we know about him. The rhetoric used by Texas state health department focused on mercury poisoning, and the threat of it spreading from the Rio Grande to the rest of the country, much in the same way that illegal immigrants and illegal drugs spread, another strain of the diseased alien, the alien as disease.

Mixing mercury skin cream with acne medication was a homemade version of the already existing development of the skin cream industry, which replaced mercury with hydroquinone and dark skin with "discolored" skin, which might include acne. *La Crema de Belleza-Manning* was a persistently mercury-containing preparation. Texas authorities traced it to Mexico. Mexican health officers raided the factory where it was made. That source was shut off, but jars of the cream, under other names, continued to appear on the shelves of the small stores.

Notices in the Centers for Disease Control and Prevention's *Mortality and Morbidity Weekly Reports* warned communities in a widening arc of distribution of further cases of mercury poisoning associated with use of the beauty cream. A technical report used the epidemiological term "prevalence" to describe the effects of persistent application of the cream in border communities of Texas, Arizona and California. All 330 women who contacted their state health departments with symptoms of mercury poisoning were users of the cream and were shown to have elevated urine mercury levels. "In 104 (5%) of the 2,194 [Texas border] households surveyed, at least one person reported having used Belleza-Manning in the past year; 820 (37%) had heard warnings about the cream." It was an epidemic from the other side of the border.

New York health authorities, advising users to seal the jars in plastic and dispose of them in the household trash(!), traced mercury-containing *Crema Blanqueadora,* and *Jabon Germicida* to the Dominican Republic. That prosperous Spanish-speaking country shares the island of Hispaniola with Haiti, whose poorer residents, distinguishable by their darker skin color, are both exploited as laborers and barred from crossing the border. It is a social laboratory for the development and commercialization of skin products that allow Dominicans to maintain their separateness while tempting Haitians to take part in whiteness, which is then exported to New York, Miami and other Dominican-Haitian population centers.

As messages of the dangers of mercury spread, it ceased to be an ingredient listed by manufacturers of beauty soaps and cream for those uneasy about their skins and their skins' colorings. That unease became vaguer in the advertising, a matter of hygiene rather than race, but kept in association through imagery rather than wording.

Nadinola, Dr. Fred Palmer's Skin Lightening Cream and several other old mercury compound names persist in the Internet market as hydroquinone preparations. The names are too well known to disappear. But now other words appear in the titles, "cleansing," "germicidal," "beautifying," which imply skin lightening as part of a health program and promise to deliver it through a list of ingredients with chemical names, none including mercury. "Fade cream" sells its ability to remove "discolorations." There are some that advertise that they do not include mercury in any form and claim to achieve their cleansing-sanitizing effect using herbs and mushrooms, the same components of many another soothing bath oil. The practice of advertising against mercury persists in the markets where mercury is still available.

A team of Danish scientists who investigated the penetration of mercury into the bodies of gold miners in Tanzania undertook a parallel study of mercury in the blood of soap and face cream users. The Tanzanian government had officially banned mercury-containing personal care products, but the researchers found that they could easily purchase at open-air markets three brands of packaged soap which openly declared 2 percent mercuric iodide content on the packaging. The two brands of face cream made no such declaration. All of the products identified themselves as contributing to a lighter skin, and all but one was manufactured in the United Kingdom and imported into Tanzania. Chemical analysis of the soaps showed an actual mercury content slightly less than what was advertised in the soaps, and no mercury in the face creams, which were based on hydroquinone.

The soaps produced in the United Kingdom and imported into Tanzania were packaged with printed claims of skin-lightening properties. They must have been the source of the greatly elevated body mercury levels found among Tanzanian women tested: 122 milligrams of mercury per kilogram of body mass. Tanzanian miners and amalgamists working with mercury to extract gold from ores had a body mercury content of 3 milligrams per kilogram, compared with 1.1 milligrams for male non-miners in the same population. The average mercury of Danish citizens tested was 0.6 milligrams. The mercury soaps were the most efficient system for the delivery of mercury to the body through a popular culture practice.

Use of mercury soaps to lighten skin induced a much higher mercury level in Tanzanian women than was found among the next highest concentration, in fish consumers in the Brazilian Amazon tributaries where there was considerable small-scale gold mining. The concentration of mercury in the soap can enter the body directly from the entire area of the skin being washed and lightened with the soap. The concentration of mercury entering the miners and refiners is at first modest but it is magnified in the fish living in the water that receives the mine waste and runoff and again in the people who depend upon the fish.

Hydroquinone and other compounds can replace mercury in skin-lightening soaps and creams, and cyanide can replace mercury in gold and silver extraction. As the mercury disappears from the soaps and creams it also disappears from the bodies of their users (though if they were pregnant the effects may linger in the child). Even if other means replace mercury in getting at the gold and silver, the mercury that already has been used to obtain the present stores of the precious metals is in the water and is rising in the fish. The gold ring on your finger, the soap to lighten your skin, and the fish you had for supper converge in the same body.

9

〜〜

The Rivers of California

Three men went out looking for oranges and found a mercury mine, a "cave of cinnabar." Their wives prospered.

"Cave of cinnabar," *dan xue* in Chinese, was an expression that also meant the interior of a woman's vagina, its color similar to the reddish oranges the men were seeking and the red-orange mineral deposit they found. The resultant prosperity, though measured in taels of gold, can only have been an increase in the number of children who would have emerged from the cave of cinnabar.

This story, from the *I Lin* (Forest of Symbols) section of the second-century C.E. Chinese classic the *I Ching, Book of Changes,* identifies what mercury was to the Chinese, a color called "vermilion" in European languages. Vermilion was the color of mercury in the earth and into which mercury was transformed from its metallic form.

There are several stories like this in early Chinese ritual and historical literature, where the discovery of the peculiar red-orange in the ground signals a chance to delve successfully into the body of the earth to uncover the body of the woman and of the family.

The pictographic interpretation of the Chinese character *dan,* which stands for cinnabar, the color vermilion and the elixir of life, is often taken to be a drawing of a writing stone on which a piece of vermilion sits ready to be moistened before being used in writing with a brush. Or it is an opening in the earth like a pit or a well with vermilion inside. Or it is an alchemist's crucible in which cinnabar is heating. Or a pill ready to be swallowed by the seeker of immortality.

Vermilion or cinnabar, *dan,* was a more fundamental object of commerce in ancient China than mercury itself. It was a color seen, tasted, felt, inscribed, and transmitted. In the early twentieth century, as industrial mining of mercury was taking hold in China, mining's chief purpose was still to produce vermilion. When the large cities on the coast of China were cut off from the mercury sources in the interior or those sources could not send enough mercury, they imported mercury from California to make vermilion: concentrated, artificial cinnabar.

Master Sung Ying-hsing marveled that the redness of fire is the source of the deepest black ink (lampblack). The whiteness of mercury can be transformed into the vermilion ink used for imperial rescripts ("vermilion pencil") on state decrees written in black ink. "Hence law and order are proclaimed across the land!"

Chinese scholars and officials who wrote about mercury minerals described the appearance of the specimens best suited for making the elixir of immortality. These mineral specimens were uncovered in configurations defined by royal imagery. "Twelve pieces of cinnabar make up one throne. Its color is like that of an unopened red lotus blossom, and its luster is as dazzling as the sun." The relationship between the visible configuration of the mineral deposits and the metaphysics of monarchy was carried forward in the use of cinnabar crystals to make vermilion ink.

By Sung's time, a transition from metaphysics to industry was visible. Writing in his *Manufactures Under Heaven* (*T'ien-Kung K'ai-Wu*) in 1637, Sung says that the highest grade cinnabar was used to polish arrowheads, mirrors and the like. The mercury in the ore amalgamated with the metal of weapon and mirror making the surface shine.

Mercury, cinnabar and vermilion are the same substance according to Sung, capable of transformation, one into the other. Cinnabar can be distilled into mercury liquid which heated with pieces of sulfur mineral makes artificial vermilion of different grades. Naturally occurring cinnabar is crushed with rollers and the resulting powder is placed in a jar and covered with water. Over three days the low-grade ore, useful only to make mercury, floats to the top of the jar. The high-grade ore that falls to the bottom is crushed to a powder, formed into vermilion paste and molded with glue into sticks for use as ink. Vermilion ink cannot be converted back into mercury. There, Sung writes, the works of heaven are exhausted.

All forms of mercury are sorted into hierarchies that reflect the quality of the material and the nobility or baseness of use. Gleaming weapons for imperial warriors and costly mirrors for court ladies are primary uses for the high-grade mineral, as is vermilion ink which carries official orders and scholarly commentaries from the center of power to the provinces.

Vermilion paint derived solely from crushed crystals of cinnabar covered the interior of aristocrats' tombs from ancient times onward. Some of the "oracle bones" which are the earliest evidence of Chinese writing are covered with cinnabar powder, probably to preserve them from mildew. It would have to be the interior of tombs and buried bones since vermilion mercuric sulfide on exposure to sunlight becomes black mercuric sulfide, metacinnabar. Less visible mercury compounds also were found to be used as a preservative of buried bodies—mummies.

Color uniquely provided by mercury compounds was carried over to medicines, paints and inks. When Sung was writing, the medicines and paints were for lower-rank users, while the ink used in writings of the officials was the highest form of the color.

The formation of reds by the combination of yellow sulfur with silvery mercury seemed to be a blooded, vital process in the earth. In China, a perfection of vermilion color achieved through refinement of mercury became the possession of royalty. The "red chamber" (*hong lou*) in which the foppish son of the nobility dreams in an early Chinese novel was only an approximation of the sleep of kings of bygone ages. It was not a vermilion chamber.

Mercury mines in China were not adits and shafts occluding faces, but open pits from which the minerals were viewed and drawn out by daylight. The vision of cinnabar is therefore a view of how it lies in the ground, symbolic mineralogy becoming symbolic geology.

The hierarchy of uses extended to the location of cinnabar deposits in the ground. The deeper the rock the higher its grade. Sung wrote that "top-grade cinnabar ore is reached by digging some 100 feet below the earth's surface." The first appearance of the seam has the look of white stones, and is called "cinnabar bed." Some of the pieces found at that point are the size and color of hen's eggs. The low-grade ore, for use in medicines, paints and making mercury, is not usually accompanied by white stones, but appears only a few dozen feet below the surface amid dark or yellow stones and sand. Deeper down, cracks in the white bed show a bright red substance, and this is the ore extracted, crushed and sorted by flotation grading. "This kind of ore is produced mostly in Ssu-yin and T'ung-jen in Kwei-chou province, but is also found in Shan-chou and Ch'in-chou [in Shensi and Kansu, respectively]."

Today these excavations are still active mines, but they also are the source of mineralogical specimens sold to rock fanciers world-wide. Unique single pieces of cinnabar taken from these mines and carved into bowls and figurines were exported along trade routes, to be found in the imperial treasury of Japan and in ancient Roman collections. This stone carried such a signature of preciousness that an entire industry of vessels made from wooden molds lacquered vermilion with vegetable dyes developed in China. Museum gift catalogues feature this production today.

The main mercury export from China was powdered vermilion, which also made its way along trade routes both east and west out of China. The quicksilver extracted by heating inferior quality cinnabar and other minerals was made into vermilion by combining it with sulfur. That industry became so well developed in China that at one time the mercury imported from America was processed into vermilion and exported. The managers of the New

Almaden mine in California even considered importing the Chinese vermilion-making process, which would have meant importing the workers. By the middle of the nineteenth century, however, there were complaints that Chinese vermilion was adulterated with powdered glass, and was no better in quality than French or more robust American vermilion.

Sung's description of cinnabar deposits suggests digging into the ground in the manner of pit mining. A twelfth-century text on mineral resources fills in some of the details that cannot have changed much by Sung's time. A pit was dug several hundred feet down to the white cinnabar seam, wood was piled in and a fire was started. After it had cooled and the ashes were removed "shrines" housing bright red crystals of cinnabar were visible in the cracked white stone. These were withdrawn and pulverized to make the precious powder.

These were not the extraction methods used when in the late nineteenth and early twentieth centuries Chinese miners were placed at the command of European and American mining engineers who supervised them in the construction of shafts and systems to transport quantities of the ore to the surface. The band of mercury deposits stretching across Guizhou and Gansu provinces attracted foreign investors and expertise when the value of mercury to local and international commerce exceeded the cost of removing it from the ground, processing the ore and transporting it to where it was used industrially.

Wanshan in Guizhou province had cinnabar deposits extensive enough to warrant tunneling, while much smaller local excavations continued as they always had. Cinnabar was no longer primarily a red crystalline monarch enthroned in white or an exclusive device for imperial and scholarly rule. Sung's description of grading techniques suggests the quality and quantities of rock brought to the surface, but later the vision of single precious specimens gave way to a stream of ore to be processed in mills. The precious specimens were left to museums and mineral fanciers.

As described in the early twentieth century by a European engineer who was occupied with the industry of mining, the work at Wanshan reflects elements of the older mining practices. There were two varieties of ore at Wanshan, one a bright transparent red and the other a dark opaque red.

> In extracting the ore the miner follows a stringer or mineralized band where it leads, resulting in irregular workings. The miners use iron drills pointed with steel, and the holes are usually about 15 in. deep. Gunpowder is used for blasting.... The ore is sorted in the mine and brought to the surface in bamboo baskets of about 3 lb. capacity. It is further cleaned and caused to pass through a ⅛-in. bamboo sieve. If the cinnabar is of the red variety, the crushed ore is panned and the clean cinnabar removed, the tailings being retorted. The dark ore is treated directly without panning.

To the engineer's disapproval, the Chinese miner followed the colored vein when planting the charge holes, rather than studying the strata and removing the entire mass to form an adit leading to a rock face. The broken rock was sorted and carried out of the pit, not removed after a fire had cracked it.

There were block-printed illustrations of pieces of cinnabar in Chinese texts long before there were depictions of miners, accounts of their work and disasters. There also was a system equating the formation of red, white and black deposits of mercury geomantically with three directions and with other associated minerals. The cinnabar veins that repaid commercial exploitation were not unearthed in pits with fires to crack the stone; they were brought up by driving down into the dark where no colors were visible.

As late as 1908, vermilion production was the main objective of mining cinnabar at Wanshan. That only changed with the development of industries in China that used elemental mercury in electric switches, fluorescent tubes and scientific instrumentation, among many others. Wanshan is one of the few mercury mining areas in the world still active today.

The records of Chinese working in mercury mines in California do not attribute to them any knowledge of the mineral they were removing from the earth. They were likely to have come from coastal provinces in south China where there are no significant deposits of mercury. They worked in the mercury mines as in the gold mines, or making bricks, or cutting tunnels through mountains for railroads.

"The celestials," according to Helen Rocca Goss, the daughter of the superintendent of the Great Western Mine in Lake and Napa Counties, California, 1876–1900, "varying in number from about two hundred to two hundred and fifty, did most of the manual labor at the Great Western." Goss's reminiscences about the Chinese workers places them at a distance, inside their barracks or huts, eating rice or working in the mines. They are the familiar exotics of opium dens and laundry shops, passive and incomprehensible, prone to sudden violence, superstitious and mysterious in their ways, led by the few well-educated men among them, the only ones named.

As with all the other aspects of Goss's account, there is little attention to the work in the mine itself. She does, however, write of the "sootmen" who crawled into the hot condensers and removed the accretions. The condensers were where the quicksilver was precipitated from mercury vapor arising from crushed, heated ore, only these condensers were much larger than the enclosed retorts that Sung described centuries earlier. Goss quotes from her mother's diary the phrase "shaking, toothless wrecks" to describe the state of the men after they had performed this job long enough to regularly inhale powerful mercury fumes. She even names one of the men, Ah Cat, who could scarcely hold a cup steady as he drank. Ah Cat sometimes helped Goss's mother Lilian with the gardening, at one time suggesting in all seriousness that her parents drown their third child, a girl, because the first two children were girls. This was taken as a curiosity, not as a reflection of a background so harsh that it would cause a man to earn his living by crawling into mercury condensers.

There was no vermilion coming out of the Great Western Mine, only flasks of mercury which were used at other mines to extract the gold from the strata exposed by hydraulic mining. The coinage and architectural gilding of the American empire was finished by mercury, the American empire's gold was mercurial.

Mr. Parrott, the president and director of the Sulphur Bank Mining Company, was arrested for having Chinese employees. A California law passed under pressure by organized labor excluded Chinese workers from many occupations that they had long held. Judge Sawyer decided in the subsequent trial that the state law violated federal law and a treaty with China that would permit the Chinese to immigrate and work. The empire always has been uncertain about this, even about extending the opportunity to become shaking, toothless wrecks for miserable wages. The Chinese continued to extract mercury from the American ground, but not in peace.

The properties of cinnabar, according Marcus Vitruvius Pollio, are very strange. The clods the miners dug out were reddish in color and covered with red dust. Under the blows of the digging tools it shed tear after tear of quicksilver, which was collected by the miners. When the lumps of ore were dry, they were crushed in iron mortars, and repeatedly washed and heated until the impurities were gone, and the colors came. The process of making vermilion was as tedious as the mining itself.

When the cinnabar had given up its quicksilver, and had lost the natural virtues that it previously had, it became soft in quality and its powers were feeble. Hence, Vitruvius added, vermilion turns black on exposure to sunlight and moonlight, giving the example of an official who's had the walls of the peristyle of his house stylishly painted in vermilion only to see it turn a mottled black within thirty days. If you want to keep the vermilion color in the light, he advises, apply an overcoat of Pontic wax, which will prevent the sun and moon from "licking up and drawing the color out" of the polished surface.

Vitruvius included these prescriptions in the section on architectural colors in Book VII of his *Ten Books of Architecture* (first century B.C.E.). He explained that vermilion was what was left in mercury after the quicksilver was gone, assimilated by potent heavenly bodies. Cinnabar showed red because it was underground, and it was the red that guided the attack of the skilled miner. The color brought out by washing off the mercury was unstable and needed to be protected from light. This was a light-developing property of mercury compounds forgotten when vermilion became one of the many colors that could be fixed as paint, dye or ink and made permanently fast on stone, paper, and hair.

Cinnabar was drawn from the mines and produced artificially from mercury and sulfur. There were formulas for making it in treatises on painting, giving varieties of different hue and tone. Natural cinnabar is not distinguished from artificial in writings until the sixteenth century, and it is not possible to tell the two apart in the color chemistry of artworks. What writers called "cinnabar" could also have been hematite, a red iron-oxide pigment; and "minium," red lead coloring, also referred to what we call cinnabar. "Vermilion" is a specialized term that came to apply to all red mercury pigments.

Iron, copper, nickel, gold, silver, salt, sulfur, coal, potash and many other metals and minerals were extracted from veins and deposits identified by their color and texture. Mercury was hardly unique in that tints and feel and smells guided those who pursued it. The chemistry of its bodies and its interaction with other metals made a color array that extended from the earth to the body, something that requires some imagining to recapture today, when machinery intervenes in all mining, even small-scale operations. Miners formerly sank pits to follow surface colorations which, if they continued, became tight underground passages artificially lit and in danger of collapse, flood, and explosion. Chinese mercury mining for a long time was trained upon the color, whereas in Europe the color only existed in the dark, drawing in the body of the miner to meet it.

Mercury is unique in being a liquid that is mined both in its native form and in the minerals from which it can be smelted. Ramazzini wrote that mercury "flees on sandaled, winged feet" from heat, associating it with the Roman god Mercury, the messenger of the gods, a divinity who delivers hidden hermetic truths, and is the patron of thieves. The earth grows warmer the further down the mine shaft is driven; as the cinnabar is exposed, mercury vapor enters the air — and the lungs of the miners laboring in the enclosed chambers. Ramazzini also wrote that mercury mining was the most dangerous mining of all because of the penetrating vapors.

Ignoring Vitruvius, he said nothing of colors down below. There is none of the vermilion or the other colors of mercury that the Chinese found and fixed into the directions and character of the earth. Mercury gained color when it turned to gold in the hands of gilders who covered everything with gold, while mercury corroded their faces and nerves. Ramazzini's continued irony of contrast between the afflictions suffered by artisans and the beauty of their work was strongest in his description of the use of mercury by gilders. One of Ramazzini's most dramatic images, imported from another writer, is of a gilder whose brains boiled out his eyes.

Gold and silver were the surface and currency of empire in China, as in Europe and America. While in China vermilion locked this surface, in the rest of the world it was mainly called upon to bring forth gold and silver. The punitive darkness and misery of the gold, silver and mercury mines, brought forth the shine and flash of the royal courts and celebrity bling, the dazzle of the churches and corporate offices, the gilding of a gilded age. This rise from the mines yielded several unique states of color contrast, a silvery photography and an explosive red.

Miners suffered lack of fresh, moving air, and endured the presence of noxious vapors and moisture where they remained entire days, where it didn't matter whether it was day or night. The threat of cave-ins and floods collapsing and blocking shafts and tunnels also surrounded the lives of mercury miners, as of all other miners. The mercury mines more than any other intensified the danger of the workers absorbing the element being sought. The known consequences for the body were a numb state, almost dreamlike, as much from heavy labor as from poisoning. Shaking and confused, prone to accidents, even expendable conscripts were restricted in the amount of time they spent in the mercury chambers.

Perhaps the sensations of mining freed of the tedium and danger were carried forward into the use complexes of mercury aboveground. The vermilion of the Chinese emperor's notations was the red shock amid the white stone and dark other matter suddenly discovered in a heated pit. The dreams of the alchemists and chambered kings, and the painful health of syphilis sufferers selectively reproduced the condition of the miners who raised the mercury the elites deliberately inhaled.

As the larger mercury mines became state enterprises linked to gold and silver production, the emerging professional classes began to investigate the effects of the mercury on the health of the miners. This was part of a general trend toward the study of occupational illness first centered on mining, noticed since antiquity as a source of specific damage to the bodies of long-term laborers in the shafts and pits. The motives of the study were at times charitable and humanistic, seeking to lessen the suffering of those condemned to work by sentence and then by poverty. As the production of the mines became proportional to the hours of labor available, the well-being (and supply) of miners became an economic asset. Ultimately the mines became a venue for doctors and scientists to observe and experiment with the long-term effects of mercury absorption on living tissue. The miner's body emerged from the dark interior like another silvery resource.

The Almaden mine in the Ciudad Real area of La Mancha, about 200 kilometers to the south of Madrid, has been yielding high-grade mercury ores through a matrix of lengthening tunnels for over two thousand years. The mercury content, or tone, of the Almaden ores ranges from 7–25 percent, compared with 0.65 percent at the Idria mine and an average content of 0.38 percent for California ores. The relative richness of mercury concentrations in Almaden minerals may be a reason why the miners were more strongly affected by the fumes in that mine than in the others.

The Carthaginians and the Romans used the mine's stone for decoration and for mercury production. The word "mine" *la mina* has its origins in an Arabic word used for the Almaden deposits worked by the Arab overlords of Spain until the reconquest. Granted by the Spanish crown to a military order of knights, from 1525 to 1645 the mine fell under the control of the Fuggers, an

Augsburg merchant and banking family. They used their war-debt hold on the Hapsburg emperor Charles V to corner the lucrative market in syphilis treatments. They both monopolized the importation of the tropical wood guiac and managed a major source of quicksilver, for a time owning both vegetable and mineral remedies for the disease.

Medicinal calomel and vermilion recovered from mercury deposits were sidelined by the introduction of the amalgamation method of gold and silver extraction, which required quantities of distilled quicksilver to dissolve and purify the gold and silver from crushed ores and objects they coated. The ability of fluid mercury to dissolve gold and silver (and, unfortunately, lead) was used by the Romans and their heirs to withdraw precious metals from unwanted combinations. In the middle of sixteenth century the method was described in several books on mining and goldsmithing, demonstrating that it had been in use for a while as a professional secret.

Amalgamation allowed promoters such as Johann Becher to thrill would-be investors with gold extraction from sands. The quantities of gold obtained were so limited that they did not justify the cost of the mercury used. The increased use of "raw" mercury in medicine in the late seventeenth and early eighteenth centuries may simply be a reflection of its availability for gold amalgamation. More than one wit pointed out that mercury could extract gold from bodies as well as from rock.

Mervyn Lang claims that amalgamation was in use in Mexico to extract silver from ores before it became well known in Europe. By the 1550s it became apparent that the known precious metal deposits, laboriously worked by the natives and the European invaders simply by burning the ores until the silver was released, could be forced into much greater production with the use of mercury. The demand for raw mercury impelled the search for new and more accessible mercury resources.

The discovery of the Huancavelica mine in Peru in 1563 seemed to give the Spanish Crown a chance to bypass the Fuggers and supply the silver mines at Potosí with mercury from a closer source, but colonial mercury production never approached Almaden's. The Spanish vessel that the HMS *Triumph* salvaged in 1713, giving English doctors their first chance to observe mass mercury vapor poisoning, was carrying mercury from Spain to the mines in Nueva España (New Spain, Mexico). The New Almaden mine in California, named according to a hope it inspired, matured with the loss of Spanish control of California to the United States, in time to provide amalgamation stock for the nearby goldfields.

There was every motive for the old Almaden mine's operators to drive as deep as they could in quest of mercury. During the five-year period from 1600–04, the mine yielded 3,041 Castilian quintals (46 kilograms or about 101.4 pounds per quintal) of mercury; by 1894–99 it produced 35,026, with only a few interruptions and severe drops during the intervening centuries. The number of workers employed at the mines also increased over the three-hundred-year period, as a small city grew up to house them and their families.

In 1566, the Fuggers succeeded in getting the Crown to assign convicts sentenced to hard labor in the galleys to work in the mines, and they continued to press for more labor as the mercury and thus the gold flowed in response to the added muscle. "Moriscos" (black Muslims of Northern African origin), Gypsies and slaves formed the bulk of those pressed into this service. Eventually the workforce became voluntary and intergenerational, as at others mines.

This growth of production, population and infrastructure occurred at the other mercury mines, but was limited by the extent of the deposits, and by the ratio of demand to cost of extraction. Idria, Monte Amiata, Huancavelica, New Almaden and New Idria are now closed as major mining operations, with only some artisanal mining and mineral collecting still pursued in the area. At Idria and Monte Amiata there are major concerns about contamination of ground water and living things. Almaden operates a few months per year. Only Wanshan remains open and producing full time. People living in the vicinity of Huancavelica will demonstrate condensing mercury from heated rock if you ask. Mercury mining still goes on in Turkey, Kazakhstan and Algeria, at locations and under conditions not described in the literature.

Most of the mercury now used is derived from recycling. The United States exports recycled mercury generally to be traded in Amsterdam, and imports a small amount of newly mined mercury from countries where there are fewer restrictions on mining and smelting.

Ancient writers who visited mercury mines viewed them in terms of the materials extracted there rather than the people who worked there. The little comment they made on the miners just reinforced their statements on the potency of the mercury. The early Chinese and Western writers on cinnabar discoursed on shapes and colors, sometimes naming the location of a mine but only remarking on the precautions taken by miners to escape the worst effects of their labor.

The pig's-bladder masks that Pliny wrote workers wore in a mine (Sisapon) which may have been Almaden later became glass masks, which cannot have been very practical. The Roman Senate closed down the Monte Amiata mercury mines in the second century C.E., and for unknown reasons the Romans imported their mercury from Almaden while the mines supposedly remained idle. Several were reopened by the revived Italian kingdom in 1848 and all were closed for good by 1981. During a strike in 1968, forty-eight miners remained below in the tunnels for two weeks to press their demands for higher pay and better work conditions, using the dangers of the mine for the workers to pressure the private owners. Now the mine is a historical park with a museum.

A Tang-dynasty alchemical work advises those who make mercury by roasting and distilling the vapors to eat large quantities of pork. "If they did not eat this the chi of the mercury would enter their stomachs and their five viscera would become stopped up." Joseph Needham notes that this would have been a valid practice, since mercury vapor would bind to pork fat and be carried out of the body.

A brief practical guide to avoiding the noxious fumes of lead, silver and mercury, written in 1473 but not published until 1524, was intended by its author for goldsmiths. Ulrich Ellenbog was city physician in Augsburg, known for its goldsmiths who shaped the metal of its commerce shaped by the Fuggers. Ellenbog advised the workers to remain in the open air, avert the face while heating the materials, sprinkle wine on the smelting coals, and take sarsaparilla and other aromatic medicines to clear the blood. Ellenbog's handbook was apparently unknown to Georg Agricola, a teacher of Latin and Greek in the Saxon city of Zwickau, who made suggestions (1556) for minimizing the intake of harmful vapors, humidity and dust in the mines, saying to wear thick boots and insulated clothing and ventilate the tunnels through shafts.

Paracelsus wrote a treatise on "the miners sickness," probably while he worked as a metallurgist at the mines operated by the Fuggers in Villach, but it wasn't published until 1565. He called the vapors that entered the miners and attached themselves to the interior of their lungs "mercurius." He generalized from the vapors of mercury mines to those of all mines: every metal had its mercury, and the essence of that mercury was pure quicksilver in flight. From the experience of miners, Paracelsus formed a medical-chemical theory of poisoning and healing.

From this basis, the Central European writers on mining urged abating the fumes and dust of volatile metals underground. Their advice was carried to New World mines by German and Cornish miners, but it was not consistently followed.

The first account of the bodies of the workers in the Almaden mine was not a physician's prescription but a secret imperial report by a *contador*, appointed as a visiting judge. The Spanish state administrative council, the *Consejo de Ordenes*, in 1593 commissioned Mateo Alemán to investigate the condition of forced labor at the mines. Outwardly humane in intent, this mission proceeded against resistance by the Fuggers and their allies on the Interior Council, *Consejo de Hacienda*.

Over a period of fifteen days, Alemán summoned miners, posed questions and had the answers concurrently recorded by a scribe. He did not examine the workers' bodies; he inquired about food, clothing, health, and work conditions. For the first time anywhere, within the highly constrained framework of Spanish imperial judicial inquiry, the workers were able to speak. Miguel del Aldea, a native of Tarasona in the Kingdom of Aragon, told the interrogator that he was condemned to eight years of labor for various crimes.

> Asked if he knows the number of forced laborers in this works and if they are in keeping with the mandate and if the said laborers receive the treatment that his majesty commands in necessary clothing, healing arts and medicines for their

sicknesses and if what is done for them suffices and is freely given so that their treatment and life conditions are not so hard that they are made to die quickly and who is to blame for all that is done here and what provision can be made for the future. He said: he did not estimate the number of forced laborers there are in the said works but could not say any more, and when this witness was given the space of a day he recovered his memory; he declared how many forced laborers there were in it a day later; at the present it appeared to him there were forty, more or less, and that the treatment the witness declares is done to him and he has seen done to others is a plain routine in which a man can drink, and he declares he is satisfied with the ration they give to him and after he is not wanting because they give him each day two and a half pounds of good bread and a quart and a half of wine and a pound of meat and a chard for greenery. And [the] clothing they give him each year consists of some gloves and a tunic, some half leggings and a cape of colored broadcloth and two shirts and three pairs of shoes, so that when it comes to food, dress, and shoes the necessities are not lacking. And about his illnesses this one declares that there is a proper pharmacy for the forced laborers and slaves of the works and there he has seen when any of them are sick they cure him and provide for him giving him a confection and medicines and other things the doctor orders sufficient for the health of any sick person.

Miguel del Aldea continues, saying that in 1592 he was given four purges at different times, together with needed medications. But then as he begins to relate the conditions of the work itself, his account quickly turns darker. The foreman Luis Sanchez brutalizes the water carriers, the main workers in the mine, binding them hand and foot with a board across the back and driving them to bloody collapse. One miner named Domingo Hernandez, from the city of Santander, had his mouth so covered with sores from the mercury fumes and dust that he could not eat, yet Sanchez would not hear his pleas ("for the love of God") not to kill him by driving him hard.

As a result of his and other complaints, the administrator appointed by the Fuggers ordered that this punishment be discontinued. Not long afterward Luis Sanchez himself died.

It is true that taking being present where mercury is being made is very dangerous for the health ... many will lose their reason and others remain mercurialized (*azogados*) ... those who carry the mercury flasks from where they wash them to the storage chamber where they are locked up and guarded and to deepen the diggings because they are not protected it enters them through the mouth, eyes, nostrils and ears and since they are warm scrapes their feet.

Miguel then lists at length the companions who have died from the mercury. Miguel himself was shaking so much with mercury poisoning that he was unable to make his signature to certify his testimony.

Azogados were a distinct category of person, not the same as those who had lost their reason. However paternalistic the mine administration might have been, and however cruel the foremen in direct command of the men, the mercury killed indiscriminately. Some through an ability of their own or through the help of the infirmary, may have become mercurialized without suffering lethal consequences.

Mateo Alemán filed his secret report with the *Consejo de Ordenes* and it rested in the archives until brought to light almost four centuries later. Though intended to be a report on the treatment of the prisoners sent to the mines, the *informe* did not change anything.

Alemán, a descendant of marranos, Jews who concealed their identity to avoid expulsion from Spain, went on to write the novel *Guzman el Alfarache* (1599). Guzman is a *picaro*, an adventurer who takes advantage of what he can. In the end he is sentenced to the galleys for theft and makes himself a servant on board ship. He escapes by betraying his comrades. He does not go anywhere near mercury mines. The testimony that Alemán collected years earlier contains statement after statement that the condemned men would have preferred serving out their sentences on the ships rather than in the mines, and in his fiction reflecting their lives and adaptations Alemán respected that preference. Guzman typifies the survival tactics of people shifting about in the underground of the golden age, including educated, ambitious men like Alemán.

Buoyed by the immense popularity of his novel, Alemán emigrated to the colony of Mexico, where he faced the questions of the Inquisition, but continued his writing. The sequel to the novel was the work of another author.

The operations of mercury on the bodies of the miners underground were never again described by the miners themselves. There are no autobiographies of mercury miners as there are of gold, silver, coal, diamond and sulfur miners, to name a few. Secondhand information, the petitions for assistance by the families of deceased miners, studies of working methods by those who sought to improve output or study disasters, tell what happened to the miners, but not how they reacted to it. Words and images come through, penetrating aboveground like the mercury released by the ground heat, the underground fires and the industrial process of distillation that also went on in the mines.

> Cinnabar is a sulfur compound of mercury, and the opening of enclosed, unventilated passages following its concentration in the rock, released gaseous sulfur into the warm spaces. There are no aromas other than the fetid sweats of the miners, the corrupt odors of the slime, the terrible stench of the sulfur that pervades all of the mine. In our subterranean world there are no flowers other than mineral pieces nor balm other than the odor of the dust and the drippings of the candles, of the rotting mud, of the vapor of sulfur and other minerals.... This subterranean world does not bask in the light and warmth of the sun, of the moon or stars. This is a world without sun.

Jose Pares y Franqués, the second physician in charge of the Royal Hospital at the Almaden mine, wrote those lines in 1777, summing up his examination of the health of the miners and the horrible disaster that had occurred with the fire and collapse of tunnels in the Almaden mine, that killed miners and took the mine out of service for years. The expression "*mundo sin sol*" ("world without sun") concluding this passage reflects the prayer formula of Christian hope, "mundo sin fin" ("world without end"), only in this world there is no hope.

The light and warmth of the Spanish sun above did not reach the galleries and chambers of the polluted mine below. This world belowground was reproduced wherever Spain extended the search for mercury. In greatest contrast to the air and sun above, the most isolated sectors of the mine galleries held pockets of sulfurous mercurial vapor instantly lethal to the diggers who opened them ("which kills as soon as it is breathed").

Antonio de Ulloa, colonial administrator and naturalist who served as superintendent of the Huancavelica mine in Peru from 1758 to 1764, transmitted in his *Noticias Americanas* (1772) the word *umpé* used by the Quechua Indian workers who opened these spaces frequently enough to have a word for them. Their precaution was to pierce a small cavity into any hollow encountered and hold a lighted piece of straw to the opening. If the fire died they did not continue probing in that direction.

Ulloa studied the properties of the air in these spaces, its effects on the flame of the candle, but he was unable to ascertain what the gas was made of, only to determine its barometric pressure and temperature.

> People who encounter where an *umpé* begins not having its full force, feel a great shivering in the body, particularly in the extremities, in the face, and in the head; ringing and much sound in the ears; the eyes squeezed as though they want to leave the skull, the same as if a vacuum pump removed the air....
>
> Those who become mercurialized (*se azogan*) practice an easy remedy, which makes them well in a short time, when they can no longer stand it because their bodies shake in all the limbs. Strained and emaciated, they transfer to some pit warm in temperature. There they apply themselves to working the ground, with which they sweat much and expel the mercury, recovering in every way; and afterward they return to take up the old tasks without any damage.

The use of a Quechua term to name a lethal mining event reveals the source of the labor the European masters found to exploit the Peruvian mine. Indigenous people were obliged to dedicate a certain amount of time to work in the mine: their labor was a fixed entitlement of the colonial nobility that could be inherited and assigned. The *mita* system assured that it would be underclass Indians who were encountering pockets of gas as they reached for mercury ore to supply the colonial silver mines with amalgam stock. The Incas had long used the cinnabar to carve into bowls and figures; smashing the rock to distil into quicksilver and then transporting it to other mines was a product of the imposed international imperial economy. Only a scientist like de Ulloa, with an administrative interest both in Indian culture and mining technology, could open the underground of mercury with the report of a word.

Ulloa became superintendent at the time of the most devastating collapse of the overextended Santa Barbara mine. His succession of predecessors had pushed the largely Indian work force to extend the tunnels strictly in the most exploitative direction, without regard for safety. Not long before the 1758 collapse, the workers had removed pillars propping up the ceiling.

Leon Crosnier, a French engineer hired by the Peruvian government to do a survey of the country's mercury resources in 1851, recounted the tale of a parish priest who the previous year had his parishioners dig a trench extending from the Huancavelica town wall. Liquid mercury began to accumulate in the bottom of the trench, to the amount of 40 quintals within a few weeks. But after that there was no more. This event brought up records of mercury seeping into a pit dug closer to the town, around the year 1700, which caused a digging spree that nearly undermined the foundations of the town's dwellings. It is not clear where the mercury could have come from since mass deposits were not found where they might have been predicted from the geology of the area. Possibly this was a pre–Christian ceremony refashioned into a Christian miracle. The Huancavelica mine played out and various attempts to revive production were not successful.

The history of the Almaden and Huancavelica mines is a history of economic, social and political struggles between mine labor, usually members of a colonial underclass, and mercury users, determined to fix the quicksilver in silver and gold. Even more than in most other kinds of mine it was a struggle over the worker's body, the health of which was the efficiency of the mine, captured at complex limits of expendability and endurance. The science and medicine of the authorities there met an already existing practice of maintaining life in a mercury environment more concentrated than the polite laboratories and the enclosed workshops of the European cities. Like the "strong mercury" sometimes released in these places, the *umpé* marks the limit of mercury in the body of the miner.

In the voluminous testimony recorded in the case *United States v. Castillero*, Jacob L. Leese, an enterprising prospector who is thought to have built the first wooden house in San Francisco, was asked if he knew anything about the discovery by Andres Castillero "of metal in the ore taken from the place now called the New Almaden mine."

Leese told of a dinner at the mission of Santa Clara with Padre Real in late November or the first of December 1845 at which Castillero was present. During the dinner the men conversed about the mine, and Castillero remarked that he thought he knew what the metal was.

> He got up from the table and ordered a servant to pulverize a portion of this ore; after it was pulverized he ordered a servant to bring in a hollow tile full of lighted coals; he took some of the powdered ore and threw it on the coals; after it got perfectly hot he took a tumbler of water and sprinkled it on the coals with his fingers; he then emptied the tumbler and put it over the coals upside down; then took the tumbler off and went to the light to look at it; then made the remark that it was what he supposed it was, "quicksilver." He showed all who were there the tumbler

and we found that it was frosted with minute globules of the metal, which Castillero collected with his finger and said it was quicksilver.

Castillero was an engineer, originally from the province of La Mancha in Spain, the home of Alonso Quijana (Don Quixote) and of the Almaden mercury mines. Castillero worked as an agent for the Mexican government in California, settling disputes among officials, and most recently he had been assigned to purchase the property owned by Jacob Sutter, where newly discovered gold deposits were already attracting adventurers. Castillero understood the proportional relationship between mercury resources and precious metal extraction. He was unable to secure either the gold or the mercury mines for Mexico. California, like Texas before it, fell to the Americans. The title to the land was disputed in a long and voluminously documented court action that is a major source of information on the discovery of the mine.

The reddish color of the cinnabar hills in that section of the California coastal range attracted Native Americans, who according to trial testimony and travelogues about the area "from time immemorial" powdered the vermilion nuggets called *mohetka* found in caves and ravines to make a body paint. Indians from as far away as the Columbia River in Oregon came to collect the coloring, or traded for it, as evidenced by their own stories.

The Spanish missionaries recorded a cautionary tale told by the Ohlone Indians, that a group of men having colored themselves fell deathly ill. Many of them died before a black-clad female spirit came to advise them to bathe in a spring and drink its waters. A few survived to pass on the word, which steered the Indians away from immodest practices and toward using *mohetka* to paint the mission chapel walls. It is not clear whether it was padres familiar with architectural vermilion or the Indians, trained to paint religious figures, who thought to take advantage of this paint source.

James Alexander Forbes said in his 1857 testimony that when he received possession of the mine in 1846, it consisted of an adit, a horizontal entrance, 20–25 feet to the rock face, and a pozo, a well or pit. The personnel were a majordomo, a blacksmith, and two or three Indians, one of whom remained constantly at the mine and slept in it. There already were brick furnaces built at Castillero's direction for heating the ore to sublimate and collect the mercury. Using Indian labor, Forbes expanded the mine pit, and installed iron retorts at a nearby hacienda to extract mercury from the ore. In 1848, the Rev. C. S. Lyman found Forbes about to set sail for Europe to obtain distilling equipment.

Mrs. S. A. Downer, visiting the mine in 1854, passed a little hamlet of cottages for the mine superintendents. Being taken to the mine in a wagon carrying four hundred pounds of blasting powder, she imagined a catastrophe, but saw the lush wildwood along the road. In the entrance chamber there was a niche forming a shrine of Nuestra Senora de Guadalupe, after which the subterranean topography of the mine spread out in precarious passages named after Catholic saints, and, running out of them, after animals. The teams of Mexicans who worked in the mine were divided into those breaking the rock, and those carrying the pieces of cinnabar out of the mine to deposit in the cars that brought it downhill to the furnaces. According to Mrs. Downer, "We inquired the average duration of life of the men who work under ground, and found that it did not exceed that of forty-five years, and the diseases to which they are most subject are those of the chest; showing conclusively how essential light and air are to animal as well as vegetable life." The *tenateros* who carried the loads out of the mine had "a Doric build," continued Mrs. Downer.

> How gaily they work! They receive three dollars a day but they live so improvidently no provision being made for sickness or age, when that time comes, as come it will, there is nothing for them to do but like some worn out old charger, lie down and die.... Notwithstanding the precautions used, the escape of arsenic with the sulphate of mercury, has a deleterious effect upon those who labor among the furnaces. Each man works one week out of four, and then changes to something else. Even cattle, if allowed to browse at large in the vicinity during the dry season, become salivated and die from its effects.

Mrs. Downer was certain that the New Almaden ore was richer than the ore of the Almaden mine in Spain, with which it competed for the Mexican silver mine market, the major use for its mercury despite the increase of gold production in California.

In 1865, J. Ross Browne had nothing to say about the health of the miners, but commented on the noxious vapors emitted by the reduction works. The workmen who stood near them "were frequently salivated, are liable to palsy, vertigo, and other disorders of the brain." With improved methods of reduction, the health of the operators had improved, but "persons of delicate nervous organization" were peculiarly susceptible to the mercury fumes. "Instances have occurred of ladies, who, in casually passing, became salivated," said Browne. It is untrue, however, that the vegetation in the vicinity of the reduction works had been destroyed. The vapors dissipated in the open air.

The only health provisions the workers had gained in the years between Downer's and Browne's accounts were improvements in the technology to contain the mercury vapors slightly. There was nothing of the worker strategies for survival that inspired the picaresque novel, or the Spanish imperial paternalism that sent in investigating judges and eventually established a hospital to look after the treatment of forced laborers. The everyday health of the miners' communities depended on their home remedies and possibly a resident doctor. They did not use their earnings to provide for themselves; they were more likely to die young than the administrators of the mine. The effects of the mercury vapor on animals in the vicinity was obvious, but the lush growth was not really affected. The robust workers could withstand the noxious fumes, but ladies would succumb.

The Indians who worked at the mine at the beginning had vanished, replaced by laborers from Mexico with experience in the silver mines, migrating along the same route that brought New Almaden's mercury to the silver mines in Mexico. These were the robust miners and smelter workers seen by visitors to the mine, minimally clad in a slightly erotic hint of life underground. Either because they had already been mercurialized, azogados, or had learned strategies to manage mercury behaviorally, the Mexican miners endure, though they did not live long. The use of blasting powder, creating unpredictable structural weaknesses underground and starting fires that couldn't be extinguished, raised even greater quantities of dust, some of which contained mercury compounds.

Mercury always was a global commodity. Its production was in the hands of the manly American worker who faced dangers and ill health to bring out the ore, and in this particular case casually "becoming salivated" was a standard of resistance. The international composition of the New Almaden work force was keyed to overseas mining traditions rather than more general labor.

Cornish miners who had worked the dwindling tin deposits in their native

Miners in Randol Shaft, New Almaden mine, California, by unknown photographer, 1885. Courtesy of Library of Congress Prints and Photographs Division.

county of England were brought over to the mercury mine because their expertise might prove more profitable there. They had the advantage of speaking English, and of not being aware of the consequences of mining this particular substance. An "English village" grew up alongside the Mexican one.

A few Chinese workers also were included in the personnel, primarily as house servants to the mine's superintendent. The Chinese usually worked in the smaller, boom-and-bust mines in Sonoma and Napa counties further to the north, where they were subject to the same exploitation and racism that occurred in the cities.

New Almaden was the limit of the Hispanic mercury-mining tradition that originated in the Almaden mine and spread to Mexico, Peru, Texas and California. In the Mexican and Peruvian mines, Indian workers amalgamated with immigrants or natives of Spanish, possibly Jewish and Moorish origins, to form a variant of the hierarchical mixing in these societies. Like grape-vine pruners and pickers much later in the California wine industry, this heavy labor was specialized and fairly well compensated. The amalgamation that went on in California was of mercury with gold, and between Hispanics and Anglos.

The New Almaden mine's operations fluctuated depending on the demand for mercury and the richness of the deposit, that is, the ability of minimal investment in labor and equipment to achieve maximum profit for the mine's operators and investors, which included the supervisors. The narrative of the New Almaden mine, like other narratives of industry at work, was in the hands of magazine writers and novelists, who constructed an ideal mine apart from the dangers of mercury and mining

As described by Bret Harte in his 1860 novel *The Story of a Mine*, Carmen de Haro, a "boyish" young woman of Mexican descent, is invited to visit the Blue Mass mine by Royal Thatcher, who is operating the mine in defiance of several other claims being advanced in the courts, including one by Carmen's uncle, for whom she has forged title papers. Thatcher wants Carmen, a watercolorist, to make an image of the Blue Mass mills "turning out tons of quicksilver through the energies of a happy and picturesque assemblage of miners." He is disappointed with the study of the ruined red-rock furnace that the realist artist makes, and especially alarmed by a figure lying down wrapped in a serape at the entrance to the mine. Carmen insists that it is a figure she has placed there to balance the composition. "It's only poor Concho." And where is Concho, Thatcher asks. He's dead, Carmen responds, "murdered by your countrymen."

Carmen and the reader, but not Thatcher, know that Concho was the man who discovered the mine, finding mercury in the water he collected for his mule. Concho was abandoned by his prospecting companions, led off by a wily "metallurgist," who recognized the value of the mercury. A doctor in town who treated Concho also saw the silvery fluid for what it was worth and put together a committee of investors. Concho, however, was shot at the claim while sleeping wrapped up in his serape. From there began the convoluted legal and political history that was the real story of the mine. It was not mercury but greed that killed Concho and deposited him at the entrance to the mine in Carmen's watercolor. He was not one of the "happy and picturesque miners" seen in the magazine articles and many other drawings.

Harte, a migrant from New York who had become a prominent newspaper writer, published the novel (in New York) after he had been secretary of the United States Branch Mint in San Francisco for several years, and had gained knowledge of the intrigue and litigation accompanying mine claims. The novel ends in Washington, D.C., where the various parties converge to press legislators to decide the claim on their behalf. The dead Concho who haunts the only picture of the mine's operations is already an image of the declining Hispanic mining tradition.

Idwal Jones's *Vermilion* (1947), a historical novel published (again, in New York) after the New Almaden mine had petered out, reflects the mine's history in more detail. Jones also was a newspaper writer migrant to California from New York, where his father had been inspector of mines for the state. Jones ties the history of the mine to the fortunes of a single family: "The Copes had been miners since the Age of Bronze, and mercury, like a lodestone, had drawn Thomas Cope from Cornwall to Spain, to the Andes, and then to these Santa Cruz mountains." Thomas Cope marries the daughter of a Spanish majordomo, and their son Pablo, after studying the art of mining in his father's native Cornwall and in Spain, returns to California accompanied by a skilled but devious mining overseer to develop the Five Apostles mercury mine on the property of his grandfather. The mine is important enough to national security, to assure the continued production of gold, that Abraham Lincoln summons Pablo to obtain his support for the Union during the Civil War. Pablo's son Gervase opens the Canton branch of the mercury firm, supplying the unstable Chinese market from overseas with the crucial ingredient of vermilion, and a trusted Chinese servant comes to America to attend to Pablo during his declining years. Pablo's other son Roger is more caught up in a succession of mistresses than in preserving the mine, and Roger's sons enter into other enterprises. Paula, the cousin from Canton, nicknamed Miss Vermilion from the color of her hair, neglects the management of the mine as its quicksilver ceases to be profitable.

Jones is reverent about mercury and its trade, but he mainly copies the magazine articles about the tunnels and the lives of those who actually dig, blast, carry and smelt the ore. He consolidates the ethnic origins of the diverse people who make the mine into one family stream, merging the Spanish and the Cornish but only going as far as hair color to include the Chinese. Where Bret Harte's novel is about the politics of mining claims and not about mercury mining, Idwal Jones' novel is about the family heritage of mining interests and not about mercury mining. Jones acknowledges the effects of mercury on the health of the miners and the miners themselves in a very limited way. In the manner of the historical novel, he prefers to marshal the facts about the New Almaden mine in an epic of personalized capitalism, starting with Pablo Cope's smuggling mercury from China and ending in Paula's visit to the abandoned mine.

Other writings about the New Almaden mine, and the state park and museum that eventually took the mine's place after it closed in 1960, recall the people, structures and tools that formed the enterprise, an inducement of memories that exist for fewer and fewer people. New Almaden is the only California mine memorialized this way. Others are a set of decaying buildings and fences with signs warning interlopers to stay away. In the newspaper obituaries of some people who lived their lives in the area it might be recalled that they worked in the mercury mine, or even owned and operated a small mine.

The gold deposits in California are inland, on the eastern side of the central valley, associated with the Klamath-Trinity Mountains and Sierra Nevada range and peripheral hills. It is both in the form of placer gold combined with loose sand and gravel, and hardrock deposits. The mercury deposits ranging from the Pine Top and Mount Diablo quicksilver districts to New Almaden, are located on the eastern side of the valley in the Coast Range. Mount Diablo in Contra Costa County has sporadically worked cinnabar seams on one flank of the mountain and a defunct metacinnabar pit mine on the opposite flank.

From around 1854, placer gold was secured by hydraulic mining, training monitors—forceful jets of water — onto the soil, sand and gravel above the bedrock, and directing the resulting slurry into sluices. As the upper layers of gravel were washed away, systems of tunnels were constructed to carry away waste water and debris, and to shelter the sluices. The water's forceful passage was directed by systems of ditches, canals, and pipes.

Mercury shipped in 76-pound iron flasks from the mine-smelters in the Coast Range was added to turbulently flowing water in the sluice beds, and amalgamating with the gold fell to the bottom. The water was made to churn by bars (riffles) in the bed of the sluice, which collected the gold and mercury fallen from the continuing flow. Much of the mercury "floured": it separated into smaller globules and was carried away with the water and sand. The sluice bottom became coated with mercury, which leaked into the soil and bedrock, as it did at the poorly shielded smelters.

It was estimated that under the best operating conditions 10 percent of the added mercury was lost, but usually it was 30 percent. Mercury also leaked from stamp mills that crushed gold-bearing rock obtained by hardrock mining, and from drift mining and dredging. A court decision in 1884 prohibited discharge of mine debris in the Sierra Nevadas, and that plus the introduction of cyanide in the place of mercury, caused an abrupt drop in mercury use.

But the gold rush was by then a global furor, rising and falling with the price of precious metals. Alaska, the Amazon watershed of South America, parts of China, Tibet and Africa all received their doses of mercury and cyanide as the miners churned up the surface rock.

How the mercury in the mines actually affected the miners was repressed knowledge that has returned in fears of mercury in the environment. Mercurialism is deferred from the human body that works the mercury-bearing rock into the water and soil. It is projected from mine tailings into bacteria and thus again into bodies as part of a hemispheric cycle of mercury mass.

The Idria mine in Slovenia has, like Almaden, a slowly developing record of interest and attempts to remedy the work-related illnesses of the miners, most recently in studies of the effects of long-term exposure on emotion and personality traits of former miners.

The New Idria mine in San Benito County California, closed in 1972 after many years of operation, after having been the top-producing mine in the western hemisphere early in the twentieth century, became a derelict area. The owner of the property was allegedly storing on-site containers of paint, solvents, grease, and cleaning compounds that his work crews were supposed to be disposing of according to regulations. Authorities charged the owner with hazardous-materials violations and public-nuisance crimes, but they could not address the issue of mercury runoff from the mine into San Carlos Creek. The drug offenders in the mine owner's private drug-treatment program were being rehabilitated by transporting chemical waste from industrial plants to the site. They were something like miners in reverse, already afflicted by substances before encountering mercury.

The pattern of mercury escaping through the processes associated with mining, becoming buried and then returning as an environmental threat, has recurred with every mine large and old enough to attract notice. Many mines and mining districts were the subject of geological studies undertaken by scientists working for federal, state, county and university departments. And those studies often examined the technique and machinery of mining, but paid little attention to the personnel. Later there were equally technical studies made of tailings, runoff and biomodification of mine wastes into environmental toxins, but again with little attention to those affected.

Edwin A. Roberts wrote in an unpublished memoir preserved in the Healdsburg, California, library that the Socrates mine, where he worked as a young man, was called the Forty Thieves because of the number of lives it took. Roberts describes the stopes falling from the ceiling of the mine tunnel leaving a space in which noxious gas accumulated. "The miners would get very sick. Your teeth would get loose and your hands shake so bad you had to be fed." A longitudinal map of the mine prepared by the United States Geological Survey shows four levels of tunnels, each of which is broken by a few stopes, named and numbered. Roberts wrote that the earth in the mine crept, making passage so narrow that the ore carts were caught between rock masses. A white fungus that grew on the walls was called "the ghost of dead miners." "Fifteen Mexican miners are in here." On clear, sunny fall days a breeze would cause the mouth of the tunnel to make a moaning sound.

The Socrates mine closed for good in 1928, leaving the shell of an abandoned crushing mill and a row of brick furnaces on the surface. For years afterward the local newspapers reported accidents that took place on the property: a pair of men injured when the tractor they were using to haul firewood capsized on the slope; a young woman found dead after she had apparently fallen off a cliff while hiking. The mine was a point of reference for these events, which could have occurred in any undeveloped area. When record floodwaters threatened to carry mine tailings down a local creek into the Russian River, there was concern that this might add unwanted mercury to the water. The moaning ghosts of the dead miners had become apprehensions of the toxic wash of their excavations.

When state Geologist Walter Bradley visited the Sulphur Bank mine on the shore of Clear Lake in 1917, he found hot springs, a thick layer of sulfur overlaying the cinnabar deposits and an accumulation of tailings and piles of blinding white rocks left by past mining activities. Learning that the temperature rose to 176 degrees Fahrenheit only 300 feet down, he called it a "source of wonderment" that anyone could breathe near the open sulfide-gas-expelling vents in the rock, no less actually work in the mine. A dead rat lay near one of the openings. Strands of vermilion water reached down to the lake.

The 120-acre mine reserve, of such geological interest that it is still visited by school groups, was worked first for sulfur and then for mercury. It figured in the reminiscences of men who had found occasional employment in the mine over the years. Its last heavy activity was during World War II when mercury was in demand for use in manufacturing explosives. Operations ceased for good in 1957. During the 1970s, members of the Elem Indian Colony brought rock slabs from the site to their reservation about an eighth of a mile away to build houses. The 23-acre mine pit filled with water to the depth of ninety feet was used as a swimming hole. Many people fished in the lake. Pregnant women and children under the age of six were warned by the state health department not to eat the fish.

In 1991, Sulphur Bank was declared a Superfund site by the Environmental Protection Agency, and testing in 1993 revealed slightly elevated levels of mercury in the blood of Elem tribe members. A plan to fill in the impoundment with the mine waste and cover it with soil was not funded. A "white yogurt-like substance" extending from the shore of the mine to the deepest part of Clear Lake was identified as clay materials likely to be the matrix for large populations of bacteria biomethylating mercury. There was some sinking of holes to collect and test the runoff.

The year 2001 was the last year that the EPA Web site on Sulphur Bank reported any Superfund activity. The Elem community maintains a Web site devoted to the mine and its spread.

Of the hundreds of mines, diggings, pits and excavations listed county by county in the second edition of *Mercury Resources of California* (1918), most have vanished from local memory, been submerged beneath pavement and building foundations, lost in ever-receding newspaper and unpublished journal mentions.

The mines are forgotten then recalled as a source of contamination and therefore disease or as a vaguer threat. Helen Porter Goss wrote that her father was superintendent of the mine for twenty-four years and felt no ill effects of mercury, but the Chinese workers were afflicted. Walter Bradley does not allude to a single case of mercury poisoning in his 1908–1918 survey of mercury exploitation and removal. It was the Bradley Mining Company of San Francisco that last owned the Sulphur Bank mine, operated it during the Second World War, then ignored complaints about runoff and toxic waste. The Elem tribe next door to the mine used its unearthed materials to build houses then stopped their children from swimming in the impoundment pool and gave up fishing in Clear Lake because of the mercury found in the water.

Every rainy winter, every chemical survey of mercury in fish flushes out fears of mines otherwise forgotten. In May 2006, California state Regional Water Quality Control Board officials held a community meeting with residents of the area around Soulajule Reservoir in western Marin County. The officials wanted to address concerns that mercury from a group of privately owned mines near and beneath the waters of the reservoir was contaminating the water, the crappie, largemouth bass and channel catfish taken from the water, and the grazing cattle that drank it. The open pit mines had operated during the 1960s and 70s while it was moderately profitable to supply military users from such diggings. When the military needs declined, the mines closed, and to provide additional water and recreational facilities, the reservoir was constructed on top of and beside several of them. The lessors of one of the mines had constructed a retaining wall to prevent tailings from entering a creek that fed the reservoir. The high mercury levels of the predatory fish and bottom feeders called for guidelines to be issued and informational articles to be published, causing the mines to reenter local consciousness.

The rivers of California flow from east to west down from the central mountains through the coastal range and into the ocean. Too small and rough to be used for heavy transport, they were adapted to agriculture, mining and water supply. They cross the acres of disappearing gold mines and carrying with them the thousands of pounds of quicksilver thrown into the water from iron flasks brought inland from the mercury mines the rivers also cross. And they can be seen, as the floods increase, dislodging the rubble of the mercury mines. There are no more miners, or everyone is a miner in the path of runoff disgorged from the flooded pits and tunnels.

A news report in early 2007 described a gold miner pouring liquid mercury from a yogurt container into a pan containing crushed ore to begin the amalgamation-extraction process. The mine manager explained to the reporter that the people working at this mine, in the Andean region of Colombia, have problems because of the mercury in their bodies. A Canadian mining corporation is exploring the region for deposits worth exploiting with technology more advanced than the antiquated stamp mills that have long been inefficiently operating there. Colombia could produce far more gold than it does. There does seem to be sufficient labor and sufficient water for the operations.

10

⸎

Red Mercury

I didn't know what red mercury was when someone offered to sell me some. While I was living in Eldoret, Kenya, in 1991, a Gujarati merchant I knew asked me if I would like to buy for fifty dollars a container of red mercury he had purchased from "a Russian." The seller assured him the material was radioactive and could be brokered to knowing agents of interested foreign governments for a heady profit. Suresh admitted he was disappointed with the red mercury; it was just a silvery liquid in a glass tube with red paint particles adhering to the sides. A chemist he knew in Nairobi declared it a fake as soon as he looked at it. A fake of what?

Suresh said that as an American sophisticated in the materials of nuclear warfare I would want to buy the tube from him. He was half-attempting to pass along the fraud by flattering me into taking it off his hands, and half-hoping that I could front the red mercury for him in some mysterious Cold War market I would know more about than he did. Red mercury precipitated in this juxtaposition of deceit and self-mystification. Far from being Paracelsus's winter on the skin, mercury has become hot indeed. The man-made moon has turned into a thousand suns hidden inside a metal vessel resembling a bomb.

This incident was on the outer wave of a surge of technological fraud that followed the collapse of the Soviet Union in 1990. Soon Soviet weapons materials were being sold by clandestine operatives free to make claims about vast scientific research projects producing supernatural fluids that could fit in a bottle or at least be sold in one. Red mercury cropped up again and again among the packages of plutonium, uranium and missile-guidance systems trafficked in the growing international arms trade. A U.S. Department of Energy study published in 1992 enumerated at least twenty-five attempts to sell red mercury on the international arms market since the 1970s. It also stated, and this was repeated many times by a number of government authorities, that red mercury does not exist and that its sellers were running a scam.

Red mercury projects a technology in fulfillment of a dream, the same kind of cultivated guesswork attached to real and imaginary manipulations the made alchemical gold and quacks' panaceas. It is an item in the technological popular culture of the nuclear age, when closely guarded secrets were revealed at a price to those who believed in the value of what they were being offered because they didn't understand it. The atomic bomb was one of the few projects in which science actually generated a new technology. The buyers of red mercury wanted the technology cheap and ready to use, assuming that the science was already in place.

We can get to red mercury by way of uranium, which does exist. The authentic role of mercury in making some forms of hydrogen bomb leads to the myth of red mercury.

A large enough mass of uranium isotopes, like a large enough mass of mercury fulminate isomer, will explode spontaneously. The reasons for the explosion are different. Mercury fulminate crystal structure breaks down under weight or with a strike, causing a release of a great volume of nitrogen gas that pushes outward at great speed. Uranium and the heavier element plutonium, in pieces above a certain size, generate such concentrated radioactivity that the atoms themselves tear apart in a chain reaction, releasing energy much greater than any chemical explosion.

Yet a nuclear blast must be initiated by a chemical one. The scientists gathered to construct the first atomic bomb for the wartime Manhattan Project could not test a nuclear detonation on a small scale as a chemical explosion could be tested. They had to calculate the energies that would be released when two sub-critical masses of uranium-235 or plutonium were forcibly combined to form a critical mass. The force they chose to combine them was a chemical explosion, impelling them together in a gun-like single blast in one design, or in another design imploding them from all sides with a series of synchronized explosions to form a critical-mass sphere.

To appeal to the military imagination, the yield of fission explosions was measured in thousands of tons of TNT. The July 16, 1945, Trinity test, the "beginning of the Atomic Age," was measured afterward at 18.6 thousand tons (kilotons) of TNT, a quantity of the chemical explosive which could never have been made to burst all at once.

Fissionable concentrations of uranium-235, the unstable isotope, were obtained by tediously enriching naturally occurring uranium, to a lesser degree for nuclear reactors (5–10 percent U-235) and to a much greater degree for bombs (90 percent U-235). Plutonium, not available in terrestrial nature, had to be generated in a nuclear reactor. The Little Boy bomb dropped on Hiroshima was a gun-type U-235 bomb; the Fat Man bomb dropped on Nagasaki was an imploded plutonium bomb. The chemical explosion had to join the separate pieces of bomb-grade uranium into a chain-reactive mass without disintegrating them and the casing before the chain reaction took place.

Precisely what chemistry was used to initiate the explosions is information not readily available in the copious writings on the development of nuclear weapons. It is not unreasonable to suppose that the detonator compound fulminate of mercury was included in some way. Fulminate in the making goes through a red fuming stage when the mercury is first dissolved in the nitric acid, but it is far-fetched to suppose that this was the radioactive red mercury.

The next phase in the development of nuclear weapons was a fusion bomb, originally proposed as a tube of deuterium, an isotope of hydrogen, attached to a fission bomb. The heat and pressure of the fission reaction would cause the hydrogen atoms to fuse and form the next heavier element, helium, releasing the bonding energies as heat and radiation in the process. Eventually it was realized that the radiation from the fission, and not the slower material waves, was fast enough to cause fusion before the explosion tore apart the materials. That always was a consideration in nuclear bomb design: bringing together the critical mass or exerting the decisive force before the components themselves were blown apart.

Hydrogen is the simplest chemical element, atomic number 1, counting only one proton. It has two isotopes, deuterium and tritium, which add one and two neutrons respectively to the proton in the nucleus. The atomic number doesn't change but the weight of the element does. The next element in the periodic table, helium, atomic number 2, has two protons and two neutrons. The lighter the element the less energy needed to bring about fusion, but one proton hydrogen, protium, can't fuse to become the next element helium, since it lacks neutrons to form a helium nucleus. That makes neutron-holding deuterium and tritium the candidates to yield helium by fusion, which would shoot out neutrons with the force of breaking sub-atomic bonds.

The chemical explosion forced a chain reaction which by its output of radiation forced fusion. The hydrogen-bomb designers sought an element that was light enough to be fused and dense enough for that fusion to yield the greatest energy possible. Deuterium alone and then a combination of deuterium with tritium were proposed and studied.

The fission bomb was defined by the critical mass of fissionable material needed to reach a chain reaction. The fusion bomb could be made from any quantity of material capable of fusing under the influence of immensely powerful radiation and pressure.

The first hydrogen bomb, a building-sized construction on a Pacific atoll detonated in 1952, went off with a force measured at 10.4 megatons (millions of tons of TNT) on a scale much greater than the kilotons of the atomic bomb that began and finished it.

The history of explosives was reiterated in the hydrogen bomb. Chemical blow-up into nuclear, into thermonuclear, with a nuclear chaser. The unenriched uranium tamper that surrounded the refrigerated deuterium-tritium fuel was forced by the heat and pressure into a fission reaction of its own.

In the 1950s American bomb designers worked to make "cleaner" fusion bombs by reducing the fission element to a minimum and allowing the energy to be released as speeding neutrons. The uranium tamper was replaced by a lead and then by a titanium graphite "pusher" which would focus the radiation without itself exploding. The redesign made smaller bombs possible. Downsizing the fission component of the bomb could only go so far before there was not enough energy to provoke fusion.

As Soviet scientists trying to catch up with the West attempted to piece together their own thermonuclear device, the suggestion was made that a combination of the element lithium with deuterium would be a more efficient core than deuterium or deuterium-tritium. The early Soviet designs, devised with minimal knowledge of the American bomb's structure, were a layered pastry (*sloika*) of chemical explosives and deuterium. The first Soviet thermonuclear bomb detonated was an enhanced fission device rather than a true fusion bomb. It took years before the atomic bomb was introduced as the initiator. The first Soviet hydrogen bomb was a lithium-deuterium core irradiated into fusion by a fission explosion.

Lithium with three protons in its nucleus is the third element on the periodic table and the lightest solid in nature. Its isotope with three neutrons, lithium-6, could act as a preliminary stage in a fusion reaction. When bombarded by neutrons from a fission reaction it yields tritium, helium (two protons, two neutrons) and the energy of breaking bonds. The resultant tritium in the presence of deuterium further irradiated combine to form the most readily attainable fusion reaction.

An atom of tritium forced to combine with an atom of deuterium gives forth helium, a neutron and 17.6 million electron volts of energy. Tritium is difficult to generate and store. Lithium is a convenient way of introducing tritium into the reaction.

Lithium-6 is the basis of this "dry" fusion reaction (not requiring heavy water), but it is far less common in naturally occurring compounds than lithium-7, which has three protons and four neutrons. This is where mercury enters. Lithium-6 has a greater electrochemical affinity for mercury than does lithium-7.

> A lithium-mercury amalgam is first prepared using the natural material. The amalgam is then agitated with a lithium hydroxide solution, also prepared from natural lithium. The desired lithium-6 concentrates in the amalgam, and the more common lithium-7 migrates to the hydroxide. A counter flow of amalgam and hydroxide passes through a cascade of stages until the desired enrichment in lithium-6 is reached.

I quoted this U.S. Department of Defense description of the process for the two uses of the word "desired." The tritium essential to a fusion reaction has a radioactive half-life of a little over twelve years and is very expensive to produce and maintain. Lithium-6, which generates tritium when exposed to radiation from fission, is not itself radioactive and does not require a nuclear reactor to generate. As the Department of Defense *List* puts it, "the presence of a lithium-6 enrichment facility is a good indicator that a proliferant state has confidence in its fission primaries and seeks more powerful weapons."

The United States stopped making lithium-6 in 1963 because enough had been separated to supply planned weapons. The other nuclear states presumably have their supplies. North Korea, Pakistan, or, reputedly at one time, Iraq, could be seeking lithium-6 to join their deuterium and fission bomb in a fusion weapon.

Red mercury might be the lithium-mercury amalgam that is the first step in making lithium-6, or it might be the mercury recovered from the process and reused, acquiring a reddish tint from the red mercuric oxide that accumulates. Or red mercury might just be "red" (communist, Soviet) mercury in the usage of the time. It was, however, genuinely mercury and perhaps genuinely red. The red mercury flowing in the international arms trade was a shadow of this substance answering a need for a powerful, tradable bomb material. Only a catalyst in the manufacture of fusible lithium, it gained the reputation of being a nuclear material itself.

The buyers in the arms trade want high-yield, low-cost weapons that can easily be transported. As information about the design of the atomic and hydrogen bombs made its way through the various levels of popularization, quasi-scientific rumor and science fiction, they fostered thoughts of a less cumbersome, more readily deliverable nuclear weapon. Nuclear warheads would obliterate a battlefield: states loudly aim them at each other for that effect. Smaller bombs could be used to blackmail nuclear states and corporations into making concessions.

The image of a "briefcase bomb" or a "backpack bomb" made from some vaguely powerful radioactive substance allows stateless groups and even individuals to threaten radioactive devastation without an airforce of their own. Red mercury projects the transition from nuclear armed states menacing each other with remotely detectable bomb tests to bomb-planting terrorists upgrading to nuclear.

A television documentary entitled *The Hunt for Red Mercury* aired on British CTV and the Discovery Channel in America in late April 1993. The commentary mystified the substance into a "short-cut to the bomb" being traded by the Russian military and the Russian mafia on the nuclear black market, together with plutonium-239 and other fissile materials. The atmosphere of menace and intrigue that had suffused the later Soviet era was perpetuated in the idea of a Soviet-developed small-bomb fuel that could be passed around in the metal jackets pictured on television.

Articles in technical journals quoting former Soviet experts plainly describing red mercury as lithium-6 did nothing to dispel the red mercury rumors. What historian of technology Donald MacKenzie titles "the uninvention of nuclear weapons" was going forward in the "tacit knowledge" of red mercury and other nuclear materials. According to MacKenzie, fictional substances like red mercury were worked into weapons structures. The resulting weapons were oversimplified versions of originals that replaced functional design elements with the magical power of the new ingredient. Experts were emerging to take charge of this tense, willful ignorance.

In 1994, the nuclear physicist, proliferation specialist and television commentator Frank Barnaby published two brief articles in *International Defense Review*, a publication of Jane's Information Group, the standard journal on military forces, weapons systems and munitions. The first article asked simply how many nuclear bombs exist among the various players, the second raised the question, "Red mercury: Is there a pure fusion bomb for sale?"

By a "pure fusion bomb" Barnaby meant a thermonuclear weapon that dispenses with the initiating fission bomb and achieves fusion by use of a powerful explosive, a carryover from the first Soviet hydrogen bomb design but now treating the lithium-deuterium mass as an explosive mass named by the code phrase "red mercury." That name evokes an appearance which in turn assures a purchaser that something resembling mercury which is red is the real thing.

Barnaby cites his discussion with an unnamed former–Soviet scientist (proliferating along with nuclear materials) who told him that quantities of this red mercury were stockpiled and are the material that is now being marketed by arms dealers and rogue scientists. Barnaby's version of red mercury was a dense red gel, a union of mercury, antimony and oxygen created in a nuclear reactor. According to his sources, red mercury had been first produced by the Soviets in 1968, and was manufactured in Soviet military cities in several different forms. This red mercury was denser than any known substance, but was not especially radioactive. Its value could only be proven in a nuclear bomb.

Barnaby diagrammed two nuclear devices, each using red mercury as a key enhancement, but in different ways. In the fission device red mercury is injected into a channel surrounding the plutonium core. It acts as a tamper reflecting neutrons back into the plutonium and preventing it from being blown apart by the chemical explosion before fission takes place. In the second bomb an outer shell of high explosives causes a shell of red mercury to release concentrated energy into the deuterium-tritium core, precipitating a lethal volley of neutrons.

In the fission bomb, red mercury is a shield and a focusing lens. It is the best "pusher" of radiation into the core of the bomb. In the neutron bomb, red mercury is a source of the great energy needed to provoke deuterium-tritium fusion. In that contradictory pairing of uses, the self-promoting technologist suggests the ambiguous power of red mercury. These two bomb designs mark a transition from science-based technology to technological popular culture. By adding red mercury to bomb designs you could produce a cleaner fission bomb or a neutron bomb. It was clearly something nuclear powers would want to have and prevent others from getting.

Barnaby's 1994 article put in clear diagrams and weapons-business prose the red mercury of the early nineties. Following the end of the Soviet Union, some parties took advantage of this emerging mercury mystique to formulate a sales pitch. Except for a brief period at the beginning of the nineties, their activities were without official Russian support.

From February to March 1992, a decree signed by Russian Federation president Boris Yeltsin granted a Russian company, Promekologiya, rights to produce and sell red mercury abroad, the gains to be used to fund worthy domestic projects. The decree was quickly rescinded with no further comment. Into the mid-nineties a series of Russian government and independent specialists conducted investigations and made public declarations that red mercury was simply a name for a harmless substance or that there was no such thing. A government commission headed by Major General Aleksandr Gurov released its report in 1995 stating that weapons-grade red mercury was a fake. They found the physical substance was quicksilver with some red nail polish added and was not at all radioactive.

The year 1995 also saw the release of a Russian film *Ostorozhno: Krasnaya Rtut* (*Danger: Red Mercury*), which conveyed the sentiment that red mercury was now a byword for gullibility. None of this prevented the Bosnian Serb leader Radovan Karadžić from paying $6 million (and promising $60 million more) for a nuclear device centered on red mercury, a brass vessel which when opened turned out to hold red jelly. All that Russian government officials could tell Karadžić was that he had been swindled.

Likewise Osama bin Laden, one of whose agents was said to have purchased a quantity of red mercury to no avail. The naiveté of Bosnian warlords and al–Qaeda operatives prolonged the life of red mercury. Any scientifically undereducated antagonist would want to have what red mercury promised. Mythical superweapons funded by non-state actors with state ambitions and no research budget have to have a credible mystique. The same with the gold of the alchemists, which also was a state project urged on by private experts. As with alchemical gold projects and syphilis cures, red mercury created a public theater of tragicomic intrigue wherever it gained believers.

Writing under the pseudonym Max Barclay, the American writer Ben Sherwood turned himself into a specialist on red mercury available for television interviews and screenplay consultations by publishing a spy novel, *Red Mercury* (1996). The Beverly Hills press that issued the book was named Dove Books, hinting at the code name for a fusion weapon that magazine articles had reported was being developed. The paperback version remains in great numbers on the used book market today. Its progeny is not a movie but a videogame that still has its enthusiasts. Sherwood himself has disowned the book.

Among aspirant nuclear states, South Africa was a graver venue for the red mercury transactions. A white minority was defending its entrenched position against the political, economic and social gains of the black majority. The apartheid system was crumbling, and the security forces were seeking powerful weapons to help them defend it. At the time of his election in 1994 as first president of a post-apartheid South Africa, Nelson Mandela inherited a "nuclear nightmare."

An executive of the Britain-based Thor Corporation, which ran a chlor-alkali operation in a remote area of South Africa (see the next chapter), was found murdered in November 1991, his body mutilated and covered with a mercury-containing alkyd resin. The investigating officer initially was skeptical of red mercury as a motive for the murder, but gradually the investigation was overwhelmed by the belief that the Israeli intelligence agency Mossad was responsible.

According to journalists Peter Hounam and Steve McQuillan, whose book on the "red mercury killings" was published in 1995, this and other murders of red mercury traders inside and outside South Africa were the work of an Israeli government determined to prevent Arab countries from taking possession of the potent substance. The South African government had built up its own stockpile and used it to power not only nuclear weapons but also attack helicopters that used red mercury to bore their way through solid steel shielding.

It was fortunate that I did not let my curiosity get the better of me and lead me to purchase red mercury. After Peter Hounam became involved in the attempted purchase of a container of red mercury, a caller with a "Middle Eastern accent" told him his life was in danger. A photograph of the container is included in the book.

Hounam and McQuillan's pages on the South African red-mercury trade are grounded in the assumption that there is a genuine red mercury, but what was passed around on the market in the early nineties was "commercial grade" or an outright hoax. Hounam and McQuillan tell of a prospective buyer of one sealed vessel of red mercury who recounted to them that with the owner's permission he sawed it open. The two journalists report that the result was the same as in other instances of opening containers of the precious substance: some liquid mercury poured out in the company of a magnet.

With all their involvement in red mercury dealings, Hounam and McQuillan never saw red mercury, only containers allegedly holding it, much less did they ever see it used for anything, only stories about its potential. There were flasks of red mercury (and tritium) hidden in a warehouse in Zambia and secret reports identified but never seen. "There is sensitivity over mercury compounds internationally," as the brother of the murdered executive dryly put it.

Commenting on a British television producer's trips to Russia, where he obtained confidential reports detailing the nature of red mercury and the intense international trade in the substance, Hounam and McQuillan declare: "The trips to Russia showed one thing at least: it was difficult to dismiss the idea that red mercury was simply an invention of fraudsters and rouble-launderers, as had been alleged in the West." They and Frank Barnaby and their followers did everything they could to dismiss the idea of deliberate fraud, while providing information that must lead to that conclusion. That is the system of red mercury: an atmosphere of suspended disbelief that never quite becomes belief. And never is tested.

Red mercury may have motivated the murder of a few disappointed buyers or deceitful sellers in South Africa, but the more serious harm came when it was turned into an element in the civil war in neighboring Angola. Soldiers of the rebel movement UNITA sold artillery shells and rockets they could not use to villagers, telling them that the shells contained red mercury which could be sold for $300 a kilogram. The purchasers tried to saw off the tips of the ordnance to drain out the fluid, usually causing it to detonate and leaving scrap metal which the soldiers could then sell to dealers.

It was probably these scrap metal dealers who brought the lethal hoax over the border to Namibia, where they marketed the red mercury quest to the Ovambo people, who were similarly deceived and similarly destroyed by resulting explosions. An Associated Press news story put the number of dead at seventy-eight with many more injured. Another version of this story puts the going price of red mercury at $40,000 a kilogram, which the author, citing Namibian police officials, says drew people from Namibia to the Angolan border with their savings in hand to buy the alleged mercury repositories.

That no one actually saw or sampled and analyzed red mercury did not keep it from becoming enshrined in nuclear lore. The dynamics of this belief lay in presumed consensus of experts. At the Pugwash Conference in 1994, one speaker said that even if no red mercury had been seen, the fact that so many nuclear experts believe it exists was reason enough to close loopholes in the international atomic energy safeguards. If this had been done at the time, it would have further substantiated the threat of red mercury. Around the same time the story spread that red mercury was a hoax engineered by American government intelligence agencies to lure terrorists into exposing themselves as they tried to contact sellers.

Red mercury survived by not being seen. It was described on specifications sheets and its name was written on the labels of weighty flasks, but when it put in an appearance it was what the bold Radovan Karadzić saw when he opened his $6 million brass bottle: red jelly which could only be tested in a nuclear bomb.

The black market in nuclear material is greatly subject to deceit and double-dealing, and red mercury was made for this trade. It is simply too convenient to the needs of small states, radical factions and nuclear experts ever to be let go. Consider its role in the American neutron bomb.

Sam Cohen was a junior member of the team that constructed and tested the first nuclear weapons. His calculations of the neutron yield of early bomb tests were included in classified manuals, and he devised an equation that fixed the relationship between a bomb's energy yield and the thickness of its casing. Cohen returned from a visit to war-devastated Korea in 1951 with a vision of the usefulness of tactical nuclear weapons. "I'm not implying here that seeing Seoul in ruins put the neutron bomb bee in my bonnet," he wrote in his 1983 book advocating that weapon, "but it certainly did make me wonder about the advisability of using atomic bombs of the 1950s vintage to force the enemy out of cities." His recommendations were not well received by the United States Air Force, who considered atomic bombs only to be weapons of "totality" and "terror." Cohen designed a nuclear bomb that would attain specific tactical objectives, not annihilate entire cities.

If the fuel of a hydrogen bomb could be caused to emit the same radiation it did in fusion with a much smaller physical blast, then it would be destructive only to living tissue, not to land and infrastructure. This could be accomplished by not placing the uranium tamper and setting the least fission blast able to cause a fusion reaction.

It would be an enhanced-radiation bomb spreading death-dealing neutrons far and wide. A 10-ton neutron bomb would be the life-destructive equivalent of a 1-kiloton fission bomb. The neutron bomb's zone of physical devastation would be less than one half of the fission bomb's but the reach of the gamma rays (speeding neutrons) would be ten times as far, closer to the range of the radiation spread by a hydrogen bomb. Set off in the upper atmosphere over an enemy army it would kill only soldiers. It also could wreck the guidance system of incoming nuclear missiles, which made it a part of another expensive defensive strategy, the Strategic Defense Initiative.

The development of the poison gas lewisite during the First World War was fostered by similar thinking. Its advocates pitched it as a humane weapon because it would kill enemy combatants by searing their lungs rather than tearing them apart with shrapnel.

Cohen had been "selling" the neutron bomb project since his Korean War experience, and succeeded in getting it into development during the presidency of Richard Nixon only to see that halted during the presidency of Jimmy Carter and revived during the presidency of Ronald Reagan.

There were two plans for a neutron bomb, one using a "minimum amount of fission-produced energy" to trigger the fusion reactions, the other a pure-fusion device impelled by "an ingenious detonating mechanism." Cohen never specified what this device might be. He quoted a 1957 paper by the Soviet nuclear physicist L. A. Artsimovich referring to a charge of conventional explosives, "such as TNT or something more powerful," which would implode a capsule of deuterium or a mixture of deuterium and tritium. The Soviets had been conducting secret experiments which they do not report. If the Russians were able to complete this project, Cohen announced, they would have a significant edge over the United States in neutron bomb development.

Cohen believed, or at least repeatedly stated, that pure fusion, one without an initiating fission bomb, did not produce "the long-lived dangerous radioactivity that fission weapons produce." This explosive, spurring an unimpeded release only of neutrons, is crucial to Cohen's neutron-bomb pitch. Nowhere did he identify the explosive or cite a successful test of a pure fusion bomb. This lack of test results allowed Cohen's claims that fusion explosions do not release long-term dangerous radioactivity to render property unusable but only neutron bursts that disable soldiers. The explosive remains a blank, and fortunately the only tests are under wraps.

Cohen did not mention red mercury in his initial writings on the neutron bomb. It was an excellent candidate for the explosion that causes pure fusion when it became available to him in the 1990s. It suddenly appeared in his writings around the same time others noticed it, in 1993, in an article for the politically conservative American magazine *National Review*. The title of the article, "The DOVE of War," refers to the unexplained code name DOVE (an acronym?) that designates a class of small fusion weapons Cohen had learned about during a visit to the Lawrence Livermore laboratory in California. Red mercury, a "ballotechnic" explosive, was a primer for these fusion weapons.

Cohen pointed to another article published earlier that year in the finance magazine *Barron's* that apparently alerted him to the need to include red mercury in his neutron bomb writing. Red mercury was at the intersection of investment and weapons development. Cohen never discusses the red mercury trade; red mercury was a secret the United States possessed, a lever in the Cold War.

Cohen's praiseful description of red mercury in his autobiography *Shame* (2000) bears the contradiction of its role in the neutron bomb: "The triggering material, red mercury, is a remarkable non-exploding high explosive." The "father of the hydrogen bomb" (and therefore the "grandfather" of the neutron bomb, a paternity he did not accept), Edward Teller, called red mercury "nonsense" at a conference Cohen attended. This miffed Cohen but did not deter him.

In an article he coauthored in 2003, Cohen looked back over the statements by high-ranking officials during the early nineties indicating that they had produced a pure fusion device "as small as a baseball and weighing around 10 pounds." An exotic new material, red mercury, was the key to this device. Cohen had finally got wind of the "Soviet" reports earlier used by Frank Barnaby, the British television producers and the South African journalists. Those high-ranking Russian officials who in the early nineties said that red mercury was a sham had not reached Cohen.

The pure fusion bomb, he and coauthor Joe Douglass wrote on the eve of the American invasion of Iraq on March 11, 2003, would be ignited by a "ballotechnic" explosive unlike conventional high explosives. The ignited material does not explode. It stays intact long enough to reach high temperature and pressure needed to spur a "pure fusion burn" in the deuterium-tritium. The radiation of a thermonuclear device spreads without the attendant shockwave and fireball; it is purely an enhanced-radiation weapon.

In order to cover the reports that red mercury was a lie, Cohen added that when Boris Yeltsin took over as president of the Russian Federation, he secretly authorized the sale of red mercury on the international market. "Sometimes the price was very high; sometimes fake versions of it were offered to gullible buyers. The United States may have been one of these." For there to be fake versions of red mercury there had to be a real one. The Western nations, of course, not wanting it to be known that such a potent weapon was available on the black market did their best to discredit red mercury.

One country with a history of making oil and arms deals with Russia was Iraq, which was interested in this new addition to the arms catalog and was not likely to be cheated. A horrifying new weapon of mass destruction, easily deliverable, could have been in the hands of Saddam Hussein.

Cohen had conflated the fulminate of mercury that might implode the atomic bomb with the atomic bomb itself and come up with a definition of red mercury appropriate for a pure fusion weapon. This could have allowed rogue states like Iraq to skip the costly intermediate stages of developing and maintaining nuclear armaments, and to possess baseball-sized devices deadly to soldiers and civilian populations.

Fusion weapons require a large quantity of short-lived deuterium-tritium, or lithium deuteride. By making red mercury a powerful conventional explosive, Cohen avoided the issue of fuel and invented a bomb that small states and terrorists could assemble from what they could acquire on the arms market. Exploding like a mass of mercury fulminate, red mercury emits deadly radiation like a neutron bomb.

In the most recent (2006) edition of his autobiography, with a taunting title aiming an obscenity at the unnamed chief executive, Cohen works through his neutron-bomb idea but does not mention red mercury at all.

This was the old alchemical mercury transformed out of its fulminate history into a quasi-nuclear material. Experts like Cohen from the 1990s onward instilled the image of a small, high-yield bomb with no detectable radiation potentially smuggled into large countries by secret agents and terrorists. It allowed the experts to link such events as the attack on the World Trade Center to "the Russians" rather than to Saudi extremists, and to conceive a weapon that the Russians might easily pass on to their Near Eastern allies for potential use against "the West."

Alchemy and chemistry had left a heritage of techniques for making substances that look like a red-colored mercury fluid. One Internet commentator went so far as to say that the Russians employed an alchemist to make red mercury in a nuclear reactor. Another printed a diagram and instructions for producing red mercury "based on information supplied by a Russian scientist": "antimony sesquioxide" is combined with red mercury oxide and heated for two days at 500 degrees Centigrade, the resulting compound is then to be dissolved in quicksilver added to the container which then is to be placed in a nuclear reactor again at 500 degrees for twenty days. The cherry-red liquid that forms supposedly has a honey-like consistency and is packed in capsules for use in bombs.

A diagram shows a layer of mercury placed in a beaker over a copper plate that is attached to a positive terminal of an electric source. The entire beaker rests on copper attached to the negative pole of the source. The result would be that the mercury dissolves the copper and becomes a reddish-tinted sponge. Red mercury.

The nuclear reactor apparently with a controllable temperature has become a stage in a set of color transformations. The author relates the process to the surprisingly prescient *Secret Book of Artephius*, a brief and obscure set of instructions first printed in the seventeenth century for making a gold-forming powder from a long-heated mercury-antimony mixture. There is no nuclear reaction suggested, but there are color transformations, another mercury spectrum consummated in a red liquid.

The author of the contemporary red mercury recipe has replaced the arcane language and religious imagery of thirteenth century Latin book of secrets with plain statements that include an unlikely resort to a nuclear power plant. But it is true, mercury antimony oxide is red and might appear to tint iron gold, and fissionable plutonium while not red in color, is yielded by a nuclear reactor. Mercury fulminate crystals also are not red, but the first stage of their manufacture, when quicksilver is dissolved in nitric acid, is red and fuming. These alchemical-chemical imageries have been imported into the world of nuclear weapons and the groups that want to show they have them. The alchemist is an arms dealer, with the mercury flow and color of his product its selling point.

The history of chemistry provided ample merchandising techniques to position substances materially projecting nuclear potency to buyers. The current arms market, a farrago of popular beliefs with highly technical grounding, provided the context. Sometimes it is possible to get a glimpse of this in the news.

In early October 2004, Scotland Yard charged three men with violations of England's new anti-terrorism law, for trying to buy and deliver the components of a "dirty" bomb. Mazher Mahmood, a reporter for Rupert Murdoch's tabloid newspaper *News of the World* posed as "a Muslim extremist" and offered to sell the men a "kilogram of radioactive red mercury." The men told the undercover reporter they had a buyer in Saudi Arabia.

The event represented to the public the status of red mercury amid renewed warfare in the Near East. But now it is the oil-wealthy Saudis who are looking to acquire the fictional substance to carry out their fanatical purposes. The entire event is staged by a newspaper to gain a headline mounting the word "terrorist."

After a trial lasting three months in mid–2006, the three men were acquitted because they did not intend to use the red mercury in a "terrorist weapon." They in fact did not know what red mercury was for; they just wanted to make some money buying and selling it. Mazher Mahmood was a well-known deceiver of celebrities, gathering sensational news by posing as a Saudi sheikh. The arrest and the news that followed were just one more performance in the red-mercury theatre.

Now red mercury is an ingredient in a dirty bomb, which is the next step in the evolution of destructive mercury that began with fulminate of mercury two hundred years ago. It is a reversion to the origins of explosive mercury that relies entirely the imagery of its appearance and reputed power.

A "dirty bomb," implicitly the opposite of a "clean" fission or fusion bomb, simply sends masses of radioactive "dirt" scattering over a wide area contaminating both people and property. It is a neutron bomb manqué, replacing the irradiative fusion at the center with an explosion that disseminates cancerous dust. It is a cheap bomb using the more readily available nuclear waste to make a lasting mark on a population like the mark that the only fission bombs used in war made on the people of Hiroshima and Nagasaki.

A "dirty bomb" is an easier terrorist threat to make understood and to sell than fission or fusion weapons. A film produced in Britain titled *Red Mercury* (2005) has a bitter young Muslim physics student holding people hostage with his "dirty bomb" impelled by the legendary red mercury. As befits the nature of this threat, the thing never explodes.

Hafnium is a chemical element solely encountered as a by-product of nuclear reactions. There are no hafnium minerals or hafnium mines. There are several other elements in this same position, but hafnium, so it is explained, has an isomer, a different arrangement of the same protons and neutrons that seems likely to split open if properly nudged, and release vast energies. The hafnium isomer bomb concept is the product of a physicist's imagination.

The hafnium, or isomer, bomb is proposed by an expert who needs research funding to prove that the reaction takes places. He uses a dental X-ray machine to irradiate a tiny hafnium sample into generating more energy than was put into it. His test procedures are questioned by other physicists who cannot replicate his results, but the hafnium physicist is persuasive and is able to entrench his research in the secretive works of the American defense establishment. Once again the threat of a small, highly portable bomb has supplied impetus to a belief that science cannot deny.

The hafnium bomb is imaginary technology projected from authentic science. The red mercury bomb is imaginary technology projected from prior technology, the atomic and hydrogen bombs, in which mercury had a small role. They are different imaginings with different roots. They both, however, answer a need to have nuclear bombs small in size and widely devastating in their effects. It is a perceived need of nations and factions with threats to publicize, and of technicians and scientists who want to have another Manhattan Project funded to turn science into a usable weapon. There might be any number of these projects at diverse stages of development and funding right now.

Mercury, red or any other color, is only one element in these material imaginings. Red mercury and secret reports thereon are still available for purchase over the Internet. Apart from Mossad's murder campaign during the early 1990s, there hasn't been a concerted effort to block this trade. Anyone buying red mercury deserves what they get. Heavy water, uranium-235, plutonium-239, osmium, and hafnium, and the means of producing them, will have to be sought elsewhere.

Russian prosecutors' announcement in December 2006 that they had found mercury vapor in places frequented by murdered dissident Mikhail Litvenenko was an attempt to turn away from radioactive materials and to a reliable atmospheric toxin. Neither Russia nor the mercury was red any longer. The black comedy of nuclear proliferation that had been played out with red mercury was fading to traces of the old poisoners' melodrama, as North Korea tested a first atomic bomb and Iran publicly stated their intentions to make enough fissionable material for their weapon.

Meanwhile, a little-noticed type of mercury bomb actually was releasing the metal into the water and air of many countries.

11

⊶

Cycling and Recycling

> I have known in this city of Paris several personages of great authority and credible who have drawn quicksilver not only from mineral bodies but from plants and from dried human blood.

Jean Béguin in his *Cours de Chimie* (1630) does not say which plants were used or where the blood came from, but any plant growing near human activity would have absorbed mercury from body wastes. The unguents, fumigations and pills introducing mercury into human body wastes also introduced it into the blood.

Béguin then gives detailed instructions for recovering mercury from silver by dissolving the silver in acid and distilling the liquid. Mercury extracted and refined silver from its ores, and was absorbed into the silver of coins and jewelry from any casual contact. The coins and jewelry also made contact with the skin where they delivered their mercury into the body and its fluids.

Béguin giving his instruction for the recovery of mercury illuminates small curves in what already was a mercury cycle extending from the natural world into humans and back out again. Humans could learn to operate upon these streams to put mercury to their own uses. All of the uses and accidents of mercury described in this book are seconds and minutes in this cycling that grows wider, more voluminous and leakier as humans introduce more mercury and create diversifying channels for its passage.

We have long responded to this cycling, implementing it intuitively until the inquiries of science forced us to quantify and make rules for it. Mercury's ability to enter and leave compounds and associations with other forms of matter gives it cycling impetus. The volume of mercury humans have recovered and the ingenuity of our uses speeds the existing cycles and creates new ones.

A surprise like the appearance of mercury out of a sample of blood exhibits the energy of the mercury movement we have added.

As the mercury cycling has picked up speed, breadth and complexity, science has formed more categories to incorporate it and control it, and yet it has moved beyond any possibility of control. In fine ways and global ones mercury, is on the move. To make the cycles ours, we called some part of these cycles "recycling."

The Roman god Mercury was a patron of merchants: the same syllable "mer-" begins both words. These were the traders who managed the grain traffic with the Greek cities on the coast and in Sicily during the years Rome faced famine. Mercury's patronage guided the trade without interference and supplied bread during the winter months. He presided over a vital movement.

The Romans already used a Greek word for the liquid metal, *hydrargyrum*, "water silver." Probably as a result of trade with the Greeks, the Romans associated their Mercury with Greek Hermes, a divine messenger, master of thieves and boundaries, and as physicians sometimes pointed out, the conductor of the dead to the nether world. It was not until the medieval period that the name "mercury" and the horned lunar symbol were used for the liquid metal.

Explanations for this association centuries afterward read the attributes of the composite god back into the physical nature of the substance. Like the messenger god, mercury took flight; like the shape-shifting god, it always was changing. Like the thieving god, it took away gold; like the bringer of mysteries, it entered the body and the brain. Its uses to drive out worms, clear the skin, and heal syphilis, and its colorful transformations only confirmed the divine identity traits.

All these divine characteristics have one theme in common, they are all in motion, as mercury is, incessantly sublimating, escaping, penetrating containers and barriers. The primary social motion of mercury is com-mer-ce.

The Roman historian Livy wrote in his account of Rome from its founding that the grain merchants dedicated the first temple to Mercury in 395 B.C.E. Ovid in his description of Roman festivals recounts how they celebrated the god's feast day, the fifteenth (ides) of May, by marching to a spring near the temple and sprinkling their heads with water droplets from olive twigs dipped in the water. They declared that the guilt of their deceits was on their heads like the water. The god of merchants was the god of thieves.

Neither mercury nor hydrargyrum is mentioned in Livy's account. It doesn't take much imagination to see that the glistening droplets of hydrargyrum would be very decorative for this celebration, intended to mimic and invoke the fructifying rain and the seeds it was to fertilize. And the shining wealth of the merchants.

The Romans, not the Greeks, made the nymph Maia the mother of Mercury. Among Rome's many gods and godlings, she was the spirit of the rising juices of the earth during the lean time as the previous winter's stores were exhausted and gave way to growing abundance formed when the fluids met the sun's rays. The Egyptians, the Chinese, the Assyrians, the Persians and the Greeks each had a mythology that configured this tense time of first fertility in human and animal figures. The Romans included mercury, god and liquid metal, who, or which, would always have two names, one for the divine and one for the chemical, mercurio and azogue, mercury and quicksilver.

Mercury for the Romans, who bestowed their abstraction on Romance Europe, was both trade and natural motion. Trade was the movement and exchange of goods which had its season and the natural motion was the yearly cycle of planting, cultivation, harvest and fallow times. Christianity remade by the Romans into an official religion with dogma and public officers accepted and spiritualized mercury cycles as no other state cult did.

Mercury always was peripheral to the ceremonies and theology of the Christians and it was always being worked into them by marginal believers and entrepreneurs who drew upon the greater practical experience of Muslims and Chinese as that contact progressed. The sixteenth- through eighteenth-century revival of the pagan gods as images and secrets to be discovered gave numerous opportunities to equate chemical researches with mysteries being recovered from antiquity and from exotic foreigners. And there was mercury's relationship with gold and silver, and with the human skin.

The name "mercury" caught the flash of a motion simultaneously commercial, spiritual and medical. The mercury in medicine had to be recoverable from the body and its surroundings; the mercury in photography refined that recovery to a long second of captive light.

As mercury moved out of the laboratory and the mines, it moved into industry. Hamilton Y. Castner, an American chemist working in England in the 1880s, was prepared to begin large-scale extraction of sodium metal to be used in making aluminum when an aluminum process that did not use sodium greatly reduced demand for sodium.

Over the following decade he found other uses for the sodium as the basis of industrial chemicals, including sodium cyanide, which was a lower cost alternative to mercury in gold mining. The discovery of gold deposits in the British colony of South Africa created a burgeoning market for cyanide.

The increased demand for sodium to make cyanide set Castner to refining his production techniques. The impurity of the caustic soda (sodium hydroxide) he was breaking down to yield the sodium limited the volume of sodium yield, and Castner turned his attention to making purer caustic soda.

Caustic soda does not exist in extensive natural deposits, and has to be made artificially. It was known since Cruickshank's work in 1800 that if an electric current is passed through a solution of salt in water, caustic soda and hydrogen gas are formed at the negative pole (cathode) and chlorine gas is released at the positive pole (anode).

Michael Faraday developed an electrochemical explanation of these events which later were described in terms of ionizaton. The positively charged sodium ions (Na+) in the salt solution migrate toward the negative charge where they meet negative hydroxyl (OH-) ions the electricity has dissociated from the water and unite with them to make sodium hydroxide (NaOH), the extra hydrogen being released as a gas. The negatively charged chlorine ions (Cl-) are attracted to the positively charged anode where they join into molecules and rise out of the solution.

Electrolysis is one laboratory procedure that can be made into a production technique if a strong enough current is continually available. Industrial electrolysis of bauxite to mass-produce aluminum put Castner out of the aluminum business, but the stronger continual currents that made this process possible put him in the caustic soda business.

To manufacture caustic soda it is necessary to pass a current through a dense salt solution, brine, which generates amounts of soda at the cathode sufficient to warrant the initial investment of materials and power. But the caustic soda collected is mixed with the salt not yet broken down. This is the impure caustic soda that Castner determined to refine.

Castner substituted a layer of mercury in the bottom of the electrolysis cell for the graphite cathode. The positive sodium ions in the brine amalgamated with the negatively charged mercury mass before reacting with the brine water to form caustic soda. The negative chlorine ions headed upward toward a row of anodes where they exited as a gas.

The sodium-laden mercury was then piped to a separate compartment, the mercury cell, where it reacted with fresh water to form caustic soda. By pulling out the sodium ions, the mercury delayed the sodium-water reaction long enough to permit formation of a much purer caustic soda.

A rocking device caused the mercury to circulate and maximize its surface contact with the brine which was regularly restored by circulation. The mercury relieved of its sodium cycled back to the electrolysis cell. The cell was a renewable cycling system in which mercury was the only component not transformed into something else.

Purer caustic soda had a greater market beyond gold mining chemistry. It also was the alkali component in soaps, detergents, and cleansing agents, in papermaking and in other industrial processes. The chlorine gas emerging from the mercury electrolysis cell had growing commercial and, unfortunately, military applications. As the century progressed chlorine edged out alkali as the chief product of the mercury cells, hence the name for the industry, "chlor-alkali."

As he sought investments for expanded production facilities, Castner found that an Austrian chemist, Carl Kellner, had conceived of a similar production system. Kellner planned to build a facility in Austria but had sold European rights to the Solvay Company of Belgium, which already controlled the ammonia-soda process for making another important industrial chemical, sodium carbonate.

To avoid costly litigation, Castner agreed to a joint venture with Kellner, and in 1897 they built a plant for the mercury-cell production of caustic soda and chlorine at Runcorn in close proximity to salt deposits in England. Castner-Kellner Alkali Company, the makers of SeeKay brand chemicals, published a series of informative pamphlets in the 1920s, one of which was on chlorine and chlorine products in relation to public health, that is, how they benefited public health as disinfectants.

The Castner cell design (in 1894, before Kellner) was used in a chlor-alkali plant built in the United States near Niagara Falls, to take advantage of the current generated by the turbines at the falls. To bypass the patents and use less costly materials, American inventors developed a production cell with an asbestos diaphragm that allowed the sodium separated from the brine on one side to react with the water on the other. The mercury cell was not supplanted by this and other new technologies, but was used for a large portion of chlorine generation in the United States, and was adopted as a component of Japan's industrialization.

Though the Minamata Bay poisoning originated in a mercury catalyst used in vinyl manufacture, the Japanese government eventually responded in 1972 by banning the industrial use of mercury and its compounds, which had its greatest potential impact on the chlor-alkali industry. The ban was conditional and had several major exceptions gained by industry claiming that the cost of

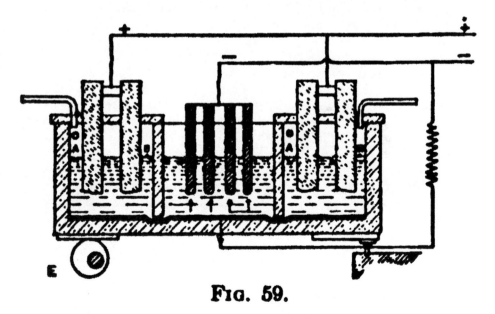

Fig. 59.

Castner-design chlor-alkali cell, illustration in Thorp and Lewis, *Outlines of Industrial Chemistry* (1920).

refitting plants would be ruinously expensive and would cause them to raise the price of key chemicals. The new American diaphragm technology, which did not use mercury, recreated the old problem Castner devised the mercury cell to solve, impure alkali. The membrane technology was only beginning to become feasible.

As one historian of the chlorine industry makes clear, it was not pollution from mercury cells that caused the Minamata disaster, but the Minamata disaster called attention to all such prominent uses of mercury and was used by labor activists and environmentalists to agitate for government bans and remediation of polluted areas and facilities.

The mercury cell was engineered to conserve a valuable resource, and its internal recycling of mercury, progressively made more efficient, was not planned to keep the mercury from attacking the workers. Of the twenty-two workers compensation claims the Ontario provincial government paid workers who came down with mercury poisoning between 1955 and 1975, two were employed in the chlor-alkali industry.

Mercury that was agitated and heated in closed vessels was certain to escape and enter bodies nearby. The steadily cycling charge of mercury had to be recharged to maintain its volume. Castner had set up conditions for the perpetual reuse of mercury within a productive system, but this also established a pathway for the perpetual release of mercury into air, water and flesh. Improvements in the mercury cell were aimed at greater volume of production at lower cost. Reduced emissions of mercury were only to cut costs, not to reduce the amount of mercury released

The attempt to create cycles of reusable materials was one of the chief economies of scale needed to sustain a chemical industry. The Solvay process of making soda ash was built out of conserving and recycling ammonia and carbon dioxide, but ended up releasing quantities of both. The chlor-alkali production cells were built to contain and therefore concentrate their reactants and components. The inputs of electricity and water drew upon resources not returned; the vessels and their components wore out or leaked, no matter how well-regulated the combination of ingredients. Those ingredients also escaped.

The Swedish chlor-alkali industry, for one, monitored mercury exposure of its workers from 1946 onward, and did eventually make technical modifications to the process that reduced blood mercury levels. If there was less hydrogen discharge during the electrolysis, then less mercury vapor was carried out into the air to be breathed. If the composition of the electrodes was changed from graphite to a dimensionally stable material, then workers would not have to spend so much time in direct contact with the trough maintaining the equipment. The Swedish industry had lowered the level of exposure so effectively that when the international call came to phase out mercury cells entirely they hesitated.

That the Minamata poisoning was not caused by escaping chlor-alkali

Chlorine cell, Pittsburg Plate Glass Chlorine Plant, New Martinsville, West Virginia. Photograph by Gottscho-Schleisner, Inc., 1943. Courtesy of Library of Congress Prints and Photographs Division.

mercury was beside the point. The disaster in Japan named a sickness that extended to other industries and initiated a trend toward government regulation and civil litigation that redefined the internal cycle of the plant to include the world around any plant using mercury. Phrases such as "phase-out" of mercury and "remediation" of plant buildings began to be used in the reported conferences, hearings and planning statements of industry and government. The transformation of metallic mercury into an unqualified poison initially led to a coverup of its use in the chemical industry as in the vaccine industry, followed by formal declarations of intention to eliminate it entirely.

A chlor-alkali industry was an important feature of any chemical economy, and the aspect of it that used mercury created a demand for new mercury once the cells began functioning at production capacity. As the industry matured there existed a reservoir of mercury cycling and recycling within its precincts. The mercury didn't exit as a part of the product or as a by-product. It didn't exit into the world of use and discards like the mercury encapsulated in dry cell batteries. At the beginning of the end of mercury chlor-alkali production, the countries with mature chlor-alkali facilities found themselves with large quantities of used mercury no longer needed in their factories.

Spain, the one European country where mercury mining still was feasible, tried to connect the chlor-alkali reservoir to inhibiting new production by arranging for chlor-alkali mercury to be sold at a low rate to the mining interests. This ideally would limit both the appearance of new mercury and the storage or export of used mercury, and stop the cycle. Spain was unique in attempting this.

The mercury cycle was preparing for one large international turn.

Such substances as mercury sludge and chemical waste that included mercury compounds joined numbers of other toxic substances buried in barrels at abandoned works, or sent abroad to disappear in countries with loose regulations and little regard for worker and environmental safety.

India's economic development coupled with its lack of internal mercury sources made it a destination for mercury wastes and spent mercury from chlor-alkali plants in America and Europe. The implications of the presence of mercury in the chlor-alkali industry was just being publicized without attention to its sources.

By the 1990s the Indian chlor-alkali industry was using mercury at a rate half again as great as the world average, and accounted for as much as forty percent of mercury pollution. The life-cycle analysis of mercury loss from mercury-cell plants in India was put at 142 grams per metric ton of caustic soda produced, and what tests were done showed elevated levels of mercury in the hair and blood of workers and people living in the vicinity of the plants and their effluent.

Indian members of the United Nations Environment Program who urged manufacturers to move away from mercury use were not obtaining much of a response. They found themselves at the horn of the cycle and unable to do anything to stop it other than make suggestions on how that might be accomplished.

In the latter years of the twentieth century, the price of crude mercury became volatile. Natural deposits of mercury had diminished in commercial productivity and it became more economically feasible to obtain crude mercury by recycling than by mining. The fund of mercury held by the chlor-alkali mercury-cell users was the least impure and therefore the most expensive. The mercury wastes of other industries which had in the past been clandestinely discarded now approached usefulness. As in mining, however, their value was strictly determined by the cost of extracting usable mercury from them in relation to the value of mercury on the ever constricted market.

Mercury recyclers were insulated from mercury price fluctuations by getting paid for receiving the waste and again when they sold the derived mercury. Recycling acknowledged that mercury continued to move in circles, but only in contained and controlled circles. Improvements were made in what basically was a technology of heating refuse in retorts or other tightly enclosed chambers to vaporize and condense the mercury. Gradually small enterprises began to accept a greater diversity of discards in smaller quantities. The recyclers placed great emphasis on the wide presence and dangers of mercury, and the enclosed safety of their operations. But they had and have much less to say about what becomes of the mercury they extract. There long were varieties of waste they would not consider.

South Africa, ruled by the apartheid government, was a place where toxic wastes could disappear. The government assisted operations that absorbed mercury discharges from abroad by declaring waste mercury a raw material. The mercury was needed by South African industry. There were no mercury mines in the otherwise mineral-rich country.

When Thor Chemical Holdings, Ltd. announced in 1987 that they were accepting mercury wastes for recycling at their South African plant, several American chemical firms responded. But chemical producers now faced export regulations that limited their ability to send abroad containers of liquids now deemed polluting. Countries whose economic elites had been casually receiving the discards of industry for disposal in their less advantaged sectors now were subject to scrutiny by the international environmental movement.

In 1989, a group of United Nations members signed the Basel Convention which was an agreement that hazardous wastes would not be exported, except for recycling. Thor Chemical operated a vinyl chloride plant where mercury had been used as a catalyst, and they could make a convincing argument for skill in recycling mercury to avoid another Minamata, which had been caused by vinyl chloride producers. Thor charged $1100 American per ton of waste mercury. American Cyanimid and Chemet Corporation were among those shipping barrels of sludge with as much as 40 percent organic mercury.

For its part, the post-apartheid South African government in 1993 banned the import of mercury for disposal ("destruction") but not for recycling. Disposed mercury was toxic; recycled mercury would be contained within factories and products.

Thor Chemical Holdings, Ltd. constructed what they claimed was the world's largest mercury-recycling plant in a remote area contiguous to Zulu lands and the Umgoni River. The siting of the plant is in part explained by the cheap labor of Zulu people, and as a work opportunity in an area destitute of other than agricultural employment.

Before long workers at the plant were displaying the symptoms of mercury poisoning, and subsequent tests of the soil and river water detected dangerously elevated levels. A government inspection team in 1994 found a large pond of mercury fluid and a warehouse full of barrels of the same. Rather than recycling the mercury, the company was storing and allowing it to leak away.

A legal precedent was set when a British court allowed disabled South African workers to combine their lawsuits against Thor with lawsuits filed by British workers in British courts because the South African courts were considered a biased venue. Thor has paid damages to some of the workers with claims, and the company has pledged some part of the total amount estimated to be needed for the cleanup.

In books on mercury published since 1995 there are diagrams of the movement of mercury in the environment, between land, water and air. One writer differentiates three types of cycle: mass balances between atmosphere and ocean, a terrestrial cycle and a marine one. The mass balances are what we usually think of as a cycle, where the same amount of mercury passes through changing physical states while remaining constant in mass. The other cycles, which include chemical changes, are not well studied. We hardly know, for instance, what becomes of mercury in the sea, other than that it appears in the tissues of marine animals and in bacteria.

In the Arctic, over 71 degrees north latitude there occurs a "mercury sunrise." As the times of the year come when the sun begins to rise over the horizon to the point that it causes a change in temperature in the ice, the mercury collected there sublimates and enters into chemical combination with the ice in ways that do not seem to change further.

Mercury in human bodies is like a mercury sunrise. Human heat and activity brings it into our skin and brains and kidneys where it remains until released by final decomposition, as the eventual melting of Arctic ice will release more mercury.

The Chinese *Book of History, Shi Chi,* describes the tomb of the first Chinese emperor Shih Huang Ti, in this way:

> In the tomb-chamber the hundred water-courses, the Chiang [the Yangtze River] and the Ho [the Yellow River], together with the great sea, were all imitated by means of flowing mercury, and there were machines that made it flow and circulate. Above [on the roof] the celestial bodies were represented; below [presumably on the floor or on some kind of table] the geography of the earth was depicted.

Since the time of the legendary emperor in the third century B.C.E., the model of the earth that surrounded him in death has come closer to being the world we live in.

12

⊶∞∞⊷

Persistence

Images of mercury are maintained long after mercury itself has vanished from view. The cycle is one image that allows the mercury to disappear but keeps it diagrammatically present in one phase of the cycle. Mercury persists in human usage in moments that expose the impetus of the cycle.

Popular culture is a matter of images not subject to the critical testing of science or the aesthetic validation of art, but drawing upon both. The qualities of mercury that best serve popular culture are those that best serve science, technology and art. It is both poison and elixir, both solid and liquid, both appearing and leaving all the time. It was a vague substance taken into the body to drive out disease found in the body. In turn it became resident in the body and its surroundings to be driven out by newer substances exact in their composition.

Technology backed by science calls for replacing teeth and blood with mercury. The mercury then inside the body threatens to be the source of inexplicable disease. Dental amalgams containing mercury call for the extraction of the teeth that contain them and vaccines administered to prevent specific diseases are themselves prevented from causing disease by mercury, which then has to be removed from the body. Mercury begins in a practical and effective use that is studied and experimented with but then becomes subject to fantasies and beliefs once it is inside the body. Science and pseudo-science join in the imagery of the escape of and from mercury.

When the master violinist Niccoló Paganini in the early nineteenth century had to call upon a team of dentists to operate on his rotting teeth, there was no question that his dental condition was caused by the mercury preparations he persistently used to relieve his syphilis. At the same time Paganini was consuming a vegetable medicine whose maker declared in its advertising that mercury was the greatest enemy of mankind. This mild plant remedy was supposed to cure the more violent mineral one. Paganini, his voice gone and his decaying jaw bound in cloth, had to retire from performing and like Ulrich von Hutten, who lost his teeth to mercury while praising guiac, died a recluse.

Persistent use of mercury is not simply use of mercury. It is use of mercury in the face of an opposite, which is thought to supply what mercury does not accomplish and restrain the worst ravages of the poison medication. Mercury's benefits are gained at the cost of damage caused by mercury. It partially cures the disease and partially causes another. It shows the mirror-maker his face ravaged by mercury. It is mercury against vegetable remedies or against hydroquinone. When it is mercury against penicillin, however, mercury loses and the debate is over. Mercury lingers and remains powered in its cycles of elimination and penetration.

There are two contemporary debates about mercury use in the body that don't seem capable of resolution. The older use seems to have provided the debates' framework, but both intensified in the late 1980s. A number of separate factors confined to technical journals became popular images projected by entrepreneurs.

In both cases, mercury initially used to promote health is suspected to be its antagonist, and no amount of evidence cited or authoritative assertion can put the suspicion to rest. One group for whom mercury is a profitable convenience maintains its use in the face of others who are sure it damages them and their progeny. I refer to the use of mercury to make dental amalgams and the use of thimerosal as a preservative in vaccines. In neither case has a penicillin appeared to replace mercury entirely.

The mercury that causes gums to suppurate and teeth to loosen and fall out also is used to save decaying teeth. The oral effects of taking mercury medication began with salivation and oral lesions and progressed, if exposure continued, to full dental collapse of the kind that destroyed Paganini. Often writers discussing the ravages of mercury would call to witness its effects upon the miners at Almaden and Idria.

Théophile Roussel, physician and legislator, visited the Almaden mines in 1848 and reported his findings in a series of letters cited by French and English (but not Spanish) hygienists for the rest of the century. Roussel found reason to doubt the belief that working in the mines forestalled disease symptoms in miners with syphilis.

He wrote of the tremors and fatigue caused by breathing the vapors and, unique among visitors to the mines, he gave an account of the acute stomatitis that softened and corroded the gums of some laborers after a few days. The teeth blackened, sank, became loose. and ended by falling out, incisors and molars. The decay was slow enough for the workers to continue at their tasks, and after the teeth were gone the infections ceased. Roussel reported that the miners were thankful when their teeth at last were completely gone. "No more teeth, no more diseased mouth," was a saying loosely attributed to the Almaden and Idria miners. While still young, the miners were said to resemble elderly men with faces sunken from loss of teeth, at thirty years bearing "the mask of age." Other writers might point to the absence of dental caries and mouth lesions among these same miners.

There was no escaping the dual nature of mercury. Robert James Graves, in one of his clinical lectures on the practice of medicine, declared that the teeth that fell from the jaws of people poisoned by mercury were not themselves damaged, but he didn't go so far as to say that the teeth were preserved by the mercury.

The most visceral description of mercury's effects on the mouth is in Aaron Snowden Piggot's comprehensive 1854 treatise on the chemistry and metallurgy of dental materials. His remarks are not in the section on mining and smelting mercury. Mercury, used in excess, "spends its force" on the mouth. "Sometimes the ulcerations attack the gums, break them down, seize upon the periosteum, penetrate the bone, which becomes carious and spongy, and finally exfoliates, leaving the most hideous gaps in the face." Piggott firmly rejects mercury in any dental preparation — he favors porcelain replacement teeth — but he never says that teeth fall out due to mercury. In all his writing of rotting jaws and collapsing faces he doesn't mention teeth at all.

Mercury affected the emergence of teeth in children. A doctor discussing the oral ravages of mercury in one of his lectures warned his colleagues to consider mercury administered to infants against smallpox and scarlet fever and not the disease when the children's permanent teeth came out black and distorted. It is the mercury used to treat the disease and not the disease itself that causes the developmental defect.

These stark and mutually opposed accounts of the effects of mercury on the teeth and mouth form a background to the use of mercury in dental amalgams.

When mercury dental amalgam was first introduced in the 1830s, oral surgeons resisted using it, not because of the damage it did to teeth but because it was so easy to use that any charlatan could fill teeth.

Gross cutting away of diseased gums, extraction and replacement of teeth and refitting the mouth with plates do not give the full measure of the finesse required to preserve teeth from caries. Dentists scraped, abraded, and filed at the diseased sections of individual teeth, removing the darkened areas and covering the exposed pulp with pieces of gold leaf or gold pellets they smoothed into conformity with the remaining shape. The tooth could then remain in the jaw impervious to attack from bacterial toxins and mouth acids. These were the skilled dentists.

As the century progressed, the variety of filling materials increased, gutta percha, mastic and metal alloys joined mercury-silver amalgam, but in publication after publication practicing dentists declared the superiority of gold. In

America, where gold-leaf making was perfected, professionals forming the American Society of Dental Surgeons as one of their first official acts in 1841 passed a resolution forbidding members from employing the mercury amalgam.

A pair of brothers bearing the name of the widespread family of dentists Crawcour had arrived from France and set up shop plugging teeth quickly, relatively painlessly and cheaply. Their work did not eliminate the decay, caused the filled teeth to crack when the amalgam expanded and discolored the other teeth when the saliva interacted with impurities in the mercury. A ten-year "amalgam war" resulted, as the organized oral surgeons denounced amalgam work because of its crudity. At the same time the members of the association were quietly adopting the use of amalgam and by the end of the decade they rescinded their resolution.

Another mercury pattern of embrace and denial was established from the arrival of amalgam in dentistry. It resembled using mercury as a remedy for syphilis that caused its own disease while relaxing some syphilis symptoms, or mercury used in smelting that released the gold and also noxious fumes. In dentistry mercury was opposed to gold and absorbed silver (and other metals, including tin, platinum and gold) while suspected of having bad effects.

The "crepitus" of the dental assistant's metal spatula as he mixed mercury with silver powder is a sound described in turn-of-the-twentieth-century texts on dental metallurgy, and which I recall from my own youth, the times I was seated in the dental chair. By then opponents of dental mercury had found several types of bodily harm caused by the mercury going into the mouth rather than through it. It had the same effects as syphilis remedies, embarrassing and dangerous, including loss of teeth. For Alfred Stock it caused loss of memory and disorientation in laboratory scientists and dental workers. More recently it might be at the base of multiple sclerosis, autism or Alzheimer's disease.

The continuing battle over dental mercury came as mercury was removed from consumption and became part of the environment. There was less experience with the effects of real mercury deliberately taken as a remedy and in the workplace, and a wish to explain frightening conditions of the mind and senses. The mercury enclosed in the teeth releasing its vapors to affect the brain became the culprit. Late-nineteenth-century writers against dental mercury claimed that it made its victims salivate and ulcerate. By the late twentieth century, syphilis and its remedies gone, this hidden mercury was affecting only the mind, like a philosophical mercury gone bad.

The earliest preparation of mercury amalgam was silver scraped from a pure ingot, or more likely a silver coin, and mixed with quicksilver to make a paste, "Royal Mineral Succedaneum" as the Crawcours pompously advertised it. Its potential for covering decay with a neutral, even attractive layer, was second only to gold. Louis-Augustin O. Taveau, the first to publish a formula for making mercury-silver paste for teeth (1827), titled it a *"ciment oblitérique,"* a "covering adhesive." It was a dental cosmetic from the start.

Another, most valuable, is the device of Dr. D. D. Smith.

No. 1.—For filling undercuts generally.

Nos. 2 and 3.—For crown and buccal cavities in upper and lower molars.

Nos. 4 and 5.—V-shaped fissure pluggers for filling anterior and posterior V-shaped fissures in molars and bicuspidati.

Nos. 6 and 7.—Right and left V-shaped fissure pluggers for right and left V-shaped cavities in molars and bicuspidati.

FIG. 162.—AMALGAM CUPS.

FIG. 163.—FILE FLAT.

Nos. 8 and 9.—Adapted for working in anterior and posterior approximal cavities, and specially useful in removing excess of amalgam when finishing.

No. 10.—For commencing a filling in the cervical portion of an approximal cavity.

Nos. 11 and 12.—Burnishers, applicable to a great variety of cases.

FIG. 164.—AMALGAM PLUGGERS.

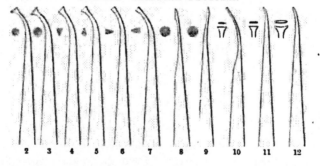

Illustration in Amalgam Practice.—We take as an illustration in making an amalgam plug an irregular cavity, dipping in part beneath the gum; situate upon the side of an inferior molar. Rubber dam or napkin in place, the plastic mass, kept pliable by being held in the warmth of the palm, as directed, is taken up by cup or file flat, preferably the latter, and, being carried to the bottom of the cavity, is condensed by tap-blows, particle after particle being added until the hole is full. To finish, a match-stick bevelled to a feather

Dental tools for inserting amalgam fillings into teeth. Illustrations from Garretson, *A System of Oral Surgery* (1884).

Dentists reformulated the adhesive to make it less likely to leak and stain other teeth, and less prone to expand and crack the teeth it filled. Amalgams formed of several different metals, the usual silver with tin, copper, bismuth, zinc, and even antimony gave a variety of colors and weights for different purposes. By the end of the nineteenth century, dental metallurgy texts were setting students to prepare six or seven different mercury amalgams, each with a different color and consistency.

Amalgam became entrenched because it was cheaper and required less skill to administer than gold, and also because it could be formulated by individual practitioners in a mystique like the medicinal formulations of apothecaries. Acceptance of and opposition to mercury were continual and graded. There always were those who rejected using it, but the majority used it, often apologetically, pointing to the positive results.

The presence of amalgam at any time and place in the practice of dental care is skewed. Those who use it do so quietly, trying to conceal its presence in the teeth with restorative craft and proprietary mixtures. Those who oppose amalgam often link it to whatever current ill-repute mercury has, whether as a poison, a contaminant or a hindrance to child development. And they often have an alternative to sell.

Dr. Joseph Head, giving a paper on "The Dental Filling" at the 1895 meeting of the American Dental Association, concentrated on the danger of poorly prepared fillings leaking bacteria. He was certain that gutta-percha, a vegetable paste long used in fillings, was a "hotbed of bacteria" and often caused fillings to fail. He had nothing but praise for gold leaf and soft gold, but was ambivalent about amalgam, saying that it also could spread bacteria, largely due to incomplete excavation of the carious area by the dentist. The long-established association between use of amalgam and low operative skill now was expressed in terms of bacteria, a new explanation for oral infection.

There also was the beginning of a link drawn between "the evils of bad dentistry," meaning both bad procedure and use of amalgams, and other areas of ill health. The otologist Samuel Sexton wrote that he had seen many cases where hearing loss was preceded by acid developed from food interacting with dental mercury to yield the mercury chlorides, calomel and corrosive sublimate, in people who had no other exposure to the metal (as in syphilis remedies).

Sexton also concluded that amalgam mercury could combine with the sulfur in vulcanite, a hard rubber used by dentists since the 1850s to create pliable plates for installing teeth. Mercury plus sulfur made vermilion which stained the mouth. Both the mercury chlorides and sulfides created lesions that encouraged the growth of bacteria which in turn traveled internally to the ear.

Sexton advised the removal of teeth that were so decayed they lacked their center pulp, rather than saving them by having them filled with amalgam. He did not explicitly recommend taking out teeth that might spill mercury.

Bacteria and bad dentistry acquired a further dimension when it was discovered that unsterilized dental instruments could spread syphilis from one dental patient to another altogether innocent of the other interactions that could lead to syphilis infections.

The antibacterial and disinfectant properties of the mercury in amalgams was touted as a reason to employ it over other less protective fillings. Even this property of mercury fillings could be turned into a negative when researchers discovered late in the twentieth century that by continuously killing bacteria, the mercury in fillings led to antibiotic resistance in the bacteria that survived. Mercury fillings thus became implicated in oral infections, stomach disorders and heart attacks precipitated by antibiotic resistant bacteria.

Motorized drills, general and local anesthetic and X-ray machines all progressively became standard equipment of the dentist, making him or her reliant on manufacturers and drug suppliers, while reducing the amount of skill necessary for painless operations. Dental materials continued to be supplied from specialized sources, but their preparation remained in the hands of the individual dentist, aided by devices to shake the compound of silver alloy powder and mercury to make amalgams.

The practice of amalgam-making resisted prefabrication longer than any other area of dentistry. It represented an area of investment for the practitioner, who did not want to make more than was needed for a particular filling. Dentists continued to "hand mull" (mix in the palm of the hand) the amalgam mixture and spill mercury about their offices into the 1970s, when a series of studies of dental practices and dental offices interfaced with the mercury anxieties of the times to produce strong cautions against the practice. The adoption of mechanical mixers, shaking machines called "jiggle bugs," reduced the hand exposure but still allowed mercury vapors to escape into the office air.

As memory of the specific toxic effects of mercury medications grew more distant for everyday users in industrialized countries, the freedom to associate mercury with various chronic conditions increased. The telltale signs of mercurialism known to calomel users, miners and hatters were no longer in view. At the same time at least one long-known disease was revealed to be mercurial in nature.

Acrodynia, "painful extremities," had been named by a clinician who observed multiple cases caused by arsenic in Paris in 1828. It was a state of extreme sensitivity in the limbs and bluish-pink discoloration of the extremities accompanied by listlessness and convulsive movements. Infection by minute worms, nutritional deficiencies and the use of opium were suggested as causes. In 1948, two physicians connected an elevated blood mercury level to acrodynia symptoms and the consumption of "teething powders" by infants.

Doctors had long been denouncing teething powders and soothing syrups given to infants who were irritated by the eruption of their permanent teeth. Without knowing the contents of these powders, doctors deplored feeding them to cantankerous children because they often had deleterious side effects.

One pediatrician in his textbook rejected teething powders but approved calomel, saying that children could tolerate calomel better than adults. Children were likely to receive calomel in a variety of medications and cleansing agents besides teething powders. Some children might receive more mercury than they could readily eliminate short of showing acrodynia symptoms. The disease was a benchmark in a popular saturation with mercury less visible in adults.

While most medical authorities accepted calomel as more helpful than harmful, or casually condoned its use, they also conceived the possibility that calomel, mercurous chloride, might be converted to corrosive sublimate, mercuric chloride, by the action of digestive fluids. A few cases of fatal gangrene of the mouth reported in children and other instances where acrodynia progressed to mutilating infections of the limbs and face caused the administration of calomel to be accompanied by castor oil or saline laxatives for quick passage through the body.

Calomel and other mercury compounds were so pervasive in over-the-counter drugs that many who used them did not receive this advice. As the same symptoms developed in adults and in children of the same family it might even seem that it was a hereditary disease and not due to the same substance. The same discovery about the cause of these afflictions was made again and again, or it was not. As mercury compounds were replaced by other ingredients in mass-marketed medications, they lingered in teething powders. Acrodynia became a condition of children between one and five years old.

During the Second World War, cases of acrodynia diminished in Britain where teething powder was among the many scarce items, and rose again afterward as the powder became available. As late as 1998, acrodynia in twin girls was explained as the result of being given teething powder their parents brought from India. The correlation became obvious, but the acrodynia was not eliminated by knowing the correlation but by removing calomel from teething powders.

Demonstrating the calomel contents of the teething powders as the cause of acrodynia (pink disease) symptoms encouraged the belief that finding hidden mercury and removing the product containing it from the market could eliminate a troubling disorder of unknown cause. Government intervention was required to assure the removal.

Those who opposed dental mercury began to visualize their cause as a matter of public education and lobbying. Mercury in the teeth, they said, taken up by oral bacteria, could become methylmercury and travel to other parts of the body, eventually leading to serious damage to the brain, stomach and kidneys. Notions of simple inorganic mercury poisoning from amalgam were succeeded by an internal mercury cycle originating in the teeth.

Those wanting to illustrate the ravages of mercury poisoning have a fund of images to draw on. The well-publicized environmental mercury poisoning in Minamata provided pictures of what creeping organic mercury could do to adults and children. Dental mercury activists also reach back to the older industrial mercury toxicology, the "mad hatter" syndrome and other occupational mercurialisms. Often added to this imagery is the claim that Sweden and Germany have banned dental mercury, which creates a compelling reason for the United States to do so as well.

These images and assertions can overwhelm considerations of how much mercury can in fact be released into the body by mercury amalgam fillings over time, and what effects those with fillings actually experience.

The Scandinavian contribution to the popular imagery of amalgam disease was in the notion of "oral galvanism." This was the belief that metal fillings in the teeth generated an electric current, something like a mercury battery, which in turn electrolyzed mouth contents and released lethal vapors attacking the brain. During the 1970s and 80s belief that this was going on throughout the dentally treated population reached a peak of epidemic hysteria. Government-sponsored studies were commissioned and clinics were opened to treat the mental illness of those who believed that the fillings had to be removed from their teeth for them to regain health.

Simply persuading a patient that certain sensations in the mouth were signs that current was rising made business for a few dentists, who could back up their diagnosis with devices that gave a current reading or a mercury vapor density measure. The urgency eventually died down, but a few profiteers continued offering mercury removal services to uneasy people with undiagnosed illness.

Patrick Stortebecker, a Swedish dentist who had relocated to Florida, helped focus the American version of amalgam illness when in 1986 he published an English translation of his book calling mercury poisoning from dental amalgam a hazard to the human brain. Oral galvanism is there, and so are the mad hatters, spreading the chagrin of the Swedish government and dental establishment to a new population.

As with all controversies over mercury from Thomas Dover's time onward, backers of each position can cite the views of sympathetic professionals and the results of scientific studies to support their views, but one position especially relies on proposing their conjectures to the fears and biases of their public. The test that proves the validity of the belief about mercury never happens because its affirmative outcome is so strongly fixed in popular culture that only those who accept the concrete interventions of science can get around it.

In 1985, a Sonoma County, California, court awarded a $100,000 settlement to a woman who had suffered nerve damage to the roots of five of her teeth after a dentist removed their amalgam fillings. The dentist, designated as "Doe" in the pleading, used a device called the Dermatron to read the mercury concentration in the woman's body through her skin. This test convinced the woman that she was in danger of a severe intestinal condition from the mercury falling off her teeth. The need for remedial surgery on two of the teeth and extraction of two others convinced the court that the woman had been defrauded.

Starker still was the case of an Iowa man suffering from multiple sclerosis who was convinced by a dentist that his symptoms would abate if his amalgam-filled teeth were removed. The symptoms did not abate, and the state dental board suspended the operator's license for nine months.

Extraction of all amalgam-filled teeth might also be an earnest attempt to cure mercurialism resulting from occupational exposure, as in the sad case reported from the literature by D'Itri and D'Itri, of a thermometer-factory employee who had all his teeth removed by a dentist who diagnosed pyorrhea caused by the fillings themselves. After the oral amalgam was gone a skin rash and tremors succeeded.On June 21, 2006, the Dental Board of California, the state regulatory authority, brought an accusation against James Shen, DDS, who practiced dentistry in Huntington Beach, California. In May, a Board investigator, P.M., had visited Dr. Shen without disclosing his identity, complaining of tooth pain. Shen took a dental X-ray, intraoral photographs, and examined the man's mouth using a dental mirror, but did not use any instruments to explore the mouth. He placed his fingers on P.M.'s teeth, then in each of his ears and had him open and close his mouth. Then he pulled on P.M.'s arm with his mouth shut and then with it open.

Dr. Shen claimed to have discovered galvanism in P.M.'s mouth and said that the mercury needed to be removed from his teeth for health reasons, and that removing the amalgam fillings would make him feel better. Shen explained how bad mercury is and discussed "Mad Hatter disease." Shen did not send P.M. to a medical doctor for evaluation and testing of mercury poisoning, and on a return visit told him he had mercury everywhere, and would think and feel better after amalgam removal.

In similar cases an individual may commit herself or himself to costly dental surgery, or be offered that surgery, based on a pseudoscientific connection between mercury amalgams in the teeth and a real or potential health condition.

Perhaps manual gestures or a junk science device bridges the gap between the dentist's self-interested diagnosis and credible measured evidence of the threat. The dread of possible illness (think of those mad hatters and toothless miners) or the frightening unknowability of an existing one (multiple sclerosis) can be enough to drive a patient's agreement to dental action.

A three-year case-control study of dental amalgams as a risk factor for multiple sclerosis (MS) found no statistically significant correlation between the number of teeth filled with amalgams and the likelihood of MS. However, Dr. Hal Huggins, a dentist no longer licensed to practice in Colorado, in a book published in 1999, tells of his studies of the cerebrospinal fluid (CSF) of people with multiple sclerosis both before and after removal of dental amalgams.

Before removal the CSF contained proteins characteristic of MS lesions; afterward the proteins were gone. And so, Huggins maintains, were the MS symptoms.

A group of psychiatrists at the Huddinge University Hospital in Sweden examined a number of patients who believed that their physical symptoms were the result of mercury in dental fillings. They found that these patients were much more likely to exhibit psychiatric disorders than a group of controls, and they had a greater number of physical conditions, but not so many that it supported their beliefs that they were much less healthy than others. Making the suffering of these patients a medical problem related to amalgams, the researchers found, deprived the patients of psychotherapy they needed.

All the parties to this debate about mercury from dental amalgams contribute to the creation of the concept of an amalgam illness. Scientifically tested or pseudoscientifically explained, amalgam illness exists to the degree of being a mental illness for some. The rich popular imagery of mercury in the body, the mad hatters and toothless miners, is there to give flesh and character to the presence of the metal. A pair of writers who identify "dental amalgam dementia" as a distinct disease follow their brief account of the disease with a long list of trades and occupations using mercury.

Controversial from their first use, amalgams literally remained in place holding mercury as other medical and occupational uses of mercury slid into the background and became part of the modern environment. The fact that the mercury used to protect teeth from decay could also make them loosen and fall out was never quite resolved, and simply was absorbed, like the mercury itself, into the body at hand.

Many unexplained and incurable diseases can be immediately addressed with a concrete explanation and simple solution. An operation as drastic as removing all the mercury, amalgam fillings from teeth, or the teeth themselves, is certain to have an effect on the patient, though perhaps not the one expected. Amalgam illness is a repudiation of the entire course of human involvement with mercury, and a memorial assertion of everything mercury has done in humans.

Professional associations such as the American Dental Association, an umbrella group of dentists and oral surgeons, have made policy statements defending the use of mercury yet assuring the public that it is kept at a minimum. The U.S. Food and Drug Administration in 1991 and again in 2006 sponsored a review by scientific advisory panels of studies of the effects of mercury amalgam on the health of populations and its connection to disease. The conclusion both times—that mercury entering the body from tooth fillings does not rise to a level that can clearly be associated with ill health — has been decried by groups organized to maintain pressure on the government to act in this and related matters of public health.

The dental mercury debate centers on the poison/remedy dichotomy that has always characterized mercury's uses, including suspicions of mercury's stealthy, penetrating nature. It is like many other debates about toxic substances implanted in bodies by heedless commercial interests who can forestall investigation, disclosure and government action.

The dental mercury debate is unique, however, in that the mercury already is inside the body, placed there to assure dental patients of continuing health. Its presence instead is inverted into a source of continuing ill health, and of diseases with no explanation and cure. The dentists' response to this criticism is conciliatory. They assert that dental mercury is safe, but they assure their critics that they are reducing its presence.

Autism was one of the conditions blamed on amalgams, in this case mercury from the teeth of a mother poisoning the development of the offspring. Mercury from the teeth could be used to explain neurological conditions arising at all stages of life, from autism first noticed in children, multiple sclerosis and amyotrophic lateral sclerosis in early adulthood, and arthritis and Alzheimer's in later years. Autism caused by the mother's dental mercury resembles the mercury poisoning caused by "metallic impregnation" by the father employed in a mercury-using industry. The metal penetrates intergenerationally.

"Amalgam illness," emerged from occupational and medicinal mercury use, moved into the background, and the holdover presence of mercury in the teeth, always controversial, became strange, linked with the entire history of mercury images. "Autism as mercury poisoning" arose similarly, but with two great epistemological differences. This mercury had been concealed, and it was not inside those most affected by it.

There are theories equating the historic identification of multiple sclerosis with the first uses of dental mercury. Both amalgams and MS emerged in the 1830s and continued a parallel increase afterward. Autism was not identified as a distinct condition until the early 1940s, after dental amalgams had been used for over a hundred years.

The use of mercury that seemed to coincide with autism's discovery was in the vaccines administered against childhood diseases. Not the vaccines themselves, but the preservative that made mass-vaccination campaigns safer. The vaccines had to come into routine use, in children so young that developmental issues could be linked to the vaccines, and given to so many that they arrived in multi-use vials preserved against contamination. Unlike amalgam, the preservative was far from controversial or even from being known.

Morris Kharasch doesn't name thimerosal in the U.S. patent application (June 29, 1927) that describes the chemical make-up and production of an "alkyl mercuric sulphur compound," nor does he assign the patent to the Eli Lilly Company as he did a number of his later patents. The heading for the patent application places him in College Park, Maryland, the location of the

University of Maryland, where he was then a professor. But the affidavit at the end of the patent declares his location to be Indianapolis, Indiana, where the Eli Lilly Company was headquartered.

This patent, referred to by later patentees as the source of thimerosal, describes a chemical structure and manufacturing process for making many slightly different organic mercury compounds. Kharasch illustrates many of them with structural formula and chemical name. Thimerosal, a very general name, could be any of these. In the patent, there is only a fleeting mention of the new compound's properties as a germicide, and more frequent reference to its water-soluble properties and suitability for injection.

Kharasch patented water-soluble organic compounds of arsenic and antimony shortly after this mercury compound. He used a general method, the subject of his first patent filed in 1926, of introducing organo-metallic compounds into a water solution using acids containing sulfhydryl (sulfur-hydrogen) groups. He placed the old medicinal metals in molecules that might be selectively active against invading bacteria and fungi while not damaging the host.

Kharasch went on to formulate mercury-based organic molecules for controlling fungus in soil and on sprouting seeds. But the soluble combination of a mercury atom with thiosalicylic acid, thi-mero-sal, was the product that came to the fore in medicine.

Years later, as a professor at the University of Chicago, Kharasch reportedly advised students of Jewish ancestry in his chemistry classes to change their names if they wished to succeed in science. In 1928, Eli Lilly and Company registered a version of thimerosal under the trade-mark Merthiolate, "sodium ethyl mercurithiosalicylate or organic mercury compound solution, useful in antisepsis and treatment of nose and throat infections."

Animal tests, and then attempts to use thimerosal to halt an outbreak of bacterial meningitis in Indianapolis in 1931 did not signal a promising future as an injectable antibiotic. Critics and lawsuits later singled out this as the only trial of thimerosal as an injected agent.

A "Therapeutic Desk Reference" published by Eli Lilly and Company in 1932 contains a section on Merthiolate, "a new organic mercurial germicide and antiseptic distinguished by its potency and non-toxicity." Merthiolate is easily mixed with water or alcohol, does not stain skin or fabric or tarnish instruments and has no appreciable odor. According to this reference entry, Merthiolate's "most desirable property" and the one that makes it unique among bactericidal agents, "is its tendency to accelerate healing."

This property exceeds what would be expected from Merthiolate's ability to destroy bacteria alone and must be "due to the substituted sulphydryl radicle present in the Merthiolate molecule."

The forward-looking physicians who were the audience for this desk reference would have known about the healing potential of sulphydryl groups.

These chemical groups were eventually recognized as having a chemical action diminishing the severity of radiation poisoning and the cellular mutations of cancer.

Kharasch had engineered the molecules to include both mercury, the old metallic remedy, and the sulfur-hydrogen radical in the same patented compound. This was not so difficult because sulphydryl groups have a great affinity for mercury. Later too, almost ironically, sulphydryl groups would form an important component of chelating agents (dimercaptol) created to remove mercury from living systems. For the present, the Merthiolate package was completed by the addition of a sodium ion, which would facilitate transport into living bacterial cells.

Injection treatment and vaccine preservation were not among the uses for Merthiolate listed by the physicians' desk reference. It was entirely for application to skin wounds and inflamed mucus membranes. It was a colorless fluid, also available in a red tincture for painting the surface of the skin prior to surgery. This was the form which use by hospitals and physicians in their offices helped spread to the home medicine cabinet.

Merthiolate, or its parent compound thimerosal, had antibacterial, antifungal properties that made it a candidate for another contemporary use, one more for the convenience of a pharmaceutical company and their doctor clients than for the patient.

In the late 1920s there were several tragic incidents of children dying from vaccines contaminated by bacteria. A good preservative was clearly needed. Merthiolate could not be a vaccine, but it could protect the vaccines just as fulminate of mercury could not be an explosive, but it could be a detonator of explosives. The fierce initial action of organic mercury compounds had to be utilized in a specialized way.

Merthiolate became the preservative of choice for vaccines that had to be produced in quantity to inoculate children against infectious diseases. The bacterial disease diphtheria, for instance, remained a significant threat to children because it could arise suddenly, before vaccines could be produced and administered. The antitoxin vaccine for diphtheria was known since the late nineteenth century. Being able to prevent diphtheria didn't protect the vaccine itself from invasion by, for instance, staphylococcus bacteria.

Yet it is not clear when thimerosal was first used as a vaccine preservative, or how extensively. Only much later did a group of researchers draw a line between the introduction of thimerosal into vaccines and first-case descriptions of autism. They did this at a time when there was greatly increased emphasis on early childhood vaccination. The connection, made in the 1990s, was applied retroactively to the time when thimerosal was first present in vaccines in the thirties. The thimerosal-autism link, or any mercury-autism link, was not claimed by those who named and observed autism. It took the circumstances of the early nineties to forge that link and inject the mercury poisoning imagery into concerns about the effects of extensive vaccine administration on infant development.

In 1988 the Centers for Disease Control, the national infectious disease authority in the United States, recommended that infants receive three Hepatitis B immunizations and three Haemophilus B immunizations within the first six months of life. The first Hepatitis B immunization was to be given at birth, and all of these were in addition to other immunizations already routine for newborns and infants. At that time, all of these vaccines contained thimerosal as a preservative, as well as other preservatives such as phenol.

The amount of these vaccines that had to be available to hospitals for these immunization schedules to be met required the use of multi-dose containers which could last long enough under refrigeration not to go to waste. Parents were conscious of the increasing load of preventive medication given to their children and when their offspring started to show unsociability and self-absorption it was likely to begin not long after some vaccination or other. At least in a few cases there was anecdotal association between the condition, which was lasting, and the vaccination.

Thimerosal was still a "little-known" ingredient of vaccines. When it was publicized that thimerosal and therefore the vaccines contained mercury, the public was ripe for the mercury-autism equation. The mad hatter imagery then was connected to a fluid being shot into the vulnerable bodies of infants whose development was closely watched by parents and caregivers.

A 2001 article in the journal *Medical Hypotheses* gave an informed cast to the fears and suspicions that autism is "a novel form of mercury poisoning." Basing their argument on a "thorough correspondence" between the traits of autism and those of mercury poisoning, the authors correlated the onset of autism with the timing of vaccine administration in individual cases and the historic increase in autism prevalence as vaccination increased. The sex ratios of autism and mercury poisoning, males favored in both cases, and genetic predisposition to both mercury poisoning at low doses and autism also were entered into evidence. Finally, there were "parental reports" of "autistic children with elevated Hg [mercury]."

The authors argued that children in the first two years of life were receiving doses of mercury that exceeded safety guidelines through the thimerosal in vaccines. Autism, they contended, was the consequence.

This article was by no means the only source of this speculation. It exemplifies the construction of the mercury-autism correlation by identifying distinct categories for which the actual data are limited and arguable. Potential for debate replaces testable conjectures, though there was no shortage of tests on any side.

The presence of mercury in the blood of autistic children could be dismissed by critics as not indicative because the same concentrations can be found in children who are not autistic. The proponents of the mercury-autism link then rejoin that the autistic children are those who don't process mercury as well as the others, and that the blood was not tested at the right time or in the right way. This in turn brings the response that the differences in processing mercury do not account for the presence or absence of autism symptoms, and so on.

Each of the arguments raised in favor of the hypothesis is opposed by a counter-argument with its own body of data. More males than females show signs of mercury poisoning because the workers in mercury-using industries tend to be male, whereas more males than females are autistic for unknown reasons. But then males and females working in the same mercury industry are differentially affected. Now, however, the information is so limited that it can support any side of the dispute.

In 2004, one of the coauthors of the 2001 article joined two new coauthors to publish in the same journal another article plaintively titled, "Thimerosal and Autism? a plausible hypothesis that should not be dismissed." From the 2001 assertion that autism was a form of mercury poisoning comparable to the known types, the contention has now receded to the defensive posture that autism might plausibly be associated with thimerosal.

Leo Kanner's first paper (1943) on "autistic disturbances of affective contact" did not offer a cause for the pattern of social withdrawal and aloofness that he found in each of the eleven children whose cases he summarizes. The last line of the paper adds the word "inborn" to "autistic disturbances of affective contact."

Kanner wrote that the parents were highly intelligent, and obsessive in the demands they made of their children. Very few of them made really warm-hearted mothers and fathers. The immediate family was preoccupied with abstractions of a scientific, literary or artistic nature, leaving the child alone. It is difficult to attribute the later social isolation of the child to relations with the parents because there weren't much in the way of relations with the parents. Instead, Kanner wrote, "we must assume, then, that these children have come into the world with innate inability to form the usual, biologically provided affective contact with people." Using a phrase from bacteriology, he referred to these children as "pure-culture examples" of inborn autistic disturbances.

Kanner was the first to use the word "autistic" to describe these children. As author of a primary text on child psychiatry and organizer of the first child-psychiatry department in a medical school, Kanner applied labels and made observations with some authority. The cases in this original paper would be considered "high-functioning" today. Kanner's final turn to the inborn nature of the autistic disturbances could encompass the much more severe inability to interact socially that became known as developmental disability. These children were unable to engage in the full range of interactions that defines a member of society; it appeared that their development was stalled. Such a range of abilities and inabilities was observed that the term "autism spectrum disorder" (ASD) was coined.

The suggestion that parental remoteness initiated autism mutated into the so-called "refrigerator mom" image: the mother was blamed for being so cold and enclosed that the child could not learn how to relate to others at this crucial period. This image was proposed and rejected: another attempt to place the burden of upbringing entirely on women.

The alternative to parental remoteness, that the autism was inborn, required parents to believe that the autism of their child had a precedent in their own family background. This might be difficult to verify, and in any event meant that nothing could be done to prevent a child from growing autistic. As the number of autism cases increased, there was pressure to discover an outside cause in early childhood that did not indict the parents. There was an impetus to make autism the result of infectious disease or poisoning unknown to the parents.

If the vaccines eliminated the possibility of disease, the mercury they contained was the poison. Hence the wording of the title of the first *Medical Hypothesis* article: a novel form of mercury poisoning. The spectrum of autistic conditions that made up ASD could then be explained as differential exposure and individual response to exposure. Autism completed its transition into popular culture on the currents of mercury-poisoning imagery.

Parents who were helpless if their child's developmental delays were due to heredity had courses of action opened for them if they were due to mercury from vaccines. They could halt their child receiving more mercury; they could seek to prevent the poisoning of other children and they could try to clear the mercury out of their own child. Only some parents, those already caring for autistic children and those who feared for the safety of their newborns, accepted the autism-mercury link, and only some of them acted upon that. The circumstances and affiliations of the image sustained and helped disseminate it through protest and accusation, testing and attempted remediation.

Autistic children and their parents became incorporated into the existing picture of mercury poisoning for everyone else to see. Autism was linked to dental amalgams, to industrial pollution and food-borne mercury reaching children. "Autism as a Minamata disease variant" is the title of an article that carries bears the picture of disabled children amid the technical details. The development of thimerosal was rewritten in legal pleadings to center around the mercury it infused into an autistic child.

At first thimerosal was described as a "little-known additive" to vaccines. Nothing tangible, nothing purchasable in bottles, was labeled "thimerosal" or known to contain it.

Lilly abandoned the trademark Merthiolate in 1982; it was acquired briefly by another company and now is in the public domain, being used to name a topical antiseptic that contains no mercury. Thimerosal in itself was out of the picture.

Thimerosal was mentioned by public officials only to state that it was being removed from vaccines. The only significant remaining use was in flu vaccines for adults, which had to be prepared and distributed rapidly. A notice to California state employees informing them of upcoming flu vaccinations in October 2006 included in the list of those who should not receive the injection anyone who is "allergic to Thimerosal (lens cleaning solution)." This admitted that thimerosal was in the vaccine by referring it to the liquids sold to keep contact lenses free of bacteria and fungi. Fewer of them contain thimerosal today, but it is the only available referent.

There was no way to see, touch or taste thimerosal as there was to look at, feel or, allegedly, taste amalgams. Thimerosal was known to break down into ethyl mercury inside the body. Ethylmercury could in turn be placed alongside, or confused with, methylmercury, the lethal compound that mercury became when acted on by bacteria. Thimerosal was supposedly the source of the same compounds that caused public health officials to issue warnings to pregnant woman not to eat certain types of seafood, or feed it to their young children. The children of Minamata again flashed in the foreground of mercury-autism imagery.

To chemistry and medicine, thimerosal was a range of compounds, but it was not tangible to popular culture. Stating that thimerosal was 46 percent mercury by weight gave it an elusive substance. Thimerosal in a vaccine meant mercury in a vaccine. And mercury had turned entirely into an essence that entered bodies and come manifest as disabilities and disease. In the popular model of syphilis, the mercury cure became the disease. For those who believed mercury was the agent of autism, mercury was the cause of the disease, and eliminating it meant eliminating the disease.

Putting pressure on government regulatory agencies to prevent manufacturers from including thimerosal in vaccines was one way to exclude this mercury from bodies, and prevent the diseases it caused. It followed that removing it from bodies where it already was would eliminate the disease it was causing in those bodies. This required thinking of autism, as a disease or poisoning condition which could be reversed and ended with the ejection of mercury. It also required thinking of autism as a disease which could be cured, not as a permanent disruption of normal development.

For those who accepted a direct relationship between the mercury within and the external signs of autism a clearing agent was the solution. There was no antidote to mercury; it had to be expelled from the body. A remedy for mercury poisoning would be a remedy for autism.

Recognizing autism as mercury poisoning inverted past beliefs of mercury in the body. Autism was not a worm to be rushed through the digestive system by drinks of raw mercury, nor was it a foreign substance to be purged up by swallowing calomel or corrosive sublimate. It was mercury itself embedded in the flesh. Fumigations of mercury vapor, unguents containing mercury or liquids in which the mercury globules were so finely divided they could penetrate the tiniest vessels— none of these could carry away the poison if it was mercury. Autism was not a composite disease like syphilis, made up of a poison and the mercury chasing it. Autism demanded a treatment that cleansed the body of mercury, repudiating the entire past of mercury in the body while using different means in the same way mercury always was used.

The obvious treatment was one already used in cases of mercury poisoning. Chelation was developed as a response to the possibility of an attack using poison gas, the organic arsenic compound called lewisite. The attack never took place and the gas remained in leaking stockpiles as the potential combatants turned to nuclear and other weapons of mass destruction.

British Anti-Lewisite (BAL), later known as dimercaprol, consisted of two sulfhydryl groups joined by a hydroxyl group. The "mer-" in its chemical name was the second syllable of "dimer-" for the two sulfhydryl groups, and had nothing to do with mercury.

It was called a "chelate" (key-late) after the Greek word for claw because it was supposed to move through the circulatory system in a claw-like way, grasping heavy metals from the tissues as it went. The metal ions would be eliminated from the body together with the chelate. The image was of a complete cleaning. It resembled what mercury once was supposed to achieve with foreign bodies, carrying them away by its weight and force, in great smooth masses or fine globules. Only the claw was much rougher and more thorough, and like mercury too it had side effects and did not work as well as its image suggested.

By the time autism was being treated with chelation therapy, dimercaprol had been succeeded as a treatment for heavy-metal poisoning by several other compounds. EDTA, an organic compound with hydroxyl and amino groups, added to foods to prevent metal ions from catalyzing degeneration, has a high potential for attracting mercury lodged in human tissues. The chelation concept was irresistible. The visualizable action of the molecules of the chelate was an advertising point. One chelating compound was sold by showing it as a basket gently collecting the heavy metals from living cells.

Autism was one of a number of different conditions that chelation therapy was supposed to address. It cleared out the mercury from the internal organs of autistic children. It cleared out the plaque from the arteries where it accumulated and thus prevented heart attacks. Chelation purified the body of foreign obstructions in a way that could be sold to non-specialists, but explained further in terms of molecular imagery if that was required. The spread of the Internet has created opportunities to perpetuate this ancient concept of healing as purging and elimination, now as a wave of smoothly searching molecules pervading the body and carrying away noxious influences. This is like the finely globular mercury that was popular later in the career of mercury medicines. But now clearing out the body means removing the mercury.

Perform a thought experiment. Imagine yourself the parent of a child who shows the signs of Autism Spectrum Disorder. You might accept the child's isolation, poor communication skills as a fault in development and strive to compensate for that with constant attention and specialized training.

The idea that this is a remediable illness is tempting and if that is accepted, that the illness is caused by a specific agent, one arriving in food or placed in childhood vaccines by a pharmaceutical corporation concerned only with profits. You learn of a treatment that can clear the noxious agent out of the child. If that does not promise to heal him entirely, it at least may heal him some day. You arrange for the treatment and are surprised by the changes in the child's behavior, but for some reason the doses can't be continued. There is no permanent alteration. The chelating agents, for that brief time, promised a better life from clearance of mercury. You at least are left believing that the disorder is due to encroaching mercury.

Worms in the intestines, the rigors of mining, syphilitic "virus" and improved skin, the management of explosions, manufacturing chlorine gas and the intention to recycle, these things and activities successively perpetuated the presence of mercury. Their patterns may have existed since the beginnings of matter. Appropriately mercury ends up in the human brain, from where it is always about to be swept away in the lasting flood.

Appendix A

Cocles on *The French Disease*, 1504

Excerpt from Cocles. 1504. *Anastasis* VI, 243, De inauditis ac malignis egritudinibus (Thorndike 1941: Appendix I), translated from the Latin by Richard Swiderski.

... And this disease [morbus gallicus] is almost incurable, returning with a leap even as it recedes. Some doctors rub the sick with various unguents. I cured some as described after regular evacuation of digested matter. Recipe: combine one pound pig grease, three ounces quicksilver, one ounce of the common salt of litharge and one ounce and a half of rose water. And extinguish the quicksilver with the said ingredients in a mortar and the resulting unguent bind up and place in a well-covered vessel and let it remain with three changes for three days. This causes sweat and evaporates the material up to the palate, and when the gums ulcerate I cured it by often washing them in water with egg white. I will not speak of abscesses because it is not my intent.

Appendix B

From *The Dialogue of Mercury and Gaiac*, 1527

Excerpt from the *Dialogue of Mercury and Gaiac exposing their virtues and rival pretensions in the cure of venereal disease*, de Béthencourt (1871: 81–90), translated from the French by Richard Swiderski.

Mercury: It's a god who gave me his name, the god of commerce and eloquence, the messenger of Olympus. It's a planet who gave me some of his power. Impossible for me not to glory in such an origin. I carry in myself, to cure men, divine and hereditary virtues.

Gaiac: You don't blush with shame speaking like that! Glorying in your origin is exalting someone else's merit. If you descend from gods, if you receive from them precious virtues, the glory is not yours but theirs. What makes nobility is not birth but personal merit.

Mercury: Do you ignore the esteem I am given among physicians, alchemists, those curious about nature, who work incessantly to transform my substance into a metal yet more precious?

Gaiac: I know that; but I also know the results of these chimerical efforts.

Mercury: Today I socialize with kings, princes, generals, prelates, bishops, all the great personages of this world. I cure all their evils, even the most incurable.

Gaiac: All their evils? Are you sure?

Mercury: Most of them: leprosy, for example, psoriasis, lichen, phthiriasis. And I cure them thanks to the conformity of my nature with their humors. Is there anything, in fact, that would have more affinity for me than men's semen or saliva? These two humors, you know, can only be expelled by movement. And is there anything more mobile than I am?

Just as well I can claim with good right the privilege of curing venereal disease, which proceeds primarily from sperm and secondarily from spit.

Gaiac: I would be at ease if your pretensions were legitimate. That would be said without jealousy, because I flatter myself with curing the same evil, not only by my own virtues but with the help of nature. It is true that I cure it by a method very different from yours. I cure it by the Penitent Fast marvelously appropriate to the cure of such an evil. This evil, in effect resulting from the ardor for intercourse and the disorder of the passions, it is greatly to the point to combat it with a treatment which imposes on the body and soul the just chastisement of their sins.

Mercury: You boast about your merits quite well. Since you take this tone with me I propose a tourney in which each of us, turn by turn, pleads his cause and says what he would have valued.

Gaiac: So be it! I accept your challenge. Begin.

Appendix C

Mercury-Containing Skin Applications, 1928

Adapted from the American Medical Associations Bureau of Investigation (1928:1–25).

Anti-Freckle Lotion
Recamier Moth and Freckle Lotion
Berry's Freckle Ointment
Bradley's Face Bleach
Clear Plex
Freckleater
Freckleless
Gouraud's Oriental Cream
Hill's Freckle Lotion
Hubert's Malvina
Ingram's Milkweed Brand Cream
Kingsberry's Freckle Lotion
Kintho Beauty Cream
McCorrison's Famous Diamond Lotion, No. 1
Mercolized Wax
Nadinola Skin Purifier
Othine
Palmer's Skin Whitener
Perry's Moth and Freckle Lotion
Rohrer's Artesia Cream
Ruppert's Face Bleach
Stillman's Freckle Cream
Tan-A-Zin
Utopian Medicated Beautifiers

Chapter Notes

At the end of each chapter I will list in order the sources of the information and statements encountered in the text. Quotations in the text are identified with the first few words followed by the source, and, in the case of translations, the original language. All citations are keyed to the References section by name and date.

Preface

Dr. Pontaeus's green salve show is described by Thompson (1993: 54–55). The "miniature inferno" illusion is in the magicians' guide arranged by Hopkins (1898: 87–97) and the use of mercury as a surrogate for molten metal in battery-plate casting is mentioned in a patent review in the early automotive journal *The Horseless Age* (1900, vol. 7, no. 17: 33).

Caliph Abd al-Rahman al-Nasir's mercury reflecting pool in the caliphal palace hall at Madinat al-Zahra was included by al-Maqqari in his travelogue (Ruggles 2002: 47).

Mercury in the Litvinenko case (Schreck 2006).

Boys (1959: 66–68) considers mercury bubbles prettier than soap bubbles. Classical authors besides Aristotle alluded to Daedalus's mercury-balanced automata, often skeptically (Newman 2004: 12–13). The *rin-no-tama* or *ben-wa* usually contain metal balls, but the mercury was an enhancement (Stanley 1995: 579). Frances Hauksbee, "curator of experiments" for the Royal Society, studied "barometric light" and found that it could be pro-

duced without mercury, but he couldn't explain it (Hankins 1985: 58–59).

Chapter 1

"The whole tract was found to be lined..." Alexander Small, appended to Victor (1733).

"In the year 1727..." and "He had a succession of fevers..." Fitzgerald (1882: vol. 2, 57–58) is the source of the quotes from Theo Cibber's description of Booth's illness.

Benjamin Victor is the likely author of the *Memoirs of the Life of Barton Booth, Esq.* (1733), the chief contemporary source on the life and death of the actor.

Dewhurst (1974) contains a brief life of Dover and a replica of Dover's *Ancient Physician* (1742).

Daniel Turner (1733) includes his analysis of Booth's autopsy in an attack on Dover's "repugnant practice." On Turner's own career and use of mercury, see Wilson (1999).

"Sir, The Benefits..." Edward Lisle's letter is printed in Dover (1742: 167), as is Captain Colt's (38–41).

Sarton (1927: 84) plainly states that Galen

considered mercury a poison and would not experiment with it, while Krebs (2004: 106) though also noting that Galen found it a poison, says that he advised using it to promote salubrious salivation.

Debus (2001: 13) contrasts Galenic humors and Paracelsian chemistry.

Viscountess Dupplin's letter is in Dewhurst (1957: 128).

Dover (1742: 119–20) tells of his smallpox cure.

"Let them take a trip to Hungary..." (Dover 1742: 74–75).

Belloste (1733: 8) is the source of the sequel to Dover's story of mercury theft by miners.

Campos Navarro (2000), compiling writings on empacho from the sixteenth to the twentieth century, including an excerpt from Barrios, gives evidence that it was Europeans who introduced into the New World mercury for blockages.

"He that rightly considers..." Dover (1742: 83).

The pamphlet war that Booth's death precipitated is examined by Dewhurst (1957: 156–63). Dewhurst counted fourteen books and pamphlets on the merits and dangers of mercury published during this time, and this probably is not all of them.

John Goodyer's translation of the section on hydrargyrum (liquid mercury) from Dioscorides first century C.E. De material medica is in Egenhoff (1953: 21).

Dr. Madden's letter (1734).

Paré's essay "On Bezoar" is translated in Keynes, ed. (1968: 197–200).

Elkins (1999: 20) sees Aethiops mineral from mercury into vermilion.

The "faeces" of mercury are a product of the analysis of mercury performed by the exacting alchemist George Starkey (Newman and Principe 2002: 121–22).

Cohen, ed. (1919) contains a Dutch translation of Boerhaave's account of his mercury experiments, the only version I could find. Polehamton and Good (1818: vol. 6, 319–21) review Boerhaave's mercury publications questioning alchemical assumptions.

"In a purely metallic state..." Long (1839: vol. 15, 105).

Von Ziemssen (1881, vol. 7: 650–52) expatiates on findings about the action of metallic mercury in the stomach and intestines, and does recommend using it.

Michelon (1908: 40) quotes Fourcroy citing the experiments of Vogel (1812) saying that if mercury seems to oxidize it actually is "the metals it encloses."

"Nothing is more common..." (Taylor 1858: 167).

Chapter 2

"M. le Duc, Physician..." Belloste (1733: 8). This translation from the French original is by the author.

Thorndike (1958: volume 8, 209) identifies M. Dodart's Journal des Sçavans article.

"The Indians at the Malucco Islands..." Dover (1742: 69).

Hippocrates, On Ancient Medicine (Book 22) states that the uterus and other organs receive fluids from the outside. Hippocrates' Aphorisms tells of its wanderings. Veith (1970) offers a history of the wandering uterus explanation of hysteria.

Thompson (1936: 48) also notes that the Assyrians used mercury to eliminate worms and heal skin lesions.

"For medisons given..." This passage is from Simon Forman's 1580 "Matrix and the Pain thereof" printed in Traister (1991: 443).

"It first got into Use..." Egenhoff (1953: 19) reproduces John Hill's 1746 translation of Theophrastus's History of Stones with Hill's commentary.

"The case of a girl..." Blyth (1885: 578). Compare to Taylor (1880: 156, 576) both from Gibb (1873).

"Metallic mercury, although a supposed abortifacient, is no doubt innocent." (Taylor 1884: 104).

"Pregnancy is no contraindication..." Forchheimer (1908: 139).

"Introduction into the vagina of a colpourynter..." Taussig (1910: 162–63).

Chinese women drinking mercury for an abortion, for instance expressed by Lane (2001: 35). Mercury contraception. An entry from the Chinese pharmacopeia Pen-ching on shui yan (mercury) stating that it treats scabies but might cause miscarriages, is translated by Unschuld (1986: 83). Medvei (1993: 10) gives a mercury contraceptive recipe provided by the seventh-century c.e. Taoist physician Sun Si-Mao. Guerrero (1977) is a survey of traditional contraception in the Philippines, which includes asoge (mercury).

The mercury-caused genital deformity of Joson is mentioned by Faure (1998: 161n59).

Lead oleate pills. Shorter (1990: 211). Brown (1977) analyzes a number of late nineteenth century "female pills" and discovers a reputation for abortion hinted at by the iron they contain.

The sexual basis for using mercury in Ayurvedic rejuvenating pills is discussed by Suoboda (1988: 173–76). The chief Ayurvedic formulary, the *Bhaisajyratnavali* composed in the mid–nineteenth century by Shri Govinda Dasji, while containing these recipes, also has a chapter of remedies for mercury disease.

"For a Foetus is too weak..." De Blegny (1707: 286). Quoted by Tanner (1868: 235n).

"as well as those infected by nurses..." Hamilton (1821: 57), "it is to be hoped..." (59).

"No embryo can live..." citing Magendie, Hempel (1865: 623).

D'Itri and D'Itri (1977: 190) cite an instance of a male using mercury contraceptive.

Brodie (1994: 74) on the use of bichloride as a spermicide in nineteenth-century America.

Storer and Heard (1868: 199) refer to the case of *Regina v. Wilson* in which the provider of "some preparation of mercury" to induce a miscarriage was found guilty of criminal abortion.

"Always mix this solution..."Sanger (1914: 8) is the first of two editions; the same advice is repeated in the 1917 edition.

Johnstone (1931: 501) reports on three cases of vaginal bichloride poisoning among twenty-one cases of acute mercurial poisoning. Rabinowitch (1933) is the 300-case survey and Rabinowitch (1938) is the single case with "unusual findings."

Barnes (1885: 353) summarizes the Lizé study.

Ornoy and Arnon (1993:385) provide evidence of the mercury's preferential attraction to the fetus.

Harada (1986) examines congenital Minamata disease, and George (2001) is a political history of the disease and the movement to force the corporation and the government to take responsibility for ending it. Shkilnyk (1985) is an account of how mercury, by disabling children, destroyed community at Grassy Narrows. Parker, et al. (2004) review the literature on thimerosol-containing vaccines and autism. Kirby (2005) details the politics of the mercury-autism controversy. Ziff and Ziff (1987) accuse dental fillings of infertility and birth defects (detail in chapter 12). Irregulartimes.com/mercuryman.html associates environmental mercury with abortion.

Chapter 3

"One to whom neither a gorgeous home...." The full quote is in Partington (1962: vol. 2, 293) and in Brock (2000: 79). Jaffe (1976: 30), in a long section on Becher, quotes a stripped-down version. The original can be found in the preface to Becher's *Physica subterranea*, in the 1733 Leipzig Latin edition edited by George Stahl, a Becher disciple, who pronounced the book "a peerless work."

Smith (1994), a survey of Becher's life and work drawn from a reading of his writings, does not quote or cite this passage, nor does Thorndike in his section on Becher.

A Western comment on *rasayana* that betrays Western ambivalence about mercury is Hauck (2004: 155).

Cosimo's letter to the Pope describing Tarentius's and Arnelius's demise is summarized by Thorndike (1934: 346–47).

"These are merely proofs...." The eighth century Chinese text is the *T'ai ch'ing shih pi chi*, the passage translated by Sivin (1968: 143n114).

"Eugenius Philalethes died..." (Wood 1817: vol. 3, 722)

Boyle and Robert Child on Starkey's illness and death. Newman and Principe (2002: 97, 225).

Glauber "seized with Sickness..." (Packe 1689: 72). Glauber's *De Purgatorio Philosophorum* is in Packe (1689), the first and last English edition of his works. Read (1957: 109–11) summarizes Glauber's productive career and destitute end.

"Can some of the alchemists' convictions be traced back to mercury, lead and arsenic poisoning?" (Sivin 1968: 30) is asked of Chinese alchemists, but could be asked of Arab, Indian and Euro-American alchemists as well.

"In the furnace changes...." Dioscorides in John Goodyer's translation is also excerpted by Egenhoff (1953: 21).

"On being shaken...." Pliny the Elder's description of minium (cinnabar) mining, use and the precautions taken by those exposed to the dust is in Book II of his *Historia Naturalis*, which concerns silver mines and refineries. Egenhoff (1953: 29–30) excerpts the 1601 Philemon Holland translation.

Geber (Egenhoff 1953: 54–56) in Richard Russell's 1678 translation.

Pachter (1961: 146–49) recounts Paracelsus's opposition to guiac bark and guarded support of mercury treating syphilis. I use guiac for the name of the bark otherwise spelled guaiacum everywhere except where direct quotes use the longer name. Hutten (1991: 219–20) gives an interesting phonetic discourse on the origin of the name.

Sendivogius's dialogue between the alchemist and mercury is in his *Novum lumen chymicum,* in English translation on the web at www.levity.com. Szydlo (1994) has published a demystifying biography of the alchemist, in which he gives evidence that Sendivogius discovered the element oxygen long before Priestley and Scheele (who may have stolen the discovery from the unknown Pole).

"With this Chanoun I dwelt...." Chaucer (1975: 98–99)

Hamilton and Hardy (1974: 131) outline the sequence of personnel in the mines.

Gilder and Gilder (2004) include a translation of the formula for Tycho's tubith mineral elixir in their account of the Kepler's intrigue against the astronomer.

Newton's biographers generally are skeptical of mercury as an explanation for his periods of withdrawal and erratic behavior. Westfall (1993), the most detailed recent biography, doesn't mention it at all. Gleick (2003: 99,229n) collects recent references on Newton's mercury madness. The case for the airborne mercury poisoning as the cause of Newton's madness is made by the neurologist Harold Klawans (1990: 30–7).

Emsley (2005: 10–19) introduces the poisonous values of mercury through its reputed effects on Newton and King Charles. He also mentions Boyle's exposure and lack of disability, possibly because his experiments were performed by apprentices.

Jardine (2004: 214–34) examines Robert Hooke's health and the "largely unhelpful" remedies he took, but doesn't suggest mercury poisoning.

"Chemists boast..." Ramazzini (1983: 46–52) contains the 1713 Latin text and Wilmer Cave Wright's 1940 English translation.

Lancillotti's 1685 *Farmaceutia mercuriale,* never reprinted or translated, but contributing recipes to later works, contains a print of *The Triumph of Mercury,* showing a procession of the crowned deity in a chariot which mirrors many other mythological triumphs, including that of Antimony in Lancillotti's other book.

Crow (2000) is another cautious, liability-skirting description of mercury use in India. Crow didn't encounter a Lancilloti or a Ramazzini among the practitioners there.

Boerhaave's unchanging heated mercury pot is an often-told tale of chemistry marking the end of alchemical aspirations and apparently the beginning of an accurate chemistry of mercury. It is reported as chemical legend by Jaffe (1976: 61) and Ripley and Dana, eds. (1873: vol. 4, 361), but as an actual experiment by Pole-hamton and Good (1815: vol. 6, 320).

Cavendish lab contamination. Williams (1998: 158) citing an unpublished 1995 report.

Partington (1957: 126–30) describes the context of Lavoisier's identification of oxygen, and includes a copy of Marie-Anne Pierette Paulze's drawing of Lavoisier's gas collection apparatus. The title of Anne Treneer's biography of Humphry Davy, *The Mercurial Chemist* (1963), refers to her subject's temperament, quoting Davy's nitrous oxide and sodium reports, and Joseph Cottle's cautions (47–48).

Roberts (2005) describes the death of the sensuous chemist.

Burnett (1823) is the belated report on the HMS *Triumph* and Earles (1964) assembles a compact note on the matter.

Faraday's recent biographers all embrace the aloof master scientist image and do not allow him to be poisoned by his research materials. For instance, Hamilton (2004), and Hirshfeld (2006). Stock's views are reported in the Massachusetts Institute of Technology campus newspaper *The Tech* (1927).

Goldwater (1972) devotes an entire chapter to dental mercury and Stock's role in the amalgam wars. Stock (1926a) appears on the Internet in a translation by Birgit Calhoun (www.stanford.edu/~bcalhoun/AStock.htm). Stock (1926b) explains that mercury vapors are generated from mercury amalgam fillings in teeth.

Winderlich (1928) also had a health encounter with mercury in the chemistry laboratory.

Frisch (1979: 39) tells of trying to invent a mercury-vapor detector.

Centers for Disease Control (1988) reports the Connecticut high school chemistry experiment gone toxic.

Chapter 4

"Phony fish scare?" in the weekly Saturday newspaper insert *USA Weekend* (January 5–7, 2007: 4); the EatSmart feature by Jean Carper cited William Lands, "a leading expert on the benefits of fish oil" for the selenium in fish news. The mercury toxicity reducing properties of selenium have been studied for some time (Ganther, et al. 1972).

"The apparatus was demolished..." Bunsen is quoted by Partington (1957: 236–37).

Frankland (1852) tabulates the organic-metal-containing bodies he was able to generate.

Russell (1996: 52) cites Frankland's physiological experiments, and quotes his description of the gas explosion (53) and his list of equipment for his lectures to the farmers (51).

Hamilton (1974: 136) comments on the looseness of laboratory practice with respect to mercury and the infrequency of accidents.

Edwards (1865) describes the first recorded dimethylmercury deaths.

"In consequence..." Russell (1996: 251–52) quotes the *Cosmos* article and the resulting defense by Frankland and his supporters.

Banda (1937: 209, 211) on the potential of Granosan to free "the generative power."

Most of the cases of occupational organomercury poisoning given in tabular summary by Bidstrup (1964: 88–109) are laboratory workers.

D'Itri and D'Itri (1977: 34) give a brief summary of the 1952 paper on the flour from mercury-treated seed being the cause of developmental disability in Swedish children.

Panogen: Bagnall and Derow, eds. (2004: 173) is a translation of the grain receipt. Courlander (2002: 153–56) is "The Wall of Millet," the tale of a once-rich man who dies after he eats seed grain.

United States Congress (1970: 109; 135) is the testimony that mentions the Japan and earlier Iraq poisonings.

Waldron (1970) is the first detailed article on the Huckleby family in the *New York Times*. It was preceded by a brief notice and followed by seven more notices and articles on the health of the Huckleby children and the outcomes of the lawsuits. An editorial on July 24, 1970, discussed the inconsistent regulatory reaction to the poisonings. Toward the end of the NBC Evening News on January 30, 1975, commentator John Chancellor gave a 40-second report on the decision in the federal lawsuit. D'Itri and D'Itri (1977: 41–46) devote a section of a chapter to "The Huckleby Poisoning." Roeuché (1970) is an account of the investigation that led to the discovery that the Huckleby children were suffering from "Minamata disease" which at the time Roeuché was writing had not been defined as industrial in origin.

Hyder's testimony is in U.S. Congress (1971: 265).

Relying on reports by "travelers" since the Iraq government blocked coverage, the *New York Times* ("Mercury poisoning in Iraq is said to kill 100 to 400," March 6, 1972: 3) assembled an account of the mercury-seed poisoning and the government reaction.

On Cargill's involvement, see Broehl (1998: 387n10).

Hamza (2000: 55–56) gives a brief inside look at the Iraqi response to the epidemic.

World Health Organization (1976) is the record of the conference on the 1971–73 Iraq "intoxication." Bakri, et al. (1973) is the first scientific publication by Iraqi specialists studying the clinical aspects of the poisoning.

D'Itri and D'Itri (1977: 29–32) summarize and reference the discovery of mercury poisoning in Swedish birds, following a chapter on Minamata.

Jensen and Jernelov (1969) announce the discovery of biomethylation of mercury by micro-organisms.

Bidstrup (1972) absorbs the 1971–73 Iraq poisoning into a general account of clinical symptoms of mercury poisoning.

Clarkson (2002) summarizes the discovery of the chain of bioaccumulation and biomethylation and the results of research on the mass poisoning in Iraq.

World Health Organization (1990) follows an earlier, less conclusive, less well-referenced set of Environmental Health Criteria for mercury in 1976, updated in 1980.

Mahaffey (2005) on the development of the mercury reference dose.

Harada (1986) updates his studies of mercury-caused congenital defects in Minamata, from 1968 onward. Amin-Zaki, et al. (1978) concentrates on the latent effects of methylmercury on Iraqi children over the two years following the epidemic. Cox, et al. (1995) takes an overview of the child-development data from Iraq, and Moore (2003: 53–55) places the Iraqi children amid international controversies about pollution and development.

Vibert (1900: 250) describes the experiment with raw mercury poisoning and fish.

United States Department of Health and Human Services and United States Environmental Protection Agency (2004) is the joint mercury-in-fish advisory.

Waldman (2005) is the commentary on the advisory, and Roe and Hawthorne (2005) is the report on the *Chicago Tribune*'s survey.

Seafood and neurodevelopmental outcomes study (Hibbeln, et al. 2007)

Renner (2005) on the complications that "hot spots" pose for the cap-and-trade system and Swamimathan (2007) on the discovery of hot spots in North America.

The most accessible account of Karen Wetterhahn's exposure to dimethylmercury is Endicott (1999), which is available on the Internet. Weiss, et al. (2002), of which Thomas Clarkson is a co-author, compares several examples of latency and neurodegenerative disease.

Nierenberg, et al. (1998) reviews the anatomy and physiology of Wetterhahn's poisoning. Feldman (1999: 95–96) gives the transport model for methylmercury and discusses its tissue biochemistry. This is accompanied by a magnetic resonance image of the brain of a thermometer worker exposed to elemental mercury and a man with "Minamata disease" (organic mercury poisoning).

Wheeler (1996) sets a timeline of environmental mercury awareness events that includes the WHO declaration. Pirrone and Mahaffey, eds. (2005) is a survey of natural mercury cycles and human exposures worldwide.

Trasande, et al. (2005) calculates the economic cost of the loss in intelligence resulting from methylmercury absorption by developing children.

Chapter 5

Allen (2000: 54) includes a copy of an engraving, *The Martyrdom of Mercury*, which illustrated a 1709 tract, *The Scourge of Venus and Mercury* by J. Sintelaer.

"The sick person is placed..." Ulrich von Hutten's Latin essay was translated into German, French, Italian and English not long after its appearance. My translation is from a modern German version, *Über die Wunderbare Heilkraft des Guajakholzes und die Heilung des Franzosenkrankheit* (Hutten 1991: 207–95).

The detail on Paracelsus's response to Hutten and subsequent French disease writings is from Pachter (1951: 146–49)

Theodoric of Cervia cited by Walsh (1911: 286). The French Disease and syphilis (Arrizbalaga, Henderson and French 1997).

Guiac says to Mercury... "The translation into French of Bethencourt's Latin *Nouvel Carême* by the mid–nineteenth century syphilologist Alfred Fournier (1871) is the source of my translation of the contest of Guiac and Mercury which, by the way, Mercury starts with his bragging. The entire dialogue is translated in Appendix B. Appendix A contains my translation from the Latin of Cocles (1504) of a formula for a mercury unguent for French disease sores.

Ramazzini (1940: 43) identifies mercury's use as a scabies treatment as the source of its use against syphilis.

Frascatoro's turn from mercury to guiac is the subject of the fourth and last-written book of his poem.

On the early history of syphilis and the guiac-mercury battle, see Quétel (1992: 9–32). Arrais's (1642) cautious mercury prescription is rejected by Henriques (1715).

Cellini (1910: Chapter 59 and Chapter 102) covers Benvenuto Cellini's brushes with syphilis and *sollimato*. Fenton (2002: 317) makes a case of the connection between the two.

The "unexpurgated" translation of Casanova's *Memoirs* by Machen (1894) contains several references to mercury, mercurials and venereal disease. Ramazzini (1940: 39) is citing a work by Martin Lister which recommends guiac for treatment of mercury poisoning.

Murthy (2002–04: vol. 2, chap. 51) translates the *Bhavaprakasa* on "the Frankish disease" and proposed treatments.

Dr. Profily's *Easy and Exact Method* is described in terms of an actual case of its use by Mary Margaret Stewart (in Merians 1996: 108–9).

The title of J. J. Gardane's 1773 handbook in French (*Methode sure et facile de traiter les maladies vénériennes*) is very similar to the title of Profily's book.

Susan P. Conner (in Merians 1996: 28–29 and 30n8) describes the Bicêtre method.

Bateman (1817: 256) describes "mercurial eczema."

Ritter von Plenck's *Methodus nova et facilis argentum vivum aegris venerea labe infectis exhibendi* was followed by a more comprehensive work on the treatment of venereal disease and an extensive typology and compilation of treatments of skin diseases.

Colby (1846: 43) offers the recipe for Dr. Elijah Smith's Anti-mercurial Syrup.

"I therefore give the title of mercurial disease..." (Mathias 1811: 21).

"The mouth feels unusually hot..." The account of mercurial disease is by Rothstein (1972: 51).

The following two chapters explore variations on this theme concerning and independent of syphilis.

Kussmaul's *Jungenerrinerungen einen alten Artzes* (*Youthful Memories of an Aged Doctor*) is the basis of the biography by Bast (1926).

Kussmaul (1861) is the source of the translations and the account of his mercury/syphilis studies.

Aldinger's thesis is quoted on 112–13 and Case 37 is on 158.

McLoughlin's 1861 pamphlet, "Proofs of the Non-Existence of a Specific Enthetic Disease," is described and quoted by Spongberg (1997: 65), as is the response of the Select Committee of medical men formed by Parliament to evaluate extension of the Contagious Diseases Acts.

"The bath should be administered..." Parker (1868: 3–5). Parker (1874) is the edition compiled by John W. Foye and includes Henry Lee's lecture on the calomel vapor bath.

Durkee (1859: 303) recommends the vapor bath with qualifications. Beaney (1869: 141) doesn't recommend it at all.

The Aachen methods. "At Aachen a course of treatment consists usually of sixty immersions in the hot sulphur bath, followed by sixty inunctions, each of five grams of mercurial ointment."

Allbutt, ed. (1905: 345).

The discovery and testing of Salvarsan is recounted by Marquardt (1951) and an early treatment manual is by Wechselmann (1911).

Fleck (1979: 1–19) examines with skeptical acuteness the origins of the modern concept of syphilis.

Arsphenamine/Salvarsan's reception by the medical profession and interested public in America can be traced in a series of articles and advertisements in the *New York Times*: "Finds a Specific for Blood Disease" (August 3, 1910: 5); "A Victory of Healing" (August 4, 1910: 6); "Brings from Europe Ehrlich's Remedy" (October 5, 1910: 5); "Curing Soldiers with '606'" (May 27, 1912: 7); "'606'/To the Public" (March 19, 1911: X11); "Present Status of Ehrlich's Remedy" (November 30, 1910: 10).

Kolmer and Schamberg (1912) give the results of human and animal tests of Salvarsan.

McDonough (1915) gives a précis of the use of both mercury and Salvarsan in treatment several years after the new remedy's introduction.

Captain Nichols's medication program is outlined by Gillett (1995: 349–51).

Wallhauser (1997) is his recollection of the introduction of Salvarsan in New Jersey.

Federal Trade Commission (1922: 65–66) states the reason for granting patents to American manufacturers to make their own Salvarsan.

Jones (1993) is the revised edition of the comprehensive account of the Tuskegee study.

Benedek and Erlen (1999) offers an assessment of the "science" that contributed to that study's course.

Moore (1946) is an evaluation and study of the use of penicillin to treat syphilis, written soon after such treatments began.

Chapter 6

"...a pound of quicksilver..." Ellis (1758), at www.soilandhealth.org/03s0v/0302hsted/030205ellis/030205cheapmedicine.html

Michelon (1908: 181–83) on the efforts to validate mercury water.

"Mercury is more or less effective..." translated from quotation of Malouin by Michelon (1908: 35)

"When crude mercury is taken..." The opening quote is my translation of Belloste (1733: 74), which is the edition of the *Traitez de Mercure*, first published in 1696, included in the supplement to *Chirurgien d'hôpital*. All quotes and paraphrases are from this edition. The latest republication of the *Traitez* I have been able to trace is Belloste (1754), but there was an English translation published by Carlile (1843). Belloste (ca.1733) is a partial translation into English by an otherwise unknown Michel-Antoine Belloste. Le Minor and Clair (2001) trace Belloste's transition from military surgeon to mercury therapist.

"Take an ounce of mercury..." Diderot and d'Alembert (1758), "Mercure" at diderot.alembert.free.fr/M.html/.

Macilwain (1853) comprises the life and works of Abernethy without once mentioning blue pill.

Abernethy (1811, vol. I: 50–52) covers Case 2. The "surgical" part of the title is dropped in some collections. *Surgical Observations of Diseases Resembling Syphilis* follows *Surgical Observations of the Origin and Treatment of Local Diseases* in the 1811 collection and later ones.

"Neither Abernethy nor others could explain more than that it [biliousness] requires blue pill." Gibson (1912: 402).

Goddings, ed. (1835: 327) reports Elliotson's outburst, "Had Mr. Abernethy lived a hundred years and done good all the time..." "To remedy this evil [excessive use of blue pill]," Graves (1864, vol. II: 243–44) recalls Elliotson's colocynth mixed with minute amounts of croton oil, which also is "liable to serious objections." Elliotson (1843) instances the painless surgery of the mesmerized.

Bell (1833: 34–36) on the mercurial medication of Mr. H. and advice to another patient to leave off blue pill (105).

"Most indescribably disagreeable sensations" treated in part by blue pill (Johnson 1827: 653–54).

"Blue pill is the favourite remedy..." (Graham 1827: 11).

"Abernethy Medicines. These originally consisted..." (Cooley 1846: 9).

"He watched the powers of nature..." and "In small doses..." Sigmond (1840: 46–48), the source of the quotations, has not been reprinted.

"Mercury is one of those agents..." Philip (1834: 41).

The New York Daily Times/New York Times pages are noted in the text.

The "Medicine for the Mayor" piece was printed in the *New York Times*, December 1, 1857: 1.

The list of medical supplies for the Lewis and Clark expedition is at www.voyageofdiscovery.com/historical/medical_supplies.shtml.

Lowry (2004: 33; 80) writes of Rush's Bilious Pills on the expedition and the evidence their use left.

In an excerpt from the *Charleston Courier* in the *New York Times* (July 15, 1864: 7), the medical purveyor of Columbia, South Carolina, requests that Confederate ladies collect rose leaves to help make blue pills for sick soldiers.

Wittstein (1871) compiled the researches into secret remedies at the time.

"But what are three blue pills..." Hepworth (1971[1864]: 206)

"Abernethy's insidious remedy...," Advertisement for Holloway's Pills, *New York Daily Times*, June 2, 1856, page 8.

Vote for Wood, "Medicine and the Mayor," *New York Times*, December 1,1857, page 4.

Pesterments—Not Troubles, *New York Times*, September 4, 1852, page 2.

The Blighted Being, Amusements, *New York Daily Times*, December 4,1854, page 4.

Death of John W. Williams, "The Death of Farmer Williams, Unsatisfactory Result of Coronor's Inquest," *New York Times*, January 5, 1881, page 3.

"Tu me fais l'effet d'un pillule!" The Kind of Pill Not Specified, *New York Times*, January 5, 1881, page 3.

The report on the poisoning of Lincoln through blue pills ("Failure to poison Mr. Lincoln") is in *The New York Times*, July 18, 1865, page 3.

Hirschorn, Feldman and Greaves (1999) suspect Lincoln's blue pill consumption was the cause of his outbursts.

Walker (1997: 157–79) begins his account of Corbett with reference to his hat-making mercury exposure, and takes it as predisposing to his actions.

"An individual accustomed to high living and a sedentary life...,"Campbell (1894: 395)

"The analysis of a specimen of blue pill..." *New York Times* (October 29, 1859: page 3).

Hewlett, et al. (1916: 112) represents the inclusion of blue pill and blue mass as cathartics in the then current U.S. Pharmacopeia. They ceased to be listed after that.

Dr. Roger L. Williams, vice-president and CEO of the U.S. Pharmacopeia, in Congressional testimony (2002) used the coloring of bichloride pills blue in the early twentieth century as an example of how medical errors can be reduced: US Congress (2002: 29).

Chapter 7

Ricord (1863: 17) recounts his rejoinder to the pretensions of Dr. Giraudeau.

Giraudeau (1858) himself published a long treatise on venereal disease in which he discussed the many forms of mercury treatment and the alternatives.

Lasky and Wandruszka, eds. (1973) provide background on van Swieten.

Van Swieten's liquor was still used in France in the mid–nineteenth-century, to treat infants with congenital syphilis, to the dismay of iodized mercury advocates (von Pfaundler and Schlussman, eds. 1908: vol. II: 563).

Brookes (1828: 116) has several entries in Brooke's catalog of his collection of anatomical specimens (a human breast, the mesentery and intestine of a turtle) prepared with mercury.

Beddoes (1802: 48–49) records his experiment with mercury injected into puppies.

Bellet's biography in the standard biographical dictionaries is little more than a list of his publications.

An Isaac Bellet was among the Huguenot refugees to the English colony of Virginia in 1700 (Brock, ed. 1886: 38, 41, 43).

Dunn (2000: 38) connects Huguenot refugees with the transmission of hat-making technology to North America.

Thomson (1868: 29–30) describes the process of secretage.

Ramsey (1994: 52–54) follows the convoluted history of the *rob* Boyveau-Laffecteur amid the secret remedies. Eamon (1994: 357–58) places secret remedies in the context of the long-continuing books-of-secrets tradition.

Bellet (1768) defends his syrop.

Horne (1769) exposits his study of mercury preparations.

Roux (1770) discourses on the "sweetened spirit of nitre" made by Bellet, and may even have written Horne's study.

Laffecteur (1785: 8) describes his presentation before the intendant of Paris.

Rivet (1803: 292–93), a revolutionary disclosure of secret remedies, prints an improved formula for *sirop de Belet*, as well as for Belloste's pills (185–86) and *rob de sureau* (elderberry rob) (251–52), and even *liqueur de Vans-Wieten* (1805: v. 2: 17–18) but not for *rob Laffecteur*. Robs can be made from dwarf elder, currants and buckthorn, all of them purgatives. Rob elder is a name in English for the source plant. Richard Burton, in his notes to the "Tale of the 34th Night" in his 1882 complete translation of the *Arabian Nights,* writes that Arab "rubb"=syrup, a word Europeanized by the "Rob. Laffecteur." (Burton 1962: v.1, 375).

Van Mons, *Pharmacopie usuelle* cited by Villebrun (1939: 23) is the source of the herbal recipe for *rob de Laffecteur.*

Michelon (1908: 190–93) outlines the attempts 1811–28 to find mercury salts in the *rob,* and quotes Henry and Guibourt's advice (197).

N. J. B. Guibourt, who published his chemical analyses of a number of secret remedies in the case of *rob Laffecteur,* asked in the title of his paper (1828), "does it or does it not contain corrosive sublimate?" He determined that it did.

"It is amazing..." Swediaur (1817: v. I, 232).

A copy of the *arrêt* is in Laffecteur (1785: 21–25), a softbound pamphlet that contains documentation of Boyveau-Laffecteur's efforts.

"As long as the venereal disease..." Extract of the *Gazette de Santé* article, Laffecteur (1785: 26–28).

"When I gave an account..." Laffecteur (1785: 1).

"I have not wanted to quarrel..." Laffecteur (1785: 3).

The words of Giraudeau's decree copy are printed by Zlatagorskoi (1862; 555).

Hoffman and Gouzil are mentioned by Ramsay (1994: 53).

Sarrut and Saint-Edmé (1836) is a laudatory biography of Giraudeau and an account of his drive to remove mercury from syphilis treatments.

Villebrun (1939: 32–34), a doctoral thesis on the *rob,* discusses Giraudeau's merchandising.

"These pustulous bandages..." Barthélémy's 1851 poem, *Syphilis* in Villebrun (1939: 40–430).

Payenneville (1910), by a physician-medical historian who planned the campaign against syphilis in the city of Rouen, writes another history of the *rob.*

Daudet (2004) describes his resort to many medications, especially morphine.

Giraudeau (1858: 501–69) discourses on the actual state of prostitution in Paris, where it had been legalized ostensibly to assert police control over venereal disease.

"The brochures of Giraudeau..." Testimony before the Paris correctional police tribunal, May 2, 1829 (Michelon 1908: 195).

Philadelphia Medical Society (1827) is the source of the story of the origins of Swaim's Panacea, and of the cases cited. Summarized and quoted in the *Christian Spectator* (1828: 431–35).

Young (1961: Chapter 5) introduces Swaim, his methods and the reaction from the medical profession.

Swaim (1822) is the basic treatise republished several times and usually has the Nancy Linton lithograph as a frontispiece.

Helfand (2002) reproduces the Linton lithograph in color.

Swaim (1827), a pamphlet on Nancy Linton only in the collection of the University of Pennsylvania library and the United States Library of Congress, was that same year collected into a compilation of cases.

"A skeleton in a bride dress, grinning horribly..." Morleigh (1842: 7).

"The Academy of Medicine..." January 17, 1857.

"For Negroes who are confined..." Swaim's advertising quoted by Kiple and Kiple (2003: 165)

Stewart (2002: 142) and Bell (1987: 237 [picture of a bottle]) give evidence of the use of Swaim's Panacea on Georgia plantations.

"Take a man who has never..."Drake (1844: 474–76).

Gura and Bollman (1999: 138–40,278–79n 8) on Swaim's legacy and banjo-making progeny.

"The French method of curing pox..." Gunn (1860: 431).

"Being nothing more than an old friend..." Gunn (1830: 439).

The equation of *rob de l'Affecteur* with Swaim's Panacea also was stated by Ellis (1854: 88). Ellis plainly stated that both medications have similar vegetable contents combined with corrosive sublimate.

Chapter 8

Tairov and Bushmakin (2002: 189) on cinnabar-tattooed skin in *kurgan* mound burials; Lubeck and Epstein (1952) on the complications of World War II veterans' tattoos.

Joyce (2001: 44) and Marder (2005: 20) on Mayan cinnabar burials and Cook (2004: 159) on Andean burials.

Valhouli (2006) on the mineral makeup revival.

The look of raw mercury on the skin is from my own recollection.

Prasad (2004) on subcutaneous mercury amulets.

Modine (1996: 79) on the face paints of Ancient Greek men, Lewis (2002: 133) on women's pyxides, and Needham (1976: 127) on Chinese opera white faces. Bastedo (1918: 524) parenthetically mentions the case of a man with mercury poisoning who had worn "Indian make-up."

Palmer, Goodwin and McKinney (2000) study the movement of a mercurous-chloride beauty cream in the skin.

The cinnabar-powdered Moche mummy is described and displayed by Williams (2006).

El-Daly (2005: 31) writes that the first reference to Cleopatra the chemist is in the *Murun* by Al-Masudi (d. 956 C.E.), but he believes this is an older tradition emerging.

Thorndike (1958: 145) briefly describes Carolus Ludovicus de Maets's "secret chemical college."

De Laguna's denunciation of *solimán* is in his *Annotationes in Dioscordiem*, his commentary on the material medica of the Greco-Roman physician Dioscordes. Philippy (2006: 24) quotes the English translation used by Thomas Tuke in his *Discourse on Painting* (1616). In Book 5, chapter 49 of his commentary, de Laguna denounces the crones who feed children spoonfuls of *solimán* for an affliction. He swears he never saw a child live after receiving this treatment. The old procuress in de Rojas classic novel *La Celestina* makes *solimán* among other suspect activities (Chapter 4, line 152).

Firenzuola (1892: 123–24) is an English translation of Mona Lampiada's intervention in the 1548 original.

"The Excellencie of this Mercurie Sublimate..." (de Laguna trans. by Arnold in Tuke 1616: B3).

"And dost thou think it lawfull..." (Tuke 1616: 13).

Vives (2000: 95) is the passage from Book I: Unmarried Women, Chapter VIII: Adornment that draws the face and body of a mercury user.

"gums like a Spanish mule..." Lomazzo (1598: 130)

Drew-Bear (1994: 80–84), Pollard (1999) and Karim-Cooper (2006) comment on Renaissance face-painting on stage and in society, and reproduce some of the passages cited.

"Alas, your palms..." Herford and Simpson, eds. (1986: vol. 4, 44) is the scene from Ben Jonson's play.

Philippy (2006: 5–7) instances della Porta's recipe as one of the egregious examples of dangerous cosmetics, and gives examples of the countervailing invective literature.

"Curious fine white..."quoted by Thompson (1993: 211). The only references to mercury Thompson found in his examination of the collection of quacks' handbills in the British Museum were to reject it. "Beware of Quacks..." (251)

Fona (2002: 30) on the British counter-enterprise to French mercury cosmetics in the seventeenth and eighteenth centuries.

Gill (2004: 154) on the Saikaku character and Richie (2003: 159) on mercury cosmetics in Japan.

Needham (1976: 125), who quotes a translation of Ma Kao's chronicle story of Hsiao Shih and Lung Yu, is primarily concerned with establishing the earliest instance of production of mercury chlorides in China.

Jin Zhongher's suicide in the erotic novel *Trails of Immortals in the Green Wild* is used as an example of women's condition in eighteenth century China by McMahon (1995: 243) and Zamporini (2001: 82).

"The Greek women at Smyrna..." Von Egmont quoted in translation by Conder (1824: 110n).

Martin (2005) reviews the medical imposition on women's *toilette,* including Le Camus' anti–mercury advice.

Brinton and Napheys (1870: 271–72) medically deplore yet cosmetically advertise the use of secretage for hair styling.

Pushkareva (1997: 115–16) reviewing Russian women's adoption of cosmetics, presents Samuel Collins's remarks on the origins of teeth blackening.

Hawthorne's story "The Birth-Mark" was collected in *Mosses from an Old Manse* (1846).

MacDonald (2006: 34–37) while describing Knox's procedures, doubts that he was a necrophile.

Shoemaker (1890a: 250) is his program for the mercury treatment of syphilis. Shoemaker (1890b: 251, 352 404, 419) contains his formulas for remedial cosmetics using mercury compounds. Both books were issued in several different editions by various publishers. Shoemaker (1901: 432–57) is the section of his "practical guide to material medica" on medicinal hydragyrum, and an ambivalent set of prescriptions it is.

Ayer (1902: 136) advises keeping bichloride away from "children and ignorant persons."

Ayer's life history was set down by her daughter (Ayer 1957) and makes no mention of the mercury content of some of her products. Most summaries of the biography follow suit. "And what are they?" Oleson (1892: 12). Kay (2005: 12–13), in a history of legislation regulating cosmetics, outlines Ayer's career with no mention of what her products contained.

Hammond (1891: 922) instances the young woman trembling because she used bichloride pimple remover.

Schroeder, ed. (1971: 797) features the Lily White Face Wash.

Berry's Freckle Ointment. Bureau of Investigation. American Medical Association. (1928: 2–3).

Stillman's Freckle Cream entry (21) refers to the Indiana state chemists' report and Wiley's "1001 Tests." Compa (2005: 12) prints Sid Kaufman's diary entry.

Advertising News and Notes, *New York Times* (September 9,1948: 40) contains the note on the Stillman Freckle Cream advertising contract in Peru.

Kerr (1990: 44) is the last reference to Stillman's that I can find in an American source. Gonzalez Ortega (n.d.: 299n 25) is the author's comment on Crema la Belleza Aurora advertising in Costa Rica. *The Philippine Magazine* is one of the periodicals that named Stillman's and Crema la Belleza Aurora together.

I purchased a jar of Stillman's through the Internet in early 2007. I tested it by leaving a small sample in a glass jar and watching for condensation on the sides,

Rush (1799) is the printed version of a lecture he gave in 1797, in which he makes his medical observations on leprosy and skin color. Baynton (2000: 40) sees Benjamin Rush's suggestion as prognostic of using disability as a justification for racial inequality.

Peiss (1997: 41) comments on African-

American use of skin whiteners, on Nadinola (272) and on Madam C. J. Walker's refusal to make skin bleach (113). Collins (2004: 290) on patent-medicine-related hair loss as one of the motives for Madam Walker inventing her hair care products.

The mercury-blocking effects of skin pigments was ascertained by testing mice (Al-Saleh, et al. 2004).

Brooke (1988) reports on the "gold rush" of cosmetics into Nigeria, in this case the drive for gold moving the mercury.

Earth Summit Ireland (2002:14–15) is an environmentalists' report on Killarney Enterprises and Rising Tide (n.d.) refers to the "toxic racism" of continued European mercury cosmetics production for export as the products were banned in Europe (and Africa).

DeFaoite (2001) links production of the soaps and creams in Europe to their presence in ethnic shops in Europe and points to the mercury soaps produced in Ireland and sold in African shops in Dublin.

Campbell, Dixon and Hecky (2003) review the Lake Victoria studies.

Ebuomhan (2005) tells of TURA International Limited's measures to protect their brand. Fuller (2006) reports on the cosmetic aspirations of young Thai women.

Al-Saleh, et al. (1997) is the skin-lightening cream survey for Saudi Arabia.

The "whitened face woman" is the subject of a paper by Suo, et al. (2003).

The "Tale of La Crema de Belleza" about the acne-conscious Texas boy is part of the Window on State Government series posted on the Internet by the Texas Controller of Public Accounts (www.window.state.tx.us/border/ch08/crema.html). The episode also made local newspapers in September 1995.

Villanacci, et al. (1995) is the *Mortality and Morbidity Weekly Reports* notice and update of the spread of the beauty cream across border states, and Weldon (2000) is the comprehensive epidemiological study of *Crema de Belleza* poisoning.

New York City Department of Health and Mental Health Alert #3 (January 27, 2005) takes off from the case of a 22-year-old woman with elevated urine mercury to warn about Dominican Republic skin-lightening products.

Mire (2005) is an exposé of the "emerging" skin-lightening industry.

Glahdet, Appel and Asmund (1999) is the Danish study of mercury soaps in Tanzania, and contains a chart of mercury burdens in different populations around the world.

Kawai, et al. (1994) is a medical case history of contact dermatitis in a woman who used skin-lightener while wearing a gold wedding ring.

Chapter 9

Needham (1976: 3) cites the *I Ching* "cave of cinnabar" discovery story, and others.

Eberhard (1988: 66) includes the vaginal significance of "cave of cinnabar" in his definition of cinnabar, *dan*.

Sung (1996: 279–81) discourses on the manufacture of vermilion, its uses and how it can be found.

Wieger (1965: 30 and 270) represents the mine and alchemist's crucible interpretation of the character *dan*. Hongyuan (1994: 197) favors the writing palette interpretation.

"Twelve pieces of cinnabar..." from "Alchemical Preparation of Numinous Cinnabar," a Chinese text dated 712 C.E., translated in Needham (1980: 237–39).

As Needham observes, "The excellence of the configuration of numinous cinnabar lay in its resonance with the metaphysics of monarchy..." Needham (1980: 242).

St. Clair (1997) concerns the trans-Pacific mercury-vermilion exchanges between California and China.

Youman (1872: 262), an entry on vermilion in a "dictionary of everyday wants," appraises the relative merits of French, Chinese and American vermilion paints.

Golas (1999) surveys the history of mining in China, making reference to the use of cinnabar to color the interior of tombs (143). Keightley (1978: 55) tells of chemical analysis of the oracle bones' surface powder revealing it to be cinnabar. Mallory and Mair (2000: 177) mention instances of mercury used in preservation of the dead.

Gil-Martin (1995) identifies the first known use of vermilion 5000 years ago to preserve bones in a Spanish dolmen burial.

Shuck (1889: 74) recounts Judge Sawyer's decision in the case of Mr. Parrott's Chinese employees.

"In extracting the ore..." Ingalls, ed. (1909: 747–48) describes mining practices at Wanshan in the early twentieth century.

Goss (1958: 73) encounters the "sootmen" and Ah Cat.

"As they passed the crucifix hung in the entrance of the gallery, the Mexican workmen crossed themselves." That is about all there is concerning the labor and the interior of the Five Apostles mine that is the source of the Cope family fortune (Jones 1947: 201).

Morgan (1960: 215–17) translates Vitruvius on cinnabar and vermilion.

Merrifield (1967, vol. I: clxxi–clxxii) on natural and artificial cinnabar, and ccxxviii–ccxxvix on the variety of names given to colors.

Ramazzini (1983: 35, 39): Gilder's brain boiling out his eyes from Fernel, *Lues venerea* and mercury's flight on sandaled feet.

Ransome (1919: 157) gives the mercury tenor of Almaden, Idria and California ores processed 1916–17.

The production history of the Almaden mine is tabulated and graphed by Menendez Navarro (1996: 24–25).

Lang (1977) offers a general history of the mercury trade in New Spain, 1550–1710.

Watras and Huckabee, eds. (1994: 617, 621–29) describes the state of current mercury production and the recycling industry.

Preite, et al. (2002) is an industrial archaeology of the fourteen major Monte Amiata mines, the earliest opening in 1847 and the last closing in 1981; Goldwater (1972: 37–38) on the obscure history of the Monte Amiata mine; and Foriana, et al. (1998) on remediation at the mine. Trakhtenberg (1974: 48) is the only mention of the Monte Amiata strike.

According to the Hu Kang Tzu, "People who make mercury by roasting eat much pork and drink much wine." Needham (1980: 80) speculates that the pork fat divides and carries away the mercury

Teleky (1948: 7–8) introduces Ellenbog's and Agricola's works on mining. Koelsch (1965: 101–2) contains what detail there is on Ellenbog.

Sigerist, ed. (1941: 43–126), Paracelsus's *Treatise On the Miners' Sickness and Other Miners' Diseases* translated from the German by George Rosen, identifies the "mercury" of metals which enters the bodies of miners and causes the sickness.

"Asked if he knows..." Bleiberg (1977) reprints with an introduction Mateo Alemán's *Informe secreto;* I translated the testimony of Miguel del Aldea from the Spanish (374–75) as literally as possible.

"Cinnabar is a sulfur compound of mercury..."Alfredo Menendez-Navarro (1996) reflects the fundamental contrast in illumination in the title of his book on the history of the health of the workers in the Spanish Almaden mine: *Un Mundo sin Sol (A World without Sun)*, where he quotes the passage from Pares y Franques partially translated here (frontispiece, 100).

"People who encounter where an *umpé*..." de Ulloa (1772: Entretemiento 18) relates his researches on and the miners' precautions against the *umpé*.

Berry and Singewald (1922: 22–23, 43) on the history of the Huancavelica mines, and on Crosnier's accounts of the mercury pits.

Young (1970: 73–9) examines the procedure devised in Mexico for silver extraction using mercury.

"He got up from the table..." Johnson (1963: 15) quotes Jacob Leese's testimony in the long-running lawsuit initiated by the contest over Castillero's discovery.

United States Navy Lieutenant Joseph Warren Revere wrote in his 1849 manuscript, *A Tour of Duty in California*, "This place has been resorted to by the Indians from time immemorial, for vermillion, to apply to their interesting persons; but the value of the deposit was first ascertained by Senor Castillero." (Egenhoff 1953: 107).

Forbes's, Pico's and Leese's testimony in *United States vs. Andres Castillero* are in Egenhoff (1953: 87–105), accompanied by other testimony and a selection of graphics, photographs and maps of the mine, as are the magazine-published pieces by Downer (113–23) and Browne (136). Johnson (1963) is a history of land claims around the New Almaden Mine, which also makes use of these sources.

"We inquired the average duration of life..." (Downer in Egenhoff 1953: 113)

Lanyon and Bulmore (1967) offer a nostalgic historical account of the mine, illustrated with many photographs of groups, buildings, and operations, published a few years after the mine's final closure.

Harte's novel is rare in print, but readable as an e-book on the Project Gutenberg website.

Idwal Jones's novel is long since out of print, and the vermilion ink used to print part of the dust jacket has tended toward orange with time.

United States Geological Survey Fact Sheet FS-061-00 is a succinct and diagrammatic survey of the mercury contamination consequences of gold mining in California.

Isenberg (2005) gives a broader environmental picture of the practice and consequences of hydraulic mining in California.

Scopolo (1761), summarized by Slavec (1998), initiates occupational medicine at the

Idria mine. Ransome (1919: 159) comments on the productivity of the New Idria mine early in the century.

Cone (2000) and Woods (2000) are local newspaper pieces on the fate of the New Idria mine. Evans (2005: 73–78) contains Edwin A. Roberts's reminiscences about the "Creeping Earth" or Socrates mine of the Sonoma County (Pine Flat) Quicksilver Mining District.

Mason (1995) narrates a lethal accident near the town of Mercury.

Bradley (1918: 63–68) is his account of the Sulphur Bank mine.

Callahan (1994), (1995), and (1996) chronicle the Environmental Protection Agency's flirtation with the Sulphur Bank mine and the Elem community's response to the dangers of the site. Nacht, et al. (2004) is a technical study of atmospheric emissions and mercury speciation at the Sulphur Bank Mercury Mine Superfund Site.

The Soulajule Reservoir sites are reported by Prado (2006) in an article printed on the same front page as a headline on the development of a policy putting greater emphasis on coal to meet America's energy needs.

Mercury from a yogurt container in Colombia: Harris (2007).

Chapter 10

Swiderski (1995: 134–35) is my earlier account of the red mercury purchase offer, in a book on technology in the Kenyan city of Eldoret. At the time of its publication, I did not have the resources to identify red mercury.

Block (1999: 223) refers to the 1992 U.S. Department of Energy study denying the existence of red mercury.

DeGroot (2005) describes the plain life of the atomic and hydrogen bombs.

I have not seen *The Hunt for Red Mercury* (1993), but only read descriptions (Knelman 1999: 83).

Hibbs (1993) is cited by MacKenzie (1998: 319n20) in his discussion of the "uninvention" of nuclear weapons, by which he means what Barnaby does in the sequel, precisely describe bomb designs that can't work — but look as if they should.

Barnaby (1994) initiates the technical side of the rumor.

"A lithium-mercury amalgam is first prepared..." United States Department of Defense (1998: II,5: 54–6) describes the lithium-6 enrichment process.

Hounam and McQuillan (1995) is an un-sourced journalistic account of the "red mercury killings" in South Africa that reflects the convergence of popular science and espionage thrillers. They write an entire chapter (85–98) of seemingly astute anecdotes on the red mercury trade.

Burgess and Purkitt (2001: 47–48) say Thor Chemical was a South African Defense Forces operation and that red mercury was used to produce the drug ECSTASY.

Roberts (1996: 58–59n63) cites the Namibia deaths due to red mercury quest.

Lamprecht (2002) brings in the UNITA soldiers and gives the $40,000 per kilogram figure.

Rotblau, ed. (1994: 11) is the Pugwash notice of red mercury.

Butler and Duali (2004) is the best informed study of the red mercury scam.

Cohen (1983: 33, 37 and 160), the source of the quotations, does not mention red mercury.

Vilensky (2005) tells the nauseating story of lewisite.

Cohen (1993) describes his first inclusion of red mercury in the neutron bomb.

"The triggering mechanism..." Cohen (2000: 447).

Cohen and Douglass (2003), in an editorial for an online investment journal, brings red mercury pure fusion into the Iraq invasion rationale.

Cohen (2006) makes numerous references to the neutron bomb but none to red mercury.

The Web page mmmgroup.altervista.org/e-mercur.html offers a sequence of mercury power stories from Vedic flying saucers to the secret Russian reactor design.

Weinburger (2006) describes the United States military establishment's pursuit of the hafnium bomb. She makes the useful distinction (137–38) between pseudoscience, junk science and pathological science. Red mercury belongs in the first two; and would belong to the third only if it's real.

Chapter 11

"I have known in this city of Paris..." Jean Béguin, Cours de Chimie quoted by Michelon (1908: 26).

Bertholet (1898) states that the name "mercury" was not used for the element until the Middle Ages.

Livy, Ab condita urbe (The History of Rome) (II, 21, 27) on the founding of the Mercury temple.

Ovid, Fasti (V, 673–) on the celebration of the ides of May.

The description of the mercury (chlor-akali) cell and of Castner's business dealings is based on Derry and Williams (1960: 550–51), Aftalion (1991: 61) and Burgess and Cravens (1914: 34).

Castner-Kellner Alkali Company (1920) is the SeeKay brochure.

Sällsten, et al. (1990) on the Swedish chlor-alkali industry's mercury measures.

The impact of the Minamata poisoning on the chlor-alkali industry is observed by Stringer and Johnson (2001: 19) and the inefficiency of diaphragm technology discussed by Howell, ed. (1990: 18).

Shkilnyk (1985: 257n4) summarizes the Ontario workers' compensation cases.

Harris (2001: 19–20) notes that cell mercury does have toxic emissions, and that there were exceptions to the ban in Japan and regulatory disinterest in the United States.

Pirrone, et al. (2003: 26–27) on the Spanish compromise.

Centre for Science and Environment (www.cseindia.org/dte-supplement/mercury-menace.htm) is a supplement to their publication Down to Earth reporting on chlor-alkali mercury in India and the effort to raise awareness of its contribution to mercury pollution.

Health Care Without Harm (2001) lists and briefly describes mercury waste recyclers. The website of Mercury Waste Solutions, Inc of Union Grove, Wisconsin (www.mwsi.com) contains links to many public sources on the dangers of environmental mercury, and a five-minute video produced by the medical school, University of Calgary, Canada, How Mercury Causes Brain Neuron Degeneration, but is sketchy about what becomes of the mercury they recycle.

Why build the mercury recycling plant in KwaZulu and not closer to the source of mercury to be recycled, in America or Europe? (Martinez-Alior 2002: 183). Clapp (2001: 63–64) summarizes the Greenpeace investigation of the recycling plant. Worldwatch Institute (2006: 104–5) in a survey of environmental issues in South Africa, singles out Thor Chemical.

Ebdon, et al. (2001: 132) diagrams the mercury cycle and Sigel (1997: 54) does too, identifying three separate cycles. Johansen (2003: 69) on the "mercury sunrise."

Needham (1959: 582) quotes the translation of the Shi Chih passage on the tomb of Shih Huang Ti.

Chapter 12

O'Shea (1988) quotes the sources on Paganini's tooth troubles from mercury use.

Roger (1905: 71), mistakenly translated to place Almaden in Idria, says that the miners suffer from gingivitis. Bumstead (1861: 516), writing on the treatment of venereal disease, credits the miners with teeth free from caries and gums free of gummy tumors.

He changes focus in later editions of the book, simply denying that syphilitic bone degeneration is due to prior mercury treatments.

Graves (1864: vol. 1, 577) on whole teeth falling from mercurial jaws.

Gallard (1877: 599–600) repeats Roussel's observations and says he can't find anything like that in other firsthand descriptions of mercury poisoning, but he does see faces like the ones Roussel described among those who come to his clinic with acute mercury poisoning.

"the mask of age" and "no more teeth, no more diseased mouth," translated from Hallopeau (1878: 133).

Talbot (1899: 93) repeats but does not give the source of the tale that Almaden miners were glad to have their teeth gone.

"Sometimes the ulcerations attack the gums..." Piggott (1854: 447).

Richardson (1860: 199–201) on the teeth effects of mercury given to children mistaken for the results of "eruptive disease."

Préterre (1884: 147), following a detailed account of the technique of aurification, dismisses all other methods of tooth repair.

American Academy of Dental Science (1871: 63–71) relates the phases of the "amalgam war" in America from the American Society of Dental Surgeons' resolution in 1841 to its withdrawal in 1850.

Hodgen (1914: 84) recalls the crepitus of amalgam mixing: "the peculiar, softly grating sound produced by compressing and rubbing the mix in the hand."

Hillam ed. (2003: 251–52) locates the Crawcours in England in 1799 before they took up amalgam.

Taveau (1827) self-published a 16-page pamphlet entitled "Notice on a covering adhesive to arrest and heal dental caries, offering a new method of treatment for those teeth which are affected without having recourse to the extraction of these precious organs."

Amalgam formulas (Hodgen 1914: 83–84).

Dr. Head's paper "The Dental Filling" is summarized in an article, "Dentists in Convention," the *New York Times*, August 11, 1895: 24.

Sexton (1888: 95–97) on the effects of bad teeth and mercury used to repair them on the health of the ear.

Syphilis spread by unsterilized dental instruments (Buckley 1894: 190).

Liebert, et al. (1997: 447–60) on dental mercury inducing antibiotic resistance in bacteria.

Neale (1831: 135–42) gives a description of acrodynia soon after it was discovered, and the worm theory of its origin. Kark (1994: 373–75) is a more recent account of acrodynia.

Hanks (1862: 99–115) has an entire chapter on the dangers of teething powders and soothing syrups, but no mention of mercury or calomel. Day (1881: 50) denounced teething powders, but stated that children receive calomel "with far greater impunity than adults."

Warkany and Hubbard (1948) find mercury in the urine of children with acrodynia.

D'Itri and D'Itri (1977: 197–201) on the historic descent of acrodynia to infants.

Weinstein and Bornstein (2003) on the two "pink ladies."

Royal (1991) brings together the mad hatters, Minamata and the Swedish ban to argue for the liability dentists face from continued use of amalgam.

Wahl (1995) counters the myth of the Swedish ban.

Bondeson (2001: 175) uses oral galvanism in Scandinavia as an example of epidemic hysteria. Molin (1990) gives a brief account from the viewpoint of dentistry.

Stortebecker (1986) offers the belief to Americans, and Huggins (1993: 112–13) takes him up on it.

Barrett (2006) cites the California and Iowa amalgam-removal cases, and much else of the "mercury toxicity" scam.

D'Itri and D'Itri (1977: 215) on the thermometer-factory employee suffering mercurial symptoms after tooth extraction.

Dental Board of California, Case No. DBC 02–2005–2168, In the Matter of the First Amended Accusation Against: James Shen, DDS (June 21, 2006).

Bangsi, et al. (1998) is the MS/amalgam correlation study. Huggins (1999) is titled after his latest theme, *Uninformed Consent*.

Bagedahl-Strindlund, et al. (1997) is the psychiatric group study of those who believe amalgams cause their (often genuine) illness.

"Dental amalgam dementia" Casdorph and Walker (1994: 131–33).

American Dental Association Statement on Dental Amalgam (www.ada.org/prof/resources/positions/statments/amalgam.asp).

U.S. Food and Drug Administration, Center for Devices and Radiological Health, Consumer Update: Dental Amalgams (*www.fda.gov/cdrh/consumer/amalgams.html*).

HealthDay, September 7, 2006, "FDA Advisors Reject Safety Report on Dental Fillings."

Morris Selig Kharasch, "Alkyl mercuric sulfur compound and process of producing it," U.S. patent number 1,672,615 (June 5, 1928).

"Water-soluble compound of antimony and process of producing it," U.S. patent number 1,677,392 (July 17, 1928)

"Water soluble metallic organic compound and process of making the same," U.S. patent number 1,589,599 (June 22, 1926)

Kharasch assignor to E.I. Du Pont de Nemours, "Germicides, fungicides, Etc., for soil sterilization and methods of using the same," U.S. patent number 1,787, 581 (January 6, 1931)

"Seed disinfectant composition," U.S. patent number 1,820,001 (August 18, 1931)

Edwin O. Davisson, assignor to Eli Lilly and Company, "Stabilized thimerosal," U.S. patent number 2,864,844 (December 16, 1958)

United States Patent and Trademark Office, Word Mark: Merthiolate, Serial number 71272568 (September 17, 1928)

Eli Lilly and Company (1932: 56–61) on the professional uses of Merthiolate.

Kharasch's advice to his Jewish students: Milton Orchin quoted in Hargitai (2000: 226)

Bernard, et al. (2001) is the first *Medical Hypotheses* article and Blaxill, et al. (2004) is the second. The common author is L. Redwood, who has assembled a large collection of autism case histories associated with thimerosal vaccination.

Kanner (1943) has been much anthologized, often in abbreviated versions.

"Autism as a Minamata disease variant" (Stoller 2006).

Plaintiff's Response to Eli Lilly and Company's Motion for Summary Judgment (www.redflagsweekly.com/legal/2002_nov.18.html) is a legal pleading from 2002 that sets out the history of thimerosal from the viewpoint of the advocates for the parents of an autistic child.

Vilensky (2005: 78–85) on BAL in a general study of lewisite.

References

Abernethy, John. 1811. *Surgical Observations, Vol. I: On the Origin and Treatment of Local Diseases; and On Aneurysm.* London: printed for Longman, Hurst, Rees and Orme.

Aftalion, Fred. 1991. *A History of the International Chemical Industry.* Philadelphia: University of Pennsylvania Press.

Agate, J. N., and Buckell, M. 1949. Mercury poisoning from fingerprint photography. *Lancet* 2: 451.

Al-Saleh, Iman, and Al-Doush, Inaam. 1997. Mercury content in skin lightening creams and potential health hazards to the health of Saudi women. *Journal of Toxicology and Environmental Health* 51 (2): 123–30.

Al-Saleh, Iman, et al. 2004. Comparison of mercury levels in various tissues of albino and pigmented mice treated with two different brands of mercury skin-lightening cream. *Biometals* 17(2): 167–75.

Albus, Anita. 2000. *The Art of Arts: Rediscovering Painting,* translated from the German by Michael Robertson. Berkeley: University of California Press.

Allbutt, T. Clifford, ed. 1905. *A System of Medicine, vol. 2, pt. 1.* London: Macmillan.

Allen, Peter Lewis. 2000. *The Wages of Sin: Sex and Disease, Past and Present.* Chicago: University of Chicago Press.

American Academy of Dental Surgeons. 1871. *A History of the Dental and Oral Sciences in America.* Philadelphia: Samuel S. White.

American Medical Association. Bureau of Investigation. 1928. *Cosmetic Nostrums and Allied Preparations.* Dearborn, Michigan: American Medical Association.

Amin-Zaki, L., et al. 1978. Methylmercury poisoning in Iraqi children: observations over two years. *British Medical Journal* 11: 613–16.

Arrais, Duarte Madeira. 1642. *Methodo de conhecer e curar o Morbo Gallico....* Lisbon: Por Antonio Craesbeeck de Melo.

Arrizabalaga, Jon, John Henderson and Roger French. 1997. *The Great Pox: The French Disease in Renaissance Europe.* New Haven: Yale University Press.

Ayer, Harriet Hubbard. 1902. *Harriet Hubbard Ayer's Book: A Complete and Authentic Treatise on the Laws of Health and Beauty.* Springfield, Massachusetts: King-Richardson Company.

Ayer, Margaret. 1957. *The Three Lives of Harriet Hubbard Ayer.*

Bagedahl-Strindlund, M., et al. 1997. A multidisciplinary clinical study of patients suffering from illness associated with mercury release from dental restorations: psychiatric aspects. *Acta Psychiatrica Scandinavica* 96 (6): 475–82.

Bagnall, Robin S., and Peter Derow, eds. 2004. *The Hellenistic Period: Historical Sources in Translation.* New York: Blackwell.

Bain, H. Foster. 1933. *Ores and Industry in the Far East: The Influence of Key Mineral Resources on the Development of Oriental Civilization.* New York: Council on Foreign Relations.

Bakri, F., et al. 1973. Mercury Poisoning in Iraq. *Science* 181: 230–41.

Banda, Francisco. 1937. *Posibilidades Agro-economicas del Ecuador.* Quito: Imprenta Nacional.

Bangsi, Dieudonné, et al. 1998. Dental amalgam and multiple sclerosis: a case-control study in Montreal, Canada. *International Journal of Epidemiology* 27: 667–71.

Barger, M. Susan, and William B. White. 2000. *The Daguerreotype: Nineteenth-Century Technology and Modern Science.* Baltimore: Johns Hopkins University Press.

Barnaby, Frank. 1994. Red mercury: Is there a pure fusion bomb for sale? *International Defense Review,* 27, 6: 79–81.

Barnes, Robert. 1885. *A System of Obstetric Medicine and Surgery.* Philadelphia: Lea.

Barrett, Stephen. 2006. The "mercury toxicity" scam: how anti–amalgamists swindle people. Quackwatch (*www.quackwatch.org/01 QuackeryRelatedTopics/mercury.html*).

Bastedo, Walter Arthur. 1918. *Materia Medica.* Philadelphia: W.B. Saunders.

Baynton, Douglas C. 2000. Disability and Justification of Inequality in American History, in *The New Disability History: American Perspectives,* ed. by Paul Longmore and Lauri Umansky. New York: New York University Press.

Becher, Johann Joachim. 1733. *Physica subterranea....* Leipzig.

Beddoes, Thomas. 1802. *Hygeia; or, Essays Moral and Medical on the Causes Affecting the Personal State of our Middling and Affluent Classes.* London: R. Phillips.

Bateman, Thomas. 1817. *A Practical Synopsis of Cutaneous Diseases.* London: Longman, Hurst.

Beaney, James George. 1869. *Syphilis: Its Nature and Diffusion.* Melbourne: George Robinson.

Bell, George Hamilton. 1833. *A Treatise on the Diseases of the Liver.* Edinburgh: Bell and Bradfute.

Bell, Madison Smartt. 2005. *Lavoisier in the Year One: The Birth of a New Science in an Age of Revolution.* New York: W. W. Norton.

Bell, Malcolm. 1987. *Major Butler's Legacy: Five Generations of a Slaveholding Family.* Athens, Georgia: University of Georgia Press.

Bellet, Isaac. 1768. *Exposition des effets d'un nouveau remède denommé syrop mercuriel.* Paris.

Belloste, Augustin. 1733. *Suite du chirurgien d'hopital, contenant differns traitez.* Paris: La Veuve d'Houry.

_____. ca.1733. *An analysis of Belloste's pill, and*

its effects upon the living body ... with instructions for its use. London.

_____. 1754. *Traitez de mercure.* Geneva: Emanuel du Villard.

Benedek, Thomas G., and Erlen, Jonathon. 1999. The scientific environment of the Tuskegee Study of Syphilis, 1920–1960. *Perspectives in Biology and Medecine* 43: 1–30.

Bernard, S, et al. (2001). Autism: a novel form of mercury poisoning. *Medical Hypotheses* 56(4): 462–71.

Berry, Edward Wilber, and Joseph Theophilus Singewald. 1922. *The Geology and Paleontology of the Huancavelica Mercury District.* Baltimore: The Johns Hopkins Press.

Bertrandi, Ambrogio. 1786. *Opere anatomiche, e cerusiche: Tomo VII, Malattie veneree.* Turin: I Fratelli Reycends.

Béthencourt, Jacques de. 1871 (1527). *Nouveau Carême de Pénitence et Purgatoire d'Expiation,* trans. from the Latin into French by Alfred Fournier. Paris: Chez Victor Masson et Fils.

Bidstrup, P. Lesley. 1964. *Toxicity of Mercury and Its Compounds.* Amsterdam: Elsevier Publishing Company.

_____. 1972. Clinical symptoms of mercury poisoning in man. *Biochemical Journal* 130(2): 59P–60P.

Blaxill, M., et al. 2004. Thimerosal and autism? A plausible hypothesis that should not be dismissed. *Medical Hypotheses* 62: 788–94.

Bleiberg, German. 1977. El "informe secreto" de Mateo Aleman sobre el trabajo forzoso en la Minas de Almaden. *Estudios de Historia Social: Revista del Instituto de Estudios de Sanidad y Seguridad Social,* 2–3: 357–443. (Published separately, London, 1983).

Block, Alan. 1999. Bad business: A commentary on the criminology of organized crime in the United States, in *Transnational Crime in the Americas,* Tom J. Farer, ed. (New York: Routledge), 217–44.

Blyth, Alexander Wynter. 1885. *Poisons: Their Effects and Detection, vol. I.* New York: William Wood and Company.

Boerhaave, J.H. 1734. *Some Experiments Cconcerning Mercury.* London: J. Roberts.

Bondeson, Jan. 2001. *The London Monster: A Sanguinary Tale.* Philadelphia: University of Pennsylvania Press.

Boys, Charles V. 1959. *Soap Bubbles.* New York: Dover.

Bradley, Walter W. 1918. *Quicksilver Resources of California,* California State Mining Bureau Bulletin No. 78. Sacramento: California State Printing Office.

Brinton, Daniel G., and George H. Napheys. 1870. *Personal Beauty: How to Cultivate and Preserve it in Accordance with the Laws of Beauty.* Springfield, Massachusetts: W.J. Holland.

Brock, R. A., ed. 1886. *Documents, Chiefly Unpublished, Relating to Huguenot Emigration to Virginia.* Richmond, Virginia: Virginia Historical Society.

Brock, William. 2000. *The Chemical Tree: A History of Chemistry.* New York: W. W. Norton.

Brodie, Janet Farrell. 1994. *Contraception and Abortion in Nineteenth Century America.* Ithaca, New York: Cornell University Press.

Broehl, Wayne G. 1998. *Cargill.* Hanover, New Hampshire: University Press of New England.

Brooke, James. 1988. "Gold Rush" of Cosmetics into Nigeria. *New York Times,* August 22: D10.

Brookes, Joshua. 1828. *The Museum of Joshua Brookes.* London: printed by Gold and Walton.

Brown, P.S. 1977. Female pills and the reputation of iron as an abortifacient. *Medical History* 21(2): 291–304.

Buckley, L. Duncan. 1894. *Syphilis in the Innocent (Syphilis Insontium).* New York: Bailey and Fairchild.

Bumstead, Freeman J. 1861. *The Pathology and Treatment of Venereal Diseases.* Philadelphia: Blanchand and Lea.

Burgess, Charles W., and George W. Cravens. 1914. *Applied Electrochemistry and Welding: A Practical Treatise of Commercial Chemistry.* Chicago: American Technical Society.

Burgess, Stephen, and Helen Purkitt. 2001. *The Rollback of South Africa's Chemical and Biological Warfare Program.* Darby, Pennsylvania: DIANE Publishing.

Burnett, William. 1823. An account of the effects of mercurial vapors on the crew of His Majesty's Ship Triumph in the Year 1810. *Philosophical Transactions,* 113, 405.

Burton, Richard, trans. 1962 (1885). *The Book of the Thousand Nights and a Night.* 3 vols. New York: The Heritage Press.

Butler, Kenley, and Duali, Akaki. 2004. A Short History of Scams involving Red Mercury and Osmium-187. Monterey Institute of International Studies. www.nti.org/e3_42a.jhtml.

Callahan, Mary. 1994. EPA offers a clean-up plan for abandoned Clear Lake Mine. *Santa Rosa Press Democrat,* September 21.

_____. 1995. EPA cuts endanger clean-up of Lake Mine. *Santa Rosa Press Democrat,* August 29.

_____. 1996. Mine site cleanup plan hits hurdle. September 30. *Santa Rosa Press Democrat.*

Campbell, Harry. 1894. *Headache, and Other Morbid Cephalic Sensations.* London: H.K. Lewis.

Campbell, L., Dixon, D.G., and Hecky, R.E. 2003. A review of mercury in Lake Victoria, East Africa: implications for human and ecosystem health. *Journal of Toxicology: Environmental Health B Critical Reviews* 6(4): 325–56.

Carlile, R. 1843. *A Treatise on mercury, exhibiting its wonderful power when taken in a crude state.* London: Dredge.

Casdorph, H. Richard, and Morton Walker. 1994. *Toxic Metal Syndrome: How Metal Poisonings Can Affect Your Brain.* Avery.

Castner-Kellner Alkali Company. 1920. *Chlorine and Chlorine Products in Relation to Public Health.* Liverpool.

Cellini, Benvenuto. 1910. *The Life of Benvenuto Cellini,* translated from the Italian by John Addington Symonds. New York: P. Collier and Sons.

Centers for Disease Control. 1988. Mercury exposure in a high school laboratory-Connecticut. *Mortality and Morbidity Weekly Report,* March 18: 153–55.

Chaucer, Geoffrey. 1975. *Canterbury Tales,* ed. by A.C. Cawley. London: J. M. Dent and Sons.

Clapp, Jennifer. 2001. *Toxic Exports: The Transfer of Hazardous Wastes and Technologies from Rich to Poor Countries.* Ithaca, New York: Cornell University Press.

Clarkson, Thomas. 2002. The three modern faces of mercury. *Environmental Health Perspectives* 110, supplement 1: 11–22.

Cohen, E., ed. 1919. *Herman Boerhaave en Zijne Beteknis voor de Chemie.* Amsterdam: Nederlandsche Chemische Vereeniging.

Cohen, Sam. 1983. *The Truth about the Neutron Bomb: The Inventor of the Bomb Speaks Out.* New York: Morrow.

Cohen, [Sam] S. T. 1993. The DOVE of War: The arms-controllers won't even think about fusion weapons. But that won't make them go away. *National Review,* December 27.

Cohen, Sam. 2000. *Shame: Confessions of the Father of the Neutron Bomb.* X-libris.

Cohen, Sam, 2006. *F*** You, Mr. President! Confessions of the Father of the Neutron Bomb,* 3rd edition. Los Angeles: www.ath

enalab.com/Confessions_Sam_Cohen_
2006_Third_Edition.pdf.

Cohen, Sam, and Douglass, Joe. 2003. The nuclear threat that doesn't exist — or does it?
Financial Sense, March 11.

Collins, Gail. 2004. *America's Women: Four
Hundred Years of Devils, Drudges, Helpmates
and Heroines*. New York: HarperCollins.

Compa, Elizabeth. 2005. Sid Kaufman's od-
yssey out of Spain. *The Volunteer: Journal of
the Veterans of the Abraham Lincoln Brigade*
26, no. 2: 12–14.

Conder, Josiah. 1824. *Syria and Asia Minor*.
London: J. Chapman.

Cone, Tracie. 2000. Mine owner charged with
hazardous material violation. *The Pinnacle*
18: 44.

Cook, Anita G. 2004. Wari art and society, in
Andean Prehistory, ed. by Hulaine Silver-
man (Malden, Massachusetts: Blackwell),
146–66.

Cooley, A. James. 1846. *A Cyclopedia of Several
Thousand Practical Receipts*. New York: D.
Appleton.

Counter, Alan S. 2003. Whitening skin can be
deadly. *Boston Globe*, December 16.

Courlander, Harold. 2002. *A Treasury of
African Folklore*. New York: Marlowe and
Company.

Cox, C., et al. 1995. Analysis of data on delayed
development from the 1971–73 outbreak of
methylmercury poisoning in Iraq: assessment of influential points. *NeuroToxicituy*
16(4): 127–30.

Crow, David. 2000. *In Search of the Medicine
Buddha: A Himalayan Journey*. New York:
Jeremy P. Tarcher/Putnam.

Dandraut, C.-A. *Textuel: Procès Orsini*. Turin:
Imprimerie Nationale de G. Biancardi.

Daudet, Alphonse. 2004. *In the Land of Pain*,
edited and translated by Julian Barnes. New
York: Knopf.

Day, William Henry. 1881. *The Diseases of Children*. Philadelphia: Presley Blakiston.

Debus, Allen. 2001. *Chemistry and Medical Debate: Van Helmont to Boerhaave*. Sagamore
Beach, Massachusetts: Science History Publications.

DeFaoite, Dara. 2001. Irish link to toxic skin-
whitener: investigation into the sale of
dangerous mercury soap in ethnic shops.
Guardian Unlimited, May 27.

DeGroot, Gerard J. 2005. *The Bomb: A Life*.
Cambridge, Massachusetts: Harvard University Press.

Dewhurst, Kenneth. 1957. *The Quicksilver Doctor: The Life and Times of Thomas Dover,*

Physician and Adventurer. Bristol: John
Wright and Sons.

_____. 1974. *Thomas Dover's Life and Legacy*.
Metuchen, NJ: Scarecrow Press.

Dickson, Donald R, ed. 2001. *Thomas and Re-
becca Vaughan's Aqua Vitae non Vitis*.
Tempe, Arizona: Medieval and Renaissance
Text Society.

D'Itri, Patricia A., and Frank D'Itri. 1977. *Mercury Contamination: A Human Tragedy*.
New York: John Wiley and Sons.

Drake, Daniel. 1844. Abuse of calomel by
southern physicians. *Western Journal of
Medicine and Surgery* VI: 474–76.

Drew-Bear, Annette. 1994. *Painted Faces on the
Renaissance Stage: The Moral Significance of
Face Painting Conventions*. Lewisburg,
Pennsylvania: Bucknell University Press.

Druide de Lacerda, Luiz, and W. Salomons.
1998. *Mercury from Gold and Silver Mining: A Chemical Time Bomb*. New York:
Springer.

Dunn, Walter S. 2000. *The New Imperial Econ-
omy: The British Army and the American
Frontier, 1764–68*. Westport, Connecticut:
Praeger.

Durkee, Silas. 1859. *A Treatise on Gonorrhea
and Syphilis*. Boston: John P. Jewett.

E. J. Woodson Company. ca. 1920. *A Complete
Catalogue of Platers' and Polishers' Supplies*.
Detroit, Michigan.

Earles, M. P. 1964. A case of mass poisoning
with mercury vapour on board H.M.S. Triumph at Cadiz, 1810. *Medical History* 8(3):
281–86.

Eamon, William. 1994. *Science and the Secrets
of Nature: Books of Secrets in Medieval and
Early Modern Culture*. Princeton: Princeton
University Press.

Earth Summit Ireland. 2002. *Telling It Like It
Is: 10 Years of Unsustainable Development in
Ireland*. Dublin: Earth Summit Ireland, Ltd.

Ebdon, L., et al. 2001. *Trace Element for Environment, Food and Health*. Cambridge:
Royal Society of Chemistry.

Eberhard, Wolfram. 1988. *A Dictionary of Chinese Symbols*, translated from the German
by G. L. Graham. London: Routledge.

Edwards, G. H. 1865. Two cases of poisoning by
methide of mercury. *St. Barts Hospital
Notes*. 1: 141–50.

Egenhoff, Elisabeth, ed. 1953. *De Argento Vivo:
Historic Documents on Quicksilver and its
Recovery in California Prior to 1860*. Supple-
ment to *California Journal of Mines and Ge-
ology*, October. San Francisco: Division of
Mines.

El-Daly, Okasha. 2005. *Egyptology, The Missing Millennia: Ancient Egypt in Medieval Arabic Writings.* London: University College Press.

Eli Lilly and Company. 1932. *Distinctive Products of Lilly Research Laboratories.* Indianapolis, Indiana: Eli Lilly and Company.

Elkins, James. 1999. *What Painting Is.* New York: Routledge.

Elliotson, John. 1843. *Numerous Cases of Surgical Operations without Pain in the Mesmeric State.* London: H. Bailliere.

Ellis, Benjamin. 1854. *The Medical Formulary, Being a Collection of Prescriptions.* Philadelphia: Blanchard and Lea.

Ellis, W. 1750. *The Country Housewife's Family Companion.* London: James Hodges and B. Cullen.

Emsley, John. 2005. *Elements of Murder: A History of Poisons.* Oxford: Oxford University Press.

Endicott, Karen. 1999. The trembling edge of science. *Dartmouth Alumni Review.*

Evans, Robert G. 2005. *Pine Flat: A Quicksilver Boom Town.* Healdsburg, California: Robert G. Evans.

Faure, Bernard. 1998. *The Red Thread: Buddhist Approaches to Sexuality.* Princeton: Princeton University Press.

Feldman, Robert G. 1999. *Occupational and Environmental Neurotoxicology.* Philadelphia: Lippincott-Raven.

Fenton, John Joseph. 2002. *Toxicology: A Case-Oriented Approach.* Boca Raton: CRE Press.

Firenzuola, Agnolo. 1892. *Of the Beauty of Women,* translated from the Italian by Clara Bell. London: James P. Osgod, McIlvaine and Co.

Fitzgerald, Percy. 1882. *A New History of the English Stage, from the Restoration ... 2 v.* London: Tinsley Brothers.

Fleck, Ludwik. 1979. *Genesis and Development of a Scientific Fact,* translated by Fred Bradley and Thaddeus Trenn. Chicago: University of Chicago Press.

Fona, Lynn. 2002. Cosmetic differences: the changing faces of Britain and France, in *Studies of Eighteenth Century Literature,* ed. by Catherine Ingrassia and Jeffrey S. Ravol (Baltimore: Johns Hopkins University Press), 29–54.

Forchheimer, Frederick. 1908. *The Prophylaxis and Treatment of Internal Diseases.* New York: D. Appleton and Company.

Foriana, R., et al. 1998. Atmospheric mercury in abandoned mine structures and restored mine buildings at Monte Amiata, Italy, in *Mercury Contaminated Sites: Characteriza-tion, Risk Assessment and Remediation,* ed. by R. Ebinghaus, et al. (Berlin: Springer-Verlag), 249–58.

Frankland, Edward. 1852. On a new series of organic bodies containing metals. *Philosophical Transactions of the Royal Society* 142: 417–44.

Fuller, Thomas. 2006. A vision of pale beauty carries risks for Asia's women. *New York Times,* May 13: A3.

Gallard, Théophile. 1877. *Clinique médicale de la Pitié.* Paris: J.-B. Baillère et Fils.

Ganther, H.E., et al. 1972. Selenium: relation to decreased toxicity of methylmercury added to diets containing tuna. *Science* 175: 1122.

George, Timothy. 2001. *Minamata: Pollution and the Rise of Democracy in Post-war Japan.* Cambridge, Massachusetts: Harvard University Press.

Gernsheim, Helmut, and Allison Gernsheim. 1968. *L. J. M. Daguerre: The History of the Diorama and the Daguerreotype.* New York: Dover.

Gibson, George Alexander. 1912. *The Life of Sir William Tenant Gairdner.* Edinburgh: J. Maclehose.

Gil-Martin, J., et al. 1995. The first known use of vermilion, *Experientia* 16: 51(8): 759–61.

Gilder, Joshua, and Anne-Lee Gilder. 2004. *Heavenly Intrigue: Johannes Kepler, Tycho Brahe and the Murder behind One of History's Greatest Scientific Discoveries.* New York: Doubleday.

Gill, Robin. 2004. *Orientalism and Occidentalism: Is Mistranslating a Culture Inevitable?* Paraverse Press.

Gillett, Mary C. 1995. *The Army Medical Department, 1865–1917.* Washington, D.C.: Center of Military History, U.S. Army.

Giraudeau de Saint Gervais. 1858. *Traité des Maladies Syphilitiques ...* Paris: Chez Bohaire.

Glahder, Christian, Peter W.U. Appel and Gert Asmund. 1999. *Mercury in Soap in Tanzania.* NERI Technical Report No. 306. Copenhagen: National Environmental Research Institute.

Gleick, James. 2003. *Isaac Newton: A Life.* New York: Putnam's.

Goddings, Eli, ed. 1835. *North American Archives of Medical and Surgical Sciences.*

Golas, Peter. 1999. *Science and Civilization in China, Volume V: Chemistry and Chemical Technology, Section 13: Mining.* Cambridge: Cambridge University Press.

Goldwater, Leonard J. 1972. *Mercury: A History of Quicksilver.* York Press.

Gonzalez Ortega, Alfonso. n.d. *Mujeres y Hombres de la Posguerra Costaricense (1950–1960)*. Editorial Universidad de Costa Rica.

Goss, Helen Rocca. 1958. *The Life and Death of a Quicksilver Mine*. Los Angeles: Historical Society of Southern California.

Graham, Thomas James. 1827. *Modern Domestic Medicine....* London: "published for the author."

Graves, Robert James. 1864. *Clinical Lectures on the Practice of Medicine*, vol. 1. London: New Sydenham Society.

Grossman, Elizabeth. 2006. *High Tech Trash: Digital Devices, Hidden Toxics, and Human Health*. Washington, D.C.: Island Books.

Grum, Darja Kobal, et al. 2004. Emotion and personality traits in former mercury miners. *Psiholoska obzorja*, 13, 4: 9–11 (English abstract).

Guerrero, A.M. 1977. Age-old methods of contraception, *Initiatives in Population* 3(1): 20–25.

Guibourt, N. J. B. 1828. Rapport sur la présence ou l'absence du sublimé corrosif dans le rob de l'affecteur. *Journal de Pharmacie* 14: 332.

Gunn, John C. 1830. *Gunn's Domestic Medicine, or Poor Man's Friend....* Facsimile of the first edition, Knoxville: University of Tennessee Press, 1986.

_____. 1860. *Gunn's Domestic Medicine, or Poor Man's Friend....* New York: C. M. Saxton and Company.

Gura, Philip, and James Bollman. 1999. *America's Instrument: The Banjo in the Nineteenth Century*. Chapel Hill: University of North Carolina Press.

Guttman, Oscar. 1896. *The Manufacture of Explosives: A Theoretical and Practical Treatise*. 2 v. London: Whittaker and Company.

Hallopeau, Henri. 1878. *Du mercure: action physiologique et therapeutique*. Paris: J.-B. Baillère et Fils.

Hamilton, Alice, and Harriet L. Hardy. *Industrial Toxicology*. Acton, Massachusetts: Publishing Sciences Group, Inc.

Hamilton, James. 1821. *Observations on the Uses and Abuses of Mercurial Medicines in Various Diseases*. New York: E. Bliss & E. White.

Hamilton, James. 2004. *A Life of Discovery: Michael Faraday*. New York: Random House.

Hammond, William A. 1891. *A Treatise on the Diseases of the Nervous System*. New York: D. Appleton and Company

Hamza, Khidr. 2000. *Saddam's Bombmaker: The Daring Escape of the Man who Built Iraq's Secret Weapon*. New York: Touchstone.

Hankins Thomas L. 1985. *Science and the Enlightenment*.Cambridge: Cambridge University Press.

Hanks, Henry. 1862. *On Teething of Infants*. London: John W. Davies.

Harada, Masuzumi. 1986. Congenital Minamata Disease: intrauterine methylmercury poisoning, in *Teratogen Update*, ed. by John Sever (New York: Alan Liss), 123–26.

Harcourt, A. G. V., and H. C. Madan. 1880. *Exercises in Practical Chemistry*. Oxford: Clarendon Press.

Hargitai, Istvan. 2000. *Candid Science: Conversations with Famous Chemists*. London: Imperial College Press.

Harris, M. 2001. Phase-out issues for mercury cell technology in the chlor-alkali industry, in *Modern Chlor-Alkali Technology*, ed. by John Moorhouse (London: Society of Chemical Industry), 19–43.

Harris, Paul. 2007. Colombian gold rush. *San Francisco Chronicle*, February 6: D1, D4.

Harris, Thomas. 1734. *A Treatise on the Force and Energy of Crude Mercury, Proving the usefulness and innocency of its internal application, by a great variety of experiments and histories of cases, acute and chronick*. London: Printed for E. Symons.

Harrison, William Jerome. 1892. *The Chemistry of Photography*. New York: Scovill and Adams.

Harte, Brett. 1877. *The Story of a Mine*. New York: Houghton-Mifflin.

Hatcher, Julian S. 1962. *Hatcher's Notebooks*. Harrisburg, Pennsylvania: Stackpole.

Hauck, Dennis William. 2004. *Sorcerer's Stone: A Beginner's Guide to Alchemy*. New York: Citadel Press.

Hauksbee, Francis. 1719. *Physico–Mechanical Experiments on Various Subjects...*, 2nd edition. London: J. Senex and W. Taylor.

Havenhill, L.D. [1913]. *Practical Exercises in the Manufacture of Pharmaceutical Preparations, According to the United States Pharmacopeia, VIII Revision and The National Formulary, Third Edition, 1906*. [Topeka, Kansas: University of Kansas].

Hayden, Deborah. 2003. *Pox: Genius, Madness and the Mysteries of Syphilis*. New York: Basic Books.

Health Care Without Harm. 2001. *Going Green: A Resource Kit for Pollution Prevention in Health Care*. Washington, D.C.

Helfand, William H. 2002. *Quack, Quack, Quack: The Selling of Nostrums in Prints,*

Posters, Ephemera and Books. Falls Village, Connecticut: Winterhouse Editions.

Hempel, Charles Julius. 1865. *A New and Comprehensive System of Materia Medica*, vol. 1. New York: W. Radde.

Henriques, Francisco da Fonseca. 1715. *Madeyra Illustrado.* Lisbon: Por Antonio Pedrozo Galrao.

Hepworth, George H. 1971 [1864]. *The Whip, the Hoe and the Sword.* Freeport, New York: Books for Libraries Press.

Hewes, Amy. 1917. *Women as Munitions Workers: A Study of Conditions in Bridgewater, Connecticut.* New York: The Russell Sage Foundation.

Hewlett, A. W., et al. 1916. *Epitome of the Pharmacopeia of the United States and the National Formulary.* Chicago: American Medical Association.

Hibbeln, Joseph R., et al. 2007. Maternal seafood consumption in pregnancy and neurodevelopmental outcomes in childhood (ALSPAC study) and observational cohort study, *Lancet* 369: 578–85.

Hibbs, Mark. 1993. Red mercury is Lithium-6, Russian weaponsmiths say. *Nucleonics Week,* July 22: 10.

Hillam, Christine, ed. 2003. *Dental Practice in Europe at the End of the 18th Century.* Amsterdam: Rodopi.

Himes, Norman E. 1970. *Medical History of Contraception.* New York: Schocken.

Hirschorn, N., Feldman, R.G. and Greaves, I.D. 2001. Abraham Lincoln's blue pill: Did our 16th president suffer from mercury poisoning? *Perspectives in Biology and Medicine* 44(3): 315–32.

Hirshfeld, Alan. 2006. *The Electrical Life of Michael Faraday.* New York: Walker and Company.

Hodgen, Joseph Dupuy. 1914. *Practical Dental Metallurgy.* St. Louis: C.V. Mosby.

Hongyuan, Wang. 1994. *The Origins of Chinese Characters.* Beijing: Sinolingua.

Hopkins, Nevil Monroe. 1897. *Twentieth Century Magic and the Construction of Modern Magical Apparatus.* Philadelphia: David McKay.

Horne, Jacques. 1769. *Examen des principales methodes d'administrer le mercure, pour la guérison des maladies vénériennes.* London & Paris: Didot le Jeune.

Hounam, Peter, and Steve McQuillan. 1995. *The Mini-Nuke Conspiracy: Mandela's Nuclear Nightmare, The Hidden Story behind the Red Mercury Killings.* London: Faber and Faber.

Howell, John A., ed. 1990. *The Membrane Alternative: Energy Implications for Industry, Report No. 21.* Barking, Essex: Elsevier.

Huggins, Hal. 1993. *It's All in Your Head: The Link between Dental Amalgams and Illness.* Avery.

_____. 1999. *Uninformed Consent.* Charlottesville, Virginia: Hampton Roads Publishing Company.

Hutchinson, Jonathan. 1887. *Syphilis.* London. 1909. New York: Cassel.

Hutten, Ulrich von. 1991. *Die Schule des Tyrannen: Lateinische Schriften.* Leipzig: Reclam-Verlag.

Ingalls, Walter Renton, ed. 1909. *The Mineral Industry: Its Statistics, Technology and Trade during 1908.* New York: McGraw-Hill.

Isenberg, Andrew C. 2005. *Mining in California: An Ecological History.* New York: Hill and Wang.

Jaffe, Bernard. 1976. *Crucibles: The Story of Chemistry.* New York: Dover.

Jardine, Lisa. 2004. *The Curious Life of Robert Hooke: The Man who Measured London.* New York: Harper-Collins.

Jensen, S., and A. Jernelov. 1969. Biological methylation of mercury in aquatic environments. *Nature* 223: 753–54.

Johansen, Bruce Elliott. 2003. *The Dirty Dozen: Toxic Chemicals and the Earth's Future.* Westport, Connecticut: Praeger.

Johnson, Byron Berkeley. 1914. *Abraham Lincoln and Boston Corbett, with Personal Recollections of Each. John Wilkes Booth and Jefferson Davis.* Waltham, Massachusetts: the author.

Johnson, C. L. 1926. *A New Collection of Notes.* Memphis, Tennessee: the author.

Johnson, James. 1827. *The Influence of Tropical Climates on European Constitutions.* London: printed for Thomas and George Underwood.

Johnson, Kenneth M. 1963. *The New Almaden Quicksilver Mine, with an Account of the Land Claims Involving the Mine and Its Role in California History.* Georgetown, California: Talisman Press.

Johnstone, B. I. 1931. Acute mercurial poisoning: report on twenty-one cases with suggestions for treatment. *Canadian Medical Association Journal* 24(4): 500–07.

Jones, Idwal. 1947. *Vermilion.* New York: Prentice-Hall.

Jones, James. 1993. *Bad Blood: The Tuskegee Syphilis Study.* New York: Free Press.

Jonson, Ben. 1601. Cynthia's Revels, in *Ben Jonson*, vol. 4, ed. by C.H. Herford and

Percy Simpson, Oxford: Oxford University Press.

Joseph, Bertram. 1959. *The Tragic Actor.* London: Routledge and Kegan Paul.

Joyce, Rosemary. 2001. *Gender and Power in Prehispanic Mesoamerica.* Austin: University of Texas Press.

Kanner, Leo. 1943. Autistic disturbances of affective contact. *The Nervous Child* 2: 217–50.

Karim-Cooper, Farah. 2006. *Cosmetics in Shakespearean and Renaissance Drama.* Edinburgh: Edinburgh University Press.

Kark, R. A. P. 1994. Clinical and neurochemical aspects of inorganic mercury intoxication, in *Intoxications of the Nervous System, Part I: Handbook of Clinical Neurology,* ed. by Frederik Dewolff (Amsterdam: Elsevier Science), 367–412.

Kawai, Kyozo, et al. 1994. Allergic contact dermatitis due to mercury in a wedding ring and a cosmetic. *Contact Dermatitis: Environmental and Occupational Dermatitis* 31, 5: 330.

Kay, Gwen. 2005. *Dying to Be Beautiful: The Fight for Safe Cosmetics.* Columbus, Ohio: Ohio State University Press.

Keightley, David N. 1978. *Sources of Shang History: The Oracle Bone Inscriptions of Bronze Age China.* Berkeley: University of California Press.

Kerr, Jean. 1990. *Mary, Mary.* New York: Dramatists Play Service.

King, Cecil Y., et al. 1957. Mercury and Its Compounds. *Annals of the New York Academy of Sciences,* vol. 65, art. 5: 357–652.

Kiple, Kenneth F., and Virginia H. 2003. *Another Dimension to the Black Diaspora: Diet, Disease and Racism.* Cambridge: Cambridge University Press.

Kirby, David. 2005. *Evidence of Harm: Mercury in Vaccines and the Autism Epidemic: A Medical Controversy.* New York: St. Martin's Press.

Klawans, Harold. 1990. *Newton's Madness: Further Tales of Clinical Neurology.* New York: Harper & Row.

Knelman, Fred H. 1999. *Every Life is a Story: The Social Relations of Science, Ecology and Peace.* Montreal: Black Rose Books.

Koelsch, Franz. 1965. *Beiträgen zur Geschichte der Arbeitsmedezin.* Munich: Bayerische Landesärtztekammer.

Kolmer, John A., and Schamberg, Jay Frank. 1912. Experimental studies on the administration of salvarsan by mouth to animals and man. *Journal of Experimental Medicine* 15: 498–509.

Krebs, Robert F. 2004. *Ground-breaking Scientific Experiments, Inventions and Discoveries of the Middle Ages and Renaissance.* Westport, Connecticut: Greenwood Press.

Kussmaul, Adolph. 1861. *Unterschungen über den Constitutionellen Mercurialismus und sein Verhaltniss zur Constitutionellen Syphilis.* Wurzburg: Druck und Verlag des Stahel'schen Buch- und Kunsthandlung.

Labiniau, Brunin. 1851. *Prevention de contrefaçon du Rob-Boyveau-Laffecteur. En cause M. Brunin Labiniau, pharmacien a Bruxelles.* Brussels: G. Stapleaux.

Laffecteur, Boyveau. 1785. *Observations sur les Effets du Rob Anti-Syphilique du Sieur Laffecteur.* Paris: Philippe-Denis Pierre.

Lamprecht, Jan. 2002. Nuclear terrorism revelations ... and Middle East war news. *Etherzone* November 26 (*www.etherzone.com/2002/lamp112602.shtml*).

Lane, Joan. 2001. *A Social History of Medicine: Health, Healing and Disease in England, 1750–1950.* London: Routledge.

Lang, Mervyn F. 1977. *El Monopolio Estatal del Mercurio en el Mexico Colonial (1550–1710),* trans. from the English by Romero Gomez Ciriza. Mexico City: Fondo de Cultura Economica.

Lanyon, Milton, and Bulmore, Lawrence. 1967. *Cinnabar Hills: The Quicksilver Days of New Almaden.* Los Gatos, California: the authors.

Lasky, E., and A. Wandruszka, eds. 1973. *Gerard van Swieten und Seine Zeit.* 1973.

Lemery, Nicolas. 1675. *Cours de chymie, contenant....* Paris.

_____. 1697. *Pharmacopée Universelle.* Paris.

Le Minor, Jean-Marie, and Clair, Pascal. 2001. Augustin Belloste (1654–1730): de la chirurgie militaire a la therapeutique mercurielle. *Revue d'histoire de la pharmacie,* T. 49, no. 331.

Lewis, Sian. 2002. *The Athenian Woman: An Iconographic Handbook.* London: Routledge.

Liebert, Cynthia, et al. 1997. The impact of mercury released from dental 'silver' fillings on antibiotic resistances in the primate oral and intestinal flora, in Sigel and Sigel, 447–60.

Liebig, Justus von. 1822. Einige Bemerkungen uber die Bereitung und Zusammensetzung des Brugnatellischen und Howardschen Knallsilbers. *Reportorium für die Pharmacie,* 12. Nurnberg: Schrag.

Lloyd, J. U. 1911. *History of the Vegetable Drugs of the Pharmacopeia of the United States.* Cincinnati, Ohio: J. U. and C. G. Lloyd.

Lomazzo, Paolo. 1598. *A Tracte Containing the Artes of Curious Paintinge, Caruinge & Buildinge*, translated from the Italian by Richard Haydocke. London.

Long, George. 1839. Mercury, *The Penny Cyclopedia of the Society for the Diffusion of Useful Knowledge*, vol. xv. London: C. Knight.

Lowry, Thomas P. 2004. *Venereal Disease and the Lewis and Clark Expedition*. Lincoln, Nebraska: University of Nebraska Press.

Lozano Leyda, Manuel. 2000. *El enviado del rey*. Barcelona: Emece.

Lubeck, Glenn, and Ervin Epstein. 1952. Complications of tattooing. *California Medicine* 76(2): 83–85.

MacDonald, Helen. 2006. *Human Remains: Dissection and its Histories*. New Haven: Yale University Press.

Machen, Arthur, editor and translator. 1894. *The Memoirs of Jacques Casanova de Seignalt*. London.

Machet, J.-J. 1803. *Le confiseur moderne....* Paris: Maradan.

Macilwain, George. 1853. *Memoirs of John Abernethy, F.R.S.* 2 v. London: Hurst and Blackett.

MacKenzie, Donald. 1998. *Knowing Machines: Essays on Technical Change*. Cambridge, Massachusetts: MIT Press.

Madden, Dr. 1734. An Account of what was observ'd upon opening the Corpse of a Person who had taken several Ounces of Mercury.... *Philosophical Transactions of the Royal Society*. 291–94.

Mahaffy, Kathryn. 2005. Mercury exposure: medical and public health issues. *Transactions of the American Clinical Climatology Association* 116: 127–54.

Mallory, J. P., and Victor H. Mair. 2000. *The Tarim Mummies*. London: Thames & Hudson.

Marder, William. 2005. *Indians in the Americas*. San Diego, California: Book Tree.

Marquardt, Martha. 1951. *Paul Ehrlich*. New York: Henry Schuman.

Martin, Morag. 2005, July 1. Doctoring beauty: The medical control of women's *toilette*, 1750–1820. *Medical History* 49(3): 351–68.

Martinez-Alier, Juan. 2002. *The Environmentalism of the Poor: A Study of Ecological Conflict and Valuation*. Cheltenham, United Kingdom: Edward Olgar.

Mason, Clark. 1995. Guerneville man dies in skip loader accident. *Santa Rosa Press Democrat*, October 17.

Mathias, Andrew. 1811. *The Mercurial Disease: An Inquiry into the History and Nature of the Disease*. London: "Printed for J. Callow."

McDonough, J. E. R. 1915. The Treatment of Syphilis in 1915, in *Practitioner's Encyclopedia of Medical Treatment*. London: Oxford Medical Publications.

McMahon, Keith. 1995. *Misers, Shrews and Polygamists: Sexuality and Male-Female Relations in Eighteenth Century Chinese Fiction*. Durham, North Carolina: Duke University Press.

McTavish, Lianne. 2005. *Childbirth and the Display of Authority in Early Modern France*. London: Ashgate.

Medvei, Cornelius Victor. 1993. *The History of Clinical Endocrinology*. London: Taylor & Francis.

Mercurialist. 1733. *A short review of the quicksilver controversy In a letter to Dr. Dover. ... By a mercurialist*. London: printed for J. Brotherton; and A. Bettesworth, and C. Hitch. http://libproxy.uregina.ca:2048/log in?url=http://galenet.galegroup.com/servle t/ECCO?c=1&stp=Author&ste=11&af=BN &ae=T009130&tiPG=1&dd=0&dc=flc&doc Num=CW108813883&vrsn=1.0&srchtp=a& d4=0.33&n=10&SU=0LRM&locID=uregi-nalib.

Merians, Linda E., ed. 1996. *The Secret Malady: Venereal Disease in Eighteenth Century Britain and France*. Lexington, Kentucky: University Press of Kentucky.

Merrifield, Mary. 1967. *Original Treatises on the Arts of Painting*. 2 v. New York: Dover.

Michelon, E.-G.-J. 1908. *Histoire Pharmacotechnique et Pharmacologique du Mercure á travers les Siècles*. Tours: Imprimerie Deslis Frères.

Mire, Amina. 2005. Pigementation and empire: the emerging skin-whitening industry. *Counterpunch*, July 28.

Modine, John J. 1996. *The Clock of Ages: Why We Age, How We Age—Winding Back the Clock:* Cambridge: Cambridge University Press.

Molin, L. 1990. Oral galvanism in Sweden. *Journal of the American Dental Association* 191, 2: 281–84.

Moore, Coleen. 2003. *Silent Scourge: Children, Pollution and Why Scientists Disagree*. Oxford: Oxford University Press.

Moore, Joseph Earle. 1946. *Penicillin in Syphilis*. Springfield, Illinois: Charles C. Thomas.

Morgan, Morris Hicky, trans. 1960. *Vitruvius: The Ten Books of Architecture*. New York: Dover.

Morleigh. 1842. *Life in the West....* London: Saunders and Otley.

Most, Johann. *Science of Revolutionary Warfare*, translated from the German. n.p.: Desert Publications.

Murthy, K.R. Srikantha, editor and translator. 2002–04. *The Bhavaprakasa of Bhavamisra.* 2 v. Varanasi.

Nacht, David M., et al. 2004. Atmospheric mercury emissions and speciation at the Sulphur Bank mercury mine Superfunds Site, Northern California. *Environmental Science and Technology* 38(7): 1977–83.

Nageler, A.M. 1952. *A Source Book of Theatrical History.* New York: Dover.

Neale, Adam. 1831. *Researches to Establish the Truth of the Linnaean Doctrine of Animal Contagions.* London: Longman, Roos, Orme, Brown and Green.

Needham, Joseph. 1959. *Science and Civilisation in China, Vol. 3: Mathematics and the Sciences of the Heavens and the Earth.* Cambridge: Cambridge University Press.

_____. 1970. Elixir poisoning in medieval China, in *Clerks and Craftsmen in China and the West* (Cambridge: Cambridge University Press), 313–39.

_____. 1976. *Science and Civilisation in China, Volume 5: Chemistry and Chemical Technology, Part III: Spagyrical Theory and Invention: Historical Survey, from Cinnabar Elixirs to Synthetic Insulin.* Cambridge: Cambridge University Press.

_____. 1980. *Science and Civilisation in China, Volume 5: Chemistry and Chemical Technology, Part IV: Spagyrical Theory and Invention: Apparatus, Theories and Gifts.* Cambridge: Cambridge University Press.

Newman, William P., and Lawrence M. Principe. 2002. *Alchemy Tried in the Fire: Starkey, Boyle and the Fate of Helmontian Chymistry.* Chicago: University of Chicago Press.

Newman, William Royall. 2004. *Promethean Ambitions: Alchemy and the Quest to Perfect Nature.* Chicago: University of Chicago Press.

Nierenberg, David W., et al. 1998. Delayed cerebellar disease after accidental exposure to dimethylmercury. *New England Journal of Medicine.* 338:1672–76.

Oleson, Charles Wilmot. 1892. *Secret Nostrums and Systems of Medicine: A Book of Formulas.* Chicago: Oleson and Company.

Ornoy, Asher, and Judy Arnon. 1993. Clinical teratology, *Western Journal of Medicine* 159(3): 382–90.

O'Shea, J.G. 1988. Was Paganini poisoned with mercury? *Journal of the Royal Society of Medicine* 81(11): 594–97.

Pachter, Henry M. 1951. *Paracelsus: Magic into Science.* New York: Collier Books.

Packe, Christopher. 1689. *The Works of the Highly Experienced and Famous Chymist, John Rudolph Glauber.* London: Thomas Milbourn.

Palmer, R. B., Godwin, D. A. and McKinney, P. E. 2000. Transdermal kinetics of a mercurous chloride beauty cream: an in vitro human skin analysis. *Journal of Toxicology: Clinical Toxicology* 38 (7): 701–7.

Parker, Samuel William Langston. 1868. *The Mercurial Vapour Bath.* London: John Churchill and Sons.

_____. 1874. *The Treatment of Syphilitic Disease by the Mercurial Vapour Bath,* compiled from the fifth London edition by John W. Foye, M.D. Boston: A Williams and Company.

Parker, Sarah K., et al. 2004. Thimerosal-containing vaccines and Autistic Spectrum Disorder: a critical review of published original data. *Pediatrics* 114 (3): 793–804.

Partington, J.R. 1957. *A Short History of Chemistry.* London: Macmillan.

_____. 1962–70. *A History of Chemistry.* 5v. London: Macmillan.

Payenneville, J. 1910. *Histoire d'un spécifique de la verole au xviiie siecle, le rob Boyveau Laffecteur.* Rouen: Barnoud Laval.

Peiss, Kathy. 1997. *Hope in a Jar: The Making of America's Beauty Culture.* New York: Henry Holt.

Philadelphia Medical Society. 1827. *First Report of the Committee of the Philadelphia Medical Society on Quack Medicines.* Cited and quoted in *Christian Spectator,* 1828,. new ser., vol II: 431–35.

Philip, A. P. W. 1834. *The Influence of Minute Doses of Mercury.* Washington: Duff Green.

Philippy, Patricia B. 2006. *Painting Women: Cosmetics, Canvases and Early Modern Culture.* Baltimore: Johns Hopkins University Press.

Piggott, Aaron Snowden. 1854. *Chemistry and Metallurgy, as Applied to the Practice of Dental Surgery.* Philadelphia: Lindsay and Blakiston.

Pirrone, Nicola, and Kathryn Mahaffey, eds. 2005. *Dynamics of Mercury Pollution on Regional and Global Scales: Atmospheric Processes and Human Exposure around the World.* New York: Springer.

Polehamton, Edward, and J. M. Good. 1818.

The Gallery of Nature and Art: Or, A Tour through Nature and Science. 6 vol. London: R. Wilks.

Pollard, Tanya. 1999. Beauty's fatalities: poisonous cosmetics on the Renaissance stage. *Épistémé* (Paris III-Sorbonne Nouvelle), June 7.

Porter, Roy. 2000. *Quacks: Fakers And Charlatans in English Medicine.* Charleston, South Carolina: Tempus.

Powell, William. 1971. *An Anarchist Cookbook.* New York: Lyle Stuart.

Prado, Mark. 2006. Tainted reservoir: Fish contaminated with mercury in Marin's Soulajule. *Marin Independent Journal,* May 28: A1, A15.

Prasad, V. L. 2004. Subcutaneous injection of mercury: "warding off evil." *Environmental Health Perspectives* 112 (13): 1326–28.

Preite, Massimo, et al. 2002. *Archeologia industriale in Amiata: il recupero del patrimonio minerario, la bonifica del siele e la costruzione del parco.* Florence: Alinea Editore.

Préterre, Apollonie. 1884. *Les Dents: leurs maladies, leur traitement, et leur remplacement.* Paris: A Préterre.

Pushkareva, Natalia. 1997. *Women in Russian History: From the Tenth to the Twentieth Century:* Armonk, New York: M. E. Sharpe.

Quétel, Claude. 1992. *The History of Syphilis,* translated from the French by Judith Braddock and Brian Pike. Baltimore: Johns Hopkins University Press.

Rabinowitch, I.M. 1934. Mercurial poisoning. *Canadian Medical Journal* 30 (4): 286–93.

_____. 1938. Unusual findings in a case of acute mercurial poisoning. *Canadian Medical Association Journal* 34 (5): 429–33.

Ramsay, Matthew. 1994. Academic medicine and medical industrialism: the regulation of secret remedies in nineteenth century France, in *French Medical Culture in the Nineteenth Century,* ed. by Anne La Berge and Mordechai Feingold (Amsterdam: Rodopi), 25–78.

Ransome, F.L. 1919. *Quicksilver in 1918.* Washington: Government Printing Office.

Read, John. 1957. *Through Alchemy to Chemistry: A Procession of Ideas and Personalities.* London: G. Bell and Sons.

Renner, Rebecca. 2005. Mapping mercury: hot spot unknowns complicate mercury regulations. *Sciamer.com,* August 22.

Richardson, Benjamin Ward. 1860. *On the Medical History of Diseases of the Teeth and of the Adjacent Structures.* London: H. Baillère.

Richie, Donald. 2003. *The Image Factory: Fads and Fashions in Japan.* London: Reaktion Books.

Ricord, Philippe. 1838. *Traité pratique des maladies vénèriennes.* Paris: J. Pouvor.

_____. 1866. *Leçons sur la chancre.* Paris: Delahaye.

_____. 1863. *Lettres sur la syphilis....* Paris: Baillière.

Ripley, George, and Charles A. Dana, eds. 1873. *The American Cyclopaedia, vol. IV.* New York: D. Appleton and Company.

Rising Tide. n.d. Toxic racism: the dirty tale of the EU, soap and mercury poisoning. www.risingtide.nl/greenpepper/envracism/mercury.html.

Rivet, Jean-Baptiste. 1803. *Dictionnaire Raisonné de Pharmacie Chimique, Theorique et Pratique,* 2 vols. Paris: Brunot.

Roberts, Guy B. 1996. *Five Minutes Past Midnight: The Clear and Present Danger of Nuclear Weapons Grade Fissile Materials.* INSS Occasional Paper 8. Darby, Pennsylvania: DIANE Publishing.

Roberts, Lissa. 2005. The death of the sensuous chemist: The 'new' chemistry and the transformation of sensuous technology, in *Empire of the Senses: The Sensual Culture Reader,* ed. by David Howes (Oxford: Berg), 106–27.

Roe, Sam, and Michael Hawthorne. 2005. Toxic fish on your plate. *Chicago Tribune,* December 11.

Roger, Henri. 1905. *Principles of Medical Pathology,* trans. from the French by M. H. Gabriel. New York: D. Appleton and Company.

Rotblau, Joseph, ed. 1994. *Towards a War-Free World: Annals of Pugwash, 1994.* Singapore: World Scientific Publishing Company.

Roueché, Berton. 1970. Annals of medicine: insufficient evidence, *New Yorker,* August 22: 64+.

Roux, Augustin. 1770. *Dissertation sur la nature de l'esprit du nitre dulcifié.* Paris: Didot le Jeune.

Royal, Michael. 1991. Amalgam fillings: do dental patients have a right to informed consent? *Risk: Health, Safety and Environment* 2:141+

Ruggles, D. Fairchild. 2002. *Gardens, Landscape and Vision in the Palaces of Islamic Spain.* University Park, Pennsylvania: Pennsylvania State University Press.

Rush, Benjamin. 1799. Observations intended to favour a supposition that the Black Color (as it is called) of the Negroes is derived from the Leprosy. *Transactions of the American Philosophical Society*, old series, vol. 4: 289–97. Also in *Documents of American Prejudice: An Anthology of American Writings on Race...*, ed. by S.T. Joshi (New York: Basic Books), 265–70.

Russell, Colin A. 1996. *Edward Frankland: Chemistry, Controversy and Conspiracy in Victorian England.* Cambridge: Cambridge University Press.

St. Clair, David J. 1997. California quicksilver in the Pacific Rim economy, 1850–90, in *Studies in the Economic History of the Pacific Rim*, ed. by A.J. Latham and Dennis O. Flynn (London: Routledge), 210–33.

Sajous, Charles, ed. 1888. *Annual of the Universal Medical Sciences*, Vols. IV and V. Philadelphia: F. A. Davis.

Sanger, Margaret. 1914. *Family Limitation.* New York.

Saper, Robert B., et al. 2004. Heavy metal content of Ayurvedic herbal medicine products. *Journal of the American Medical Association (JAMA)* 292 (23): 2868–73.

Sarton, George. 1927. *Introduction to the History of Science.* Washington, D.C.: Williams and Wilkins.

Schreck, Carl. 2006. British mum about mercury allegations. *Moscow Times,* December 29: 3.

Schroeder, Joseph J., ed. 1971. *Sears, Roebuck and Co. 1908 Catalogue No 117.* Northfield, Illinois: DBI Publications.

Schuyler, George. 1999 (1931). *Black No More.* New York: Modern Library.

Scopoli, J.A. 1761. *De Hydrargyro Idriensi Tentamina Physico–Chemico–Medico.* Venice.

Sherwood, Ben (writing as Max Barclay). 1996. *Red Mercury.* Beverly Hills: DOVE.

Shkilnyk, Anastasia. 1985. *A Poison Stronger than Love: The Destruction of an Ojibway Community.* New Haven: Yale University Press.

Shoemaker, John V. 1890a. *A Practical Treatise of Skin Disease.* New York: D. Appleton and Company.

_____. 1890b. *Health, Heredity and Personal Beauty.* Philadelphia: F. A. Davis.

_____. 1901. *A Practical Guide to Materia Medica.* Philadelphia: K. Davis and Company.

Shorter, Edward. 1990. *Women's Bodies: A Social History of Women's Encounters with Health, Ill-health and Medicine.* New Brunswick, New Jersey: Transaction.

Shuck, Oscar T. 1889. *Bench and Bar in California: History, Anecdotes, Reminiscences.* San Francisco: Occident Printing House.

Sicherman, Barbara. 2003. *Alice Hamilton: A Life in Letters.* Urbana: University of Illinois Press.

Sigel, Astrid, and Helmut Sigel. 1997. *Metal Ions in Biological Systems, Vol. 34: Mercury and Its Effects on Environment and Biology.* New York: Marcel Dekker.

Sigerist, Henry, ed. 1941. *Paracelsus: Four Treatises.* Baltimore: Johns Hopkins University Press.

Sigmond, George G. 1840. *Mercury, Blue Pill and Calomel: Their Use and Abuse.* London: Henry Renshaw.

Sivin, Nathan. 1968. *Chinese Alchemy: Preliminary Studies.* Cambridge, Massachusetts: Harvard University Press.

Slavec, Zvonka Zupanic. 1998. Occupational medicine in Idria Mercury Mine in 16th century. *Vesalius* IV, 1: 51–9.

Smith, D. G., and Lowe, M. J. 1972. Mercury excretion in users of mercury-containing skin cream, in *The Use and Abuse of Drugs in Tropical Africa*, Bagshawe, A.F., et al., eds. Nairobi: East African Literature Bureau.

Smith, Dominic. 2006. *The Mercury Visions of Louis Daguerre.* New York: ATRIA Books.

Smith, William Tyler. 1858. *The Modern Practice of Midwifery.* New York: Robert M. De-Witt.

Sotham, Sieng. 2004. *Small-scale gold mining in Cambodia: A Situation Assessment.* Oxfam America.

Spurgeon, Anne. 2006. Prenatal methylmercury exposure and developmental outcomes: Review of the evidence and discussion of future directions. *Environmental Health Perspectives* 114 (2): 307–12.

Stanley, Autumn. 1995. *Mothers and Daughters of Invention: Notes for a Revised History of Technology.* New Brunswick, New Jersey: Rutgers University Press. .

Stewart, Mary A. 2002. *What Nature Supports to Groe: Life, Labor and Landscape on the Georgia Coast, 1680–1922.* Athens, Georgia: University of Georgia Press.

Stock, Alfred. 1926a. Die Gefahrlichkeit des Quecksilberdampfes. *Zeitschrift für angewandte Chemie* 15: 461–66.

_____. 1926b. Die Gefahrlichkeit des Quecksilberdampfes und der Amalgame. *Zeitschrift für angewandte Chemie* 39: 984–89.

Stoller, Kenneth P. 2006. Autism as a Minamata disease variant: analysis of a pernicious legacy. *Medical Veritas* 3: 1–9.

Storer, Horatio Robinson, and Franklin Fisk Heard. 1868. *Criminal Abortion: Its Nature,*

Its Evidence and Its Law. Boston: Little, Brown.

Stortebecker, Patrick. 1986. *Mercury Poisoning from Dental Amalgam: A Hazard to the Human Brain.* Orlando, Florida: Bio-Probe.

Stringer, Ruth, and Paul Johnson. 2001. *Chlorine and the Environment: An Overview of the Chlor-Alkali Industry.* Dordrecht: Kluwer Academic Publishers.

Sung Ying-hsing. 1996. *Chinese Technology in the Seventeenth Century: T'ien-Kung K'ai-Wu.* E-Tu Zen Sun and Shiou-chuan Sun, trans. and annot. New York: Dover.

Suoboda, Robert G. 1988. *Prakriti: Your Ayurvedic Constitution.* Twin Lakes, Wisconsin: Lotus Press.

Swaim, William. 1822. *A Treatise on Swaim's Panacea....* Philadelphia.

_____. 1827a. *The case of Nancy Linton, illustrative of the efficacy of Swaim's Panacea.* Philadelphia: Clark and Raser.

_____. 1827b. *Cases of cures performed by the use of Swaim's Panacea.* Philadelphia.

Swamimathan, Nikhil. 2007. Mercury "hot spots" found in North America. *Sciamer.com,* January 3.

Swediaur, Franz. 1817. *Traité complète sur les symptoms, les effets, la nature et le traitement des maladies vénériennes,* 2v. Paris.

Swiderski, Richard 1995. *Eldoret: An African Poetics of Technology.* Tucson: University of Arizona Press.

Szydlo, Zbigniew. 1994. *Water That Does Not Wet Hands: The Alchemy of Michael Sendivogius.* Krakow: Polish Academy of Sciences.

Tairov, Alexander, and Anatoli Filippovich Bushmakin. 2002. The composition, function and significance of the mineral paints from the *kurgan* burial mounds of the south Urals and north Kazakhstan, in *Colouring the Past: The Significance of Colour in Archaeological Research,* ed. by Andrew Jones and Gavin Macgregor (Oxford: Berg), 175–94.

Talbot, Eugene S. 1899. *Interstitial Gingivitis, or so-called Pyorrhoea Alveolaris.* Philadelphia: S. S. White Dental Manufacturing Company.

Tanner, Thomas Hawkes. 1868. *On the Signs and Diseases of Pregnancy.* Philadelphia: Henry C. Lea.

Taussig, Frederick Joseph. 1910. *The Prevention and Treatment of Abortion.* St. Louis: C.V. Mosby.

Taveau, Louis-Augustin Onésiph. 1827. *Notice sur un ciment oblitérique pour arrêter et guérir la carie des dents....* Paris: l'Auteur.

Taylor, Alfred Swaime. 1858. *Medical Jurisprudence.* London: J. Churchill.

_____. 1880. *A Manual of Medical Jurisprudence.* Philadelphia: Henry C. Lea's Son and Company.

The Tech. 1927. Faraday's death now believed to be result of mercury vapor poisoning. Monday, April 11: 2.

Teleky, Ludwig. 1948. *History of Factory and Mine Hygiene.* New York: Columbia University Press.

Thomas, T. Gaillard. 1890. *Abortion and Its Treatment.* Boston: D. Appleton.

Thompson, C. J. S. 1993. *The Quacks of Old London.* New York: Barnes and Noble. (reprint of 1935 original).

Thompson, R. Campbell. 1936. *A Dictionary of Assyrian Chemistry and Geology.* Oxford: Clarendon Press.

Thomson, John. 1868. *A Treatise on Hat-Making and Felting.* Philadelphia: Henry C. Baird.

Thorndike, Lynn. 1934. *A History of Magic and Experimental Science, Volume IV : Fourteenth and Fifteenth Centuries.* 1958. *Volumes VII and VIII: Seventeenth Century.* New York: Columbia University Press.

Tidy, Charles Meymott. 1884. *Medical Jurisprudence, vol. III.* New York: W. Wood.

Traister, B. H. 1991. "Matrix and the pain thereof": a sixteenth century gynaecological treatise. *Medical History* 35(4): 438–51.

Trakhtenberg, I.M. 1974. *Chronic Effects of Mercury on Organisms,* trans. from the Russian. Washington, D.C.: John Fogarty International Center.

Trasande, Leonardo, et al. 2005. Public health and economic consequences of methylmercury toxicity to the developing brain. *Environmental Health Perspectives* 113 (5): 590–96.

Treneer, Anne. 1963. *The Mercurial Chemist: A Life of Sir Humphry Davy.* London: Methuen & Co.

Tuke, Thomas. 1616. *A Treatise against Painting and Tincturing of Men and Women.* London.

Turner, Daniel. 1733. *The Ancient Physician's Legacy, impartially survey'd and his Practice prov'd Repugnant....* London: J. Clarke.

Ulloa, Antonio de. 1772. *Noticias americanas sobre la America Meridional, y la Septentrional Oriental....* Madrid: Don Francisco Manuel de Mena.

United States. Congress. House Committee on Energy and Commerce, Subcommittee on Health, Hearings. 2002. *Reducing Medical*

Errors. Washington, D.C.: Government Printing Office.

_____. _____. Senate Committee on Commerce. Subcommittee on Energy, Natural Resources and the Environment. 1970. *Effects of Mercury on Man and the Environment: Hearings, Ninety-first Congress, Second Session.* Washington, D.C.: Government Printing Office.

_____. _____. Senate Committee on Interior and Insular Affairs. 1971. *Problems of Electrical Power Production in the Southwest.* Washington, D.C.: Government Printing Office.

_____. Department of Health and Human Services and United States Environmental Protection Agency. 2004. *What You Need to Know About Mercury in Fish.* (EPA-823-R-04–005).

_____. Federal Trade Commission. 1922. *Annual Report of the Federal Trade Commission.* Washington, D.C.: Government Printing Office.

_____. Geological Survey. 2000. Mercury Contamination from Historic Gold Mining in California. Fact Sheet FS-061–00.

Unschuld, Paul. 1986. *Medicine in China: A History of Pharmaceutics.* Berkeley: University of California Press.

Ure, Andrew. 1870. *A Dictionary of Arts, Manufactures and Mines.* 2 v. New York: D. Appleton and Company.

Valhouli, Christina. 2006. Skin deep: makeup, excavated from a mine. *New York Times* August 24: Style 1.

Vibert, Charles. 1900. *Précis de toxicologie clinique et medicolegale.* Paris: J. Baillère et Fils.

[Victor, Benjamin.] 1733. *Memoir of the Late Barton Booth, Esq....* London

Villanacci, J., et al. 1996. Mercury poisoning associated with a beauty cream: Texas, New Mexico and California. *Mortality and Morbidity Weekly Report* 45 (19): 400–03. Update 45 (29): 633–35.

Villebrun, Joseph. 1939. *Un remède antisyphilique aux xviie et xixe siècles: le Rob de Laffecteur. Petite contribution a l'histoire de la syphilis.* Paris: Libraire Le Francois.

Vitruvius. 1960. *The Ten Books of Architecture,* Morris Hicky Morgan, translator. New York: Dover.

Vives, Juan Luis. 2000. *The Education of a Christian Woman: A Sixteenth Century Manual,* translated from the Latin and edited by Charles Rantazzi. Chicago: University of Chicago Press.

Von Pfaundler, Meinhard, and A. Schluss-man, eds. 1908. *The Diseases of Children.* Philadelphia: J.B. Lippincott.

Von Ziemssen, H. 1881. *Cyclopedia of the Practice of Medicine, Supplement, vol. VII.* New York: William H. Wood.

Wahl, Michael J. 1995. The clinical and logical mythology of anti-amalgam. *Quintessencce Ingernational* 35: 525–35.

Waldman, Peter. 2005. Mercury and tuna: U.S. advice leaves lots of questions. *Wall Street Journal,* Monday, August 1: 1+.

Waldron, Martin. 1970. Mercury in food: A family tragedy. *New York Times,* August 10: 1,24.

Walker, Dale. 1997. *Legends and Lies: Great Mysteries of the American West.* New York: Tom Doherty Associates.

Wall, B. J. 1889. *A Dictionary of Photography for the Amateur and Professional.* New York: E. & H. T. Anthony.

Walsh, James J. 1911. *Old-Time Makers of Medicine.* New York: Fordham University Press.

Warkany, J., and D.M. Hubbard. 1948. Mercury in the urine of children with acrodynia. *Lancet I:* 829–30.

Watras, Carl, and John Huckabee, eds. 1994. *Mercury Pollution: Integration and Synthesis.* Boca Raton, Florida: Lewis Publishers.

Wechselmann, Wilhelm. 1911. *The Treatment of Syphilis with Salvarsan.* New York: Rebman.

Weiss, Bernard, et al. 2002. Silent latency periods in methylmercury poisoning and neurodegenerative disease. *Environmental Health Perspectives* 110 (Supp 5): 851–54.

Weinberger, Sharon. 2006. *Imaginary Weapons: A Journey through the Pentagon's Scientific Underworld.* New York: Nation Books.

Weinstein, Michael, and Stacey Bornstein. 2003. Pink ladies: mercury poisoning in twin girls. *Canadian Medical Association Journal* 168(2).

Weldon, Minda M., et al. 2000. Mercury poisoning associated with a Mexican beauty cream. *Western Journal of Medicine* 173(1): 15–18.

Westfall, Richard S. 1993. *The Life of Isaac Newton.* Cambridge: Cambridge University Press.

Wheeler, Mark. 1996. Measuring Mercury. *Environmental Health Perspectives* 104 (6): 826–30.

Wieger, L. 1965. *Chinese Characters: Their Origin, Etymology, History, Classification and Signification,* translated from the French by L. Davront. New York: Dover.

Williams, A. R. 2006. Mystery of the tattooed

mummy, *National Geographic* 209 (6): 73–83.

Williams, C. Matthieu. 1876. Explosive Compounds, in *British Manufacturing Industries*, ed. by G. Phillips Bevan (London: E. Stanford), 157–211.

Williams, Christopher. 1998. Conclusion: The dynamics of future change, in *Environmental Victims: New Risks, New Injustices* (London: Earthscan Publications), 157–66.

Wilson, Adrian. 1995. *The Making of Man-Midwifery: Child-birth in England, 1660–1770.* Cambridge: Harvard University Press.

Winderlich, V.R. 1928. Eine Vergiftung durch Quecksilberdampf vor 150 Jahren, *Chemiker-Zeitung* 52: 29.

Wittstein, C.G. 1871. *Taschenbuch der Geheimmittellehre: Eine kritische Ubersicht aller bis jetzt Gehiemmittel.* Third, improved edition. Nordlingen: the author.

Wood, Anthony á. 1817. *Athenae Oxonienses*, ed. by Philip Bliss. vol. 3. London: Ecclesiastical History Society.

Woods, Kate. 2000. Feds tour New Idria wasteland. *The Pinnacle* 18, 44.

World Health Organization and Food and Agriculture Organization. 1974. The use of mercury and alternative compounds as seed dressings. *World Health Organization Technical Report Series No. 555.* Geneva: World Health Organization.

World Health Organization. 1976. Conference on intoxication due to alkylmercury treated seed, Baghdad, Iraq, 9–13 September, 1974. *Bulletin of the World Health Organization*, 55 supplement 1: 1–138.

Worldwatch Institute. 2006. *State of the World, 2006.* New York: W. W. Norton.

Yonten Gyatso. 1991. The secret of black pill formulation. *Tibetan Medicine* 13. Dharmsala: Library of Tibetan Medicine and Archives.

Youman, A.E. 1872. *A Dictionary of Everyday Wants.* London: F.M. Rood.

Young, Hugh Hampton, et al. 1919. Mercurochrome: a new germicide for use in the genito-urinary tract. *Journal of the American Medical Association* 73(20): 1483–91.

Young, John Harvey. 1961. *The Toadstool Millionaires: A Social History of Patent Medicines in America before Federal Regulation.* Princeton: Princeton University Press.

Young, Otis E., Jr. 1970. *Western Mining: An Informal Account....* Norman, Oklahoma: University of Oklahoma Press.

Zamporini, Paula. 2001. Untamed hearts: eros and suicide in late imperial Chinese fiction, in *Passionate Women: Female Suicide in Late Imperial China* (Leiden: Brill), 77–104.

Ziff, Sam, and Michael Ziff. 1987. *Infertility and Birth Defects: Is Mercury from Silver Dental Fillings an Unsuspected Cause?* Orlando, Florida: Bio-Probe.

Zlatagorskoi, E. 1862. *Essai d'un Dictionnaire des Homonymes de la Langue Française.* Leipzig: E. Goldberg.

Index

Numbers in *bold italics* indicate pages with photographs or illustrations.